DATAWARS:
The Politics of Modeling in Federal Policymaking

CORPS (Computing, Organizations, Policy, and Society) Series
Rob Kling and Kenneth L. Kraemer, General Editors

DATAWARS

THE POLITICS OF MODELING
IN FEDERAL POLICYMAKING

KENNETH L. KRAEMER
SIEGFRIED DICKHOVEN
SUSAN FALLOWS TIERNEY
JOHN LESLIE KING

Columbia University Press
New York   1987

Library of Congress Cataloging-in-Publication Data

Datawars : the politics of modeling in Federal
  policymaking.

  (CORPS (computing, organizations, policy, and society)
series)
  Bibliography: p.
  Includes index.
  1. Policy sciences—Econometric models.   2. United
States—Economic policy—Econometric models.   3. United
States—Social policy—Econometric models.   I. Kraemer,
Kenneth L.   II. Series.
H97.D38   1987   353'.072'0724   86-26917
ISBN 0-231-06204-4

Columbia University Press
New York   Guildford, Surrey
Copyright © 1987 Columbia University Press
All rights reserved

Printed in the United States of America
This book is Smyth-sewn.

Book design by J. S. Roberts

CONTENTS

TABLES
AND FIGURES

Tables

Figures

ACRONYMS

AFDC	Aid to Families with Dependent Children
ASPE	Assistant Secretary of Planning and Evaluation (HEW/HHS)
ASPER	Assistant Secretary for Policy Evaluation and Research (DOL)
BAD	Budget Analysis Division (CBO)
BEA	Bureau of Economic Analysis
BLS	Bureau of Labor Statistics
CBO	Congressional Budget Office
CEA	Council of Economic Advisers
CFS	Cost Forecasting System
CPS	Current Population Survey
CRS	Congressional Research Service
DEF	Duesenberry-Eckstein-Fromm model
DOE	Department of Energy
DOL	Department of Labor
DPS	Domestic Policy Staff (White House)
DRI	Data Resources, Inc.
EPL	Econometric Programming Language
EPS	Econometric Programming System
FAD	Fiscal Analysis Division (CBO)
FAP	Family Assistance Plan
FEA	Federal Energy Administration
Fed	Federal Reserve System
FNS	Food and Nutrition Service (USDA)
GAO	General Accounting Office
GMD	Gesellschaft für Mathematik und Datenverabeitung

GNP	Gross National Product
HEW	Department of Health, Education, and Welfare
HHS	Department of Health and Human Services
ISP	Income Security Policy (HEW/HHS)
JEC	Joint Economic Committee of Congress
KGB	Kasten-Greenberg-Betson model
MATH	MicroAnalysis of Transfers to Households model
MPR	Mathematica Policy Research
MPS	MIT Pennsylvania Social Science Research Council
NIPA	National Income and Product Accounts
NIT	Negative Income Tax
NSF	National Science Foundation
OEO	Office of Economic Opportunity
OMB	Office of Management and Budget
PBJI	Program for Better Jobs and Income
PITM	Personal Income Tax Model
PPRO	Public Policy Research Organization
PUS	Public Use Survey
RIM	Reforms in Income Maintenance model
SEO	Survey of Economic Opportunity
SPSS	Statistical Package for the Social Sciences
SRS	Social Rehabilitation Service (HEW/HHS)
SSI	Supplemental Security Income
SSRC	Social Science Research Council
THC	The Hendrickson Corporation
TRIM	Transfer Income Model
TSP	Time Series Processor
USDA	Department of Agriculture
WEFA	Wharton Economic Forecasting Association

PREFACE

THIS BOOK reports the results of a cooperative research project on computerized planning models and their use in federal policymaking in the United States federal government. The research reported here was conducted from 1980 through 1984 by a team of researchers from the Institut für Planungs und Entschiedungssysteme of the Gesellschaft für Mathematik und Datenverarbeitung (GMD) in Bonn, West Germany, and the Public Policy Research Organization (PPRO) of the University of California at Irvine. The research project, or IMPMOD, came about from the collaboration of Kenneth L. Kraemer of PPRO and Siegfried Dickhoven and Peter Hoschka of GMD during an exploratory study of problems in implementation of large-scale computerized models for policymaking support during 1979. That small study led to this larger research project, which was primarily supported by GMD, and which involved Dickhoven of the GMD, as well as Kraemer, Susan Fallows Tierney, and John Leslie King of PPRO.

As with many research projects, the IMPMOD project was built around a well-developed study design intended to uncover new insights about relationships between a variety of complicated and interacting variables. The project design consisted of two subprojects: a reanalysis of data collected in a 1974 survey of model use in U.S. federal agencies; and a set of detailed case studies of actual model implementation and use in selected arenas of public policymaking in agencies. The results of these two subprojects were also consistent with the experiences of many research projects, in that the genuine insights derived from the research sometimes appeared in ways not predicted by the research design.

The story that follows presents our review of existing knowledge about model implementation and use, our own framework for understanding the factors that seem to result in successful implementation and use of models, and the results of our field research on model implementation and use. The results of the reanalysis of the 1974 survey were disappointing, for the most part, in that they were ambiguous in their meaning. We did not find a convincing story of any kind in the reanalysis; its results neither confirmed nor contradicted the results from the case studies, particularly in the context of our research framework. We believe that this occurred for two reasons. First, the survey took place in 1974, while the case studies took place from 1980 to 1984. In a rapidly growing field like computer-based modeling, such a difference in timing of data collection is likely to result in collecting data on two different stories. Second, the study itself underwent a metamorphosis that made the 1974 data moot. We discovered not long after the case studies began that it was impossible to conduct a detailed investigation of model implementation without paying attention to the ways in which models are used; the reasons behind their use, the actors in the processes of use, the disputes over the appropriateness of various models and their application, and so on. The 1974 data were limited to a brief review of the models then in use and the applications to which they were put, but they did not contain precise information about the actual processes by which the models had acquired their place in the policy-making process.

This latter point is especially important to understanding the book as it now appears. The original intent of the project was to identify those factors that differentiate "successful" models, where success meant the models had been incorporated into policymaking and failure meant they had not. We were expecting that most of the variance would be explained by the design characteristics of the models themselves. Successful models, for example, would probably be technically superior, more fully documented, better supported with computing resources, and so on. In fact, we soon discovered that successful models do embody such features, but success depends on additional features of the application environment. For this reason, the study was expanded to include a careful investigation of the context of model use, especially with regard to the dynamics of the federal policymaking process. This decision was most rewarding for us, since we began to see how the "supply forces" of model characteristics and the "demand" forces of need and desire for models among policymakers interacted in the creation of the truly impressive amount of modeling that now supports federal policy-making in the United States. Perhaps the most important finding of the book is that elegant features of models will not, by themselves, guarantee even a trial run in the halls of power.

This book is the product of a team effort in every sense, and all the authors share in its accomplishments and detractions. However, in order to appropriate the praise and blame fairly, we will briefly describe the key actors in the various aspects of the research and the resulting book. As noted above, the idea for the project and its original design came from Kenneth Kraemer and Siegfried Dickhoven, with the assistance of Peter Hoschka. The reanalysis of the 1974 survey was conducted by Kraemer with the assistance of Cecelia Campbell-Klein and Debora Dunkle of PPRO. The case study of Data Resources, Incorporated, was mainly conducted by King, with assistance in fieldwork and interpretation of the results from the other authors. Similarly, the case study of the TRIM/MATH models was conducted by Susan Fallows Tierney with assistance from the other authors. Dickhoven, as part of the overall study design, conducted a special case study of a microanalytic simulation model called BAFPLAN, used by the Federal Republic of Germany for determining needs for college student financial assistance. This case study does not appear in this book, but the results of the study did help inform the analyses that appear here. More detailed results of the BAFPLAN study and related work are found in Dickhoven (1976; 1977a, b, c; 1978; 1979a, b; 1986).

Each of the substudies resulted in comprehensive reports that were reviewed by all members of the project team. Their results were synthesized into an overall project report consisting of the study write-ups and the overall findings. It was at this point that we decided to contain the story in the book to the major results of our efforts. The pieces of the various studies were split apart into a number of topical chapters, and a new structure was developed to contain them. Much of this organization and initial drafting was done by Fallows Tierney and King, with continuous review by both Kraemer and Dickhoven. The first draft was subsequently edited by Laurel Battaglia, who, through her patient efforts, revealed what was most valuable and worth passing on. Through a great deal of discussion and criticism by the whole team, a final structure for the story was developed. That story, which appears in this book, was assembled by Fallows Tierney and again reviewed by the rest of the team. The final integration and editing of the book was performed by Kraemer. In all respects, then, this book constitutes a team effort in which various participants built the substantive bases for the book and subsequently participated in construction of the present narrative.

Many people deserve thanks for their help and support in the research project and the writing of this book. Peter Hoschka of GMD was critical to the entire effort, and without him the project would never have taken place. Debora Dunkle and Cecelia Campbell-Klein provided essential help throughout the reanalysis of the 1974 survey data. Marti Dennis, Sherry Merryman, and Elaine Pezanowski provided excellent assistance in managing the daily affairs of the project at PPRO. Professional and much appreciated secretarial support for endless typings and retypings of the study reports and manuscripts was provided by Kathy Bracy, Rosa Garza, Helen Sandoz, and Julie Takahashi at PPRO and by Petra Pleil at GMD.

Beyond the loyal people in our own institutions, we extend our deepest thanks to those persons who provided us with information in the course of our case studies. Without them we could never have learned what we now know. Providing us with information on the development and use of microsimulation models were Richard Wertheimer and Richard Michel of the Urban Institute; Harold Beebout, Carolyn Merck, Miles Maxfield, and Patricia Doyle of Mathematica Policy Research; Helen Cohn of the Hendrickson Corporation; Richard Hayes of the Policy Research Group; Gary Brewer and Guy Orcutt of Yale University; Michael Barth of ICF, Incorporated; James Fallows of the *Atlantic Monthly;* Nelson McClung and Roy Wyscarver of the Treasury Department; Gail Wilensky of the National Center for Health Services Research; Joan Turek-Brezina, Richard Kasten, and Heather Pritchard of the Department of Health and Human Services; Jodie Allen and Ray Uhalde of the Department of Labor; James Springfield of the Department of Agriculture; William Hoagland and Maureen McLaughlin of the Congressional Budget Office; Carolyn Stoneberg of the House Information Systems Office; Wendall Primus of the House Ways and Means Committee; and Bruce Thompson, Frank Capece, and Nick Lanier of the General Accounting Office.

The following individuals contributed to our understanding of DRI and its model and data bank services, the use of macroeconomic models in the federal government, and econometric modeling generally. Otto Eckstein, Joseph Kaspudys, Donald McLagan, Jan Prokop, William Raduchel, and Eric Williams of Data Resources, Incorporated; Doug Beck, Sally Cleaver, Doug Lee, and Roger Whinsby of the DRI Washington office; Bob Anderson, John Haltiwanger, and Gail Makinen of the General Accounting Office; Flint Brayton, Jered Enzler, and Michael Prell of the Federal Reserve Board, Washington offices; Stephen McNees of the

Boston Federal Reserve Bank; Darwin Johnson and Robert Kilpatrick of the Office of Management and Budget; Frank DeLeeuw of the Bureau of Economic Analysis; Robert Harris, Kathy Ruffing, Mark Therber, and Steve Zeller of the Congressional Budget Office; James Lafferty, Paul Manchester, Timothy Roth, and Robert Weintraub of the staff of the Joint Economic Committee of Congress; Kem Stokes of the Senate Budget Committee staff; Peter Bidwell, James Girola, Nelson McClung, James Russell, and Roy Wyscarver of the Treasury Department; David Munroe and Michael McKee of the Council of Economic Advisers; Joseph Peckman of the Brookings Institution; Robert Lacey of the Massachusetts Software Corporation; John Henize of the Gesellschaft für Mathematik und Datenverarbeitung in Bonn; Tjalling Koopmans and Gary Brewer of Yale University; Henry MacMillan of the University of California, Irvine; and former members of the DRI team, Gary Fromm, Stephen Browne, G. Dennis O'Brien, Charles Warden, James Craig, David McLain, Stephen Brooks, Gregory George, Allen Cody, Frank Ripley, and Roseanne Hersh Cahn.

We acknolwedge the great debt of intellectual and institutional support provided by GMD and PPRO in our efforts to produce this study. We reserve for ourselves the responsibility for any errors in this book. We deeply appreciate the chance this project has given us to cooperate in a fascinating research study which, aside from adding to our knowledge of modeling implementation, greatly enhanced our understanding of U.S. and German national policymaking processes. In an era of changing trans-Atlantic relations, we feel such studies help to reaffirm the common bonds that tie together our countries. It is for this reason that we dedicate this work to American-German cooperation and friendship.

Kenneth L. Kraemer
Siegfried Dickhoven
Susan Fallows Tierney
John Leslie King

DATAWARS:
The Politics of Modeling
in Federal Policymaking

CHAPTER ONE

IMPLEMENTATION
AND USE
OF PLANNING MODELS

I N OCTOBER 1985, the *Washington Post* carried an article by Michael Schrage entitled "How You Can Profit from the Coming Federal InfoWar." In it, he predicted that "the technology of the information age will breed winners and losers." Nowhere would this be more apparent than "in the most information-intensive organization in the world: the bureaucracy of the federal government." Schrage then went on to cite a number of examples of winners and losers ranging from the Pentagon (winner) to the IRS (loser) to the Department of Commerce (loser) to the Congressional Budget Office, to the Social Service Administration (loser). For example:

Winner: An agency that has a sophisticated database system like the Pentagon's that enables it to show recalcitrant congressmen just how much defense money flows into each of their districts.
Loser: An agency like the IRS whose new large central computer systems have been a disaster from start to finish, delaying millions of refund checks, affecting the buying plans of millions of Americans for months, helping to undermine taxpayers faith in both the fairness and effectiveness of a tax system based on trust. (Schrage 1985:B1,B4)

In the spring of 1986 David Stockman confirmed, in his book *The Truimph of Politics,* what William Greider had hinted at earlier in his 1981 *Atlantic Monthly* article entitled "The Education of David Stockman." President Reagan's then director of the Office of Management and Budget had indeed massaged and manipulated economic statistics to support "Reaganomics," the supply side economics of the new Reagan administration. Speaking about the 1981 economic forecast which eventually became known as the "rosy scenario," Stockman said:

My hope for an early concensus on the economic forecast proved to be a vain one. . . . the others could agree on only one thing: that the Congressional Budget Office (CBO) forecast . . . was an ideological abomination. It assumed real GNP growth that was way too low and continued high inflation for years into the future.

So we got out our economic shoehorn and tried to jimmy the forecast numbers until all the doctrines fit. It was almost inherently an impossible forecast [emphasis added].

The essential dilemma was this: real GNP growth plus inflation equals current dollar Gross National Product or "money GNP." The Treasury supply siders wanted the biggest possible numbers for real growth. That would show the effect of the tax cut. Historically, real GNP growth has averaged about 3 percent. We therefore had to expect 5 to 6 percent. Otherwise, what was the point of the whole miracle cure we were peddling?

On the other hand, the monetarist-oriented members of the team . . . wanted the lowest possible numbers for money GNP. That was the litmus test of sound, anti-inflationary monetary policy.

When you brought the two camps back together, it was the inflation number which took it in the neck. . . . Thus, the ideal long-run economic forecast scenario was this: the Treasury supply siders wanted about 5 percent real growth; the monetarists wanted about 7 percent GNP growth. Consequently, by the third or fourth year, inflation collapsed to 2 percent because that's what the arithmetic required.

These economic numbers were a pretty good approximation of the supply-side synthesis. . . . They portrayed a world close to the ideal of inflationless, capitalist growth. By the end of January, we had a tentative forecast along these lines. . . . We had ended up with a high growth-low inflation consensus forecast on the basis of pure doctrine. Nobody was running the economic forecast through the OMB budget models to see what kind of deficit you got. (Stockman 1986:92–94)

At the end of the first week in February, however, reality began to set in as Stockman got overall budget numbers from the OMB technical staff. Using the economic forecast and the administration's planned spending program, the OMB numbers showed that the 1984 budget deficit would total $130 billion and the cumulative five-year deficit would total more than $600 billion. In an effort to deal with these numbers,

Stockman says: "I soon became a veritable incubator of shortcuts, schemes, and devices to overcome the truth now upon us—that the budget gap couldn't be closed" (1986:122–123).

What is significant about both examples is that they illustrate the powerful role of information, and of computer models and databases, in federal politics and policymaking. Schrage's winners had computers and computer databases and knew how to use them. Alternatively, Schrage's losers lacked computer capability and knowhow, or had computer capability but lacked adequate knowhow to manage them effectively. Stockman and friends' economic forecast, though purely ideological in origin, was generated in response to a forecast they didn't like from the computer model of the Congressional Budget Office. Although Stockman claims that computer models played no role in generating the 1981 economic forecast, computers did come into play later when the economic, spending and taxing policies were checked out on the OMB computer model. Then, the policies were found to be seriously flawed as the computer model showed the huge budget deficits they created.

Thus, two powerful and contrary images can be applied to the use of computerized data and models for policymaking by central government agencies. In one view, this technology is a widely implemented scientific tool which allows its users to accurately predict the outcome of various courses of action. Here, managerial objectives, such as improving the quality or the flow of information available to policymakers, account for the existence of model-based analysis in policymaking. The contrasting view is one of modeling as a complex gimmick which is subject to frequent implementation failure and political abuse. Sometimes the shortcomings or failures are laid to technical problems with the model, and at other times they are laid to problems of organizational or individual behavior, including political behavior. In this latter perspective, political objectives, such as enhancing the objective or authoritative appearance of information useful for achieving partisan political goals, are the underlying basis for agencies' interest in acquiring models for the policy process.

Whether computerized planning models are implemented and used for managerial or political objectives, they are increasingly becoming a standard part of the policy process, and federal agencies account for a large share of the multimillion-dollar market for computerized planning models. According to Roth, Gass, and Lemoine, "The U.S. Government is the largest sponsor and consumer of models in the world. Estimates have indicated that over one-half billion dollars is being spent annually on developing, using, and maintaining models in the Federal Government" (1979:214). Hence we think it is important to determine the conditions that encourage their implementation and use in public organizations.

In this book, we provide an empirical examination of these conditions and explore whether there are certain factors that lead to successful model implementation and use among federal agencies. Specifically, we examine the impacts of four factors on model implementation and use: (a) the conditions of the generalized modeling and policy environments; (b) the characteristics of modeler and policymaking organizations; (c) the features of modeling technologies; and (d) the nature of the strategies modelers and users employ to facilitate model implementation. More broadly, we analyze whether the widespread use of models results more from users' needs for models, or from modelers' promotion of their models, or from the coexistence and interaction of these "demand pull" and "supply push" factors.

THE DEBATE OVER MODEL UTILITY

Although U.S. federal agencies have used economic planning models since at least the 1950s, use was relatively limited until the 1960s, when macroeconomic modeling first gained prominence as a major economic forecasting and policy tool. Since the late 1960s, spurred by Great Society programs and the increasing social-welfare portion of total federal spending, interest also developed in the use of microanalytic simulation for assessing the distributional effects of tax policy and social programs. These and similar developments in the energy policy field (Greenberger 1983; Ascher and Overholt 1983) have established the use of social and economic planning models as a permanent feature of policy planning and evaluation in the federal government.

However, although many models have secured strong niches in federal agencies, some have been used one time and abandoned. Still others have died in the transfer from developer to user agency. Even when implementation has been successful, conflicts over the models have developed among users. Some policy analysts have been suspected of misusing macroeconomic models and of introducing partisan bias into the model results (Greider 1981; Henry 1978; Magnuson, Beckworth, and Brew 1981). Systematic studies of model performance have shown that econometric models generally do not perform as well as the judgment of experts relying on no explicit routines (Ascher and Overholt

1983; McNees 1976, 1977; Su 1978; Su and Su 1975; Zarnowitz 1978). In addition, observers have questioned continued reliance on models that proved incapable of forecasting the dramatic changes that occurred in the nation's economy over the past decade (Balogh 1980; *Business Week* 1981; Henry 1978; McNees 1982).

      Failures in the predictive power of models have raised particularly serious doubts about the utility of current models for economic policymaking, on the grounds that their underlying theory, assumptions, and structures are basically flawed (Ascher 1978; Ascher and Overholt 1983; McNees 1982; Mintzberg 1979). Most analysts agree that it is too early in the development of modeling as a science to tell whether the concepts that underlie models are irreparably flawed. Moreover, despite their problems, models serve many purposes and are heavily used in policy analysis. Even policymakers and analysts who rely on judgment, intuition, or back-of-the-envelope calculations want to know how their forecasts fit with those of available models. Policymakers who distrust the models still want to know what the models say, either to attack their credibility or to be able to answer questions and defend their own estimates against those who do believe in the models' forecasts. The widespread use of models by believers and critics alike is strong empirical testimony to the continuing importance of planning models in the policy process.

Model Success and Failure

Despite more than two decades of model experience in government organizations, the success of planning models varies greatly. On one hand are a large number of notable model successes that are accounted for in numerous studies (Brewer 1973; Fromm, Hamilton, and Hamilton 1974; Greenberger, Crenson, and Crissey 1976; Pack and Pack 1977b). Model successes attest to the potential utility of the exotic science and art of modeling, and feed the fires of investment in modeling technique and expansion in model use.

      On the other hand, however, there are a large number of modeling disappointments. Some of these disappointments are no doubt due to a shortcoming in the basic design of these models. There also are implementation difficulties that raise important questions about the conditions that favor successful model implementation and use for policymaking. For example, to what extent is the type of model—a well-packaged product or essentially a research prototype—differentially related to success? Are some model developers more effective than others in producing and marketing usable models? Do some public agencies have greater need for or make better use of models in policymaking than others? Finally, how does the political and institutional setting of model use affect modeling efforts?

The difficulties that give rise to these questions figure in many accounts of the failures of modeling systems:

- Large-scale computerized models and simulations have been used once and then abandoned (Brewer 1973; Lee 1973; Pack 1975).
- Many large-scale models have proved to be of little use to policymakers. Such models were designed to replicate a complex system with an extremely comprehensive structure and to simplify the system's operation for policymaking purposes. Yet, ironically, the actual level of the detail provided by the model was much too coarse to be of use to most policymakers (Lee 1973).
- Models have not satisfied the needs of decision makers. This is especially true in decision-making contexts characterized by immediacy and incrementalism. Public decision makers frequently have a recurring need for incremental analysis of one or another course of action. And often, immediate analysis is desired, without concern for accuracy or certainty in prediction, in order to facilitate quick decisions. Yet these decision requirements frequently conflict with modeling requirements that emphasize comprehensive and time-consuming analysis, and carefulness in prediction (Voorhees 1973).
- Models' ability to reduce the role of politics in policymaking has been grossly overestimated. Models that were designed to bring "hard" and "objective" data to a complex decision process actually resulted in increased politicization of the process by giving participants a clearer sense of which interests would gain or lose (Dutton and Kraemer 1985; de Neufville 1984; Pack and Pack 1977b).
- Model development and implementation requirements have been grossly underestimated. Considerable difficulties and delays have been experienced in operationalizing theoretical models, and

these have been compounded by appreciable data management problems. Consequently, work schedules have been drastically revised, and few models have been completed on time or on budget, often resulting in a loss of credibility for the planning effort. Alternatively, agencies have resorted to crude shortcuts, or have dropped the use of mathematical models altogether to stay somewhat close to the schedule required for decisions (Boyce, Day, and McDonald 1970; GAO 1973a; Kraemer and King 1977).

Other reports indicate that while some models are being used, their results have been far less than ideal, or their results have clouded rather than clarified complex policy issues. Even when models technically function as intended, the uses to which they are put may not be those for which they were built. Models may be used for a variety of ulterior purposes: to rationalize a policy decision already made; to delay having to make a decision; to "make work" in a project or organization; to create an illusion that progress is being made on a problem; or to justify investments in computing (Kraemer 1981; Lee 1973).

In short, the history of models has produced mixed results. Even so, the current stake in computerized planning models is large. In the national government sector, which is the focus of our interest here, nearly all larger agencies and their divisions use models. Although there are no recent surveys of model use, several earlier surveys provide some indication of the magnitude of government use of computer models. The General Accounting Office (GAO) found 450 active models within the Department of Defense alone (GAO 1973a). In another study of national economic models, the GAO identified the equivalent of eighty-three full-time staff members involved with models in nineteen federal agencies, including the Departments of Agriculture, Commerce, Treasury, Energy, Health, Education, and Welfare, Housing and Urban Development, and the Federal Reserve System (GAO 1979). Many state and local governments also use planning models (Boyce, Day, and McDonald 1970; Brewer 1973; Dutton and Kraemer 1985; Fromm, Hamilton, and Hamilton 1974; Kraemer, Dutton, and Northrop 1980; Pack and Pack 1977a, b).

For these user agencies and the public that funds them, model failure can mean the waste of thousands of dollars in development investments. Although models can be developed and run for a wide range of costs, modeling tends to be expensive (Fromm, Hamilton, and Hamilton 1974; GAO 1973b, 1979). Some indication of the level of investment is provided by the 1979 GAO study of the use of national econometric models by federal agencies; this study suggests expenditures of at least $4 million per year for these econometric models alone.[1] We estimate this number to be very conservative, with the actual figure today probably being five to ten times this estimate. The civilian agencies reporting the largest expenditures for national economic models were Commerce, Labor, and Health, Education, and Welfare, in that order (GAO 1979).

Further, the consequences of modeling "failure" can spread throughout the system. For the government user agency, an unsuccessful model can mean not only the waste of economic resources but the loss of actual or potential organizational effectiveness. For policymakers and department heads, such failures can result in the decline of personal effectiveness. For policy analysts, unsatisfactory models increase the time they need to spend on model-related problems rather than enhance their effectiveness in applying the models to decision problems. For model developers, failures mean their models are not utilized, hence a loss of opportunity and, ultimately, a loss of credibility. And for the modeling community as a whole, all of these consequences reduce the support for modeling as a policy-relevant enterprise.

In order to reduce the costs of modeling failure, there is a need to determine the conditions for effective implementation of planning models in federal agencies. If, as the literature cited above suggests, things can still go wrong even when the model itself is technically perfect, how can any of the participants avoid implementation failure and its associated costs? Are some implementation factors more important than others? Are there paths that model developers and/or users can follow to avoid the pitfalls and exploit the opportunities afforded by the application of computerized planning models? Are there factors that account for the successful matching of an agency's need for modeling and a modeler's supply of specific modeling services?

Conceptual Framework

MEASURES OF IMPLEMENTATION SUCCESS

One of the difficult questions involved in assessing the success of model implementation is definitional: what is success? If, in the modeling process, the system being modeled is clarified for users, can we say that the model was implemented successfully? If a model intended for policy analysis proved to be influential in a decision maker's selection among policy options, has the model been successfully implemented? If a model is developed for the purpose of educating its developers but eventually is used for developing new policy options, can we say that this model was implemented successfully? When we talk about implementation success or failure, we are referring to a variety of outcomes that may occur within the general modeling environment. Previous research has frequently attempted to resolve this definitional question by employing the concept of "use" as a measure of implementation success.[2] We shall do the same. Of the many possible measures of the use of models, our empirical study focuses upon three that we believe are important: policy use, political use, and institutionalization of model use.

At a minimum, the impacts of modeling technology are a function of their actual utilization for policymaking—that is, the extent to which the results of the model were applied to policy-related situations whether or not the model was initially intended for such a purpose.[3] Policy use, then, refers to the extent to which a transferred model was actually used for one or more of the following purposes: development of policies or programs; selection among policies or programs; or evaluation of a policy's or program's effectiveness. Here, the model is used to provide information to policymakers that is different from the information obtained through other means. The model provides an ability to answer "What will happen if . . . ?" questions with quantitative information. It enables policymakers to ascertain some sense of the consequences of their decisions in advance of making them and acting on them. The model's use, in this way, satisfies managerial objectives of improving the quality or flow of information available to policymakers.

A second measure of model use, political use, stems from the widespread controversy over the indirect effects of modeling in the policy process, such as the use of a model to obscure an issue, or to lend credence to a previously made policy decision. Models provide information that can be useful in answering politically relevant questions, such as who wins or loses as a consequence of a government action, or in providing evidence that is consistent with a policymaker's biases. Political use, then, refers to the extent to which a transferred model was actually used for one or more of the following purposes: to delay decision making; to give symbolic attention rather than real attention to a decision; to confuse or obfuscate decision making; to defeat a specific policy by giving explicit attention to only one side of the argument when the model could have been used to give both sides; to justify or legitimatize a decision already made without the model; or to add a sheen of technical sophistication to the reputation or position of the decision maker. Model use for political purposes is a well-documented feature of policy modeling. Some observers regard political use as "bad," whereas others see it as "good"; most view it as an inevitable feature of policy modeling. Thus we feel it is important to examine political use as a measure of implementation success.

From a broader perspective, we also consider the institutionalization of model use as a measure of implementation success. Institutionalization refers to the incorporation of specific models and of modeling per se as an ongoing part of the policymaking process. On the surface, this criterion of success seems excessively strict. Some models are never fully incorporated into the policymaking process, either because they were found wanting and were abandoned, or because they were intended for only a single application and their use terminated when that purpose was satisfied (Dutton and Kraemer 1985). In either case, these outcomes can be considered successful implementation at least from the modeler's or the user's point of view.

FOCUS ON PLANNING MODELS

In explaining these three kinds of model use, we focus on models developed for or used in policymaking in American federal agencies as our base of empirical research. We believe that these federal agency models are an interesting subset of the general universe of policy models, because their use is in the public domain and indirectly affects large numbers of people. They are accessible and, we feel, deserving of research attention. We do not insist that our sample is perfectly representative of the universe of modeling experience or even of the federal modeling experience; but our analysis of existing data, our extensive field interviews, our discussions, and our reading persuade us that our research has captured important features of federal modeling, and that the dynamics of model implementation in federal government agencies are similar to those in state and local governments as well (Dutton and Kraemer 1985).

We also are persuaded that these planning models are similar to the large-scale decision support systems (DSS) used in private organizations (King 1984; Kraemer and King 1986). The concept of DSS is relatively new, dating from the late 1970s, and successful large-scale, sophisticated DSS aimed at strategic planning are generally considered to be relatively rare and recent phenomena (Keen 1981; Methlie 1983; Naylor 1983). However, an examination of DSS concepts and definitions suggests that federal planning models do fit within the rubric of DSS. For example, Keen and Scott-Morton define DSS as the use of computers to support decision processes of managers involving semistructured tasks, with the goal of improving the effectiveness rather than the efficiency of decision making (Keen 1981; Keen and Scott-Morton 1978). DSS are contrasted with data processing (DP) and management information systems (MIS), in a way that implies an ordinal ranking of the level at which the systems' primary outputs are used: DP at operations levels, MIS at routine middle management levels, DSS at higher levels of management where strategic planning occurs. Under these characterizations the major macroeconomic and microanalytic simulation modeling systems used by federal agencies appear to fit the DSS definition.[4] They are applied to perhaps the most unstructured of decision situations—the attempt to create policy to influence an enormously complex and often uncontrollable set of economic phenomena through a highly political policymaking process. The models are intended to help improve the effectiveness of this policymaking process by focusing policymakers' attention on relevant issues, allowing sensitivity testing of different variables at issue, providing an opportunity for the simulation of possible outcomes of various policy alternatives, and forecasting baseline assumptions to assess the possible second-order effects of different policies. Finally, all of the models must operate on computerized systems, thus incorporating the component of automation frequently implied as an essential attribute of DSS. Thus, we feel these federal modeling systems are in fact large-scale DSS, and our research on successful model implementation has relevance to that literature and practice.

CENTRAL RESEARCH ISSUES

Two central research issues form the basis of this study. First, we explore the nature of implementation success: What constitutes successful model implementation? How were the models we studied actually used for managerial and/or political objectives? Did they become institutionalized as part of the policymaking process? What forces were important for successful implementation: users' "demand pull" for modeling, or developers' "supply push" for their models, or the coexistence or interaction of these demand and supply factors? How did modelers and users overcome barriers to successful implementation?

Since the outcomes of successful implementation relate to model use, we also focus on a second set of research issues in order to determine what accounts for successful model use: What constitutes successful use? What is the relationship between model implementation and model use? Are there major patterns of model utilization among federal agencies? Does the political and/or institutional context in which models are developed and used affect users' acceptance of models, the salience of models' results, and the nature of model use (e.g., its type or frequency)? What are the impacts of modeling on the policymaking process? And what is the prognosis for the role of models in policymaking in the years ahead?

FACTORS RELATED TO IMPLEMENTATION SUCCESS

Our past research on the use of computer-based information systems in public organizations (Danziger, Dutton, Kling, and Kraemer 1982; Dutton and Kraemer 1985; King and Kraemer 1985; Kraemer, Dutton, and Northrop 1980) and our assessment of the theoretical and empirical literature on model implementation suggest four possible factors which might be associated with variation in implementation success. These are (a) environmental preconditions surrounding the model; (b) the organizational attributes of the developer and user organizations involved with the model; (c) the features of the technology supporting the model and the technical characteristics of the model itself; and (d) the social and technological strategies or policies under which the implementation process is conducted.

But our assessment of the past studies on modeling in public organizations revealed an important gap: none examined explanations of implementation processes in an integrated framework that could enable us to derive conclusive statements about the relative importance or interaction of these variables.

We wanted to move beyond these studies to try to develop a way to think about model implementation that would enable us to clarify the role(s) each variable might play in the implementation process. Drawing especially on the theoretical and empirical literature, we developed a conceptual framework to illustrate the important dimensions of our research problem and to show the interconnections of these dimensions.

Figure 1.1 shows the outlines of our simple conceptual framework, which served as the overall structure of our subsequent analyses. It embodies an organizational perspective (rather than an interest group or bureaucratic politics perspective), similar to that of Ascher and Overholt (1983). In this perspective, conflict and cooperation among organizations is the central metaphor of our analysis and the central stuff of the politics of modeling. Although modelers, analysts, and policymakers are the central actors in our analysis, they operate in roles within organizations, and consequently their behavior is shaped and constrained by both the *organization's attributes* and general *environmental preconditions* toward the use of data-based arguments in policymaking. The demand for modeling stems from competition and conflict over alternative social and economic policies between and among political parties, agency bureaus, and the administration and Congress. The available supply of models within government modeling units or outside among private modeler organizations, in turn, affects the ability to satisfy this demand, and fuels it. Two *features of the technology,* its large scale and its complexity, require that modeling services themselves be organized, and the character of the organization becomes a critical factor in implementation success, as do alternative *policies for model transfer.* Policy models are adopted by one agency to gain substantive and/or political advantage for their policy position, and soon other agencies do the same. Once modeling capability is established among several agencies, a referee organization might be created independently if the organizations are in competition, or jointly if the organizations are essentially cooperative but possess different models and expertise. In this context, successful *model implementation* is some function of the substantive policy use, political use, and institutionalization of modeling within and between organizations.

We used this simple model to guide our data collection and

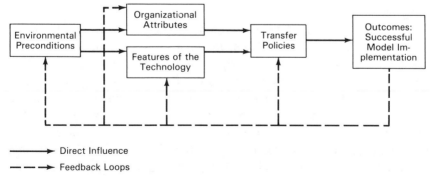

——————▶ Direct Influence

— — —▶ Feedback Loops

Figure 1.1. FRAMEWORK OF THE RESEARCH

analysis efforts, to organize an inventory of research propositions (chapter 8), and to discuss the findings of our own empirical research (chapter 9). With our framework, we hope to explore our view that the outcomes of model implementation were a function of a set of transfer policies, operating within a milieu that includes attributes of models, the characteristics of organizations involved in model development and use, and the conditions of the larger environment in which modeling takes place.

Environmental preconditions. The idea that the model's environmental preconditions will affect implementation success derives from the assumption that the level of model use will be contingent upon the opportunities and constraints in its environment. For one thing, the disposition of the overall environment toward or away from the use of modeling techniques will affect the level of financial support available to agencies for model use. For another, the flexibility or rigidity of bureaucratic behavior can affect model implementation. For example, a rigid policy for hiring civil servants, which blocks the movement of highly trained modeling personnel into federal agencies, could seriously impede the transfer of modeling expertise and, in turn, the use of a model. Further, the degree to which agencies rely upon the use of data-based arguments to support their policy decisions will set the stage for the "demand" for models to meet this need.[5] Such demand is a function not only of the individual users' needs but, in a larger sense, of the interaction of all of the policymaking agencies' needs. When one agency is using a model to rapidly analyze and defend a particular policy course, other agencies with competing policy proposals will find it expedient to follow suit with model-based analysis in order to defend their own policy choice. In such an environment, the demand for modeling pulls model development and use over and beyond that which would have existed as a result of the individual proclivity of a user agency toward the modeling techniques.

Organizational attributes. The organizational attributes of the model developer and/or user may also have major effects on successful implementation. For example, it is widely assumed that model developers situated in university settings have more difficulty obtaining government agency acceptance of their models than do those developers working within the user agency (Greenberger, Crenson, and Crissey 1976). The literature also suggests that user involvement in development increases the probability of successful implementation (Greenberger, Crenson, and Crissey 1976; House and McLeod 1977): when a user agency is involved in the development of a model from its conception, the model is more likely to be designed to meet the agency's specific modeling needs and, therefore, to be successfully implemented than a model which has simply been "purchased" from a developer. Similarly, the professional reputation of the model developer and/or model user and the type of unit using the model within the user agency (e.g., policy unit or research unit) are variables which could potentially interact with implementation success.

Features of the technology. A different view of the variation in implementation success stems from its relationship to the features of the model technology: the complexity of the hardware, software, and/or data supporting the model, and the technical features of the model itself. Some have suggested that implementation success is closely related to technical support features such as the size and adequacy of the data base supporting the model (Greenberger, Crenson, and Crissey 1976), although others posit that data issues are likely to be of importance mainly to new users (Bean, Neal, Radnor, and Tansik 1975).

Similarly, the adequacy of computing resources has been critical in the development and use of many modeling techniques (Greenberger, Crenson, and Crissey 1976). The technical characteristics of the model itself also might affect implementation success. The study of other innovations suggests that the greater the number of particular socio-technical traits associated with a particular model (e.g., its lack of complexity, ease of use, and established theoretical grounding), the more likely the model is to be successfully implemented (Hayward, Allen, and Masterson 1976; Rogers and Shoemaker 1971; Rothman 1974; Zaltman, Duncan, and Holbek 1973). Implementation success thus appears to be more likely when particular, aggregated configurations or "packages" of model characteristics are bundled together. We call models with this bundle "product" models, while we call models lacking this "packaged" quality "research" models.

Transfer policies. The final factor which appears to be closely associated with variation in the use of planning models is transfer policy. Successful model use is commonly conceived as an outcome of a multistage process involving development, or the steps involved in building a model, and implementation, the steps associated with transfer and use. The literature has characterized transfer as the movement of a specific technology from one place to another (Chaiken, Craybill, Holliday, Jaquette, Lawless, and Quade 1975; Downs and Mohr 1975; Fainstein and Fainstein 1972; Lambright 1977; Public Affairs Counseling 1976; Rogers 1962; Urban Institute 1971; Yin, Heald, Vogel, Fleischauer, and

Vladeck 1976). Usually, this concept has entailed the idea of the transferee adopting a more or less packaged technology from its developer into another site of use, often at lower cost with greater speed than that at which it was developed (King and Kraemer 1979). This conception of transfer has assumed implicitly that there is a clear demarcation between developers, who are the transferers, and the new users, who are the transferees. Transfer entails spatial movement, from one place to another. We adopt this spatial notion of transfer but add to it a temporal component to account for cases in which model transfer is effected within an agency, where transfer entails movement of technology from in-agency developers to in-agency users.

Successful implementation is in part a function of the arrangements by which a model is introduced into and adapted to a specific organizational environment. Since these arrangements are largely within the control of the developer and user agencies, we call these arrangements transfer policies. Case studies have suggested that models transferred with the permanent movement of experienced personnel to the user agency will be implemented more successfully than models transferred with only a temporary movement of experienced personnel (for example, see Greenberger, Crenson, and Crissey 1976). The policy of a highly developed marketing and service strategy, where a model developer employs a functional division of labor (e.g., for development, marketing, maintenance, and customer service), could affect implementation success. Such a strategy might result in a greater level of expert attention being applied to potential problems and opportunities that might develop during the implementation process. Similarly, agencies that are institutionally specialized in various modeling functions are likely to have greater resources at their command and are therefore more likely to be successful in implementing their models than are those where functional specialization is weak.

Prior Research

Much of the existing empirical research views the various explanations for successful implementation of models in a limited context, focusing on one or another of the explanations. Few studies have undertaken a systematic comparison of the relationships among these explanations.

Most of this research has concentrated on organizational characteristics, model attributes, and transfer policy as explanatory factors. Specific organizational variables in the studies have tended to focus on the traits of user and/or developer agencies, such as the number of employees in the organization, the user agency's level of personal involvement in the project, and/or its prior experience with innovations (Bean et al. 1975; Fromm, Hamilton, and Hamilton 1974; Greenberger, Crenson, and Crissey 1976; Manley 1975; Radnor, Rubenstein, and Tansik 1970; Schultz and Slevin 1975; Souder et al. 1975; White 1975). Model characteristics such as the appropriateness of its outputs, its ease of use, and its theoretical reliability have also been studied (Fromm, Hamilton, and Hamilton 1974; Greenberger, Crenson, and Crissey 1976; Lucas 1975; Manley 1975; Pack and Pack 1977a; Souder et al. 1975; White 1975). And finally, transfer policies such as adequacy of user training, strength of documentation, and model costs have been studied extensively (Bean et al. 1975; Fromm, Hamilton, and Hamilton 1974; Lucas 1975; Manley 1975; Radnor, Rubenstein, and Tansik 1970; Schultz and Slevin 1975; White 1975).

Only a few studies have examined the technology (Bean et al. 1975; Fromm, Hamilton, and Hami'ton 1974; Greenberger, Crenson, and Crissey 1976). Even fewer have focused on the features of the modeling environment (Greenberger, Crenson, and Crissey 1976). This latter factor, however, has received a great deal of attention within the innovation process literature. For example, the political disposition toward innovation, the flexibility of bureaucratic behavior, and the level of financial support have all been studied (Blau and Scott 1962; Costello 1971; Downs and Mohr 1975; Hayes and Rasmussen 1972; Shepard 1967; Urban Institute 1971).

One recent study, *Modeling as Negotiating* by Dutton and Kraemer (1985), is similar to our own. Their study examines the factors of context, technology, process, and impacts in modeling. They develop four political perspectives on the dynamics of modeling: the technocratic, rational, partisan, and consensual perspectives. And they examine these perspectives using four case studies, plus survey data, on the use of fiscal impact models in land use decision making by policymakers, planners, developers, and citizen groups. They conclude that modeling in the local government context is a political process, but essentially a benign one, and not primarily a partisan political process. Most generally, modeling appeared to facilitate negotiation and consensus in the policymaking process. But modeling was not politically neutral. The outcomes of modeling differentially affected the interests of various groups involved in the policy process; those groups excluded from the modeling process were unlikely to have their interests served by its outcome.

The shared conceptualization of the general research framework between Dutton and Kraemer's research in local governments and our own in federal agencies should be clear. However, there are important differences of context and technology which separate the two studies. First, federal policymaking is explicitly partisan, whereas local policymaking generally is not. Second, the policy models used by federal agencies are large scale, complex, and sophisticated, whereas the fiscal impact models used by local governments are small, simple, and relatively unsophisticated. Consequently, federal modeling is both technically more uncertain and politically more salient. Both of these features increase the difficulty of successful model implementation and use and, appropriately, tend to make modeling politically charged. Modeling is politically charged because so much hinges on what the models show and because there is often no single correct way to make forecasts using models. In this book, therefore, we explore a broad array of political and technical factors influencing the success of model implementation. In the process, we examine what we call the managerial (technocratic, rational) and political (partisan, consensual) objectives of modeling and their influences on the uses and impacts of modeling.

Despite the similarity of the Dutton and Kraemer study with our own, in general, neither the variables studied nor the outcome definitions of successful implementation are consistent from study to study. Table 1.1 summarizes the coverage of the four explanatory factors in representative empirical studies.

On balance, the major existing studies present some promising empirical grounding but are difficult to merge into a coherent package of findings. The studies vary in terms of the number of cases, the comparability of organizations, the operational measures employed, the object unit of analysis (e.g., model, user organization), and the level of analysis (e.g., organization, individual). But for us, the more serious problem is that these studies do not, in general, examine explanations of implementation in an integrated framework that could enable us to derive statements about the relative importance of the nature of environment, organization, technology, model attributes, and transfer policies in explaining implementation success and failure.

We wanted to develop a way to think about model implementation that would help us clarify the role(s) each factor might play in the implementation process. We did not hope to provide a final assessment

Table 1.1. SUMMARY COMPARISON OF EXPLANATORY FACTORS INCLUDED IN REPRESENTATIVE EMPIRICAL STUDIES OF MODELING

	Environmental Preconditions	Organizational Attributes	Features of the Technology	Transfer Policy	Extent of Use	Outcomes Degree of Implementation	Outcomes Perceived Success
Bean et al. (1975)		X	X	X		X	X
Dutton and Kraemer (1985)	X	X	X		X	X	X
Fromm et al. (1974)		X	X	X	X		
Greenberger, Crenson, and Crissey (1976)	X						
Lucas (1975)		X	X	X	X		
Manley (1975)		X	X	X			X
Pack and Pack (1977a, b)			X	X	X	X	
Radnor, Rubenstein, and Tansik (1970)		X	X				
Schultz and Slevin (1975)		X			X	X	
Souder et al. (1975)		X	X		X	X	
White (1975)		X	X	X			X

of the factors relevant to modeling success; rather we wanted to fix some boundaries around the factors that seem to matter and to ascertain the contingencies that might affect when and how the different factors influence the implementation process.

Research Methods and Case Studies

Between 1950 and 1970, most applications of economic, statistical, and operations research models were to operational decision problems that had well-understood objectives and conditions, and that were subject to formal expression and rigorous analysis. Beginning in the late 1960s, there arose a serious effort to apply modeling techniques to policy problems. Policy problems differ from operational problems in that unambiguous, rigorous representations of the problems are very difficult to construct. The fundamental objectives in policy problems are themselves unclear in many instances (Quade 1982).

In the public sector, these efforts to apply modeling to policy problems occurred under the rubric of planning models, and in the private sector they occurred under the rubric of decision support systems (DSS). Although not commonly seen as such, planning models are large-scale, complex DSS. By large scale, we mean involving around 100 structural equations and large time-series or disaggregated data bases such that computerization is a practical necessity. By complex, we mean embodying theoretical propositions and assumptions, which are interconnected in the structural equations of the model with interactive effects. As such, they "can, in theory, capture the complexity of real situations, represent intricate relationships such as mutual causation and feedback, and yield surprise implications that may not have been apparent to the analyst examining each relationship in isolation from the others" (Ascher and Overholt 1983:95).

When we began our study of modeling in federal agencies, planning models had already established a solid footing in Washington, D.C. For over two decades, scores of planning models had made their way from the desks and keypads of the modelers who had developed them to the offices of policy analysts throughout the federal government. Everywhere in Washington, there were planning models answering analysts' questions about some aspect of the American condition. While new models were still being developed, policy modeling had moved beyond the stage of development into a period of active marketing, successful commerce, and institutionalized use.

Of course, not all the planning models ever developed have been actually used by policy analysts. What enables some models and not others to move out of the hands of their developers and into settings where they can be utilized to provide information of relevance to policy analysts, managers, and decision makers? We wanted to learn more about model implementation in order to try to answer this question.

Because we were interested in refining or developing theories about the determinants of successful implementation, we decided to focus our attention on cases of models that had actually been implemented and used over several years, so that we would have an array of experience to explore and analyze. Therefore, we chose models that had been successfully implemented and used for five years or more, and that had an identifiable history that could be provided through interviews with individuals directly involved in developing, implementing, or using the models. We specifically chose not to pursue case studies of model "failures," since we felt that studying models that had never been transferred or used would reveal predictable sources of problems, such as poor model design or inappropriateness of the model for the needs of the users. Such problems had already been described as major causes of model failure (Fromm, Hamilton, and Hamilton 1974; GAO 1973b; House and McLeod 1977). By focusing our case studies only on successful modeling experiences, we hoped to be able to identify the subtle but potentially important factors that influence both implementation failure and success.

CASE STUDIES

We selected two models that had already established successful records of implementation and use, undergone an extensive period of early development, and continued to undergo refinement and change. These two models are:

1. The Transfer Income Model (TRIM) and its approximate counterpart, the MicroAnalysis of Transfers to Households model (MATH). These are microsimulation models designed to analyze the effects of welfare programs on individuals and households. TRIM, developed by the Urban Institute, was first used in 1973 and is still used by the Department of Health and Human Services. MATH was built at Mathematica Policy Re-

search, which marketed MATH to a number of federal clients. This model is also still in use. Since the Urban Institute and Mathematica Policy Research differ considerably in their organizational environments, we hoped to be able to observe the influences of organizational factors on model development and implementation.

2. The Data Resources, Incorporated, national econometric model (referred to as the DRI model). This model and its supporting infrastructure constitute the most widely used macroeconomic modeling service in the U.S. government. The DRI model was developed by DRI in the late 1960s. DRI's tremendous success in developing and marketing its modeling services, especially among federal agencies, made it an excellent subject for a case study. Also, the DRI model was part of a much larger data, modeling, and computing service company that provided an opportunity to study the ways in which the many factors related to computer-based models influence the success of special models. The large number of federal users of DRI's modeling services provided a wide range of experiences with the model, which enabled us to investigate the organizational factors associated with users of models (King 1983).

We hoped these studies of models that contained significant similarities and dissimilarities would help us identify and discriminate among the factors that affect the processes of model implementation and use. The selection of the TRIM/MATH models inadvertently provided an additional opportunity we exploited wherever we could. Our investigation into the relatively close community of model experts in the microanalytic fields led us to learn about several other models that provided interesting additional insights. Two models in particular were instructive: one was the so-called KGB model, a special-purpose model built within the Department of Health, Education, and Welfare for analysis of income-transfer programs; another was the Personal Income Tax Model, built in the Department of the Treasury to evaluate the dynamics of the income tax system. Similarly, our investigation of the DRI model provided us with an opportunity to observe, although in limited detail, other major macroeconomic models such as the Wharton model, the Chase Econometric model, and the Federal Reserve's MPS model. We did not do focused case studies of these other models and do not suggest that our comments about them in this book are either comprehensive or useful for other than simple comparisons. But these models did provide us with important "calibrating" information in the course of our two main studies, and these models are mentioned from time to time.

In order to construct our case analyses, a series of in-depth interviews were conducted using a "snowball" sampling technique. First, the developers and marketing staff of the models were contacted and interviewed about the model's development, characteristics, and transfer. Lists of the model's users were obtained from the developers. Key personnel within these user agencies were then identified and interviewed about their perceptions of the model, its transfer, and its use. In the process of these interviews, we further identified other key informants who played an important role in model implementation or use. Included in the total set of user agency interviews, then, were personnel in key policymaking positions (e.g., agency heads, division leaders, committee chairmen) and in various analyst positions (e.g., statisticians, economists, policy analysts in congressional committees and staff agencies, and federal departments).

In addition to model developers and users, we interviewed individuals who were "external" to these organizations, but who were knowledgeable about the models, model developers, model users, or experiences with model transfer and use. These people, by virtue of their historical and reputational position in the modeling and policymaking communities, were key sources of independent and expert opinion used to reconcile differences among informants, to fill in historical gaps, and to aid our understanding of how differences among the models might affect use.

Many of the discussions that arose during these interviews dealt with issues that were sensitive for personal, political, or business reasons, and often the interviewees requested that their comments not be attributed to them. Since the aim of our research was to ascertain, as closely as possible, how and why computerized planning models are used in economic analysis and policymaking, it was necessary at times to assure respondents that their comments would be treated confidentially. Therefore, our discussion of the cases in chapters 2, 3, 5, and 6 sometimes refers only to the general source for a given comment or perception (e.g., "This comment was made by a senior economist from the Commerce Department"). In most cases, the information provided in confidence was checked with at least two other sources to determine its reliability and to attempt to discover why the original source wished his or her comments to remain confidential.

LIMITS TO THE ANALYSIS

Clearly these case studies represent only a small fraction of federal modeling efforts. However, we believe they are of sufficient detail and scope to provide adequate preliminary information about the variables of interest in our study. Moreover, the correspondence between our findings and research on federal agency use of energy models is particularly encouraging (Ascher and Overholt 1983; Greenberger 1983).

Our research has expanded and refined understanding of the factors that affect the implementation and use of computerized planning models in federal policymaking. As with many research projects, this project has uncovered as many questions as it has found answers. Rather than reducing the number of important variables in model implementation, our findings suggest that many factors are important, and that different factors are important under different circumstances. Modeling appears to be a complex phenomenon, and it cannot be understood without incorporating many variables in the analysis. If nothing else, the research suggests that there are no simple recommendations for improving the state of model implementation.

There are several inhibiting factors in this research that have affected our ability to derive more comprehensive conclusions, and these deserve mention. One is the limitation of our analysis: the need to focus case analysis on only a few models and a few instances of model transfer and use; and the inherent difficulty of using case studies to develop generalizable conclusions. We believe that the situation is at least equally due to the state of the art of policy models and policy modeling itself. Policy models, especially those of the complexity and size examined in this study, are difficult to understand on their own terms as technological tools and are themselves continually evolving. In addition, while policy modeling is becoming an accepted part of national debates over economic, social welfare, energy, and other critical issues, it occurs in a dynamic political and institutional environment in which complex relationships—public and private, competitive and cooperative, professional and personal, individual and organizational—seem to defy attempts to factor out the critical from the coincidental.

Despite these limitations of subject matter and our own analysis, we believe that our use of an empirically grounded method to identify and specify the factors influencing implementation success has been an important first step toward gaining the understanding we seek. We see the next step as requiring the systematic collection of data on these variables across a wider array of models and instances of model transfer, and quantitative testing of the relationships among individual factors and sets of factors implied by the conceptual model and its further specification in the chapters that follow.

Overview of the Book

The rest of this book describes what we learned in our study of federal agencies' implementation and use of large-scale computerized planning models. The chapters which follow describe our actual observations about modeling in federal agencies, our findings about the factors' importance for facilitating model implementation and use, and our conclusions about the role of modeling in the federal policymaking process.

Chapter 2, entitled "Political and Technical 'Demands' for Models," tells the tale of TRIM/MATH's development and transfer to federal users. The story begins with the initial effort to develop an innovative technique for studying impacts of social service program changes on the poverty population. This effort responded to a demand for analysis of trends in the welfare population at a time when welfare reform first became a major, salient issue on the national political agenda. The initial model—called RIM—was developed by the staff of a presidential advisory panel working on welfare revisions. After the termination of the panel's work, the staffers moved to a research organization to continue extensive developmental work on the model under contract to a federal agency. This work produced a running model—TRIM—as well as considerable organizational turmoil, leading the key modelers on the TRIM project to leave the organization. Although they left TRIM behind, they took their knowledge of and interest in microsimulation modeling with them to their new organization, where they began to work on MATH—a model conceptually related to TRIM but packaged in a form more accessible and adaptable for new users. MATH's developers promoted their technique aggressively among federal agencies, many of which subsequently implemented MATH for analyzing various income-transfer programs.

This story raises interesting questions about the development of complex microsimulation models and their successful transfer to outside users: How was model development affected by such conditions as the state of knowledge of microsimulation modeling, the characteristics of model developers, competition among modelers, demand for policy analysis, and sources of financial support? To what extent was model transfer from developers to different users facilitated or inhibited by such factors as deliberate strategies adopted by modelers to promote model implementation and use, movement of individual modelers in and out of user agencies, costs of model acquisition and use, and technical attributes of the model and its data bases? Focusing as it does on the behavior of modelers and their relationships to users, the story of RIM-TRIM-MATH explores the imprint of these "supply push" conditions and practices on the development and spread of models to federal agency users.

Chapter 3 explores the development of a package of macroeconomic modeling and data base services by Data Resources, Incorporated, and its marketing of these services to federal agencies involved in national fiscal or monetary policy. The chapter, "The 'Push' for Model Implementation," focuses on the DRI modeling story—a unique and highly successful episode in the transfer of macroeconomic modeling out of the laboratory and into the halls of government.

Data Resources, Incorporated, or DRI as it is universally known, is the largest and most successful commercial macroeconomic modeling service in operation. The DRI case represents a fascinating example of model transfer by "commercialization." Commercialization refers to the process in which a technology developed primarily for experimental and research purposes is modified and provided with the necessary support to make it commercially available and useful to anyone who wants to pay for it. DRI's commercialization of its modeling service was part of the company's objective of creating highly usable and useful modeling services and then "pushing" those services among appropriate customers. The tremendous success of DRI makes it an important source of information on the techniques by which computerized planning models can be moved into user communities and routinized into regular user operations.

The chapter provides a brief look at the antecedents of the DRI model, a history of the movement of macroeconomic modeling into federal policymaking agencies, and the story of the establishment and growth of DRI. It also describes the features of the DRI economic services "package" and the means designed to the market it, and gives an overview of the use of DRI in federal agencies.

Chapter 4, "Accounting for Implementation Success," summarizes what these two cases taught us about implementation processes. In both cases, we found that agencies needed models to answer technically complex and politically important questions, and they obtained models from vendors willing to tailor their modeling services to fit the agencies' political needs. The implementation of the TRIM/MATH models was prompted, above all, by a demand for analysis at a time of intense political concern over welfare programs. Transfer of the models was facilitated by a high degree of movement of key individuals between modeling organizations and user agencies that enabled agencies' adoption of complex microsimulation models like TRIM and MATH, even though implementation did not necessarily lead to the institutionalization of model use in all agencies. We consider the DRI case to be an example of developers pushing for model implementation, or "implementation by commercialization." Here, the packaging and marketing of a large number of complex macroeconomic modeling and data base services by an aggressive commercial firm helped to move DRI services into federal agencies filled with economists already predisposed toward using forecasting and simulation tools for policy analysis. Here too, this implementation process was aided by a high degree of personnel transfer.

Chapter 5, "Partisan Politics and Model Use," explores the extensive use of MATH/TRIM in major political conflicts over income-transfer policies. By the mid-seventies, TRIM and MATH were being run extensively to generate highly desired information for use in specific policy-making episodes. Few participants in those discussions really understood what the models were about, or even whether the numbers they produced were any good. TRIM and MATH were "black boxes" to virtually everyone on the user side, except for those analysts and programmers with hands-on experience. The presence of a black box per se didn't seem to bother many policymakers. After all, few politicians ever enjoy—or care to acquire—sophisticated knowledge of the analytic techniques their aides employ. But with regard to TRIM and MATH, as the models gained a foothold in key policy analysis offices and produced numbers that were prominent in controversial policy discussions, a few policymakers and staff in other agencies began to take an interest in the black boxes. Clearly, where one stood on the acceptability of the models depended upon where one stood vis-à-vis the numbers they were generating. Those in political positions critical of the agencies that used MATH or TRIM became concerned over issues of model bias. Starting around 1976, MATH and TRIM began to receive focused scrutiny, just as they were gaining heightened importance in policy debates.

The chapter focuses on two lengthy episodes of the use of TRIM and MATH during major policy battles in the mid to late seventies. The first story, "The Automation of Bias," involves the role of the MATH model in an interinstitutional dispute over food stamp policy between the Food and Nutrition Service (FNS) of the Department of Agriculture (USDA) and several congressional committees. This episode spawned an investigation by the General Accounting Office (GAO) into claims that MATH was a "liberal" tool. The interconnected stories of the food stamp debate and the GAO evaluation of TRIM/MATH focus on questions of model credibility, control, and bias. The second major episode of modeling politics centers on "countermodeling" during the 1977–78 welfare reform debates, when MATH and a new microsimulation model, the KGB model, were involved in interagency rivalries and policy disagreements between the Department of Labor and the Department of Health, Education, and Welfare. This latter story highlights the role of models and of forecasts as weapons in larger political struggles.

Chapter 6, "Managerial and Political Ideology in Model Use," shifts to the DRI model and to a description of how federal agencies have used macroeconomic models for policy analysis and forecasting. The discussion does not concentrate on the technical details of use, such as how a model might answer different types of questions. Rather, it focuses on the broader organizational and political aspects of macroeconomic use by the three major economic policy-analysis groups in the federal government: the executive branch's major economic policy agencies—the Office of Management and Budget, the Treasury Department, and the Council of Economic Advisers; Congress' Congressional Budget Office; and the Federal Reserve Board.

Naturally, there are many important similarities between patterns of agencies' use of macroeconomic models like DRI and of microsimulation models like TRIM or MATH. However, there are also important differences. Of particular importance is the fact that econometric models are widely used in a continuous and routine manner by numerous federal agencies involved in some aspect of fiscal or monetary policy planning. The MATH/TRIM models, by contrast, tend to be used sporadically, in response to periodic efforts by legislative and executive bodies to evaluate or reform federal income transfer programs. So, unlike chapter

5, which presents specific episodes of model use, chapter 6 examines the more routinized use of macroeconomic modeling by focusing on the nature of cooperation and competition among macroeconomic modelers, economic advisers, policy analysts, and the policymakers they serve.

The chapter tells the story of macroeconomic model use in two parts. The first part, "The Institutionalization of Need for Macroeconomic Modeling in National Economic Policymaking," describes how modeling has become embedded as an integral part of ongoing economic policymaking processes. The second part, "Macroeconomic Modeling After the 1980 Election," explores how these routine modeling and analytic procedures were disrupted when the Reagan administration brought new economic perspectives and analytic approaches to bear on the federal policymaking process. The two parts of chapter 6, which focus on the use of the DRI model, describe two different ideologies of modeling—one in which technical objectives dominate model use, and another in which political motivations control modeling and the use of model-generated information.

Chapter 7, "Accounting for Successful Model Use," presents our findings and conclusions about the technical and political roles that microsimulation and macroeconomic modeling play in the larger policymaking process and how strong incentives for users to obtain modeling capabilities influence the spread of models in Washington.

Generally, our findings emphasize the importance of political over technical considerations in model use and the complex ways in which these considerations are interconnected in policy modeling. The MATH/TRIM case emphasizes the importance of intra-agency and inter-agency rivalries surrounding income-transfer programs, and shows how these rivalries affected when, where, and how microsimulation modeling was put to use in providing political ammunition for use in debates. The DRI case raises the ideological factors that have played an important role in the institutionalization of macroeconomic modeling in federal fiscal and monetary policymaking processes. It demonstrates the role of a "managerial" ideology over issues of when and how such modeling gets used in policy debates on the economy. The chapter shows how the advent of the conservative Reagan administration and a conservative majority in the Senate turned the ideological tables on these long-established macroeconomic modeling practices in the federal government.

Chapter 8, "Critical Factors in Successful Modeling," summarizes our findings as to the relative importance of these different variables to successful model implementation and use. Overall, our analyses reveal that three groups of variables—environmental preconditions, organizational attributes of user organizations, and features of the technology— are most critical to modeling success, especially in organizations with the primary responsibility for policy analysis and development in a given policy area. In such organizations, modeling is highly demand driven. These user agencies are willing to invest heavily in acquiring techniques, personnel, and data to satisfy their need for analytic and modeling capabilities. For secondary model-using organizations (those who use modeling for general information or to check the analyses of primary users), the supply-side factors of modeler attributes and transfer policies are more important. Secondary users are less likely to invest large sums in modeling and generally adopted well-packaged product models that are backed up by the support and expertise of modelers.

We have also included an Appendix, "Propositions on Successful Modeling", as a compliment to chapter 8. The Appendix presents a comprehensive inventory of propositions we generated and examined in our research about the variables that seem to lead to successful model implementation and use in federal agencies. These propositions were discovered to be important across our in-depth case studies, and sometimes appeared in the literature as well.

In this Appendix we use the conceptual framework of our research project as presented in chapter 1 to organize our discussion of important clusters of variables: the environment of policy modeling; the characteristics of the organizations involved in policy making; the characteristics of modeling techniques; and the policies specifically adopted by modelers to facilitate model transfer. Overall, we discuss thirty propositions regarding the factors we thought might affect successful model implementation and use. These propositions, and what we learned about them, are included as an aid to other researchers.

In chapter 9, "Computer Models and Policymaking," we discuss our conclusions about successful model implementation among federal agencies. We note that models are indeed used for two distinct types of purposes, with some uses conforming to a managerial ideology of modeling, others fitting more into a political ideology of modeling, and some serving both. We also describe how model use varies according to characteristics of the models and the modeling environment: support for modeling as an enterprise in any given policy area depends upon the level of political interest in that area; support for using a specific model as the basis for such modeling depends upon the level of general acceptance for that model among the community of model users and their political backers. Models that are frequently used and broadly supported are more likely than others to become institutionalized as regular fixtures of the policy-analysis process.

The chapter also describes how the institutionalization of models and modeling results from a complicated interaction and coexistence of "demand pull" by agencies for modeling resources and a strong "supply push" by modelers for transfer of specific models. In spite of the existence of many obstacles in the way of broader implementation of models, we see a gradual move toward increased reliance on modeling among federal agencies. We think models are here to stay and we expect use of models will grow in the future as they continue to prove their value for planning and political advantage.

Overall, there are several significant findings from our study. The first is that the single most important factor in successful model implementation is the need or demand for modeling. A supply of good models and their promotion by modeler organizations might enhance model implementation and use but they will not generate use in the first instance. What generates model use is policy need, and political saliency.

The second significant finding from our study is that need is a feature of the user organizations and their policy environment—not the modeler organizations, the models, or the model transfer process. Given that modeling is technically feasible in a given situation, the question of whether it will be used depends upon the circumstances of the user organization. If the user must have modeling capability, other consideration become opportunities or constraints in the development of that capability. If, however, the user does not have a great need for modeling capability, the other factors become much more important in determination of whether modeling will be used.

The third significant finding from our study is that "need" for modeling is a broad concept. It includes technical need in the sense that a model is required to improve the substantive quality of a decision. But it also includes political and ideological need, in the sense that a model is needed to gain political advantage over an opponent or to counter the opponent's use of models. We found that model use occurs as much for political and ideological need as for technical (substantive decision) need. In fact, while technical need might often provide the initial impetus for model use within an agency or policy arena, it is political and ideological need that stimulates use within other usually competing agencies involved in the same policy arena. Moreover, it is political and ideological need that institutionalizes model use within a policy arena as competing agencies, parties, and institutions accept model results as an inherent feature of policy debate.

Our findings are especially notable because much of the writing on computer models emphasizes technical-rational approaches to successful model implementation and use. Only a small part of the literature deals with the politics of computer models and data—most treat any political problems surrounding model use as largely correctable by means of better data, models or implementation. In contrast, this book argues that politics is an inherent and appropriate part of computer modeling. It results from differences of opinion and interest regarding policy outcomes. It is interjected into computer modeling because the models' predictions are used to influence policy choices whose outcomes differentially affect the fortunes of agencies, parties, and institutions. That is, computer models influence "who gets what."

As a result, we outline in our final section some lessons from the study for the modeling field, for modelers, and for policymakers and analysts. Perhaps most significant is the observation that as long as models continue to prove their value as useful tools for planning, in the technical-rational sense of the term, their political potency as weapons in debate will remain. However, in cases where models eventually prove to be no better than guesswork, the demand for models will eventually disappear because their practical and political value cannot be sustained. In the end, models survive or die based on their ability to help policy analysts and policymakers choose appropriate courses of action from among many complicated alternatives.

CHAPTER TWO

POLITICAL
AND TECHNICAL
"DEMANDS" FOR MODELS

IN RECENT decades, the United States has engendered an enormous and costly welfare population. Social support programs for the poor have constituted a sizable portion of the federal budget: 22 percent in 1971, 15 percent in 1976, and 14 percent in 1980 (Aaron 1978:11; OMB 1980). By 1980 the annual expenditures for such programs as Aid to Families with Dependent Children, food stamps, Supplemental Security Income, and Medicaid cost U.S. taxpayers $42.5 billion, and the number of recipients of federal income assistance was still rising.

Likewise, concern has been growing over the effectiveness and expense of the nation's welfare system. Every new federal administration of the past fifteen years has pushed for reforms of existing social support programs. However, few reform efforts have resulted in legislation passed on Capitol Hill. Every set of proposals to change the structure and scope of the income-maintenance programs has met with resistance from interest groups concerned over the acceptability and uncertain impacts of changes in benefit levels and conditions.

One way in which program analysts and reformers have attempted to cope with the uncertainty and controversy associated with proposed policy changes has been to develop and utilize methodologies to forecast the effects on costs and caseloads of alternative program designs. One such methodology—known as microeconomic simulation modeling—has come to play a principal role in helping analysts compare the likely effects of alternative reforms, as well as in shaping high-level policy debates around quantitative aspects of welfare reform measures. One family of microsimulation models that began with the development in 1969 of the RIM (Reforms in Income Maintenance) model, and which later branched into two other principal models—TRIM (Transfer Income Model) and MATH (MicroAnalysis of Transfers to Households)—has become the dominant quantitative technique for forecasting the impacts of policy changes in the social welfare policy area. This chapter explores how this family of computerized microsimulation models grew in response to the demands of the welfare policy analysis community in Washington, D.C.

MICROSIMULATION MODELS

Microsimulation is a mathematical technique for modeling the behavior of individuals (such as households or firms) in a larger system. The approach utilizes survey data on the characteristics (e.g., household income, household size) of a representative sample of individual units, along with simplified models of behavior, to simulate the population's likely participation in some activity (such as childbearing, tax liability, or enrollment in an income-transfer program such as food stamps).

Microsimulation techniques are particularly useful for modeling the decision-making behavior of households or firms with respect to relatively well-understood activities, where there are either clear rules for eligibility (as with the food stamp program) or liability (for various tax brackets), or where there exist good historical data for estimating rates of participation in an activity for different subsets of the population (as with females' fertility). Microeconomic models which are computerized and programmed to analyze large, representative data sets may be capable of generating estimates of the total number and composition of households entitled to participate in an existing activity or proposed program. When these models have data on the level of program benefits available to eligible households with different socioeconomic characteristics, they can produce projections of the total costs of that program (or revenues, in the case of a tax law). Additionally, they can forecast variations in costs and caseloads associated with changes in the eligibility requirements or benefit formulas for that program.

Antecedents of Microsimulation Policy Models

Microsimulation began to show promise as a tool for policy analysis in the late 1960s. At that time, interest was growing in Washington in assessing the numerous social support programs initiated during the Great Society. Many politicians and administrators saw the need for review and possible reform of existing income-maintenance programs. Policy analysts at the Office of Economic Opportunity (OEO) and at the Department of Health, Education, and Welfare (HEW) were called upon to generate information describing the beneficiaries and total costs of existing programs and the impacts of proposed program changes. But serious gaps in data and available analytic techniques hampered the analysts' ability to produce this information. Some analysts began to search for ways to add to their understanding of the individuals or groups receiving program benefits.

These analysts were indirectly aided in their search by work already under way at several major universities in the United States. Several research economists had been developing computerized microanalytic models of the U.S. economy, using subsamples of the U.S. population as the data base for simulating the economic behavior of households. The prime mover in this research community was Guy Orcutt, who at various times worked at Harvard, the University of Michigan, and the University of Wisconsin.[1] In 1961, Orcutt had published his research with Martin Greenberger, John Korbel, and Alice Rivlin in *Microanalysis of Socioeconomic Systems: A Simulation Study.* While Orcutt's models were too experimental and unwieldy to be useful as policy tools at that time, he did propose to the U.S. Department of the Treasury in 1962 that it consider using microsimulation to analyze federal income tax programs.

For Treasury analysts, this recommendation had been premature. While they had needed some method for estimating the impacts of proposed changes in tax policy, most were satisfied that the "back-of-the-envelope" techniques they had been using for years provided a sufficient level of detail and precision. Most Treasury economists enjoyed reputations as productive, capable analysts and felt no strong need to change methodologies at the time. But at least one economist at the department, Nelson McClung of the Division of Tax Analysis, had shown interest in microeconomic analysis and had begun to promote its use within the agency. McClung has since described the attitudes of Treasury analysts during that mid-sixties period: "They were really good at paper and pencil analyses, and they didn't want to get into microsimulation and microdata and computers. For one thing, it was very difficult to work with those things: it was hard to prepare data files; computers were hard to use. So around 1963 . . . 1965, there was real resistance."[2]

McClung's interest in microanalysis was boosted at that time by the work of two Brookings Institution economists, Joseph Pechman and Benjamin Okner. They were developing a simple computerized "data file processing" technique to assess the income tax revenue effects of proposed changes in the provisions of the federal tax code (Pechman 1965). McClung described the advent of a crude microsimulation methodology for analyzing tax policy: "Interest picked up at the Treasury—the first place within the government—around 1967, 1968. . . . We got a Ph.D. economist with some computer experience and gave him the job of developing a computer model to run the magnetic files of tax returns. The Personal Income Tax Model started as a simple system, and we rebuilt it year by year. . . . It's based on filing units [married (joint and separate) and single], not households. Unfortunately, filing units bear little relationship to households."

While Treasury analysts initiated in-house efforts to build a simple, static model, interest in microsimulation modeling was growing elsewhere in the executive branch. At HEW, Alice Rivlin, then Deputy Assistant Secretary, Frank Gorham, Assistant Secretary for Planning and Evaluation (ASPE), his deputy Worth Bateman, and several staff economists wanted to be able to identify trends in the poverty populations and to assess the effectiveness of the Johnson administration's War on Poverty programs. Bateman's staff, which was already gaining a reputation for high-quality policy analysis, had been charged with the responsibility of analyzing the likely effects on employment and program costs and caseloads of policy alternatives such as a negative income tax, a universal child allowance, a complete federal takeover of welfare, and aid to the working poor. To perform such analyses, ASPE analysts needed access to disaggregated data on the poverty population and a methodology for calculating the size of the population touched by program alternatives (Moynihan 1973:128–129). In describing this early period of program analysis, Orcutt and several colleagues have written:

It occurred to a number of analysts that many of the programs that were already in existence, or being discussed, had common key features. Most had two eligibility screens; economic need and demographic category. Eligibility and benefits of many programs were based in part on actual economic need—

measured by income or assets (or both) in relation to cutoffs or maximums determined administratively or by statute. Categorical eligibility is defined by some demographic characteristic in relation to administratively or statutorily established criteria—sex, age, handicap, family type, or other characteristics. The potential cost of any program would depend primarily on the number of people eligible, and the kind and amount of benefits for which they would qualify. Actual costs, of course, would depend in addition on the rate of participation in the program by eligibles, the number of ineligibles admitted through fraud or error, and behavioral responses of individuals to programs.

It seemed obvious that a conceptually simple general purpose computer model would be enormously helpful in analysis of a wide range of programs. Certainly it could be used to make estimates of potential costs and the potential distribution of benefits. It was also clear that such a model would be most useful if it simulated the effects of a program at a low level of aggregation—such as the individual or household—so that answers to different questions could be developed by aggregation of simulated results. This would make it easier to answer unanticipated questions. (Orcutt et al. 1980:83)

This concept of a microsimulation model was well received among HEW policy analysts during the mid-1960s.

But even if the ASPE analysts had developed such a technique at that time, which they did not, a major obstacle stood in the way of investigating their programs' impacts on their target groups in an easy or efficient manner. ASPE analysts had to rely on the Census Bureau for data, since their own data on program recipients were incomplete and inaccessible. ASPE analysts had to request highly specific information from the bureau, which would answer by means of aggregated statistical tables instead of raw data. The information was typically out-of-date by the time it was released by the bureau; often it took as long as two years to obtain. This problem greatly restricted the ability of ASPE analysis to do timely and useful analyses of welfare programs.[3] So in 1966, Worth Bateman and his staff assistant Jodie Allen (who had previously used computerized analyses of Census Public Use tapes for the Department of the Army) requested the bureau to allow them to copy the relevant census tapes so that they could do their own analyses flexibly and quickly. After some initial resistance and delay, the Census Bureau eventually helped Allen with the lengthy task of converting the tapes for use on HEW computers. Thereafter, this unprecedented transfer of volumes of disaggregated data to HEW gave the ASPE office a unique and valuable resource, which in turn made ASPE the focus of other agencies' requests for data and policy analysis.

THE PRESIDENT'S COMMISSION AND THE RIM MODEL

One such group was the President's Commission on Income Maintenance Programs,[4] an advisory task force established by President Johnson to evaluate existing poverty programs and to propose welfare reforms. The members appointed to the commission were prominent business and political leaders, all of whom were both unaffiliated with the welfare programs and inexpert in program analysis and design. To help undertake its mandate to "examine any and every plan, however unconventional," the commission hired a technical staff of social scientists and policy analysts. Robert Harris, formerly of HEW's ASPE office, served as executive director of the commission's staff. Harris hired Nelson McClung from the Treasury Department as technical director.

Harris and McClung at the helm of the project had important implications for how the staff would go about its analytic work. As McClung later explained: "We had the task of answering the question of what is the government doing for the poor, with all of its programs—taxes, AFDC, veterans, retirement, etc. We had no way to understand how all the programs combined, let alone observing the distributional effects. We wanted to know the effects of changing one program on all of the other programs, and their incidence on households." In particular, the commission was interested in examining the program costs and income distributional benefits of a negative income tax scheme. Under such a plan, families could choose to receive a simple but generous cash allowance, whose amount depended upon the size and income of the family. Receipt of such an allowance would reduce the family's access to other public assistance benefits for which it would otherwise be eligible. The commission wanted to know how many families would benefit from choosing the cash allowance, what impact the program would have on the number of families below the poverty line, and what effects the program would have on the U.S. Treasury.

Given this understanding of the commission staff's job, McClung wanted the aid of a systematic methodology: a model that could evaluate poverty programs in the way that the Treasury Department's Personal Income Tax Model or the Pechman/Okner model evaluated tax programs. McClung planted the idea that the commission staff should develop such a model for the welfare programs. Harris, who in his former days at ASPE had become well versed in the problems of analyzing the effects of income distribution programs, supported McClung's initiatives. They hired Gail Wilensky, a young economist from the University of Michigan with research experience in microeconomic modeling of negative income tax schemes, to help them develop a microsimulation model.

At first, the President's Commission staff turned to the analysts at ASPE to provide them with data on the welfare population. Jodie Allen cooperated with such requests, even helping to prepare simple analyses. She also referred the staff to another consultant: her former colleague, computer programmer Herbert Miller. Wilensky and Miller worked full time for half a year to construct a model using disaggregated data and capable of forecasting future costs and caseloads of existing welfare programs and of the alternative income-supplement programs under consideration by the commission. The model eventually came to be known as the Reforms in Income Maintenance (RIM) model. It was primarily a data processing technique—a static model with few assumptions regarding the behavior of the population being modeled.

The best data base available to Wilensky was the OEO's 1967 Survey of Economic Opportunity (SEO). The survey included detailed information on 18,000 representative U.S. households plus 12,000 more households from largely nonwhite poverty areas. Wilensky designed the computer program to recreate a secondary data file, selecting for each new household record only those variables of interest to the analysis of welfare programs: marital status, size of family, race, income from different sources including public assistance, and so forth. Next, to enable the model to calculate the effects of income supplements for a future year instead of for the year 1966 when the survey was taken, Wilensky projected (or "aged") the 1966 sample forward year by year to 1975.[5]

With the reduced and aged data set, the model then proceeded to calculate each household's available cash allowance, its tax liability, and the public assistance benefits for which it would be eligible. After reading each data record and calculating these benefits, the model summed all records to obtain estimates of the total costs of the cash allowance program, including the total dollar amount of the allowances themselves, and the federal income tax implications, minus the reduction in costs of other public assistance programs attributable to the allowances' impact on raised incomes. The model did not take into account the behavioral effects of the cash allowance programs on family formation or dissolution rates, individuals' work efforts, or the positive tax liabilities needed to finance the program.

Wilensky's model was used extensively to explore alternative combinations of cash allowances and offset taxes during the lifetime of the President's Commission, which issued its executive summary and proposal for a negative income tax for all needy persons in November of 1969.

These plans were somewhat overshadowed by the activities of the new Nixon administration, which had taken office the previous January. The administration's new advisers at HEW had been rapidly and independently formulating the Family Assistance Plan (FAP) as its major welfare reform. While similar to the commission's recommended negative income tax scheme, FAP's proposed guaranteed income would be limited to households with children, and it involved more complicated interactions with other cash and in-kind transfer programs such as food stamps and child care (Burke and Burke 1974; Moynihan 1973).

The FAP analysts may have worked independently from the commission staff, but they liked the methodological approach utilized by commission analysts. Worth Bateman's staffer Jodie Allen (still at the ASPE office) and James Lyday, principal FAP economist at the Office of Economic Opportunity, had been quietly developing their own "quick and dirty" microsimulation model specifically to estimate FAP costs, as requested by Nixon advisers.[6] The Lyday technique was relatively efficient for producing FAP estimates, but it could not forecast effects or costs of other income-transfer programs without extensive revisions. The RIM model, on the other hand, worked well for most program alternatives besides FAP—for which its calculations were cumbersome and its results awkwardly presented—and Allen and Lyday also felt RIM was more adept than their model for "aging" the data base. So thereafter, ASPE relied on the RIM technique to analyze FAP and its alternatives. However, ASPE did not take the model in-house immediately.

Allen needed help in revising RIM to make it capable of forecasting FAP impacts. She contracted for programming and processing assistance from former commission consultant Herbert Miller, who by then was a partner at an independent consulting firm, the Hendrickson Corporation (THC). Allen later explained why ASPE analysts preferred this mode of handling model development at the time:

At HEW, we had a staff of three involved with this project. We were under terrific time and resource constraints. . . .

We left it with THC because we needed numbers fast. We didn't want to have to run it ourselves; it was easier for us to avoid having to learn to run it that way, so that we could use it right away. . . . I cannot overstate the importance of having a private consultant help us at the time. Miller would do anything for me. A private firm was a much more responsive system than we could have had, had it been in-house. The people at THC would stay up late, work after hours to do the job by the time we needed it. Government workers would never do that. It was quite efficient.

Over the following months, ASPE program analysts utilized this crude microsimulation model to add information to the national debate on welfare reform. Jodie Allen gradually adopted the role of mediator, linking the RIM modelers with the policymaking community. Allen had knowledge of the kinds of policy questions computer simulation models could answer as well as the kind of information policymakers would find interesting and usable. She used RIM results to prepare reports on expected FAP program beneficiaries for congressional hearings. She manually transformed the computer-generated forecasts into summaries that were

in a form congressmen could understand—showing the distribution of beneficiaries by district. This allowed them to see whose constituencies would be affected and how. This made the model's data attractive to the policymakers; it was the same output, except in a form that was readable, accessible, meaningful to them. Suddenly, they thought we knew what we were talking about. Relevance of the information made us gain credibility on the Hill—and it helped the model's credibility too. . . . People tended to believe it—to believe in its accuracy, at least in comparison with former ways of estimating costs.[7]

Participating in these 1969 welfare debates was Daniel Moynihan, who at the time served on the White House staff and later commented on the role of the ASPE's RIM model in analyses and discussions of the FAP proposal: "By early 1969, a simulation model had been developed which permitted various versions of FAP to be 'tested' and costs to be estimated. . . . In time, the Congress was to have before it the same data as the executive branch had worked from. So did persons outside government, persons for the program, and persons against it. This was a situation probably without precedent in the development of major social legislation. It disciplined and informed the debate" (Moynihan 1973:190).

Thus the RIM model played a role in policy discussions by providing a common set of numbers in a timely fashion and in a form meaningful to politicians as well as policy analysts. In the eyes of many observers, these factors helped to enhance the promise of the microsimulation technique for playing a useful role in future analyses and policy discussions of social programs. And in the years that followed, considerable federal money was invested in further development of microsimulation models for policy analysis.

TRIM Development

Starting in 1970, microsimulation for policy analysis entered into a different phase of development. The dissolution of the President's Commission on Income Maintenance a year into the new Republican administration meant that many of the top-level commission staffers, formerly associated with the Johnson administration, looked for employment outside the federal government. Many, including Robert Harris and Nelson McClung, found a home at a new nonprofit policy research organization, the Urban Institute. The institute had been established in 1968 by several former top administrators from HEW's ASPE office.[8] Early on, the institute's researchers showed particular interest in analyzing welfare programs and other social policies. After 1970, McClung headed the Income Maintenance Group and brought the RIM model with him. He also brought RIM's designer, Gail Wilensky. Shortly thereafter, Jodie Allen joined the institute. During their initial months together, the institute researchers continued to help HEW staff analyze welfare reform proposals by means of RIM.

Before long, though, McClung and his staff concluded that future reliance on microeconomic modeling for policy analysis would require significant revisions to RIM. RIM was becoming increasingly inefficient for new policy applications. When analysts wanted to experiment with changes in any given federal program, new modules were added to the model's existing programming structure, but often without documentation. The model grew in size and sloppiness, becoming complex and unmanageable, expensive to run, and difficult to use. Many analysts were no longer even certain they understood what the computer program was doing.[9]

McClung urged the institute's directors to seek public funding to enable his staff to shift their focus to development of a new, more efficient model. The institute obtained money from the Office of Economic Opportunity to modify and deliver a working model for use in analyzing the latest FAP proposals. OEO signed a one-year, sole-source contract with the institute for $30,000. This was the institute's first contract specifically for in-house development work on the RIM model. At first, the Urban Institute used its existing programming staff rather than THC programmers to salvage pieces of the old model for use in the new one, which by then was beginning to take on its own identity as the Transfer Income Model (TRIM). But the institute's internal computing resources were weak, and the time and funds budgeted in the OEO contract were insufficient to complete the rebuilding task. By the end of the year, there was no working model to show for the $30,000 spent on the year's effort.

This situation posed a problem for the project leaders at the institute. McClung and Allen saw two possible courses of action regarding TRIM's future. The institute could decide to terminate its association with the model. This would necessitate returning to OEO the $30,000 the agency had spent on the project. The alternative was for the institute to continue to build an operational model. This would necessitate the institute's investing some of its own money into the project. Additionally, it would require the institute to obtain assistance from skilled programmers more knowledgeable about microsimulation modeling. Both McClung and Allen attributed part of the failure of the institute's TRIM reprogramming efforts to the fact that the institute's systems staff were organizationally and functionally isolated from the economic analysts. Status differences within the organization meant that the programmers' tasks were defined narrowly—simply to write code, not to participate in the design of the programs they were coding. They were not encouraged to ask questions about the overall logic of the system design. When programming problems arose, they were resolved piecemeal, without an eye to their effect on other components of the system. In the long run, McClung and Allen believed that such organizational and process problems were contributing to the institute's inability to design an efficient working model.

Because both McClung and Allen firmly believed in the future usefulness of microsimulation modeling for policy analysis, they argued to the Urban Institute's president, Frank Gorham, for continued institutional support for model development. They laid out a plan which involved seeking additional funding from HEW. To assure the agency of the credibility of the institute's grant request, the institute would promise to invest some of its own funds and would subcontract to the Hendrickson Corporation for the technical assistance the institute lacked. Gorham eventually backed their proposal and underwrote nearly $500,000 worth of work on TRIM over the following years.[10]

The institute obtained HEW funding through John Palmer of ASPE's Office of Income Security. Palmer was already familiar with the potential utility of microeconomic models for program analysis as a result of the FAP experience. Allen and McClung were frank with him in explaining why the institute had failed to complete its too-ambitious OEO project on time. Palmer apparently agreed that everyone had grossly underestimated how much time and money it would take to develop a model flexible enough to analyze various social support programs. Palmer was willing to infuse the project with another $50,000 as long as the institute committed itself to eventually providing a working version of TRIM, complete with documentation and able to be transferred to the agency for in-house use.

The ensuing work arrangements between the Urban Institute and the Hendrickson Corporation proved quite effective for developing the model. A team of programmers and economists worked together at the institute's offices in Washington. Mary Frances leMat and Ann Bergsmann, both senior-level Hendrickson programmers, became immersed in the project, attempting to understand the model's purposes and conceptual framework in order to enhance their own systems design work. Several institute analysts, particularly John Moeller and George Chan, also participated in the joint design effort.

This collaborative arrangement had several benefits. First, it gave the programmers and analysts a sense of colleagueship and mutual respect. They recognized the importance of communicating among themselves, not just for moral reasons but for the interests of the modeling enterprise. They recognized the importance of each other's contribution to the project's success. This perception was reinforced by the independent status of the two organizations, where neither group was subordinate to the other. Second, the open internal communications and sense of interdependency allowed the Hendrickson programmers to discover early on the futility of further attempts to save design time and money by salvaging pieces of the existing model and constructing linkages between the separate components. Starting in January 1972, after several months of abortive efforts to save parts of the old RIM, the Hendrickson designers advised the project team to abandon the old model altogether and to start from scratch.

This new strategy involved nearly complete technical and conceptual restructuring. The new model evolved as a result of collaborative design work, where systems problems helped to point out conceptual weaknesses and vice versa. By June 1972, most of the detailed specifications for the model were complete. The overall supervisory programming systems were nearly finished, as were several of the separate modules for specific transfer programs (e.g., Aid to Families with Dependent Children, Supplemental Security Income).[11]

At that time, the Urban Institute hired Harold Beebout, a young economist from the University of Wisconsin, to help complete the TRIM project. According to Jodie Allen, the person who hired Beebout, his involvement with TRIM was unexpectedly fortuitous for the quality of the eventual product: "Beebout had a great instinct for organization as well as a commitment to modeling. He was able to motivate people" at a critical stage toward the end of the HEW contract. At this point, the project had used up nearly all of its funds, and the nearly developed model had not yet been tested. Furthermore, several personnel changes at the institute had left TRIM without a spiritual leader: Jodie Allen had become a vice president within the institute, ending her direct contact with the TRIM development team. Additionally, Nelson McClung had left the institute late in 1972 to return to his post at the Treasury Department. With McClung's departure, the institute lacked a director for the Income Maintenance Group which oversaw the TRIM Project.

Beebout took on formal responsibility for shepherding TRIM to its completion when he became TRIM project director in early 1973. Beebout was under time pressures to turn over a working version of TRIM to HEW by the summer. HEW's ASPE office staff needed TRIM, since the department had once again been directed by President Nixon to look into reforms of the ever-enlarging welfare system. (Nixon had failed during his first term to win congressional approval for his Family Assistance Plan, and his interest in tackling welfare reform was renewed as he began his second term.) ASPE economists John Palmer, head of the Office of Income Security Policy, and Michael Barth, a former staffer at the President's Commission on Income Maintenance Programs, wanted to get their hands on TRIM. They planned to use it to forecast impacts of program changes on the costs and scope of a revised income-maintenance scheme under study by the new HEW Secretary, Caspar Weinberger.

For a while, though, it was uncertain whether the Urban Institute could provide Palmer and Barth with an operational version of TRIM on time. HEW had previously specified the policy alternatives it wanted the institute to use in testing the model; but Beebout could see that there were still months to go before testing could begin. So could the institute management, which had begun to view TRIM completion as an ever-moving target and a bottomless pit in terms of its funding demands. Beebout lobbied on behalf of TRIM, emphasizing the important role the Urban Institute would play in developing a state-of-the-art tool for improving policy analysis. And despite considerable resistance by the increasingly cost-conscious management, the Urban Institute agreed to subsidize final testing of TRIM.

Beebout's team used TRIM to simulate participation in the income-maintenance programs specified by ASPE analysts. Palmer and Barth analyzed the cost and caseload results, as well as the copy of TRIM the institute had turned over to them. Finally, by June they sent word to the institute that it had completed its formal contractual obligations.

Over the following five months, ASPE analysts used TRIM, with the assistance of the Urban Institute, to investigate alternative welfare reform strategies. Palmer and Barth had a fairly sophisticated analytic staff who were used to responding quickly and capably to the kinds of questions policymakers tended to ask. They prepared background papers on the characteristics of the poverty population and on existing income-transfer programs to serve as the reference point for looking at other policy options. Then they used TRIM to estimate the effects on program costs and caseloads of changing the welfare program eligibility rules. Finally, they used it to analyze a structural change in the welfare system—a proposed reform whose logic was based on economist Milton Friedman's ideas for consolidating the federal income tax and welfare programs into a single tax system. It would involve elimination of AFDC, food stamps, and the other income-transfer programs in exchange for a minimum guaranteed income. Households with income above the minimum level would pay into the income tax system, while households below that level would receive a cash payment (a "negative tax"). To analyze the impacts of this "Income Supplement Program," Barth's staff cranked Current Population Survey data through TRIM; the estimates it produced were then used in briefings before HEW policymakers (Lynn 1980:5). This initial phase of model utilization ended when Friedman, armed with his own powers of persuasion and these TRIM-generated data, convinced Secretary Weinberger to advocate to President Nixon in November 1973 the "integration of the tax, welfare, and domestic assistance programs" (*ibid.*, p. 97). While Nixon liked the proposal, he couldn't give it the attention it would require for congressional action; other matters, such as Watergate, took up increasing amounts of the President's energies. The proposed Income Supplement Program eventually died on the vine.

HOW TRIM WORKS

The model the Urban Institute designed for the analysts at HEW was, like its predecessor RIM, essentially a data processing technique. It was large and complex in practice but relatively straightforward in concept. TRIM contained two sets of components: a "microdata" base of individuals and households along with a number of data modification modules;[12] and a set of modules designed to calculate individuals' or households' eligibility for public assistance programs (or their liability for federal income taxes).

Enormous data bases were used to simulate participation in federal public assistance programs such as Supplemental Security Income (SSI), Aid to Families with Dependent Children (AFDC), and General Assistance. In the income-transfer module, individual and household records were examined to identify those who were "categorically" eligible for aid as a result of one condition, such as physical disability or dependent children lacking parental support. Then the economic status of these categorically eligible individuals and households was reviewed to determine which ones met the "means test" (criteria of economic need) appropriate to them, given the assistance program under consideration, their state of residence, and their filing status. For each eligible individual or household, the income-transfer module calculated the amount of benefit available to it according to the transfer program's rules. TRIM recorded this amount on the individual or household's record and added the figure to each affected transfer program's tally. This module generated total figures on the size of each program's eligible caseload, the total cost of supporting this caseload, and the geographical distribution of beneficiaries and benefits.

Analysts could use successive runs of TRIM to analyze and compare the impacts of changes in, say, eligibility requirements for AFDC or benefit levels for SSI. To do so, the user would change the parameters in the transfer modules which simulate program rules. Given the large size of the data files along with the number of times each data record was read by different modules in TRIM, the time requirements for processing the data were extensive, and the cost of complete runs of the model could reach nearly a thousand dollars.[13]

TRIM IMPLEMENTATION

As the ASPE staff became more familiar with TRIM, they found that microsimulation modeling suited their analytic tasks well. There was a continuing demand for information on federal welfare programs, whose reform remained a controversial and unattained goal of policymakers in

Washington during the early 1970s. In this environment, Michael Barth (then director of ASPE's Income Security Policy Analysis Division) foresaw the need to bolster his staff's already strong in-house analytic capability for the future. Among other things, this meant making TRIM more efficient and user oriented. At the time, ASPE analysts found TRIM useful but excessively complex and cumbersome, requiring extensive training and technical expertise to run and modify. Additionally, they considered TRIM too costly to run for routine analyses.

At the end of 1973, Barth's office issued a request for proposals from firms interested in "microsimulation maintenance." ASPE indicated its willingness to invest considerable resources over at least a three-year period to work with a modeler to redesign TRIM and to enhance ASPE's modeling expertise. In 1974, the Urban Institute won the competitive bid and was awarded the TRIM maintenance contract worth $200,000 a year for three years. (Subsequently, the institute won a second three-year contract, also amounting to $200,000 a year.)

Over the next few years, the TRIM project staff at the institute worked on preparation of model documentation, revisions of the model to make it more efficient and more easily operated by nonprogrammers, provision of tapes of the model and its data files to users, and training of users to do statistical analyses, forecasts, and model modifications. The technical assistants at ASPE's Division of Computation and Modeling became the linkage staff between the institute's consultants and TRIM users at the Office of Income Security. As institute economist Richard Wertheimer has commented, the staff at ASPE have since become "highly sophisticated consumers. Less sophisticated users think of the model as a black box which produces useful information. They see it as very mechanical: 'Just give us the numbers we need.' But sophisticated users give the drudge work to the contractors and keep control over determining the assumptions, setting the parameters, doing the analyses. This is good use by analysts. They control the model—its biases, its turn-around time, its flow of information."[14]

Over the years of the maintenance contract, the ASPE office gradually developed a "soup-to-nuts shop,"[15] so that by 1977 it was capable of doing everything from collecting survey data to operating TRIM to evaluating and revising the model to writing new, small-scale microsimulation models. Still, the continued complexity of the TRIM model meant that only the handful of individuals with hands-on experience with TRIM at ASPE had in-depth knowledge of how the model worked and knew how to run and change it.

MATH Development

The Urban Institute's completion of the working version of TRIM in 1973 and its successful bid for ASPE's TRIM maintenance contract coincided with a period of organizational turmoil within the institute. Nelson McClung's departure from his post as director of the institute's Income Maintenance Group in late 1972 had left a vacuum in the group, and its members began to perceive a loss of status within the organization. The directors of the three major projects within this group, including Harold Beebout of the TRIM project, worked as a committee to run the division, but they urged the institute's management to select a new group director as soon as possible. Jodie Allen was one of the prime candidates for the position, along with several individuals from outside the institute. An intense struggle developed over selection of the director, with Beebout and others within the division supporting Allen, who had experience both in the policymaking arena and in the applied research world. She also had a history of effective leadership within the organization. The institute's management was less certain of Allen: she was a woman without an advanced degree; she was critical of institute policies, including its pay structure; and she envisioned a more aggressive role for the institute in conducting policy analyses. When the management selected outsider Lee Bawden as director, Allen decided to leave the organization. Beebout departed shortly thereafter.

Allen and Beebout soon began a search for a new institutional setting where they could pursue their interest in revising and using microsimulation models for policy analysis. Among the organizations they contacted were the Brookings Institution (where Alice Rivlin then worked), the Stanford Research Institute, Mathematica Policy Research, and the Hendrickson Corporation. Allen and Beebout chose Mathematica Policy Research (MPR), which offered them support and freedom to establish and run a for-profit, Washington-based office solely devoted to performing policy analysis and applied research for government clients. They chose to remain organizationally independent of their longtime colleagues at the Hendrickson Corporation (THC), but committed themselves to working closely with THC programmers on future projects.

The Washington office of MPR opened in early 1974, and with it arose competition within the applied microsimulation community. MPR wanted to enter the market but had no model specifically identifiable with the new organization. The Urban Institute, by contrast, had actual organizational experience in developing a model for a federal administrative agency; its overall reputation was high; and it had a working model that could be adapted for new uses in the future. However, the key individuals who had had responsibility for creating and managing the TRIM project at the institute had left the organization and set up a rival firm. A significant proportion of the institute's former microsimulation-related expertise, experience, and network of personal contacts was now located within MPR.

In fact, MPR even had the model itself. Because TRIM had been developed with public funds, the Urban Institute had no proprietary rights over its use or dissemination. The key barrier to actual use outside of the institute was the specialized knowledge required to run and modify it, which MPR obtained with its absorption of the model's experts. Allen and Beebout recognized the potential for competition between MPR and the institute. In order to avoid uncertain legal or professional problems, they decided that for its first year in the microsimulation modeling business, MPR would develop projects not in direct conflict with the institute's modeling work. MPR would compete on new requests for proposals issued by any agency but would attempt to drum up unsolicited microsimulation work only with agencies not currently holding contracts with the institute.

Since the current users of microsimulation models constituted only a small group at the time,[16] this policy left MPR with a large potential market. Allen's wide range of personal contacts in the Washington social policy community and her familiarity with agencies' behavior and needs served MPR's business-development efforts well. For example, she "cashed in on an early contact" when she got in touch with Bill Robinson of the Congressional Research Service (CRS), one of the information and analysis arms of the legislature.[17] Months before, when Allen was still at the institute, Robinson had asked her to conduct studies of trends in the welfare population and of the mathematical models being used to analyze it. (Robinson knew of the models from his former days at the Office of Management and Budget, when HEW used RIM to estimate the costs of the Family Assistance Plan.) Because of the institute's reticence to work for congressional clients, its management discouraged Allen from taking the job.[18] Now that she was independent, she offered Robinson her assistance for other studies. CRS responded by awarding MPR two small contracts together worth nearly $30,000. One was to evaluate the microsimulation model used by the Veterans Administration; the other was to assess the general state of modeling for federal income-transfer programs. These were the first contracts

Allen and Beebout obtained. They kept MPR out of the microsimulation business for the "cooling-off" period, and helped MPR clarify strengths and gaps in the state of the art and identify potential users of further modeling applications. These circumstances were useful to MPR when it attempted its first modeling contract.[19]

By 1975, MPR submitted a bid to the Social Rehabilitation Service (SRS) for a three-year model-rebuilding program. SRS, while part of HEW, was organizationally isolated from the Office of the Assistant Secretary for Planning and Evaluation, which had sponsored TRIM. SRS was less interested in welfare reform than in preparing budget estimates, which required valid forecasts of future caseloads and costs for existing income-transfer programs. To obtain those forecasts, one analyst at SRS was interested in a more dynamic microsimulation model than the static TRIM. MPR proposed to revise TRIM from a simple data processing technique to a model capable of simulating important changes in the welfare population, such as shifts in family composition or significant behavioral responses associated with changes in income-transfer programs. Additionally, MPR would estimate how many of the households who were eligible for public assistance would be expected to actually participate in the programs. The Urban Institute's microsimulation group did not bid on the SRS contract. Other firms, however, did, and MPR won.[20]

The two-year, $360,000 contract served as the core of MPR's initial modeling work, enabling redesign of TRIM to make the program more efficient and more amenable to a variety of social service programs, and to incorporate simple behavioral assumptions. Additionally, the routine for aging old data was changed.

MPR called its adaptation of TRIM "MATH," at once an acronym for MicroAnalysis of Transfers to Households and an abbreviation for the consulting firm's name. Figure 2.1 shows how the MATH system works. The conceptual structure of MATH closely resembles that of TRIM, although specific differences can be seen in the descriptions of the origins of the separate functional components of MATH in figure 2.2. Harold Beebout, in fact, considers MATH a second generation of TRIM.

MATH IMPLEMENTATION

The 1975–76 SRS contract enabled MPR to begin to rework TRIM into the MATH model described in figures 2.1 and 2.2. But before MPR analysts and THC programmers had completed their reconstruction work,

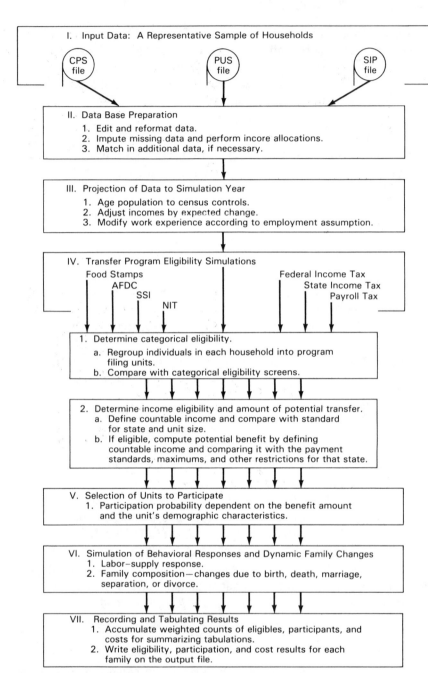

I. Input Data: A Representative Sample of Households

CPS file

PUS file

SIP file

II. Data Base Preparation
   1. Edit and reformat data.
   2. Impute missing data and perform incore allocations.
   3. Match in additional data, if necessary.

III. Projection of Data to Simulation Year
   1. Age population to census controls.
   2. Adjust incomes by expected change.
   3. Modify work experience according to employment assumption.

IV. Transfer Program Eligibility Simulations
   Food Stamps
      AFDC
         SSI
            NIT
   Federal Income Tax
      State Income Tax
         Payroll Tax

   1. Determine categorical eligibility.
      a. Regroup individuals in each household into program filing units.
      b. Compare with categorical eligibility screens.

   2. Determine income eligibility and amount of potential transfer.
      a. Define countable income and compare with standard for state and unit size.
      b. If eligible, compute potential benefit by defining countable income and comparing it with the payment standards, maximums, and other restrictions for that state.

V. Selection of Units to Participate
   1. Participation probability dependent on the benefit amount and the unit's demographic characteristics.

VI. Simulation of Behavioral Responses and Dynamic Family Changes
   1. Labor–supply response.
   2. Family composition—changes due to birth, death, marriage, separation, or divorce.

VII. Recording and Tabulating Results
   1. Accumulate weighted counts of eligibles, participants, and costs for summarizing tabulations.
   2. Write eligibility, participation, and cost results for each family on the output file.

Source: Beebout (1977c).

Figure 2.1. A DIAGRAMMATIC REPRESENTATION OF THE *MATH SYSTEM*

MPR had new microsimulation projects. Other federal agencies wanted to utilize the technique, and they were willing to support additional model-building efforts required for new applications of the model. In short order MPR had contracts with the newly created Congressional Budget Office, the Food and Nutrition Service of the Department of Agriculture, the Office of Consumer Affairs of the Federal Energy Administration, and the Division of Tax Analysis of the Treasury Department. All were new microsimulation clients—users that Allen and Beebout had identified as having a potential need for analysis that MPR could help to satisfy.

MPR developed an aggressive marketing strategy which one analyst described as "contacts and contracts." Allen and Beebout would talk to people they knew in agencies involved in some kind of income-redistribution policy. They would bring their acquaintances up-to-date on their new organizational location and their interests in accommodating a wider range of microsimulation users than in the past. They would share ideas about the agency's analytic needs and the firm's modeling capabilities, leading to discussions of how MATH could be adapted for new policy applications. Then came the wait for contract offers, sometimes in the form of sole-source contracts specifically designed for MPR and others as requests for competitive bids.

In the case of the Federal Energy Administration (FEA) contract, Allen has described how the process worked: "At the FEA, we knew a few people in the agency: John Sawhill [administrator] and others at the top. . . . But we eventually got a contract by finding a woman at a relatively low level of the organization who needed the kinds of numbers we could produce fast. [FEA specifically wanted to estimate the impacts of the 1973 OPEC oil embargo on different population groups.] Having this person push to bring us on board was much more important for getting the contract than simply knowing people at the top, although those contacts didn't hurt."[21]

The FEA's Office of Consumer Affairs wanted to use MATH as part of a larger project to create a Comprehensive Human Resources Data System, a tool for estimating the impacts of existing and proposed energy programs on household consumers. MPR helped adapt MATH's data modification routines to input data on energy use onto household records.

The Congressional Budget Office (CBO) also seemed to MPR a logical candidate for using MATH, given the purposes and leadership of the agency. CBO had been established in 1974 as an analytical support agency for Congress, providing objective analysis of the administration's

Level	Master Routine	Purpose (origin)
0 (Input/output and supervisor)		
	SUPER	Controls other master routines [b]
	RDFILE	Reads binary input file and maps input data into storage position [a]
	WRFILE	Writes output file [b]
	SUMTAB	Produces a set of standardized out tables [b]
	PRREC	Prints data from individual households [a]
100 (Initial base year recording and intermediate computation)		
	DEFSTA	Computes intermediate program eligibility status and defines variables [a]
	ALLOCS(ALLSIE)	Allocates person's income by detailed source (1977) [c]
	FUNITS	Defines program filing units except for public assistance [a]
	UNIT7	Defines public assistance filing units [a]
200 (Projections of base year data to future years)		
	POPAGE	Consistent demographic aging for persons and families (1977) [c]
	AGING	Economic aging and special purposes demographic aging [b]
	CSWORK	Unemployment and labor force participation rate adjustment (1978) [c]

300 (Transfer program simulations)

FEDTAX	Federal income taxes[a]
FICAT	Payroll taxes for OASCHI, Railroad Retirement, and federal employees[a]
PBLAST	Public assistance programs: AFDC, SSI, and GA[b]
FSTAMP	Food stamp program (1976)[c]
STATAX	State income taxes (1977)[c]
CASHBEN	Negative income taxes (1977)[c]
JOBS	Public Service Jobs program

500 (Behavioral response and dynamic simulations)

WYWORK	Labor supply response to transfer programs (1977)[c]
PAPRAT	Selection of public assistance participants (1977)[c]
MORTAL	Mortality simulation (1976)[c]
FERTIL	Fertility simulation (1976)[c]
COUPLE	Marriage formation and dissolution (1976)[c]

SOURCES: *MATH Technical Bulletin*, March 22, 1978, p. 2; MATH Users Workshop, 1979.

[a] Adapted from TRIM with minor changes.
[b] Adapted from TRIM with major modifications.
[c] Newly developed for MATH (during year x).

Figure 2.2. MATH MASTER ROUTINES BY FUNCTIONAL LEVEL, PURPOSE, AND ORIGIN

budget proposals and helping to generate and analyze alternative proposals on Capital Hill. Its director was Alice Rivlin, the former colleague of microsimulation theoretician Guy Orcutt, and a person with a long-standing personal interest in microsimulation techniques for policy analysis. Rivlin had once encouraged Beebout and Allen to join her at the Brookings Institution when they left the Urban Institute. In 1976, Rivlin was across town at CBO and Allen and Beebout renewed this contact.

Within CBO, they focused their attention on analysts in the Human Resources and Community Development Division (especially the Income Security and Employment Unit). There they found strong user demand among analysts like William Hoagland, who needed techniques to enable them to answer complex policy-impact questions quickly and to allow them to check the analyses being prepared by the administrative agencies. Hoagland explained CBO's needs:

Before CBO existed, if a congressman had an alternative proposal and wanted it evaluated, he'd have to call down to the agency responsible for developing the President's proposal and ask them, "What if . . . ?" This was rather problematic. It was easy for the congressional alternative to never be analyzed and just die. So with CBO, we can analyze Hill proposals and the President's program. To do so, though, it's especially useful to use the same models that the administration is using—to take them to the Hill, to examine them, and to run them with the same assumptions to see if we get the same results.[22]

CBO therefore had an institutional rivalry interest in acquiring the same methodologies in use across town at HEW. But instead of using TRIM as did HEW, CBO's Hoagland opted for MATH because it seemed to be the more current version of a similar model: "MATH and TRIM were the only tools around; there were no other alternatives to analyze the distributional impacts of programs. MATH was newer, more up-to-date. . . . TRIM had stopped being developed when the Mathematica Policy Research people left the institute, so it didn't really seem like the way to go."[23]

CBO's first contract with MPR was to project the annual costs of all income-transfer programs to the year 2000. For this and subsequent contracts over the next few years, CBO used MATH out-of-house. The model was too large and complex to be well enough understood and operated by CBO analysts in the short time in which they needed program cost estimates. Economist Hoagland caught on rapidly to the logic of the model, but he lacked the personal time and additional technical staffing to learn MATH well enough to operate it in-house. Hoagland used MATH for several years by sending his data bases and program instructions over to MPR, which would prepare the cost estimates with the help of THC computer programmers.

In the case of the Treasury users, it was clearly Nelson McClung who arranged for the contract with MPR; he wanted to combine MATH with the department's Personal Income Tax Model (PITM), to create a synthetic microdata file of all U.S. households in order to forecast the tax implications of proposed changes in welfare and social services policies. The Division of Tax Analysis had sufficient technical staffing, as a result of its experience with designing and running the PITM, to actively participate in adapting MATH for Treasury's need and to help in converting it for use on Treasury's UNIVAC 1108 (instead of the usual IBM 370 system used by other agencies).

At the Department of Agriculture (USDA), MPR found an unsolicited but welcome client in the Food and Nutrition Service (FNS), where analysts were struggling to respond to controversial demands of the Ford administration for large, across-the-board budget cuts in the burgeoning food stamps program. By the end of 1974, several officials and staffers responsible for the food stamp program were aware of how other agencies had used microsimulation models to forecast impacts of changing welfare programs. Both food stamp director Royal Shipp and his assistant, James Springfield, had recognized the need for such a technique to prepare cost estimates and to generate attention to the distributional effects of changing eligibility requirements for food stamps. Shipp and Springfield had already hired Carolyn Merck, an experienced RIM/TRIM analyst, away from HEW's SRS. Next, Shipp, Springfield, and Merck contacted Allen and Beebout at MPR for help in revising MATH so that it could estimate both eligibility and participation rates for the food stamp program. As Merck explained,

We went to them because we knew Allen and Beebout were the real model participants and they were no longer at the Urban Institute. We knew they'd already done some food stamp work for CBO. . . . Jodie Allen had already given some thought to food stamps and considered it a transfer program rather than a farm subsidy program. Royal Shipp knew her from her work at HEW. . . . So she was a natural choice. . . . Beebout did the modeling for us under contract. . . . We spent about $30,000–40,000 for about six months of work. Once the numbers were available, it was possible to cost out all aspects of it, and then food stamps became a real political hot potato.[24]

FNS's contract with MPR called for the consultant to run the computer for food stamp program simulations, although Merck retained control over changes she wanted to make from one simulation to the next. FNS did not have an in-house computing staff capable of reprogramming or operating MATH and could not afford to hire programmers trained in MATH (which used FORTRAN).

THE MATH SUBSCRIPTION SERVICE

These modeling contracts with FNS, CBO, Treasury, and FEA kept MPR busy during its initial years in Washington. By the mid-1970s, nearly 60 percent of MPR's work involved contracts with the MATH model, and the organization's identity was closely wrapped up with MATH.[25]

Over this time, MATH grew incrementally. MPR used the specific contracts with user agencies to build separate modules to simulate eligibility for and participation in discrete income-transfer programs within the federal welfare system. So while work was progressing on the general structure of the model, the MATH model was also growing in terms of its comprehensiveness and the range of its potential policy applications. (See figure 2.2) There were separate modules for the food stamp program, for gasoline price policies, for Aid to Families with Dependent Children, for the Social Security program, for Medicare, for tax policies, and so forth. All MATH users could benefit from the breadth of MATH's expanding program simulation capabilities, since the publicly funded model development work was available to all other users as well as the agency which directly footed the bill. Additionally, regardless of the narrowness of a single agency's program jurisdiction (e.g., FNS's concern for food stamps, or Treasury's interest in personal income taxes), all federal income-transfer programs are related in that policy changes in one program may affect households' income and therefore the costs and caseloads of other programs as well. CBO was especially interested in cross-program implications of policy changes, since CBO has to analyze the budgets of all federal programs. As CBO's Bill Hoagland explained: "The beauty of the MATH model is that its [income-transfer simulation] modules are integrated, just like the welfare system is itself integrated. It makes sense to go with a complex and growing model like MATH rather than a simpler one."[26]

As MATH grew, so did MPR's staffing needs. The Washington office expanded from a handful of analysts in 1974 (Beebout, Allen, economist Ray Uhalde, and planner Richard Hayes) to several dozen professionals, mainly economists with a few sociologists, political scientists, and applied mathematicians. Groups of analysts worked on separate portions of the model. Several programmers at the Hendrickson Corporation were also assigned full time to the MATH project. By 1975, Beebout became concerned that this complex and poorly supervised division of labor might undermine the model's internal integrity. There was a real possibility that it could go out of control.

This model was originally designed with a single worldview by a small, closely knit group of people. But the project grew rapidly and we needed more help. Also, the conditions of the environment we were modeling were changing, and we needed the model to take into account new information and knowledge. Lots of important revisions were going on. These were technical improvements as well as substantive ones. These changes could improve the model, but without coordination they could kill it too. So we definitely had to set up ground rules for how we were going to work on this ever-enlarging model in an organized way.[27]

To coordinate the project, Beebout hired Patricia Doyle and gave her the responsibility to manage and systematize future model development efforts. Doyle was an applied mathematician with no particular familiarity with policy-relevant microeconomic models like MATH. But since she was someone who could learn about such techniques and could communicate with both the economists at MPR and the programming staff at THC, she was in a good position to play the role of "go-between" and manager of the technical effort.

Because Doyle was a novice vis-à-vis MATH, she needed an efficient mechanism to familiarize herself with the guts of the model. No such mechanism existed. Doyle had to ask the individual analysts and programmers assigned to each part of the model about its different parts. The documentation that existed at the time was so terrible that Doyle came to assume that any document she saw was outdated and useless. Before long, it was apparent to Doyle that she had to focus on the documentation task as a way to save the project and integrate the work of the different participants. She set up a rigid system to transfer the personal knowledge of the staffers into written documentation, and to record changes in the model in a consistent way.

This process was important but costly. The contracts MPR held with user agencies were designed to cover model development efforts, not maintenance costs. Unlike the Urban Institute, which had the long-term contract with HEW's ASPE to maintain TRIM, MPR had no user contracts to underwrite documentation efforts. So in mid-1976, Beebout and Doyle devised a plan to offer MPR's modeling services to users on a subscription basis. This was an important innovation for enabling MPR to stay viable in the business. It would provide critical documentation funding while supporting agencies' in-house use of the MATH model.

MPR had to provide the model at virtually no cost since it was developed with public funds, but few users could get away with simply purchasing the model. Agencies could hardly understand the model, much less operate or modify it without extensive consultation, training, and detailed documentation. As Beebout and Doyle saw it, establishment of a subscription service could serve the needs of model developers and users alike. For MPR, it was a way to spread out among all users the expenses of maintaining the elaborate new recording and documenting system—procedures that were absolutely critical to the future integrity of MPR's model. The subscriptions would pay for updating old versions of the model when new modules were completed and ready for dissemination. It also seemed an attractive way for MPR to market its wares; an agency could still hire MPR to design new policy modules or revise existing ones, or even to run the models for specific policy analyses; but the agency could also take the model in-house, receive training for operating and modifying it, obtain subsequent updates and descriptions of technical and substantive changes in the model, have access to selected data files, and receive a limited number of hours of consultation with MPR staff.

MPR recognized the importance of agencies being able to fully implement the model in-house. With sufficient training and experience in operating the model, analysts in the agencies could better control its use. This in turn could increase the analysts' confidence in the model's estimates, their use of the model for actual policy analyses, and even their demand for new modeling applications in the future. Without that initial sense of independence and control, the analysts—and by extension, the policymakers who rely on them—might never get to the point of fully trusting MATH's output. And without this trust, and with insufficient expertise to independently evaluate the output, analysts might lose interest in using MATH for actual policy analysis. In the long run, the future of the MATH technique in policy analysis relied upon agencies' ability to better understand and control the model.[28] The subscription service might enable agencies to implement the model while also maintaining demand for MPR's services.

Part of MPR's modeling package included user support in the

form of Pat Doyle. The subscription package required a new role for Doyle: in addition to her continuing role as mediator between internal groups, she would also serve as a mediating agent between the modelers and the users. She was the agent through whom MPR and users interacted. She organized training sessions. She linked agency analysts with the appropriate consultants at MPR. She tracked and recorded agencies' own modifications in their versions of MATH. These functions meant that along with the new package of products and services offered by MPR came a variation of its own organizational structure.

The existence of the package also required MPR to formally separate its "development model," the one it would use for internal experimentation and modification, from its "product model," the one it would offer to users through the subscription service. MPR initially decided to release four updated versions of the model each year. On a given day, the development model would be "frozen" so that a version of it could be identified, recorded, and documented for subscribers. Once recorded, work could continue on the developmental version while the product version was being prepared for subscribers. For example, to produce the first release of the model, called "77.1" (the first version for 1977), MPR replicated the development model's source code on another tape, prepared documentation in the form of a MATH codebook and a technical description, and wrote a "user's manual" to accompany the package. For subscribers, a new release included the updated version of the model's code, a cover letter explaining technical and substantive changes in the model, and new codebook pages to replace those pages where code changes had occurred.

Within six months of the initial concept of a subscription service, the first subscription was actually placed. MPR priced the subscription by calculating their annual costs for model maintenance, dividing that figure by the number of users, and then adding on the relatively fixed costs of consultation. Thus, a larger base of subscribers could lower the prices of individual subscriptions, although not significantly, because the marginal costs of user-directed services remained high. In the first year, the annual flat rate was set at $15,000, based on MPR's estimate of its total annual maintenance costs of $150,000. The first subscriber was HEW's ASPE office, which was interested in adding to the microsimulation capabilities it already had as a result of in-house use of TRIM.

ASPE remained the only MATH subscriber during 1977, the first year of the service. This led Beebout and Allen to return to more organized marketing practices to convince potential users of the value of MPR's services. In the next year other agencies joined, including the FNS, the Division of Tax Analysis at Treasury, the Office of the Assistant Secretary for Policy Evaluation and Research at the Department of Labor, and the CBO. For each of these users, the annual subscription to MATH cost $18,000.[29] While these subscription contracts did not in fact fully cover the expenses MPR incurred in maintaining the model, they did provide a substantial base from which MPR could underwrite its microsimulation modeling work.

Microsimulation at Mid-Decade

By 1977, MATH and TRIM had clearly entered into a use stage throughout Washington, D.C. The small group of microsimulation modelers at Mathematica Policy Research and the Urban Institute had experienced noticeable success in having their models embraced by key policy analysts in every federal agency involved in income-transfer policy. Within a decade of these models' genesis at the President's Commission on Income Maintenance Programs, the social-policy analysts had adopted a new mode for examining the clientele served by federal welfare programs. Commenting on this period of model dissemination, early model advocate Nelson McCLung said in 1980: "People have finally begun to learn to live with these microsimulation models. Serious development began about fifteen years ago by the very people who needed the output. Eight to ten years ago, more people became aware of them. Five years ago, MATH and TRIM had become the basic tools of analysis within the field. . . . This marked the end of the 'disbelief' stage."[30]

CHAPTER THREE
THE "PUSH"
FOR MODEL
IMPLEMENTATION

THE UNITED States' economy is by far the world's largest and most influential. For a number of years the Gross Domestic Product of the United States has been about as large as the combined products of the second, third, and fourth largest economies (the Soviet Union, Japan, and West Germany). This dominance of the U.S. economy has existed for many years, becoming most pronounced following World War II, when the United States almost single-handedly financed the rebuilding of Western Europe and Japan.

Any economy is a product of many varied, complex, and often uncontrollable forces, including the vagaries of nature and the turns of international events. Yet it has been a goal of economists since the earliest days of the economic discipline to decipher the workings of economies and thereby develop ways to influence economic phenomena. Such knowledge would give economists the insight to advise national leaders on what course to take for improving and increasing what Adam Smith called the "wealth of nations."

The efforts of economic policymakers in the post–World War II industrial world have been encouraging on some fronts (e.g., the apparent success of efforts to avoid calamitous disruptions like the depression of the 1920s and 1930s) and disappointing on others (e.g., the apparent inability of economic policymaking to eliminate the cycles of recession and expansion that have plagued the industrial West since the late 1940s). As yet, no economist would claim that the economy of the world or of any nation is "under control," or even well understood; few would even suggest that such understanding or complete control is really possible. Nevertheless, progress has been made.

One of the most important developments in the effort to improve the ability of nations to control their economies has been the notion of "systems" of economic phenomena,[1] which holds that the many components that make up the economy behave systematically with regard to one another. Changes in one component lead to changes in others. For example, a drop in the level of personal income means a drop in purchases of consumer goods. More important, this notion holds that these systematic relationships can be identified, measured, and monitored.[2] If the economy can eventually be understood in all its systematic complexity, it might be possible to make selective interventions to achieve desired economic policy objectives.

This notion of systems in economic behavior has been developing for over 200 years. In the past century most major economists have embraced the systems notion, and the economic discipline as a whole has adopted the powerful tools of mathematics and statistics to enable construction of quantitative models of economic systems. A subspecialty within economics, macroeconomic modeling, takes existing or hypothetical data on economic conditions and runs those data through a set of mathematical equations designed to express the relationships that exist between key factors in the economy. The intended result is a simulation of how the real economy would behave given the assumed relationships. The fundamental belief in models of this kind is expressed by Klein and Young: "Every model is an approximation to the unknown, but true, underlying system of the economy" (1980:50). In other words, the economy behaves systematically and this behavior can be modeled, provided one can gather sufficient insight into these systematic processes and assemble the data necessary to provide coefficients for the variables in the equations.

MACROECONOMIC MODELS IN FEDERAL
ECONOMIC POLICYMAKING

Macroeconomic models have been used extensively as economic research tools for over forty years, in part because they serve as highly controllable laboratories for testing theoretical relationships among economic variables. But the most alluring feature of models is the fact that, if properly developed, they can be used as tools for forecasting the probable economic conditions of the near future, and for simulating the effects of possible economic policy changes. Such applications of macroeconomic modeling have been the goal of thirty years of extensive efforts to improve model performance and move modeling into the mainstream of national economic policymaking. The results of these efforts have been impressive. In the relatively short space of fifteen years, from 1960 to 1974, macroeconomic modeling moved beyond the research laboratories of universities and into the economic policymaking agencies of the federal government. Macroeconomic modeling is now well established as an important tool of analysis for national economic policymaking in the United States. Perhaps the largest and most successful macroeconomic modeling service now in operation is that of Data Resources, Incorporated (DRI).

Antecedents of the DRI Model

To understand how the DRI macroeconomic modeling service found a niche in the policymaking apparatus of the national government, it will be useful to briefly review the history of macroeconomic modeling which served as a base for the development of DRI. This historical context illustrates the basic characteristics of the models and indicates their strength as analytical tools, as well as the constraints on their utility for real-world policymaking.

A SHORT HISTORY OF ECONOMETRIC MODELING[3]
    A macroeconomic model of the economy is, by broad definition, a systematic model that deals with the larger features of the economy— the performance of the overall productive base of a nation, or a group of nations. Macroeconomics is important in setting the course of national economic policy because major macroeconomic variables such as Gross National Product are barometers of national economic health. Current macroeconomic modeling efforts rely mainly on the specialty of econometrics, which is ". . . the study of economic theory in its relations to statistics and mathematics" (Strotz 1978:188). Econometric modeling matches actual patterns of economic behavior to theoretical models of economic behavior in order to improve understanding of the economy. All the major macroeconomic modeling systems, including DRI's, are built on the traditions of econometric modeling. Strictly speaking,

their models are best called macroeconometric, to encompass both the macroeconomic and econometric components. To keep the terminology simple, however, we will use the commonly accepted term econometric modeling to refer to the antecedents of the DRI model.

Econometric models are among the oldest models used for policymaking (Greenberger, Crenson, and Crissey 1976). The groundwork leading to the development of econometric models is a product of the past sixty years. The 1910s and 1920s saw the first blending together of economic theories, statistical data bases, and mathematical techniques in efforts to forecast the likely behavior of the economy over the short run. This work was not successful at producing reliable forecasts, but it did set the stage for more serious attempts at examining the present state of the economy to decipher what the future would be like (Samuelson 1975).[4]

The first genuine econometric models of a national economy were built in the 1930s by Jan Tinbergen, a Dutch economist now regarded as the father of econometric modeling. Tinbergen built a model of the Dutch economy in 1939 and a year later built a model of the U.S. economy under the auspices of the League of Nations (Tinbergen 1939). The work begun by Tinbergen was continued in the United States during the Second World War by economists at the Cowles Commission for Research in Economics at the University of Chicago. These economists, including Tjalling Koopmans, Jacob Marshack, Trygve Haavelmo, and Lawrence Klein, expanded on Tinbergen's concepts and incorporated the economic theories of John Maynard Keynes into a model of the U.S. economy. This model, known as the Klein-Cowles Commission model, was released in 1946. It gained early notoriety by accurately predicting that the country would not experience a generally anticipated postwar recession. This success established econometric modeling as a tool of considerable promise for economic forecasting, and launched Klein's career as the foremost econometric modeler—a position he holds to this day.

With support from private foundations, universities, and eventually the U.S. government, a number of econometric models were developed during the 1950s and early 1960s. Among the most important were: the Klein-Goldberger model, developed in 1952 at the University of Michigan by Klein and graduate student Arthur Goldberger; the Duesenberry-Eckstein-Fromm model, developed in 1959 at Harvard by James Duesenberry, Otto Eckstein, and Gary Fromm; the Wharton model, developed in 1963 by Klein at the University of Pennsylvania's Wharton School; and the Social Science Research Council (SSRC)/Brookings Institution model, developed in 1964 by Fromm, Klein, Duesenberry, and others. A relatively small number of key econometric modelers were involved in the creation of these models, and they were in close communication with one another during the 1955–1965 period. This collaborative work produced most of the major tools and techniques for large-scale econometric modeling, and the formal institutional settings for modeling were established at universities and research institutes.

It was also during this period that economic policymaking agencies in the federal government began to show serious interest in model use. Government interest came in two forms. One was the interest of policy analysts in the forecasts and simulations the models produced. By 1965 models at Michigan, Wharton, and Brookings were producing fairly regular forecasts, which were being watched by the economists in policymaking agencies such as the Bureau of the Budget, the Treasury Department, the Council of Economic Advisers, and the Federal Reserve Board. Economists in both the modeling and policymaking arenas shared model results and information. The second major form of government interest was in improving model accuracy, and took the form of financial support. In particular, most of the development of the SSRC/Brookings model was financed through a series of National Science Foundation (NSF) grants. Between 1960 and 1967 NSF provided approximately $375,000 in support for this model-building effort. Through this combination of substantive interest in the results of models and financial support for the creation of new models, the federal government entered the macroeconomic modeling fraternity in an important and influential manner. The federal role helped establish a financial support structure for model development and a respected policymaking arena for the use of model results.

WHAT ECONOMETRIC MODELS DO

The models developed by these research efforts were basically mathematical models containing a number of simultaneous equations representing assumed relationships between important macroeconomic variables. For example, assuming there is a general and stable relationship between interest rates and the extent to which investors place their money in interest-bearing holdings, one could create a mathematical equation that expresses this relationship. Provided one correctly specifies the relationship, and inserts data on how the variables change, it is possible to simulate likely real-world investment behavior under various rate changes. If the data provided correctly correspond to real-world conditions, and the model incorporates other equations to account for the interrelatedness of various economic phenomena (e.g., that the amount of money available for investment also affects investment rates), the model could be used to forecast how much investment there might be if one variable changed while the others remained equal.

The conceptual foundations of most of today's macroeconomic models are the economic theories first consolidated and expounded by John M. Keynes (Greenberger, Crenson, and Crissey 1976; Klein and Young 1980). According to Keynesian theory, many variables in the economy (e.g., housing starts, interest rates, inflation rates) interact with one another in theoretically predictable ways, making it possible to build a set of equations that model many different components of the economy. If the set of equations is large enough and accurate enough, and the relationships between the variables correctly correspond to real-world relationships, a model's structure and behavior, will produce a close simulation of the actual economy.

Historically, the early simple linear models of behavior had proven inadequate for modeling the dynamic and complex economy of a modern nation. A major advancement represented by the large macroeconomic models of the 1960s was the creation of models that were nonlinear and dynamic, in which the behavior of the models was governed by such factors as the passage of time and changes in the business cycle. Moreover, the modern models were simultaneous models: changes in one set of variables affected other variables simultaneously. The result of these advancements was the creation of large models containing a great number of equations corresponding to many economic variables.

These models also formalized the basic structure of variables for macroeconomic modeling. Two major kinds of variables make up the models. *Exogenous variables* are the assumptions the modeler brings to the model; they are determined judgmentally by economists and must be specified prior to running the model. Examples of exogenous variables are "policy" variables which are assumed to be under the control of government (e.g., tax rates or government-spending levels), and "nonpolicy" variables which include the forces of nature and international events (e.g., crop conditions and foreign exchange rates). Using the values provided for the exogenous variables, the model then determines the values of the *endogenous variables*—the products of the model given the initial exogenous asumptions. Examples of common endogenous variables are the economic output values that make up the Gross

National Product, as well as other factors such as inflation, employment, and interest rates. The models draw their data from several sources, but primarily from major federal government records such as the National Income and Product Accounts (NIPA).

LESSONS FROM THE HISTORY OF ECONOMETRIC MODELING

The early evolution of econometric models reveals several lessons about what it takes to do such modeling. First, any major econometric modeling effort requires three basic components: a theoretically sound model, a highly reliable data base of time-series economic data, and the computing capability to manage the data and conduct the many thousands of calculations required. The major theoretical work proceeded from the early model builders. The major data elements, including the NIPA, were established during the 1930s and expanded during the 1940s and 1950s. Initial mergers of the theoretical models and the extensive data sets took place about the time the Brookings and Wharton models took shape. The catalyst of the merger was the advent of powerful late second-generation and early third-generation computers.

Second, the coming together of the prerequisite components of theory, data, and computing capabilities was the product of focused research efforts that required as much skill in computing and data management as they did in econometric science. These large-scale efforts in econometric modeling were hybrid, interdisciplinary projects in which the participants had to learn new skills and integrate them with their own economic specialties. This integration not only set econometric modeling apart from classical economics, in the sense that econometrics was characterized by its sophisticated tools, but it caused econometrics to acquire a large and demanding infrastructure of statistical and computing expertise without which it could not survive. Moreover, the growth of econometric modeling fueled the demands for ever-greater collection and refinement of economic data in the United States and other countries.

Finally, the growth of econometric modeling necessitated the growth of established centers for econometric activity. While gifted economists might move about from place to place, top econometricians became tied to their established facilities. The creation and maintenance of large-scale models depended on powerful and stable computing environments, a continued inflow of computerized time-series data, and all the specialized support personnel necessary to run such an operation. In many ways the large econometric modeling efforts became substantial organizations in their own right. Thus econometric modeling evolved from disaggregated efforts of individual economists to cooperative research efforts into model building, and eventually to the creation of established modeling projects at universities and other research centers. This evolution led directly to the establishment of separate institutionalized modeling centers with their own identities and budgets and engaged in model building and marketing. Perhaps the archetypical example of such a center is Data Resources, Incorporated (DRI).

The Development of DRI [5]

Data Resources owes its existence and success to its principal founders Otto Eckstein, Donald Marron, and Gary Fromm, and a group of talented people who worked with and for them.[6] Eckstein, a Harvard economics professor, had become interested in simulation during a short stay at the RAND Corporation in California in 1957. He brought his new knowledge back to Harvard in 1958 where he became involved in a macroeconomic modeling project that had just begun under the direction of James Duesenberry. Together with economists Duesenberry and Gary Fromm, Eckstein helped create the Duesenberry-Eckstein-Fromm (DEF) model, a twenty-equation econometric model of the U.S. economy. This modeling project launched Eckstein's career as a macroeconomic modeler.

Following the DEF project, Eckstein, who was well connected with Democratic party politics, moved on to Washington where he served for a time as staff director for a study of employment, growth, and price levels conducted by the Joint Economic Committee of Congress. Later he became a member of the Council of Economic Advisers in the Johnson administration. During his tenure in these positions he came to see the importance for economic policymaking of having quick access to economic data. Eckstein also established extensive contacts within the professional ranks of economists engaged in helping to set national economic policy.

EARLY DEVELOPMENT

In 1966, Eckstein left Washington to spend a year at a behavioral science research center at Stanford Univerity. During his stay at Stanford he began to develop the idea of creating an information service to provide economic data for analysis, a notion that had come up earlier in discussion with Fromm and Duesenberry during the DEF work. Eckstein's renewed interest in creating such a service was prompted by his increasing involvement as a consultant, presenting his economic analyses and forecasts to various business interests around the country.

These consulting presentations had grown out of Eckstein's association with Donald Marron of the New York investment firm of Mitchell-Hutchings (later called Paine-Webber-Mitchell-Hutchins). Marron had conceived the idea of bringing together top people in economics, political analysis, and international affairs to produce periodic forecasts and analyses to help business leaders plan their investments.[7] He retained Eckstein to handle the economic aspects of the plan, and Marron and Eckstein began to build a clientele for the service from among Mitchell-Hutchins' customers. By the time Eckstein returned to Harvard in 1968, he began to look for a way to maintain his advisory services while reducing the travel demands they made on him. It seemed that forecasts for his clients could be done in an approximate manner by giving clients access to the forecasts and the data behind them over a computer time-sharing network.[8]

In the late 1960s commercial computer time-sharing services were the darling of Wall Street. Many shrewd investors believed that companies providing such services could be profitable investments. Marron quickly seized on the idea, and arranged $1.1 million in financing to launch a new company—DRI—to provide computerized economic modeling and data services to customers over time-sharing lines.[9] DRI was founded with Marron as chairman of the board and Eckstein as president. Fromm, a man with extensive macroeconomic modeling experience as well as considerable respect among members of both the modeling and economic policymaking communities in Washington, was asked to head the model and data services part of the plan.

Marron and Eckstein headquartered their new company in small rented offices in Lexington, Massachusetts, and immediately began developing their business strategy. DRI needed an econometric model on its developing system, and efforts were made to procure the Wharton model for this purpose. After several months of negotiations, however, the deal fell through and DRI proceeded to develop its own model.[10] DRI built upon the accumulated knowledge of past modeling efforts to construct the model, although the actual DRI model was essentially new.

Eckstein built the model with the assistance of DRI employees (many of whom were Eckstein's graduate students) and several colleagues from other universities: Martin Feldstein of Harvard developed the model's initial financial sector; Lester Thurow of MIT developed the initial equations explaining the structure of unemployment; Mark Nerlove of the University of Chicago developed some stock market models (which were never really marketed by DRI); and Dale Jorgensen of Harvard developed several long-range models that influenced but were not fully incorporated into the DRI model. The DRI model was completed and available for commercial clients in 1969.

From the beginning Eckstein and Marron realized that DRI had to be more than just a computerized modeling company with time-sharing services. As the name Data Resources indicates, the company not only provided modeling capabilities but also the data services necessary to run the model under different assumptions, plus the analytical expertise necessary to construct analyses at many levels (e.g., national, regional, and sectoral) and interpret their results. This was a major departure from other modeling efforts. The other macroeconomic modeling centers were, for the most part, research centers in which economists worked primarily on developing models and provided, as a secondary activity, periodic forecasts generated by their models to an interested audience of government agencies and private concerns.[11] Unlike DRI, these academic centers did not exist to answer the specific questions of economists working in government or large corporations about the effects of the economy on fiscal or monetary matters, or on particular industries. DRI would provide the data bases, models, and analytical expertise to do whatever analyses paying customers might request. What put DRI outside the tradition of modeling projects was that it was a private, profit-making, service delivery company that put into commercial production the techniques and skills developed over years of painstaking research into econometrics, mathematical modeling, data management, and computing.

CREATING THE PRODUCT BASE

The development of the DRI macroeconomic model was only the first step in creating the range of services DRI eventually provided. To help organize the company, Eckstein enlisted the help of Charles Warden, a retired military officer who had become acquainted with Eckstein in Washington in 1950–60. Eckstein had encouraged Warden to go on to Harvard for graduate studies in economics, which Warden did. Following the completion of his Ph.D., Warden returned to Washington where, with Eckstein's patronage, he secured the position of special assistant to the chairman of the Council of Economic Advisers, a post he held from 1966 to 1969. Warden's job brought him into extensive contact with major actors in the economic policymaking process, and his managerial skills were broadened through dealing with the complicated technical and political aspects of national economic policymaking. Eckstein believed both qualities would be useful to DRI, since the company was to provide econometric modeling and data services, as well as economic consulting.

DRI's intention to make its model and its data bases available over a computer network meant that it was necessary to develop computer systems support to facilitate maintenance of a large and accurate data base of economic time-series data, and allow remote users to conveniently log-on and use the system for their needs. To build this support, Eckstein and Fromm hired John Ahlstrom and James Craig from the SSRC/Brookings project in early 1969.

Ahlstrom went to work building the computer system needed for the data management and modeling tasks, and selected a Burroughs B5500 as DRI's first computer mainframe because of its capability in handling large processing requirements at lower cost than rival machines.[12] Ahlstrom also contacted a computing services company called TYMESHARE to arrange use of its developing TYMENET data communications system, and began building the database systems that would be used to support the model. His first system was PRIMA, a primitive data base management system, capable of inputting and retrieving data and doing crude time-series processing. Of particular importance was PRIMA's matrix format that provided space for instructions at the beginning of each data set and flexible record lengths at the end. PRIMA was replaced by a more powerful system called AID in 1974. Craig set about building the data base for the model. He selected, and DRI purchased, about 350 time series from the Brookings project's data base, and by the end of 1969 he had expanded this to over 6,000 time series. More important, Craig developed elegant procedures for obtaining, cleaning, loading, and managing this large data base that allowed a high degree of quality control over the data.[13] Ahlstrom and Craig succeeded in building a technical base of computer power, data, and data management software whereby DRI could create and maintain a large data base of economic time-series data and provide customers access to this data base and to the DRI model over the computer time-sharing system.

To develop the software systems that would allow users to estimate the equations for the model in conducting their own analyses, DRI purchased Robert Hall's TSP (Time Series Processor) package of statistical regression routines. This package, developed by Hall with support from the National Science Foundation, was publicly available but not tailored to the DRI system. Eckstein hired Hall to modify TSP to fit the DRI system and its needs. The result, known as the Econometric Programming Language (EPL), was a processor that allowed for comprehensive estimation capabilities needed in macroeconomic model building. To complement EPL, DRI built a package called MODSIM that would help users construct their own small models and make industry-specific forecasts through changes in the DRI national model's structure.

EPL was the best piece of software of its kind, but its use was cumbersome. Modeling with EPL required exiting and reinitializing many small programs, making it excessively time-consuming. DRI management decided to build a more comprehensive system that would link the various aspects of the modeling process together in one program. They hired Robert Lacey, a talented young programmer from Harvard, to develop the new system. Lacey developed a program called MODEL that allowed users to quickly do complicated tasks required of econometric modeling, such as moving from a quarterly time period to an annual one, as well as creating and running multiple forecasts under different assumptions while keeping all the numbers straight.[14]

MODEL was an extraordinary system, a decade ahead of its time. It was efficient, logical, and powerful, and took much of the tedium out of doing macroeconomic modeling. Subsequently, in 1975–77, Lacey wrote a comprehensive system that linked together and expanded the capabilities of EPL, AID, MODSIM, and MODEL. This system, called EPS (Econometric Programming System), allowed a user to do almost any modeling task with considerable ease. It also had extensive capabilities for outputing formatting, report generation, and graphics that allowed users to specify what results they wanted to see and how they wanted to see them.[15]

To build up DRI's client service capability Eckstein hired three individuals to market and provide support services to clients. Donald McLagan, a Harvard MBA who had been doing cost analyses of the

Vietnam War at the Pentagon, was hired to head up consulting activities for clients and to build an organizational capability for providing continuous support. Under McLagan's direction DRI adopted a "team" approach by which each client would be served by a specific team of specialists, ranging from senior economists to systems support people. This allowed clients a consistent point of contact with DRI, and the teams were responsible for learning what the clients' needs were and making sure they got the services they wanted. This move institutionalized DRI's founders' sensitivity to the needs of analysts and decision makers, and the necessity of developing DRI services to meet them. When DRI marketed its services to the federal government, this focus on meeting needs rather than simply selling a product greatly aided the DRI effort. Eckstein also hired G. Dennis O'Brien, a Ph.D. economist who had worked in private industry, to develop marketing strategies and assist in the creation of consulting service support. O'Brien was an enthusiastic, articulate person with the ability to quickly and accurately clarify clients' desires and needs and envision a package of services they would be willing to buy. Finally, Eckstein hired Stephen Browne, an MIT Ph.D. in industrial economics, to begin to flesh out the expansion of services and products DRI could offer to different industrial sectors.

Once the technical, administrative, and economic foundations of DRI were laid, the task of selling services began in earnest. Early clients were primarily private firms that had been clients of Eckstein during the time he made rounds providing economic forecasts and advice. But this client base soon expanded to include other industrial and commercial interests who wanted to enhance their in-house economic analysis capabilities.

GETTING STARTED IN WASHINGTON, D.C.

With revenue from the private sector providing a sound financial base for expansion, DRI established a Washington office in 1969 specifically to market its products to the federal government. Fromm, assisted by Warden, was installed as the first director of the Washington office.

Selling services to federal agencies was different from selling to the private sector. The needs of federal users differed from those of private clients because of the government's unique responsibility for making fiscal and monetary policy. Moreover, federal economic agencies already employed highly competent economists, who needed extensive analytical capabilities to evaluate policies that both affected and would be affected by the economy. These economists had been using the results of existing macroeconomic modeling projects at Wharton, Michigan, MIT, and other universities, but they did not have access to the models and data bases needed to do their own analyses. DRI provided access not only to a large and respectable model and extensive data, but also to software routines that facilitated independent analysis and report writing as well.

The first federal users of DRI were the Library of Congress, which then was the primary research and analysis arm of Congress, and the Treasury Department, which had primary responsibility for analyses used by the executive branch in the creation of the annual budget. Both agencies quickly adopted DRI services because DRI provided them a unique and powerful new tool for evaluating fiscal and monetary effects of federal program changes.[16] In the early 1970s the federal government had relatively few competitive bidding restrictions on contracting, so it was possible for these agencies to simply issue a purchase order for DRI services.

The marketing of DRI in Washington soon went beyond these early contacts. In 1970 Warden went to Paul Earl, a professor at Georgetown University, and arranged to give Georgetown access to the DRI system for use in its teaching and research programs. In exchange, Georgetown students used the system to develop methods of creating regional data bases on state and local economies in order to build up the regional analysis capabilities of the DRI system. A hidden benefit to DRI came from the fact that Georgetown economics students became familiar with and partial to the DRI system, and took a desire to use DRI services with them when they went on to jobs in federal agencies. This helped seed a large number of knowledgeable economists in federal agencies who created internal demands to acquire DRI services.

This influx of new talent and tools into economic policymaking came at a crucial time. The war in Vietnam was straining the national economy, and the Great Society programs were rapidly growing in cost. It was expected that the end of the war would lead to a "peace dividend," but that the Great Society programs would continue to be growing items in the federal budget. Most of these programs had been based on liberal social ideologies, with little long-range analysis as to what they would cost in future years. In the early 1970s, this burden, coupled with the burden of the war spending, began to spur new interest in analyzing what the programs cost and whether they were accomplishing the taks for which they had been designed.

These concerns came together in 1973 when President Nixon's

impoundment of appropriated funds spearheaded a congressional reassessment of the federal budgetary process. There was considerable concern that the federal government had been buying itself into an uncontrolled spending pattern with little thought to the consequences. With the passage of the Congressional Budget and Impoundment Act of 1974 (P.L. 93–344), Congress established the Congressional Budget Office (CBO) to take over and enhance the budget analysis capability of Congress (previously housed in the Library of Congress). The Act formalized economic analysis as a part of the budgetary process, and instantly created new demand for economic analytical capability in both Congress and the executive agencies. As CBO and the Office of Management and Budget (OMB) became increasingly tough in review of programs, federal mission agencies began to build up their in-house analytical capabilities to answer the questions that would inevitably arise about their programs.

Given this context, DRI arrived at exactly the right time, and with a package containing all the right things. An example of how DRI exploited this new opportunity is its development of the Cost Forecasting System (CFS), a system designed to use past data on costs and DRI's current economic forecasts to predict the future costs of major federal programs. This service got its start when DRI's O'Brien took his marketing expertise to the Department of Defense in 1974 and proposed that DRI develop a system that would allow Defense analysts to forecast the costs of major weapons development systems being proposed to the President and Congress. Defense paid DRI $350,000 to develop this system, which became CFS. DRI then took CFS to a large number of Defense contractors and showed them how Defense was using the system to predict the costs of their large procurement programs. These companies quickly bought CFS to help them in developing their bids for Defense contracts, and overnight DRI had a new clientele. Other federal agencies quickly followed the Defense Department's lead and acquired DRI services for themselves. Shortly, both OMB and CBO were using CFS to evaluate the estimates provided by the agencies.

DRI'S GROWTH, 1970–1978

From 1970 to 1978 DRI grew rapidly in terms of the number of clients it served and the range of services it offered. Business revenues often grew at a rate in excess of 50 percent per year. The DRI professional staff grew to the point that Eckstein became fond of saying DRI had more Ph.D. economists than the federal government. Technical capabilities of the company constantly expanded. The original Burroughs B5500 computer system which could support fourteen simultaneous users was replaced in 1973 with a single B6700 machine, and later with two additional B6700s. In 1977 these were replaced with a system of four B7700s capable of supporting over 300 users at a time. Time-sharing capability also expanded, first over TYMENET, and then over DRI's own time-sharing system called DRINET.

By 1978 DRI had become almost a household name among economists and others concerned about the economy. DRI's forecasts and analyses were being quoted regularly in newspapers, and the DRI data bases had become industry standards of reference. Government agencies both in the United States and abroad discovered that DRI's data often were more accurate than their own, and the DRI data were routinely used to correct official government economic records.[17] By 1978 the DRI data bases had grown to over eight million time series, with data available on almost every conceivable economic and commerce variable in the United States and many overseas countries. DRI had more information about U.S. industry than any other organization.

DRI's macroeconomic model also underwent constant refinement and improvement during this period. This was in part due to an endemic desire among modelers to improve on the existing model. Improvement also was necessitated by the fact that destabilizing factors in the economy had begun to make forecasting difficult even with the best of models and judgmental expertise. The energy crisis in 1973, coupled with the aftereffects of the war in Vietnam and the growth of federal spending, altered the behavior of the economy to the point where the forecasts of the large models, which had once been so successful, were as seriously in error as the forecasts of economists who did not rely heavily on models.[18] The process of continuous improvement kept the DRI model at least abreast of other models and research available at that time.

During the early and mid-1970s, a large number of new product lines had been added to DRI's services. New models were developed in many industrial sectors, including chemicals, steel, paper products, agriculture, and many others. Through the marketing talents of O'Brien and the industrial economics expertise of Stephen Browne, many of these services were actually paid for in advance by the industries they served. For example, DRI received a contract from National Steel to build a large, linear programming model for investment analysis, and it worked so well that within two years fourteen of the top fifteen steel companies in the United States were using the service.

This strategy for business development worked so well that DRI never had to borrow beyond the initial $1.1 million of capital it started with. By the end of 1978 DRI had as clients 49 of the top 50 *Fortune* 500 firms, 250 of the top 300 manufacturing corporations, 50 of the top 100 utility companies, and 24 of the top 25 banks. Most of DRI's contacts were directly with the chief executive officers in these companies.

DRI also expanded its services for the federal government during this period, especially in the Department of Energy (DOE). One consequence of the major oil price increases in 1973 was a call for improved federal monitoring of energy resources that led to many efforts to create energy information banks. President Carter sank large amounts of money into the effort to improve federal data on energy, and DRI managed to secure over $1 million from DOE to develop a wide range of energy price impact models. Other agencies adopted DRI services as they became familiar with their usefulness, and by 1978 DRI had every major government agency as a client in one way or another.[19]

This rapid growth was tremendously remunerative for all those who held equity interests in DRI, but it was also stressful for the company's leadership. Fromm had left the company in 1974 after a dispute with Eckstein over his role and his compensation.[20] Other problems were due directly to growing pains and disagreements about how the company should proceed. Competitors such as Chase Econometrics began to try to steal portions of DRI's lucrative business. Often the marketing staff would promise products that the company had not yet developed, then put pressure on the technical staff to come up with the products. Also, there was a rift developing over what the main components of DRI's service mix ought to include. Some thought the company should move more heavily into direct economic consulting and specialty analyses for individual firms, while others felt the company ought to stay with its broader "generic" services to industrial sectors. This rift spilled over into a dispute about how to organize the company's markets. Charles Warden, whose calm administrative manner had helped smooth the troubled waters, left in 1977 and the pressure became more intense. In July of 1978, Stephen Browne, vice president in charge of industrial economics, left DRI with six of DRI's top consultants to start their own company called Planning Economics Group. O'Brien, the company's senior vice president of service and marketing, also indicated he wanted to leave (he soon did), and word quickly began to spread that a major breakup of the top echelons of DRI was under way. Within two weeks, Marron, who for two years had been holding off offers by large investors to buy the company, arranged the sale of DRI to McGraw-Hill for $103 million. The sale made rich many of those who held small amounts of stock gained during the early days of the company, while the principals, including Marron, Eckstein, and Fromm, made millions.[21]

The sale of DRI did not seem to damage the company, however. With backing by its giant new parent it began a program of retrenchment that has solidified its position as the leader in the macroeconomic modeling/data resources/economic analysis field. Large amounts of capital were put into expansion of DRI's computing and analysis capabilities, and new development efforts to exploit emerging technologies (e.g., microprocessor-based end-user stations) were begun. Since its start many firms sprang to compete with aspects of DRI's business, but none has ever approached the size or stability of DRI.

Status and Use of DRI Services

By the time the data collection for this book was complete DRI had become the largest purveyor of econometric modeling services in the world. DRI's services had been organized along six dimensions: models, data banks, computer services, professional staff services, publications, conferences, and consulting (DRI 1981).

DRI continued to build its large econometric model of the United States, upon which its modeling reputation was built. An overview of that model is shown in figure 3.1. DRI also had expanded to provide models of the economies of eight other free-world industrialized nations and of the Far East. It provided specialized econometric models of major industrial sectors, including agriculture, the chemical industry, oil and gas drilling, forestry and wood products, steel, transportation, and others. It provided several cross-industrial models to address such subjects as state and area forecasting, the utilities industries, and industrial cost forecasting. Finally, it had a number of econometric models specifically tailored to the financial industry. These models came to constitute the intellectual capital of DRI as far as econometrics is concerned, and the presence of these models served as a major selling feature for the rest of DRI's services.

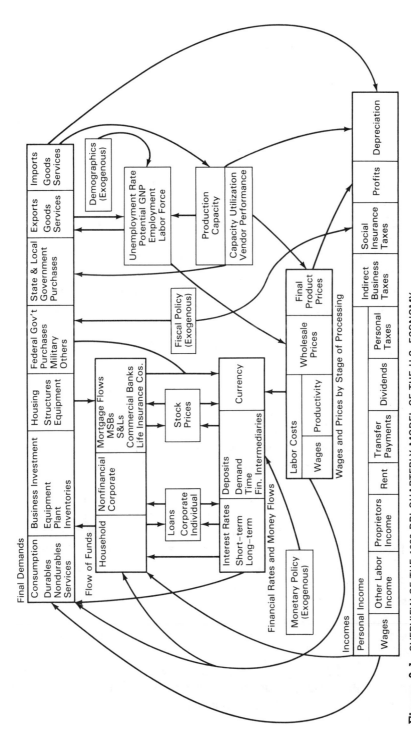

Figure 3.1. OVERVIEW OF THE 1982 DRI QUARTERLY MODEL OF THE U.S. ECONOMY

By 1981 DRI's data banks contained "millions of national, international, regional, financial, industrial, company, and special purpose data series" (DRI 1981:5). An approximate count showed between eight and ten million time series.[22] The vast majority were assembled, cleaned, and put on-line by DRI's staff of eighty "primary-source" data bankers. A few time series were obtained in machine-readable form from governmental and other organizations, although these were usually edited and documented by DRI data bankers. As with the models, the data banks were organized along functional lines. National economic data banks contained time series on the U.S. economy as a whole, on regions of the nation, and on other countries. They also contained data from international financing agencies (such as the International Monetary Fund), from international economic study agencies (such as the Organization for Economic Cooperation and Development), and from certain specific political jurisdictions (such as California and New York City). Other DRI data banks covered specific industries (e.g., agriculture, the auto industry, coal), the financial sector (funds flows, the Standard and Poor indexes), and cross-industry data (Conference Board analyses, Compustat statistics). DRI also had become a major computing service provider. The DRI models and data banks were available for use only through the DRI computers in Lexington, Massachusetts. The DRI computer center had been undergoing almost constant expansion since 1974 and consisted of an extensive remote communications network, for user dial up and access to the DRI facility, and a large processing system, extensive disk storage, and a large staff of systems and operations personnel.[23]

Beyond the basic provision of computing power, DRI provided a wide range of software packages to facilitate analysis of the data and the running of models. These included the Econometric Planning System (used to manipulate the data and models to produce desired analyses and to format output reports and graphics) and a host of other analytical and data management packages such as the Statistical Package for the Social Sciences (SPSS). Users could write their own programs in high-level languages such as FORTRAN and APL. Extensive on-line disk storage was available for users, and use of this storage generated considerable revenue for DRI.

In fact, the overall profitability of DRI was reflected by the great success of its computing services division. Billings for service often were much larger for use of these computing services than for access to the models. In many ways the billings for computer services constituted surrogate billings for access to the models and data banks and to DRI consultants at its Lexington headquarters. Moreover, DRI enforced customer underwriting of its facilities through its computer service billings, in the sense that DRI prohibited clients from taking the DRI models and data banks and placing them on client machines. Many computer service companies were able to provide the same computing power as DRI, but no other had what the users were really after: the DRI models, data banks, and software routines that facilitate modeling and simulation.

For those with no desire to use DRI's modeling and data analysis services directly, DRI began publishing many of its in-house analyses on a regular basis. These included the firm's flagship econometric modeling publication, the monthly "Data Resources Review of the U.S. Economy," as well as long-term reviews of the economies of the United States and other nations, and a "World Economic Bulletin." DRI also established specialized industry reports such as the weekly "Agricultural Service Working Papers," and periodic reviews for industries. Some publications were periodicals, others were specialized working papers prepared by the DRI staff on various subjects.

DRI also became organizer and sponsor of a large number of conferences and workshops dealing with economic analysis. Some, designed to present the results of DRI's analyses, were "Economic Outlook" conferences covering national economies or industrial sectors. Other workshops provided information on how to do analysis related to planning. Finally, DRI held conferences to explain DRI services and how to use them, and to acquaint clients and potential clients with the techniques of econometric analysis and forecasting.

In addition to its role as a service-providing company, DRI also had become a consulting firm. The company had a staff of over 200 professional economists, many with Ph.D. degrees available for consulting on econometric and data analysis. It also had built a staff of over 200 consulting personnel distributed among its offices in eleven North American cities and three European cities. The economists and consultants consulted with clients on nearly any question related to analysis using DRI's resources. In addition to these economic consultants, DRI's staff of over 60 software experts at its Lexington headquarters worked with clients to design and develop software systems for specialized analyses.

The success and growth of DRI was a function of simultaneous development of products and services and vigorous marketing of its offerings to the government and business communities. Each of the major product and service lines incorporated elements of the company's marketing strategy. The model and data bank services, for example, were designed to offer a wide variety of choices for the client and to provide the opportunity and encouragement to expand the use of economic analysis as far as possible within DRI's offerings. Similarly, the publications and conferences offered by DRI were direct advertisements for DRI services as well as vehicles for providing information and training to clients and potential clients. This blending of product and marketing efforts was for a long time unique to DRI among all the major econometric modeling organizations, and was a factor in DRI's success.

U.S. GOVERNMENT USE OF DRI SERVICES

The U.S. government became a major user of DRI services. An evaluation of the extent of use of macroeconomic modeling by federal agencies conducted by the General Accounting Office in 1978 indicated that the DRI model was being used in seventy-two activities where macroeconomic analysis is required. Table 3.1 shows a breakdown of the use of DRI in four major areas, with comparative data on the use of other macroeconomic modeling services for the same tasks. DRI was

Table 3.1. U.S. GOVERNMENT AGENCY USE OF THE DRI MODEL IN 1978

Questionnaire Responses Indicating Model Use for:	Data Resources, Incorporated	Other Models[a]
Macroeconomic policy formulation:		
Monetary	7	12
Taxing	11	19
General spending	10	20
Program impact	13	28
Other[b]	8	13
Budget formulation	4	5
Program development	7	14
Other[b]	12	18
TOTAL	72	129

SOURCE: Comptroller General of the U.S. (1979).

[a] Other models included here are the Chase Econometrics model, the Wharton Economic Associates model, the Bureau of Economic Analysis model, and several others.

[b] The responses varied. Some uses given were agricultural policy, inflation analysis, Defense requirements and production, Social Security, international economic policy, world energy markets, and reviews of the state of the economy.

clearly the leader, with a total of about 33 percent of all usage recorded by the study. Known users of DRI services include: the Departments of Agriculture, Commerce, Defense, Energy, Housing and Urban Development, Health and Human Services, Education, Interior, Labor, and Treasury; the major analytical agencies of Congress, including the Congressional Budget Office, the General Accounting Office, and the Congressional Research Service; and other agencies such as the Office of Management and Budget, the Council of Economic Advisers, the Council on Wage and Price Stability, the Environmental Protection Agency, the General Services Administration, and the Interstate Commerce Commission.

DRI services came to be relied on heavily by major economic policymaking agencies of the federal government. Details of their use of the DRI model are discussed in chapter 6, but an overview is useful to illustrate how aggressive agencies made use of DRI services. DRI's models are used by economic policymaking agencies to analyze issues of specific agency concern (e.g., the CBO uses the macroeconomic model of the U.S. economy, while the Department of Energy has made considerable use of DRI's energy model). Since agencies must access DRI models through DRI's computing system, these agencies also make extensive use of DRI's computing resources. The extensive DRI data banks provide the necessary data for estimating variables and specifying equations. Because of the complexity of using the models and data banks, DRI has frequently been called on to provide consulting expertise to agency analysts. DRI's Washington staff would occasionally perform limited special work for federal agencies beyond their contract obligations in order to maintain cordial relations with government clients.

The Federal Reserve Board (Fed) maintained on-line access to the DRI model and to the model forecasts, although it has not usually run the model. The Fed, however, has made considerable use of DRI's computing and data bank services to conduct analyses related to the use of the Fed's in-house model. The high quality of DRI's data bank and computing services has facilitated the Fed's analyses to such an extent that the Fed came to regularly depend on DRI to provide computing and data services for special Fed models.

Many government agencies purchased DRI publications. The exact publications they acquired vary, although most of the economic policymaking agencies were receiving at least the "Data Resources Review of the U.S. Economy" and the "Data Resources U.S. Long-Term

Review." Agency analysts and economists also frequently attended the frequent conferences and workshops that DRI held in Washington, D.C., and New York.

It is difficult to estimate exactly how extensively the economic policymaking agencies have used the DRI model and associated services over time. Analysts in some agencies told us they use the model daily. CBO analysts have sometimes spent eight hours a day using the model and data banks on DRI's computer, and often used DRI's computer to prepare and run other models they themselves constructed. Other agencies such as GAO have made relatively little use of the model or other DRI services, using them only a few times per month. Some, such as the Fed, have used DRI services primarily for the data banks and computing resources.

The most accessible quantitative measure of the use of DRI's model and services is the cost of such use by federal agencies. Unfortunately, it has been difficult to get precise estimates of costs for such services. Few agencies publish what they were spending for DRI services, although analysts frequently would say the agencies spend "a lot." As of 1980, CBO was spending approximately $40,000 a year for access to the model and data banks and about $400,000 a year for DRI computing services. DRI representatives were generally unwilling to say how much DRI bills the various agencies or the federal government as a whole, although a former employee of DRI estimated that DRI billed all agencies of the federal government a total of between $3 million and $4 million for DRI services in 1980. DRI representatives did not dispute these numbers. Of this sum, most of the billings were for computing services, and one former employee reaffirmed that the ratio of computing service costs to model access costs was about ten to one.

Most users believe DRI services are worth what they cost, and plan to continue using them in the future. In the federal agencies we studied, analysts reported their belief that econometric modeling has established a secure niche in the economic policymaking establishment and would endure. DRI is universally acclaimed as the most usable and comprehensive of the commercial modeling services available; and it is this utility that has allowed DRI to garner the largest share of use among federal agencies. Only two analysts we spoke with suggested that the cost of using DRI and other modeling services had ever been an impediment to their work, and even then the concern for costs was limited to trying to find ways to reduce some of the costs from less necessary usage (e.g., reducing the amount of on-line disk storage space analysts maintained on DRI's computers).[24] However, whether this open-ended attitude toward modeling costs might prevail over time is uncertain. Growth in the number of model-selling companies and increasing demands for use of models might require agencies to look at modeling costs more closely. One agency analyst said, "I think pretty soon we are going to have to start drawing the line on these costs."[25] Even if the total amount of money spent on modeling were to increase, the money would be distributed among a larger number of model service providers.

CHAPTER FOUR

ACCOUNTING
FOR
IMPLEMENTATION
SUCCESS

THE TWO case studies of the TRIM/MATH model and the DRI model reveal different clues about the dynamics of successful model development and transfer. In the case of TRIM/MATH—models designed to simulate the workings of the federal welfare system—successful implementation meant the adoption of the models by the handful of federal agencies involved in social program administration and intensive use of the models during discrete episodes of program reform. In contrast, successful implementation in the case of the DRI model—a macroeconomic model designed to simulate the functioning of the U.S. national economy—meant the modeler's success in getting dozens of federal agencies to subscribe to its model on a regular basis and to use its modeling services as part of the routine processes of day-to-day economic analysis and policymaking.

This chapter describes the results of our analysis of these cases and explains the factors that we think enabled the TRIM/MATH and DRI models to make their way so successfully into their respective policy analysis circles in Washington.

Components in the Success of TRIM/MATH

By 1977, TRIM and MATH were well known among the community of welfare program analysts in Washington. A small number of micro-simulation modelers at the Urban Institute and Mathematica Policy Research had experienced remarkable success in seeing their models used by key analysts in every federal agency involved in income-transfer policy. In less than a decade since these models first materialized on paper, social policy analysts had adopted a new mode for examining the clientele served by federal welfare programs. Characteristics of their acceptance became apparent. First, MATH and TRIM were being widely used within a relatively circumscribed social policy community. User agencies had in many cases implemented different versions of the models and had developed different kinds and levels of internal support for model use: sometimes MATH was used alone, other times in conjunction with TRIM or an in-house development model; sometimes agencies obtained MATH on a consultation basis during the long period it took uninitiated analysts to acquire the complex technical skills required to operate it. More often agencies overcame the lengthy learning process by hiring experienced model analysts or technicians away from another user agency or directly from MPR or the Urban Institute. But disregarding these variations in implementation, all of the agencies directly involved in federal income-transfer policies were using MATH or TRIM in 1977. Agency analysts were sold on the usefulness of microsimulation and they enjoyed working with it:

I love to play with these models. There's been a lot of good thinking that'd gone into them, and they make my job a lot easier in many ways and much more interesting. (Analyst from FNS)

These models are here to stay, in my opinion. They're the best thing around for looking at distributional impacts of policy changes. (Analyst from Treasury)

What else is better? They're all we have right now and they do a pretty good job. (Analyst from ASPE)

Lots of people have been educated about MATH and TRIM. They figure there's nothing better to use in the income-transfer area. There just doesn't seem to be any argument about use of the models, just only about how to resolve some of the lingering technical problems. (Analyst from DOL)

Second, distinct user agencies had exhibited various motivations for acquiring microsimulation models. At one level, analysts at all of these agencies had a need for tools to help them process and analyze the large volumes of data associated with the low-income population and the income-transfer programs; MATH and TRIM were powerful if complex and bulky information-processing techniques. On another level, one reason these analysts needed to provide detailed analyses of welfare trends was a continuing interest in welfare reform in Washington in the 1970s. Policymakers who cared greatly about reform seemed to share a common interest in understanding who was being served by welfare programs and at what public cost. As one congressional staffer explained: "Costs of government programs are an important thing to politicians. And anyone who can produce numbers that say something about costs will have an edge. It makes people who don't have models want to get one of their own so they can provide some interesting information too" (House Ways and Means Committee staff member).

This leads to another important and overriding rationale for adoption and use of these models by more than one agency: politics. Once HEW had RIM/TRIM and the ability to generate detailed microeconomic information quickly and abundantly, other agencies began to exhibit strong demand for comparable modeling capabilities. The Congressional Budget Office, for example, obtained MATH to check the reliability of the cost and caseload estimates emanating from the executive agencies already using microsimulation planning models. Congressional users were interested in exploring the possibility that when HEW or the Department of Agriculture used such models to generate information and then utilized those data to support agency policy initiatives, the data they used could be biased as a result of institutional rivalries, partisan politics, or even internal technical problems of the analytic techniques themselves.

According to agency analysts, the bottom line in motivating administrative and legislative agencies to follow the lead of the first model-adopting agency is the political power attached to quantitative data:

Some numbers beat no numbers every time. (Analyst from DOL)

It's simple: once someone has a model, you have to have one too, even if you're in the same branch, supposedly on the same side. Around here, if someone says, "The cost of the program is 'x,'" your boss asks you, "Is that number right?" You have to duplicate the other guy's method and try to figure out if that number is okay or way off. So you have to have the same models or at least another one that'll allow you to do something similar. (Analyst from ASPE)

People have no choice but to get models too. . . . If you ask lots of people whether they like these models, they say, no, there are problems, etc., but yet they still use the figures that come out of MATH or TRIM in support of positions they've taken, sometimes without realizing it.

Some people would prefer not to have any models. They think that a smart person could do the same quality of analysis without complex computer models. Yet we realize models are here to stay: Basically, you can't fight or compete with numbers coming out of a computer with numbers you've generated off the back of an envelope. Since the opponents are going to use models, you have to do it too, to defend yourself. You just can't stand up and argue (and win) that simple calculations are as good as computer models, even if they may in fact be. Modelers end up calling the shots on the mode of debate. (Analyst from FNS)

Given that an implementation momentum among federal income-transfer agencies began with the first instance of model implementation, the issue was not whether to model, but which model the agency should acquire. An important factor in this decision was the promotion and transfer strategies adopted by MPR and the Urban Institute, the model contractors. These two primary providers of modeling services—in fact the only real contenders in a highly constrained and noncompetitive microsimulation "industry"—differed significantly in their organizational structures, their package of products and services, their marketing styles, and their network of clients.

The Urban Institute had had a longer institutional involvement with developing models for implementation and use by federal agencies. The institute is a nonprofit organization, where social scientists and policy analysts conduct applied, policy-relevant research supported by contracts and grants from government agencies and private foundations. Over its lifetime, the institute has undertaken research in many areas, among which its work in developing and maintaining TRIM for HEW constitutes but a small one. The organization's identity is as a research institute, concerned with the production of knowledge and analyses with potential utility for policymaking. The institute has built its name on the reputation of the experts it attracts to work for it. And it promotes their work predominantly through publishing and distributing their articles, books, reports, and technical analyses. This marketing approach follows the relatively passive model of information dissemination with which most scholars and researchers feel comfortable.

Mathematica Policy Research stood in sharp contrast to the institute. MPR is a for-profit, private company with an array of services and products to offer to potential clients. One important package of products involves the MATH model and the consulting services available for operating, modifying, and transferring the model to fit the needs of specific clients. With MATH as a major source of its business, MPR's leaders have adopted an aggressive marketing approach to add new users to the list of clientele, to facilitate redevelopment and refinement of the model itself, and to lower per-client costs of model support. In fact, there have been many more users of MPR's MATH than the institute's TRIM, with users located in both the executive and legislative branches.

In spite of these organizational differences, the entire community of TRIM/MATH developers and users has been a relatively close-knit group over the years. This condition contributed greatly to the spread of these models. In fact, many of those active during the late 1970s had been involved in the initial stages of early development and use of the RIM model in the late sixties. Many had gone to the Urban Institute and MPR to continue to work on TRIM and MATH. Many had in turn moved to positions as agency users at a later point. Figure 4.1 shows the pattern of "personal transfer" for a number of the key participants.

Microsimulation users tended to view themselves as members of "a rather incestuous group."[1] However deliberate or unintentional, this camaraderie, colleagueship, and "revolving door," which existed even in the face of interorganizational competition (among public as well as private organizations), facilitated the process of model implementation and use. Over the long run it helped to spread the news of model availability and usefulness, it allowed knowledgeable individuals to enter into new user or developer agencies and thereby speed up the new organization's access to the complex technique, and it situated model advocates in different locations where they could create a new locus of commitment to microsimulation modeling. Many members of the "community" have recognized its importance to their work:

> I think the key to successful development and implementation of these models was the model developer's understanding of what the client needed to know. The way you did that was by establishing personal relationships and then opening up the communication lines. That's the only way to do it, and that's how it was done in this case.[2]

> In the adoption process, personal transfer was very important. Initially, I'm not sure that individuals in government would have had faith in the technique without knowing the people who were using it. A revolving door may have been very important for moving this technology to dif-

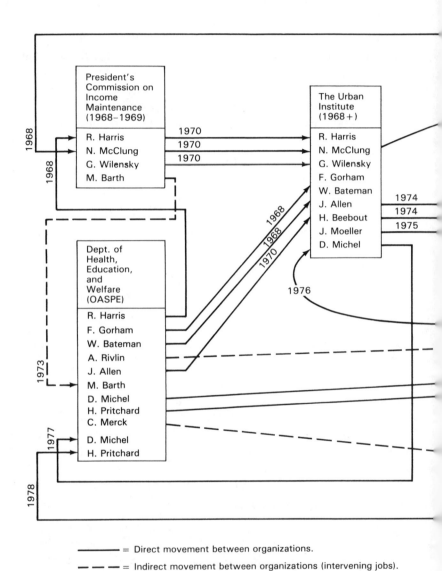

Figure 4.1. MOVEMENT OF SELECTED INDIVIDUALS AMONG DEVELOPER AND USER ORGANIZATIONS (1966–1978)

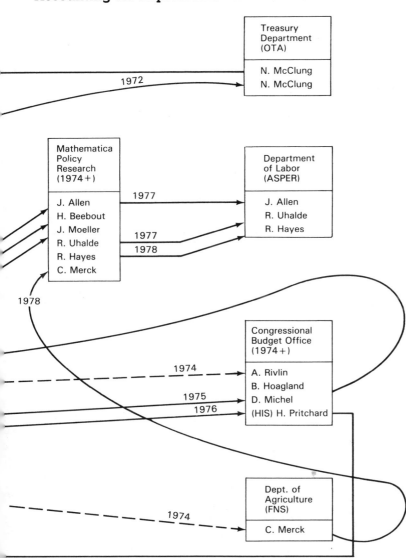

Treasury
Department
(OTA)

N. McClung
N. McClung

1972

Mathematica
Policy
Research
(1974 +)

J. Allen
H. Beebout
J. Moeller
R. Uhalde
R. Hayes
C. Merck

1977
1977
1978
1978

Department
of Labor
(ASPER)

J. Allen
R. Uhalde
R. Hayes

Congressional
Budget Office
(1974 +)

A. Rivlin
B. Hoagland
D. Michel
(HIS) H. Pritchard

1974
1975
1976

Dept. of
Agriculture
(FNS)

C. Merck

1974

ferent users. Here people were very literally the agents of transfer themselves.[3]

If you can get people who know the models, that's the quickest way to learn them. If you lose all those people before building up the necessary technical skills in other people in the organization, then you're up the creek. The Urban Institute was the principal model developer originally. When Allen and Beebout left to go to Mathematica, MPR had its heyday.[4]

By 1977, it was becoming clear to members of the income-transfer policy community that MATH and TRIM had made it to the inner circle of welfare policy analysis, having been helped en route by information demands of analysts, political imperatives of organizations and politicians, and a revolving door policy among agencies and contractors. Something else that was becoming clear was the high cost of implementing this microsimulation methodology. HEW's ASPE office alone was spending $200,000 a year for its TRIM maintenance contract. Five agencies were paying $18,000 each to MPR for the MATH subscription service. Across all federal users, an unknown but significant amount of money (estimated at $3.5 million) had already been spent on development, implementation, and use of TRIM and MATH and their data bases.[5]

The convergence of these factors—scope of model use, market control, and high cost—led to some interest in evaluating what was taking place in Washington. Concerns developed over such issues as: How were agencies actually using microsimulation models? What alternatives to modeling with TRIM or MATH existed? How accurate were the models' forecasts? How good were the data? How did model assumptions affect model output? Were the models biased? Who controlled and understood their assumptions? How much did model adoption and use cost, and was the information provided worth the expense?

Both MATH and TRIM came into intensive use and fell under public scrutiny in late 1976 and early 1977. To describe what happened, chapter 5 reviews two particularly interesting instances of model use in high-level policy debates during this time. One story involves the utilization of MATH/TRIM in an interinstitutional dispute over the food stamp program between the Food and Nutrition Service of the Department of Agriculture and several committees in the Senate and the House of Representatives. The other focuses on how rival agencies—the Department of Labor and the Department of Health, Education, and Welfare—used microsimulation models during the welfare reform debates under the Carter administration. Both stories help to illustrate the politics of model use and how agencies' demand for modeling has driven successful implementation of microsimulation models.

The MATH/TRIM implementation story was one of personal transfer. The next section examines model transfer by "commercialization" in the story of a commercial macroeconomic modeling service. This next tale differs from the microsimulation case in many ways, although both models experienced substantial implementation success.

Components in the Success of DRI

Successful model implementation in the case of DRI meant that federal agencies were using DRI's models on a regular basis. Of course, DRI had managed to get agencies to subscribe to and use its modeling services without actually transferring the model. Complete physical transfer of DRI's models to user agencies was not possible because DRI's models involved proprietary software and DRI would not sell the models as products. Access to the models was made available only through time-sharing services to DRI's computer center in Lexington, Massachusetts. Thus a number of factors typically felt to be relevant to successful physical transfer of software systems are irrelevant in this case. Rather, the story of DRI's success must focus on the question of how it managed to sell its services to so many federal agencies.

A number of important factors contributed to DRI's success. We have identified ten key factors that seem to explain the DRI story in federal agencies. They are: the DRI "package"; timing and providence; the reputations and connections of DRI principals; the "businesslike business" approach of DRI; the image of independence from DRI's commercial status; the value of DRI services as a function of cost; DRI's training and user service tradition; the movement of key persons among DRI and its client agencies; and the perceived utility of the DRI services.

Perhaps the most significant factor in the success of DRI and its model is the fact that DRI never attempted to market just the model or modeling service. Eckstein and his DRI associates saw from the beginning that the four components of model, data, computer power, and infrastructure were all required for model use and had to be incorporated into a general "package" of services.[6] Curiously, the model itself has been probably the least potent selling feature of DRI's service mix.

Many econometric models have been developed and a good number are in the public domain.[7]

The real strength of DRI came from the interactions of three other components of the package. First was the data base. DRI has gradually built up an extensive inventory of between eight and ten million time series using data from almost every available source. This gigantic data base has been a major factor in DRI's success in marketing its services to federal agencies. A number of federal agencies do not even use the forecasting capabilities of the DRI model; rather, they use the simulation capabilities of the model together with the on-line data base to analyze the probable outcomes of policy changes. Since the vast majority of the data in the DRI data base originate in the federal government, DRI has been in the enviable position of getting data from the government and selling it back to the government. However, DRI appears to have done this job of data consolidation and formatting exceedingly well, and several agency analysts remarked that it was unlikely that any federal agency would do the job as well as DRI.[8] Moreover, agency respondents felt they would never find money in their budgets to provide them such easy access to so much data.

The second feature of the package critical to DRI success is the software DRI developed to execute the model, manage the data bases, and manipulate files. Many other software systems have been developed to facilitate such data manipulation, but these have never become as useful and readily available as the tools provided by DRI. Right from the start DRI concentrated efforts on improving its software, providing good documentation, and making its systems usable for consumers who were not experts in computer programming. Among other things, the DRI software allowed economists to run their own forecasts using data they themselves selected from the data base. It also allowed the people who manage the DRI data base to clean and update it regularly. Early on, the economic analysis and data base management portions of the software system were linked together with powerful time-series processors which were written in such a way that they seemed to users to be very close to natural language. This made them exceptionally easy to use. DRI's early software tools enabled DRI users to perform analyses very quickly, and thereby respond on short notice to inquiries sent from agency policymakers.[9]

The DRI software capability was continuously improved, culminating in the completion of the Economic Programming System (EPS) in 1976. EPS was a powerful, user-centered software package that enabled nonprogrammers to manage data and do complex analyses. This system, one of the most powerful and sophisticated of its kind, has undergone continued refinement. This software development effort was exceedingly expensive; it was suggested that at least fifty person-years of senior programmer time went into it directly, not counting the costs incurred in all the earlier systems developments on which it was based. EPS was from the start a large piece of software—about 200,000 lines of source code—making it difficult to maintain. Nevertheless, it was instrumental in the success of getting economists and other nonprogrammer consumers to directly use the DRI system. This is something the competition was not able to provide.

The third factor in DRI's package is the provision of consulting services to accompany its models and data services. Consulting takes several forms. A major aspect of DRI's modeling efforts from the start was the senior-level analysis of model results provided by Otto Eckstein and other senior economists on the DRI staff. This served two functions: it enabled the DRI economists to adjust the model's outputs to fit the economists' expectations about what would happen (a policy some people have found problematic because it seems to indicate that the model's reliability is questionable if the boss has to tidy it up before releasing the numbers it produces);[10] and it has allowed for an assessment of what had gone wrong with earlier forecasts when they did indeed prove to be badly off the mark. This is, in a sense, consulting provided automatically to every DRI subscriber. More customized consulting has been provided in both the economic and systems areas. The large staff of professional service personnel in DRI's Washington, D.C., was maintained to handle inquiries from their clients. These inquiries were mainly concerned with data systems aspects of DRI services, which indicates that the running of the model has required considerably more handholding than has use of the model outputs by federal agency users.[11]

DRI's strategy of combining these components into a package created a comprehensive set of services and capabilities of interest to the federal agency users. Whether the lack of offering this package is a reason why competitors of DRI, such as Wharton Economic Forecasting Associates and Chase Econometrics lagged so far behind DRI in use in the federal government is unclear; other factors might be as important. But the fact is the competitors did not have such a package of services, and clearly the most comprehensive and extensive users of DRI services (e.g., for simulation, etc.) came to depend heavily on having these capabilities available.

Closely associated with the DRI package in accounting for DRI's success is the fact that DRI arrived on the scene at precisely the right time and under the right conditions. The sudden and explosive growth in demand for economic analysis capability in the federal government, a result of the problems of the rapidly expanding federal budget and the emergence of complex and troubling economic conditions, created a vacuum that DRI was uniquely able to fill. It is unlikely that DRI could have arrived at a better time to market its services.

Beyond the timing was the providence that brought together the talented and visionary people who created the company and made it happen.[12] It is not simply that the people involved were intelligent and creative; there were so many of them and each did his job so well. A short sketch of each of the "founding fathers" of DRI illustrates the importance of the fact that these people came together with their skills at the right time: [13]

> Donald Marron—a Wall Street leader with the ability to sense money in new investments, the connections to arrange venture capital financing, the executive skills to pilot a young and promising company to greatness, and a reputation as a person wedded to success.
>
> Otto Eckstein—an economist with extensive connections in government and business, high visibility among economic policymakers in government and investors in the private sector, and a great deal of drive dedicated to making DRI succeed.
>
> Gary Fromm—an expert in econometric modeling who helped formulate the DRI concept and assisted in the creation of its early models.
>
> Charles Warden—an executive with experience in economic policymaking in the government, an attentiveness to details, a knack for making the pieces of the puzzle fit together, and an ability to facilitate cooperation among the top DRI people.
>
> Donald McLagan—an experienced business consultant who realized the importance of providing consistent client service of high quality and who originated the "team" concept of client support.
>
> James Craig—a data expert who saw the importance of the proper management of data in an operation like DRI, and who possessed the skills to develop procedures that ensured the collection and maintenance of very large data banks of economic information.

Robert Lacey—a programming wizard who was able to quickly grasp the task to be done, develop the systems concepts necessary to carry the task out, write elegant and efficient programs to do it, and facilitate maintenance of the programs once they were running.

G. Dennis O'Brien—a marketing expert with a forceful style who could quickly ascertain what DRI's clients would be willing to pay for, the drive to get DRI to provide what the clients wanted, and the business insight to leverage each product to its maximum potential by expanding its use among clients.

Stephen Browne—a skilled industrial economist who could take O'Brien's market concepts and client requests and develop them into sound models capable of doing what clients wanted done, plus an ability to spot the specific needs of individual clients and tailor products to fit them.

DRI was able to hire experienced individuals to take over the key spots as senior members moved up or left the company. For example, Joseph Kaspudys was hired to run the Washington, D.C., office after Charles Warden returned to Lexington, and succeeded in firmly establishing DRI's position in federal agencies. He later went on to become president of the company when it was sold to McGraw-Hill and Eckstein moved up to become chairman of the board.

Another major component in the successful transfer of DRI's modeling services was the reputations and connections of its principals, especially Eckstein. Both he and Fromm were part of a small clique of acknowledged senior experts on econometric modeling.[14] Perhaps more important, both Eckstein and Fromm had had extensive experience at the advisory level within the federal government's economic policymaking structures. Eckstein and Fromm were well known among their econometric colleagues, and they had a considerable base of contacts throughout the field of econometric modeling for policy purposes. The fact that no other academics at that time were engaged in developing a modeling service for commercial sale removed the danger of serious marketing competition.

More broadly, it is possible that the reputation of DRI as a successful organization influenced its expansion. This seems likely, since the firm has enjoyed a good reputation among its users in federal agencies. DRI's success in the federal government occurred in small part because of its initial success in getting clients in the private sector. However, federal agency use was a considerable boost to its success in the private sector. The fact that DRI's services have been so extensively employed in policymaking units of the federal government has also made it worthwhile for business users to know what DRI has to say. Similarly, DRI achieved a position of having many government agency users use its services primarily because other agencies use its services. As an informant in one agency told us, it is necessary for his agency to have DRI services in order to be able to respond to questions that come from the other agencies that use DRI services. DRI's model has become something of a de facto standard for the trade, although many agencies and private firms subscribe to all the major economic consulting services in order to be able to compare their forecasts.

A fourth significant factor in DRI's success was its status as a businesslike business engaged in providing modeling and data services. This status has had three consequences. One is that as a private firm, engaged in making a profit on its products, DRI has had an incentive and a justification to vigorously market its services. Other major modeling groups tended, at least at the beginning of DRI's life, to be in either academia or other nonprofit institutions. They had neither the incentive nor the justification to pursue such marketing.[15] This meant that DRI was operating in a relatively noncompetitive market where it could actively try to sell its services to clients who might never have sought them out on their own.

A second consequence is that DRI's private character has made it possible for those regular government and business users of econometric modeling to procure modeling services on a sound, reliable, businesslike basis, from an established firm run by respected members of both the modeling and financial community. The commercial, profit-oriented concept behind DRI made it viable as a delivery mechanism for its service and also established it in the minds of users as an excellent source for a needed service at a predictable price.

The third consequence of DRI's private, for-profit nature was its ability to secure unrestricted capital with which to carry out its goals. Unlike other modeling projects, which were constrained by nonprofit status and dependence on grants and donations from foundations and private companies, DRI could accumulate the capital necessary to market its services, and it had the freedom to do so without running afoul of legal restrictions faced by its nonprofit brethren.

The commercial nature of DRI, together with its basic operating concept of providing model forecasts along with access to the model and data bases, helped create the image in the government of DRI as an "independent" source of economic information. Independence in this case meant freedom from the political or parochial biases that tend to be associated with various federal policymaking agencies. DRI was outside the government, and thus was thought to be more "objective" in how it approached problems agency analysts wanted investigated. This perceived independence was a considerable advantage in selling the DRI services to government users, since there was little chance that use of the DRI model would be seen as accommodating any particular interest group, or depending solely on the economic philosophies of key econometricians at the various modeling centers.[16]

There is reason to believe that DRI's image as "independent" did not arise accidentally. In an interesting anecdote, one informant remarked that Eckstein played his role carefully and well in building his company's image in both government and business. He was slow to criticize government policies, and some observers even suggest that he sometimes deliberately changed model outputs to allay government criticism.[17] Nevertheless, DRI's strong following among corporate users, its clearly commercial intentions, and its businesslike behavior all indicate an attitude supportive of the private sector. The dramatic growth of DRI's clientele in both business and government reinforced the image that DRI services everyone, which in itself made DRI seem more independent.

Federal users we talked to spend substantial amounts on DRI's services. The important question is what do they get in the way of value for what they spend on DRI services? Most analysts feel DRI offers reasonable value for the cost of its services. An analyst in the CBO, who had been courted by all the major commercial modeling services, maintained that the DRI services were a very good buy, and that he could never hope to be able to do what they provided on his own with his agency's budget. Chase Econometrics and others had repeatedly tried to get him to switch over to their models, but he refused on the grounds that they were not as good, that it would take a long time to learn them, and that switching-over costs would be too great when added to the service costs.[18] Government users have peculiar contract arrangements with DRI. DRI provides a blanket contract with all users within given groups of agencies (e.g., congressional offices) with certain minimum services for a flat fee. These are the most basic services—forecasts, etc.—while more extensive uses of DRI services require additional payment. It appears that DRI priced its product well, splitting the difference between what the competition's services sell for and what the user's additional cost would be to change over to the competition. This obviously takes considerable advantage of the fact that DRI got to these users first. Conceivably, DRI occasionally could subsidize its government users. The competition would probably have to sustain a loss to get the DRI business.

DRI has always provided training for its subscribers at regular conferences and classes, and it has provided seminars specially targeted to federal users' needs. By 1981 DRI was offering eight to ten classes per month. This kind of training is not unique to DRI—Chase Econometrics and the others do it as well—but as of 1981 DRI's training was the most extensive.

One of the strong suits of DRI, used in conjunction with its training classes, has been the "team" approach to dealing with clients. Teams are made up of a half dozen DRI employees, two or three of whom usually have bachelor's degrees in computer science and economics, one or two of whom have a master's degree in economics, and one of whom is a senior economic consultant who frequently has a Ph.D. in economics. Depending on the nature of the user's inquiry or problem, any member of the team might respond. The teams are permanently attached to specific clients, and the clients know that they can call up members of their "team" for information and advice. Good working relationships have been common between the teams and clients.[19] Also, it has always been DRI policy that clients could go to any level of the company to get the help they needed, though access would be through the team. Thus, if a client had a particularly difficult question or problem, it might be the company president himself who eventually would deal with it. The other modeling companies appear not to have a client relations structure as well developed, stable, or personalized as DRI's.

Many of the principal actors in the development of DRI models moved around from model-building to model-using agencies and vice versa. These personal movements of key individuals seem to have been important in the success of DRI's models and service, as they were in the case of TRIM/MATH models. Beginning with development of econometric modeling generally, and later in the formation of DRI, a small clique of model experts migrated from place to place, from one model development effort to another. Eckstein and Fromm had served with a number of economic policymaking groups in government that would become eventual clients of DRI. Some economists came to DRI from the client agencies, although DRI policy discouraged hiring personnel from the clients for fear this would anger clients.[20] Others moved from DRI into the client organizations. A common pattern was for bachelor's-level people to be hired by DRI, work for a time, and return to school for graduate work. Eventually they would either come back to work for DRI or go to work for its clients in positions where they would be able to work with the DRI services or help in bringing DRI service into the agency. A final form of movement has been for users of DRI services in one agency to move to another agency and to "take the service with them."

This kind of movement has been common in the field of economics in the United States, especially among people with advanced degrees and those in academia. It is considered proper for an economist to have direct, personal experience in several economic institutions, including government agencies, private firms, research institutions, and the academy.[21] Thus, there has been a social ecology of movement facilitating the drift of people into and out of DRI. When they drifted out, they often would take with them an inclination to use the services of DRI as well as firsthand experience in using the services—a marketable skill is not lost on clients of DRI. Thus, there has evolved what might be called a "DRI network" that helped spread DRI around Washington.

Finally, our research revealed that the perceived utility of DRI services figures critically but in unanticipated ways in their successful transfer and adoption. Agency analysts acknowledge that the objective utility of econometric modeling for making forecasts or predictions is relatively low.[22] One observer went so far as to say that no one who works with these models takes them very seriously as predictors because the models do not deserve to be taken seriously for this purpose.[23] They often exhibit poor predictive power, and they do not deal with the many noneconomic aspects of every economic policy proposal that are critical in policy outcomes. The only defense made for the forecasting strengths of the models was that they are at least as good as the intuitive (i.e., "naive," and "back-of-the-envelope") methods of forecasting.

The real utility of the models for their federal agency users has arisen not from forecasting, but from the ability of a model to simulate the phenomena it purports to represent. DRI's macro model was seldom sold on the basis of its use as a forecasting tool, even though this is what many users initially wanted to use it for. Rather, it has been sold on the grounds of utility for policy simulations.[24] Such uses require the ability to manipulate the data, the endogenous and exogenous variables, and in some cases the model itself. All these are possible with DRI services. In the end, the DRI model, and the other models provided by other services, are valuable in the eyes of analysts in policymaking agencies of government because of their role in simulation. But the models themselves are not enough. They become useful only when the data, computing resources, and manipulative software are available as well.

It appears, then, that the most critical and useful feature of DRI for actual hands-on users was the huge DRI "package" of models, time-series data bases, computing resources, and technical assistance necessary to manipulate the data and perform desired analyses. The national econometric model does form a key core component of the DRI services, and apparently has been a critical component for many private sector users. However, the major value of the DRI services for most government agencies is the availability and utility of the data and the resources to analyze them.

The "Demand Pull" and "Supply Push" for Model Implementation

A number of factors had converged in Washington, D.C., to foster the development and spread of computerized planning models among federal agencies. By the mid-seventies, models had become institutionalized, routine fixtures in federal policy-analysis processes. The period from the late sixties through the mid-seventies was the golden age of policy analysis, with administrators clamoring for more systematic management techniques and quantitative tools for program analysis. Politicians wanted to know hard facts about how federal programs were doing and what the impacts of their decisions might be.

Within the income-maintenance area, this situation translated into demands for estimates of the costs of and number of people served by social support programs, as well as evidence of the status of the "war against poverty." The seventies were a period of intense concern over the effectiveness of the nation's large, complex, and costly welfare system. Nearly all interested groups agreed that something had to be done to reform the system, but few people could agree on the best way to provide assistance to the poor while also eliminating program waste and fraud. This interest in welfare reform and the controversy over how to do it eventually combined with a generalized thirst for systematic policy analysis to make microsimulation modeling an attractive tool for social-welfare policy analysts in Washington.

The strong "demand pull" had, of course, helped to foster the development and implementation of the TRIM and MATH models. These two models were the only microsimulation models being utilized for federal income-maintenance policy analysis in the mid-seventies. Their virtual monopoly in this arena had largely resulted from several factors. Microsimulation was a relatively new technique for economic analysis, and a limited number of economists had technical training in microanalytic modeling. The key developers of the earliest applied policy models were still directly involved in modeling work. They had strong modeling experience and expertise, and records of service which gave them a competitive edge over newcomers to the field. While other analysts had access to MATH and TRIM (both publicly funded projects), the very complexity of these models meant significant start-up costs for outsiders who wanted to get into the microsimulation modeling business. In competition for agency contract work, other firms could not underbid more experienced outfits like the Urban Institute or Mathematica Policy Research, nor could they claim greater analytic expertise. User agencies had been working with individuals at the institute and MPR for years and had developed strong ties. In many cases, the revolving door employment tradition in the income-security analysis community meant that many agency analysts were in fact former employees of these two firms, or vice versa. The institute had a solid reputation for high-quality applied research, and MPR had become known as an aggressive and capable provider of packaged, user-oriented services.

These "supply push" factors associated with modelers' work was well connected with the agencies' "demand pull" for quantitative analyses, facilitating the process of implementing these microsimulation models for use in actual planning and policy analyses. Therefore, by 1976 TRIM and MATH enjoyed strong support and use.

In the macroeconomic policy arena, the demand for and supply of analytic techniques also joined to spread macroeconometric models across the terrain. A number of circumstances enabled a supply of modeling capability to become available for policy use. Several decades of theory building and research in econometric methods led to the development of numerous econometric models, and the creation of major economic data bases served as input to the models. Large-scale advanced computing capability allowed for the construction of more complex models and the ability to process huge time-series data files. Successive cohorts of economists and planners gained exposure to econometric techniques in graduate schools and led to the emergence of a professional community of skilled econometricians and data analysts.

Eventually a handful of senior economists, with an entrepreneurial bent and considerable experience in giving advice to federal policymakers, established private, for-profit firms dedicated to providing services to federal economic analysts. These analysts were eager to possess the ability to make credible economic forecasts and simulations of fiscal and monetary policy options so as to better answer the questions of economic policymakers concerned with taming the uncertainty and risks of their decisions. DRI designed a package of services to meet the analysts' needs, and it marketed its services aggressively to key users long before there was any competition from other "full service" economic consulting firms. DRI's early entry into the market and its success in getting the key economic policymaking agencies to subscribe to its services attracted other agencies as clients as well, so that they could have access to the same information as the Office of Management and Budget, the Department of the Treasury, and the Council of Economic Advisers. Thus, it was not only DRI's marketing strategies and the data, modeling, and consulting services it provided that fostered the firm's success throughout federal agencies; it was also the fact that key actors in the economic policy community believed that DRI forecasts and data bases met important analytical and political needs, and then actually relied on DRI's services to perform critical and oftentimes visible analytical tasks.

A close look at the dynamics of how the TRIM/MATH and DRI models were actually used in real political environments can shed light on the different motivations and behavior of various agencies and actors in acquiring and utilizing computerized planning models for policy analysis. These political dimensions of model use show a different side of the story behind model implementation, one which focuses less on the motivation of managers, analysts, and modelers to obtain techniques to help rationalize decision making, and more on the political interests of actors and organizations to control and use powerful resources to their advantage. The following two chapters tell stories of the politics of microsimulation and macroeconomic modeling in policymaking and political debates.

CHAPTER FIVE
PARTISAN POLITICS
AND MODEL USE

BY THE late 1970s, after nearly a decade of model development, refinement, and implementation, microsimulation models had begun to acquire a favorable reputation as useful tools for policy analysis. The key economic analysts in the income-security policy arena were familiar with MATH and TRIM, largely as a result of the important behind-the-scene roles the models had played in several major policy discussions, such as those surrounding the proposed Family Assistance Plan. And policymakers were becoming increasingly aware of the existence of computerized forecasting techniques which enabled their staffs to answer detailed questions about the likely impacts of alternative changes in the income-transfer programs.

This chapter tells the story of the politics of microsimulation modeling in policymaking and political debates. It explores two lengthy episodes of extensive use of MATH/TRIM in recent conflicts over income-transfer policies. The first story, "The Automation of Bias," involves the role of the MATH model in an interinstitutional dispute over food stamp policy between the Food and Nutrition Service (FNS) of the Department of Agriculture (USDA) and several congressional committees. This episode spawned an investigation by the General Accounting Office (GAO) into claims that MATH was a "liberal" tool. The second major episode of modeling politics centers on "countermodeling" during the 1977–78 welfare reform debates, when MATH and a new microsimulation model, the "KGB model," were involved in interagency rivalries and policy disagreements between the Department of Labor and the Department of Health, Education, and Welfare.

The Automation of Bias: MATH and the 1975–1976 Food Stamp Debates

During 1975 and 1976, there were rising concerns among many federal policymakers and administrators over the size and cost of the nation's food stamp program. It was rapidly becoming the nation's largest income-support program. Food stamps were automatically available to households receiving other kinds of public assistance, such as AFDC or unemployment compensation. Eligibility and value of benefits for other households depended upon their size, income level, and the value of various household assets and allowable deductions. During a single six-month period alone, when unemployment happened to rise dramatically, the food stamp program's caseload jumped from 14.5 million people (September 1974) to 19.5 million (May 1975). The food stamp budget for the fiscal year 1975 amounted to $3.99 billion (Shipp 1980:76).

These figures troubled the Ford administration, then bent on cutting domestic spending across all federal programs. Toward the end of 1974, the administration pushed for multimillion-dollar budget cuts at the USDA, and especially in the food stamp program, which made up two-thirds of the USDA budget. The White House policy staff and the Office of Management and Budget (OMB) were considering various food stamp reforms, including changes in the "purchase requirement" such that all program participants would have to pay some proportion of the face value of the food coupons—benefits that many participants then received at no cost.

THE NEED FOR INFORMATION

The budget savings associated with these changes were unknown, even at USDA's FNS, the bureau directly responsible for administering the program, so food stamp director Royal Shipp and his assistant James Springfield sent their newly hired analyst Carolyn Merck (a former TRIM/MATH user at HEW) in pursuit of the information. Merck soon began to figure out how to "cost out" the proposed changes. But she wanted more than just budget estimates; she, like her boss Shipp, wanted to know how the changes would affect current food stamp recipients.[1]

To a certain extent, she already had a head start on preparing these detailed estimates, since FNS had just recently contracted with Mathematica Policy Research to help in generating data on the food stamp program's "population at risk"—program participants and nonparticipating eligibles. Merck wanted information on the number and characteristics of both eligible and participating families, the size of the subsidy going to recipients, and the extent to which benefits were targeted to various income and geographic groups. Having these disaggregated data would enable Merck to analyze how changing program rules would affect program costs and caseloads.

FNS had gone to MPR because the agency lacked good disaggregated data on either the program participants or the nonparticipating eligibles. Shipp, Springfield, and Merck figured that MATH's data bases and its data projection capabilities would provide the best available estimates of the population at risk. Also, with the new food stamp module MPR was developing to simulate eligibility and participation, FNS could estimate the budgetary and distributional impacts of changing food stamp policies.

ENTER PARTISANSHIP

MATH seemed just the kind of tool Shipp and Merck needed to "catch the attention of the Secretary or the Assistant Secretary," since the food stamp officials wanted to see calculated, selective changes in the food stamp benefit formulas rather than the "hatchet job the administration was using to make its desired budget cuts."[2]

Others in Washington were of the same mind. On Capitol Hill, politicians on all sides of the food stamp issue reacted strongly to the administration's approach to budget cutting. While most could see that making everyone pay something for their food coupons would surely lower program costs, the amount this change would ultimately save federal taxpayers was uncertain. What was evident—to the politicians and the thousands of constituents who took their anger to Congress—was that the changes would hurt millions of current beneficiaries, with the largest relative burden of the changes falling on the poorest households. In February 1975, both the House and the Senate moved rapidly to pass legislation preventing President Ford from imposing his changes. Shipp described what had happened:

Forcing the Congress to take action in this way led to substantial constituent pressure on many congressmen and senators who ordinarily would have supported President Ford's attempts to reduce federal spending, particularly in a welfare program. As a result of being forced to act, the Senate passed a resolution calling for a study from the Department of Agriculture, which would include proposals for needed changes in the Food Stamp Program. The resolution specified that the study should address the problems of targeting benefits to those in need, simplifying program administration, tightening program accountability, and enhancing program integrity. . . .

Thus, the stage was set for policy development work. This was a desirable situation for policy analysts: their work would be required and would be used. (1980:77)

THE ADMINISTRATION AND ANALYSIS

At FNS, Merck was ready to conduct just such a study. The MATH module was by then operational after six months of work by MPR's Harold Beebout and the programmers at the Hendrickson Corporation (THC). Merck had MPR run simulations of hypothetical food stamp programs using different rules for program eligibility and purchase requirements. One policy change of particular interest to FNS involved replacing the itemized deductions then used to compute households' eligibility with a standard deduction—something the states had long pushed for as a way to reduce the program's administrative costs (which the states then shared with the federal government). During these simulations, Merck had discovered that

(1) itemized deductions increased program costs by about $1 billion; (2) most of this was accounted for by the rent and medical deductions; and (3) incidence and size of deductions was positively correlated with income. Hence, replacing the itemized deductions with a standard deduction would improve equity, shift benefits to the poorest recipients, place an absolute income ceiling on income eligibility, and simplify program administration. . . .

The standard deduction, while mixing important programmatic improvements, also did something else. It established federal law benefits that only varied by family size and income. Previously, the level of benefits had also depended on a particular household's living expenses. Thus, it was obvious that program costs and impacts would be extremely sensitive to the levels of the standard deduction decided on. Without a microsimulation model it would have been impossible to know what the impacts on recipients of different standard deduction levels would have been. (Shipp 1980:77–78)

Merck ran scores of food stamp simulations on MATH using alternative program rules and compared the results against current policy's costs and caseloads. She varied one by one the household income level for program eligibility, the type of deductions, the size of the purchase requirement. She played with mixtures of policy changes to discover which would reduce the program costs in amounts acceptable to the administration. With the results of these simulations, she prepared hundreds of "winners and losers" tables which detailed how specific changes would affect current food stamp recipients by income group and by geographical region. Table 5.1 shows an example of the kind of information these tables contained.

Throughout this policy design and analysis process, Merck passed the information along to her supervisors, testing the credibility of her estimates. She moved through higher and higher policymaking levels as she gained acceptance for her figures:

Within the Agriculture Department, I had no problem bringing the model into the analysis community. . . .

Once we had the model, it was an incredible policy tool. . . . With these numbers, we got the idea across to Agriculture administrators that we could take money away [from the food stamp program] selectively. . . . I had the job of explaining the model to [USDA] Secretary Butz and to the Assistant Secretaries. Butz was extremely bright and understood the logic of the program immediately. Others had more trouble. . . . We made a pointed attempt to show how economic assumptions—as in unemployment rates, food price increases— would affect the model's results. We told them we had no choice but to use the administration's economic assumptions—the official word—on employment rates and so forth, but that using other economic assumptions would change the output. . . .

After explaining it all around, we got the blessing of the Agriculture Department. . . . Then I began to work with John Palmer and John Todd at HEW's ASPE. They already knew MATH and TRIM so they understood what we were doing.

Then we sold our estimates over at OMB. But MATH wasn't news over there either. There wasn't ever any question abut whether our methodology was okay. We eventually took them to the Domestic Council and the Committee on Food Stamp Reform. We always had control of the numbers. No one had numbers on food stamps with the detail we had. So this made everyone in the administration depend on Agriculture for information.[3]

The Committee on Food Stamp Reform mentioned by Merck above was a task force set up by Ford in 1975 to study how to cut the budgets of income-transfer programs. The committee included representatives from the Domestic Council, the Council of Economic Advisers, OMB, and

Table 5.1. "WINNERS AND LOSERS" TABLE

Changes in Status of Households Participating in Food Stamp Program Under New Legislation[a] by Income Class and Census Division

| Income Class and Census Division | Status Changes of Previously Participating Households (%) | | | | | | | | | | Not Previously Participating, Now Participating | Number of Current Participants |
| | Now Ineligible | Now Eligible, Not Participating | Households Losing | | | No Change | Households Gaining | | | | |
			$51+	$21–50	$6–20		$6–20	$21–50	$51+		
Income Class as % Poverty Ratio[b]												
0 income	0%	0%	0%	0%	0%	100%	0%	0%	0%	2.9%	154,481
1–49%	0	0	0.2	1.3	3.4	47.5	47.6	0	0	2.5	1,035,037
50–99	0	0.5	1.4	7.5	15.3	50.3	23.5	1.6	0	1.9	2,671,828
100–149	20.1	0.8	1.0	4.3	20.9	43.3	7.4	2.1	0	11.3	1,062,621
150–199	79.9	0.7	1.9	1.4	9.6	5.9	0.6	0	0	10.0	256,120
200–249	96.3	0	0	0	0	0	3.7	0	0	0	48,941
250%+	30.6	0	0	34.4	0	35.0	0	0	0	27.1	4,874
All Households	8.6	0.4	1.0	5.1	13.3	47.3	23.0	1.2	0	4.3	5,343,001
Census Division											
New England	8.7	0	2.1	9.5	17.4	50.0	11.7	0.7	0	2.9	229,531
Middle Atlantic	10.9	0.5	2.6	11.7	16.0	51.1	6.7	0.5	0	2.5	981,351
E. North Central	9.7	0.6	0.2	2.1	16.4	43.4	26.4	1.2	0	7.1	797,953
W. North Central	8.5	0.5	1.0	1.1	12.2	51.5	24.4	0.9	0	3.9	322,881
South Atlantic	5.8	0.2	0.4	2.8	10.5	43.5	34.2	2.6	0	5.7	835,168
E. South Central	5.5	0.9	0.7	4.1	8.7	47.1	31.1	1.8	0	2.7	535,198
W. South Central	3.8	0.3	0.2	2.1	9.4	49.2	32.8	2.3	0	3.9	696,587
Mountain	8.3	0	3.2	8.6	11.8	46.8	20.7	0.6	0	6.2	240,638
Pacific	14.0	0.6	0.7	5.1	16.0	46.4	17.2	0	0	3.5	794,693
All Country	8.6	0.4	1.1	5.1	13.3	47.3	23.0	1.2	0	4.3	5,434,001

SOURCE: MATH simulation, November 7, 1977.

Note: Percentages may not sum to 100% because of rounding.

[a] New legislation refers to the Food Stamp Act of 1977 (P.L. 95–113).

[b] The poverty ratio refers to the poverty line as defined by the Census Bureau, *Current Population Reports*, P-60 series.

all of the administrative agencies with jurisdiction over social support programs. The committee reviewed the FNS' figures on food stamp program alternatives and approved the content of the USDA report to Congress, "Who Gets Food Stamps?" released on June 30, 1975. As requested by Congress, the report addressed several possible program changes, but its authors declined to take a position on the preferred reforms. In fact, when the Senate Select Committee on Nutrition and Human Needs reviewed and held hearings on the report, committee chairman George McGovern accused the administration of delay and even deception, claiming that OMB had deleted from the report information that the numbers of individuals eligible for food stamps would decline by 1980, if unemployment dropped as the administration forecast it would.[4]

Before long, however, the administration did announce its plan for food stamp reform. By the end of October, Ford proposed to cut out 3.4 million non-needy recipients to save the program $1.2 billion a year. The administration would limit eligibility to those whose net income was at or below the poverty line ($5,050) and would allow a standard deduction of $100 a month for all households (raising maximum gross income to $6,250). The plan would also require all recipients to pay 30 percent of their net income for their allotment of food coupons (whose actual value would still depend on household size). Because this purchase requirement resembled the proposal to which Congress had reacted so negatively that spring, food stamp officials expected that its proposal and impact estimates would be seriously scrutinized on Capitol Hill.

CONGRESSIONAL SCRUTINY
In fact, this is just what happened. Congressional interest in food stamps was at an all-time high. In short order, 200 bills were introduced in the House of Representatives; the House Committee on Agriculture began to consider them alongside the Ford administration proposal in February 1976. The main competition for Ford's plan in the House was a conservative bill, sponsored by Representative Robert Michel and Senator James Buckley. They proposed to cut the maximum eligibility level to the poverty line, with no deductions allowed, and to require all households to pay 30 percent of their gross income to obtain the coupons. In the Senate, a more liberal bill also had strong backing. The McGovern-Dole Bill would set a high maximum income ceiling, reduce benefits, but eliminate all purchase requirements, thus cutting off wealthier recipients but bringing in many low-income people who did not have

the lump sums of cash needed to purchase food coupons each month.

The committees in the Senate and House approached consideration of these bills in different ways. The Senate fight centered for a
while on the effectiveness of the three proposals in reducing federal
spending while also meeting the nutrition and income-support needs of
the poor. Several attempts were made to forecast these impacts of the
bills. The conservative Republican study group produced formal estimates indicating that its favored Buckley-Michel bill would save the
food stamp program $2.5 billion in the next year (compared with existing
policy), even though the proposal would increase the benefits of the
poorest households on the rolls. These estimates were prepared by the
bill's author, David Swoap, a former California welfare official under
Governor Reagan. Buckley, Michel, and Swoap hoped to convince Ford
to support their bill, partly as a way to help Ford's standing with conservatives in his fight with Reagan for the Republican presidential nom-
ination. The administration asked FNS to review Swoap's estimates, which
showed double the savings the administration's plan offered.

Carolyn Merck described the process of reviewing—and challenging—Swoap's figures:

I ran the Buckley-Michel proposal on MATH, which showed a saving of $360
million over the current program, instead of $2.5 billion. This was a huge differ-
ence. Our run of the administration plan, using comparable assumptions, showed
$300 million savings, so Ford decided that his own bill was just as good, so he
wouldn't back Buckley's.

Well, Swoap came down to FNS, absolutely furious at me. We had to
explain to him how our model worked, why he was wrong, and why ours was
right. It was a really horrible experience. He did not understand the model at
all.

We wanted to see his model, and he took out a piece of legal paper
with pencil scratching on it. Unfortunately, he couldn't even explain how he'd
come up with the $2.5 billion figure. He couldn't replicate his estimate. But we
could show him exactly how we'd gotten ours. This gave us the advantage for
the time being.

Finally Swoap realized we'd never change our figures or the model. So
he went after all the administrative provisions in the bill that we hadn't modeled—twenty-five components. These were things that were impossible to simulate, like a provision that when recipients were required to work, they didn't
have to take a union job. . . . So we told him how we'd try to cost out all of
those provisions manually. This was a horrible frustration for him. And he was
making life very unpleasant for me.[5]

The battle over the food stamp estimates did not end here. Word of the conflicting numbers drifted across Capital Hill to the House Agriculture Committee, which was working its way through the Ford plan, the Buckley-Michel proposal, and the scores of other bills on its agenda. Committee chairman Thomas Foley had already decided to attempt an independent study of the impacts of the various schemes. He hired food stamp specialist James Springfield away from the FNS to direct the committee staff's work.

CONGRESSIONAL ANALYSIS STYMIED

Springfield suggested to Foley that one way to gain some perspective on the credibility of the estimates generated by the administration—then the only source of detailed information on costs and caseloads of the various schemes—would be for the committee to use the MATH model on its own.[6] Springfield understood MATH and how FNS was using it. This would give the committee the expertise and experience needed to make the complicated technique useful. The committee could contract directly with MPR to run simulations on any policy option the committee wanted to explore.

The Agriculture Committee staff had never conducted its own independent quantitative analyses before. Nonetheless, Chairman Foley and several other members liked Springfield's idea. They agreed on staff use of MATH to get information quickly and to test the reliability of the FNS estimates. Resistance to the idea, however, came from Republican members on the committee. They didn't question the value of independent analysis for a congressional committee; it was one thing—and an altogether common and predictable one at that—for an administrative agency to introduce its own bureaucratic or partisan or ideological bias into the numbers it produced for Congress. What bothered the Republicans was that the MATH model might itself be biased. Word had gotten out that MATH was a "loaded" model which favored liberal interests. This struck Springfield as odd, since FNS had acquired and first used MATH under the influence of a Republican administration which had found the model's estimates to be acceptable. What had happened, of course, was that the Republicans on the committee had heard from David Swoap of the Republican study group that MATH's estimates couldn't be trusted.

Swoap had heard that MPR was involved in the results FNS was generating. . . . Mathematica already had a liberal reputation because of its previous work with the negative income tax experiments [in New Jersey]. This drove Swoap crazy. . . . He got the word out to others. For example, Congressman Steven Symms made a speech on the floor or in the *Congressional Record* about the left-wing numbers coming from the radical MPR. . . . David Kershaw [head of Mathematica's Princeton office] and Beebout [head of MPR in Washington] went to see Symms to defend their organization, and he did back down a little after they explained themselves and their model. But it didn't matter, since the symbolic damage was already done.[7]

There's no way the Republicans would believe the numbers coming out of MATH. . . . Jodie Allen [of MPR] had written an editorial in the *Washington Post* and had testified over at the Senate that she'd support significant liberalizing policy changes in the food stamp program. This was the icing on the cake as far as MPR's problems with the Republicans were concerned. It was inconceivable to them that a person could testify and take a stand and still be unbiased as a model vendor. This was all the proof they needed to say that MATH was liberal. . . . It didn't matter that the Republican administration was providing the numbers. There was the feeling that since FNS contracted for the simulations, the numbers could be fudged by MPR. . . . It was the ultimate independence issue. If you don't control the people who directly control the black box, you can't know what's going on.[8]

Despite Springfield's attempts to explain to committee members that the model itself was neutral and that they could control the assumptions used in the simulations, he couldn't convince the Republicans. They knew of Springfield's former association with FNS and MPR. More important, he now worked for the committee chairman, Foley, who also wore the hat of chair of the liberal Democratic study group. How could they trust Springfield's use of MATH when they couldn't even trust or control Springfield? Foley and the committee decided to deflect the complications of working through MPR and advised Springfield to develop his own methodology for producing estimates. He and staff economist Wendall Primus wrote a simple model to process food stamp data files for the use of the committee.

The "model" was only a dozen or so algorithms long—just long enough to allow us to come up with our own figures. It was what we used to produce all the committee estimates on food stamp proposals.[9]

Our feeling was that if the staff developed the model in-house, the committee members could ultimately have confidence in the estimates since they control the staff. It's a real question of control. . . . If you control the people who control the black box, you can have confidence in the model. . . .

Some people would have preferred not to do any modeling at all. But since the opponents were going to use a model, the committee had to too. . . .

And eventually our model produced results that jived with the interests of a majority of the members of the committee. So there was no opposition to the model itself.[10]

In the ensuing House debates, which lasted well into the summer of 1976, the Agriculture Committee continued to use its own simple in-house "model." The committee eventually reported out a complex compromise bill in August.[11] The voluminous committee report which accompanied the bill to the House floor included eighty pages of cost and caseload estimates. Three sets of figures appeared in the report: the committee staff's estimates that the bill would save $41 million for the fiscal year 1977; FNS figures showing savings of $43 million; and CBO's projections (using MATH but with different economic assumptions) indicating a savings of $38 million. Despite the near reconciliation of these numbers and the strong support for the bill within the committee, the bill came too late for action before the adjournment of Congress in the fall. This meant that in spite of the Senate's successful passage of a compromise, liberalized version of the Ford Administration's proposal,[12] food stamp reform failed to become law in 1976.

OUTCOMES OF THE ANALYSIS

A few things did come out of the battle, if not a piece of legislation. For one thing, microsimulation became an accepted technique for policy analysis in corners of both the administrative and legislative branches. The information it produced was used extensively for policy design and experimentation in both branches. Modeling policy changes made explicit the impacts of different trade-offs in program rules. It allowed fine-tuning of alternative program components to achieve an array of impacts acceptable to enough politicians to achieve consensus.

In some respects the estimates became a focal point, taking on a life of their own during some of the congressional debates. As Royal Shipp of FNS said, "The more data available, the more questions asked" (1980:79). Merck recognized the same phenomenon:

There's been criticism that numbers could run the policy issue. I don't know if they ran the policy. But they surely affected the discussions. . . . During mark-up of the bills, I would be sitting there [at committee hearings] to answer questions. The politicians didn't especially like having a low-level bureaucrat there being the one they dealt with face-to-face. But I was the one with the information they wanted. I'd sit there and they'd shoot questions at me. The questions got more and more specific and detailed and eventually got beyond what the model could do or what I knew. At first I answered using my judgment, but eventually I just asked them to put an end to the questions. . . . It got to the point where I was scared to think that these guys were actually believing what I was telling them despite all of the qualifiers we told them. It was really awesome. . . . The numbers took on a life of their own. It was really sort of frightening to me.[13]

Also involved with the increased stature of the estimates was the increased power of those who provided and controlled the numbers. The analysts provided information on expected program costs, of course, but more important, information on who stood to win and lose from legislative proposals, how current recipients would be affected, and where the winners and losers lived. Modeler Jodie Allen commented on this impact of forecasting: "Perhaps it's too bad that we even tried to produce information on the regional geographic level. I think it's turning the welfare system into a pork barrel. Now they're arguing in terms of the number of people who'll be hurt in their own particular districts. No one is willing to take a stand on the ideological issues. I think it's a pernicious effect."[14] This craving for particular kinds of numbers gave real power to the analysts who could answer questions quickly. This was a situation which no one says the analysts abused but it did have potentially serious implications. Analyst Merck was herself concerned about this issue.

Royal [Shipp] and I joke about the fact that we kept control of the policy debate here at FNS. He and I controlled policy issues because we had a model and we had numbers. It never got out of our hands because we could produce answers to any question that came up. . . . When there's only one set of numbers, they can rule. . . . If Swoap's numbers hadn't been so easy to undermine, then ours would have lost some of their authoritativeness. When the other modelers came in later on, the fact that their estimates were similar to ours gave us even more credibility. . . . No one criticized my control—but there was considerable concern that the numbers could be controlled.[15]

On another level, the fight over partisan modeling also generated interest among many policymakers to evaluate the black boxes themselves, to find out something about the models that produced the numbers that played such an important role in the policy debates on food stamps. The question of potential model bias was a sensitive issue, one whose importance was not lost on Jodie Allen herself: "One thing I learned is that one really ought not to write in newspapers when one is involved in analysis. . . . I think there's a reason to be concerned about the suspected partisanship of people like us: it's a natural thing to occur because to do these models well, you need to know a lot about the income programs . . . and after you work on them for a while, you begin to get ideas about what you think works and what doesn't. And you begin to develop an interest. It doesn't mean that you will shade your simulations, but it can make you want to." [16]

Congressional concern over model bias crystallized when the House committee formally requested that the General Accounting Office evaluate the claimed liberal bias of MATH and other microsimulation models used by federal agencies.

GAO's STUDY OF MATH/TRIM

GAO received the request in July 1976. Over the preceding months, analysts at GAO had already become increasingly aware of the need to evaluate the computerized planning models being utilized by various federal agencies. They had already initiated efforts to select an appropriate set of models to evaluate. Just before GAO received the evaluation request from the House, its analysts had determined that MATH/TRIM would be a reasonable candidate. [17] MATH/TRIM had been built and operated with an unknown but large amount of federal money; versions of the model were actually being used for policy analyses at various locations in the executive branch; and there was growing interest in and concern over expanding its use on Capitol Hill.

At GAO, three analysts were put in charge of the evaluation. The model they looked into most extensively was the version of MATH already on-line at the House Information Systems, but they also evaluated TRIM and MATH as they operated at other agencies. The analysts spent weeks trying to piece together the enormous quantity of fragmented and incomplete documentation made available to them by MPR. (MPR was just then initiating its subscription service and did not yet have extensive, accurate documentation available.) They eventually scrutinized MATH's more than 50,000 lines of computer code involved. They conducted a literature search on other evaluations of large-scale computerized planning models.

They did not actually begin to analyze MATH/TRIM until the start of 1977. It had taken that long for the team to develop the criteria to use in their evaluation and to understand the structures of MATH and TRIM well enough to evaluate them. Part of the delay was caused by organizational conflicts over use of the model at House Information Systems, which serviced both GAO and the Congressional Budget Office. These two congressional support units' separate but equal status created some conflicts over whose needs for the model had the higher priority. CBO analysts considered their interests in actually utilizing the model for food stamp analyses to be more pressing than GAO's interests in running it for evaluation. In fact, some CBO users even viewed GAO's uses as a potential threat, fearing that a negative evaluation might undercut their future access to MATH and their reliance on it for forecasting impacts of income-transfer program changes.

These delays kept GAO from completing its report in a timely manner. By the time GAO issued its final report on MATH/TRIM in late November 1977, the debate over food stamp program reforms—the main impetus for calling for an evaluation in the first place—had subsided. With the change from the Ford to the Carter administration came a revised food stamp proposal—one which totally eliminated the purchase requirement, recalculated benefit levels as though households paid 30 percent of the coupons' value, and limited eligibility to households with net income at or below the poverty line, taking into account a standard deduction and a bonus deduction for the working poor. Congress received this plan favorably and passed it in the fall of 1977.

EVALUATION OF RESULTS

The GAO report was informative, despite its failure to inform the food stamp debate. Entitled "An Evaluation of the Use of the Transfer Income Model—TRIM—to Analyze Welfare Programs" (Comptroller General 1977), it provided a nontechnical description of the model, including the distinctions between TRIM and MATH. It identified how the different federal agencies used these models. And it evaluated the models in terms of specific criteria related to the potential usefulness and appropriateness of such models for applied policy analysis.[18]

The GAO analysts applied these criteria to evaluate the information collected from interviews with developers and users, from documentation and policy analysis reports based on the models, from examination of the computer programs themselves, and from sensitivity testing of the MATH or TRIM modules. This methodology produced a number of findings:

—A number of versions of the model exist, and each version of the model has been undergoing significant modifications. This makes it difficult to determine which version or what modification of the model has been used by an executive agency for a particular policy analysis. This situation also increases the possibility that agencies using different versions of the model will make different estimates of the cost, impacts, and benefits of the same proposal.

   —Because none of the currently available data sources contain all the requisite information for analyzing welfare issues, assumptions are made in the model to compensate for the lack of accuracy, completeness, and correctness of the available data. These assumptions affect the estimate made by the model.

   —The model is difficult to use and requires a considerable investment of staff and computer resources to use it effectively. (GAO 1977:90–91)

   Many of these remarks represented GAO analysts' best effort to spot the potential problems in the design or operation of TRIM/MATH, rather than actually measure the magnitude of various errors. The report indicated that the analysts were unable to determine the actual reliability of the model's forecasts. For one thing, they contended it would never be possible to know whether forecasts of policy options not chosen were correct. For another, gaps in record keeping and reporting of program administrators made it nearly impossible, practically speaking, to substantiate the accuracy of estimates of existing programs as well. The best the analysts could do was to identify potential sources of error, conduct sensitivity testing, and then look for patterns in the direction and size of possible errors.

   The GAO report concluded that models like MATH or TRIM have limited usefulness for policy analysis. They may be appropriate if used as a tool for comparing a number of alternative proposals, but they may be problematic if relied upon for long-term projections or to provide a single, absolute point estimate of costs or caseloads for a given income-transfer program. The report identified several factors that users interested in appropriate applications of the model should take into account before using estimates generated by MATH or TRIM:

> —If used *cautiously* . . . TRIM could be used to assess the relative impact of changes in the eligible caseloads, associated dollar costs, and income-distributional effects of (1) existing tax and transfer programs, (2) modifications to these programs, or (3) proposed programs of this type. . . .
> —Probably TRIM's greatest asset is its potential for examining how existing and proposed programs interact. Thus, used as a research tool, it appears to be well suited to the task of investigating the relative effects of wholesale changes in the welfare system provided that adequate data are available. Although the model would still exhibit the inaccuracies we have identified, it would reflect the interrelationships among the transfer programs. . . .
> —In general, TRIM should not be used to provide absolute estimates of the eligible or participating caseload, associated dollar costs, and/or income-distributional effects of the existing tax and transfer programs

or proposed changes to these programs especially if no information is provided as to the uncertainty inherent in TRIM's estimates. That is, we feel TRIM cannot provide estimates which are sufficiently accurate to answer such questions as:

—How much will a given program cost in 1977 or in 1980?

—How many individuals will be eligible for, or will participate in, a given program in 1977 or in 1980?

—By how much (in dollars) will a change in a given transfer program increase or decrease that program's costs?

—What would be the dollar cost resulting from replacing the existing transfer programs with a single, new program?

—TRIM results should be used very cautiously for long-term projections (i.e., estimates beyond 4 or 5 years). (GAO 1977: 91–92)

GAO's investigation of patterns of utilization of model results revealed that in fact agency users commonly adopt these latter "inappropriate" modes when using MATH or TRIM for policy analysis:

Analysts and decision makers often need absolute, not just relative, estimates of the impact of proposed program changes. Despite its limitations when used to develop absolute estimates, it may be necessary to use the Transfer Income Model for this purpose because there are no better alternatives. However, when considering its use for this purpose, it should be noted that TRIM-produced estimates are not accompanied by any information that indicates the uncertainty inherent in TRIM's estimates. Such information should be routinely provided and is particularly vital when TRIM is used for making absolute estimates. (GAO 1977: 93)

The GAO analysts attributed at least part of the source of model "misuse" to the fact that policymakers often have poor understanding of the purposes and capabilities of the model. But they also recognized that some of the uses they called "inappropriate" are not accidental or uninformed: "When agencies use them, they tend to produce results with no bounded error term; they always talk about a point estimate, not a range of prediction. Naturally participants in policy debates want 'a' number, not a range of possibilities. An answer is politically useful, whereas a range of estimates might not be."[19]

REACTIONS TO THE GAO REPORT

Many users agreed with GAO's evaluation on this and other points. One was economist Michael Barth, long familiar with microsimulations' role in policy analysis through his staff work at the President's Commission on Income Maintenance, OEO, and more recently as the Deputy Assistant Secretary for Planning and Evaluation at HEW.

The enemies of a position [which is supported by a model's estimates] always want to hear qualifiers about the data. The supporters don't. It's as simple as that. The supporters of a policy are always pushed to an extreme to stress the quality of their evidence. They can't show the problems because if they do the other side will have a heyday. You have to be fanatical. In fact I think it's a reason why analysts sometimes get uncomfortable dealing in a political world where things sometimes have to be black and white.[20]

Economist Nelson McClung of Treasury also agreed with GAO's conclusion:

Policymakers just don't want to hear a range [of error associated with the estimates]. We've offered to give them evaluations of the estimates: 'Here's one with high confidence or with low error. Here's another with much lower or worthless confidence.' And they can't stand to hear it.[21]

Bill Hoagland, who used MATH in his work at the Congressional Budget Office, explained his perception of the utility for policymakers of point estimates versus range estimates:

If you deal with lawyers, uncertainty does devalue the numbers. They say: "Don't you know? We pay you money and you can't get us concrete information?" But most people know that economic forecasting is still an art—one that's still better than random guessing. . . . What we do is useful if, for no other reason, we tell a congressman that the impacts of his proposal are likely to be "x" or "y." We provide them with a range of uncertainty, not an answer. Some people say this is a disservice, not to give a straightforward answer. I say it's a service to show this uncertainty. It makes them vote on ideology or politics, not the numbers.[22]

In more formal reactions to GAO's report, numerous developers and users commented on the reasonableness of GAO's critical conclusions. HEW, for example, defended its extensive use of TRIM, arguing that "recognizing the high priority needs of policy makers for estimates of the impact of proposed changes in welfare programs including their budgetary impacts, we feel that microsimulation analysis, including TRIM, is superior to alternative methods of analysis, namely use of current program data or tabulated survey data" (HEW 1977: 97). MPR reacted strongly to the report's pronouncement of various uses of TRIM/MATH as "appropriate" or "inappropriate," as well as its indictment of developers' failure to sufficiently verify or validate the model:

We find that the report accurately describes the version 1 TRIM model and is a very useful piece of work. However, we want to emphasize that the current release of MATH is a substantially different and improved model. We are concerned that MATH is damned by association in the report. We also object to the dogmatic nature of the statement . . . of what the model should or should not be used for. Potential users should be cautioned, but in a world of imperfect tools may still find TRIM or MATH the best available tool. . . . We would agree that the model did not have adequate testing and validation. Most of the funding, even during the early development period, was for specific policy estimates. Because of insufficient funding by the government, we had a desperate struggle to complete the model with the effort on the brink of default. The story has been the same ever since, with many agencies wanting to use the model for policy estimates, but with money for maintenance, documentation and improvement very difficult to obtain. This problem is much broader than this model. It is a product of the government procurement process which tends to award contracts to produce the minimum acceptable product. This process is exacerbated when a public good used by many agencies is the product. Everyone wants to use the public good for free and few feel a responsibility to support its continued development and maintenance.[23]

MPR's defensive reaction differed greatly from how the Urban Institute responded to the GAO report. There, where there was less institutional identity attached to microsimulation and greater orientation toward research, the institute came out in support of the GAO findings: "[We] find ourselves in general agreement with both the tone of the paper and the conclusions. . . . [We] believe that paper should add to the knowledge of the usefulness and limitations of TRIM as a policy tool. It has always been [our] position that TRIM should not be oversold and one way to prevent this is to get more analysts involved in examining its structure and the inherent shortcomings of the data with which TRIM works."[24]

Microsimulation Countermodeling: Math and the 1977–1978 Welfare Reform Debates

As GAO was finalizing its evaluation of MATH/TRIM and as the congressional food stamp debate was drawing to an end, the MATH model was becoming entangled in another national policy battle. In this case, the arena was the executive branch where members of the new Carter administration were considering major reforms in the nation's welfare system.

During his 1976 presidential campaign, Jimmy Carter had pledged himself to a "complete overhaul" of federal welfare programs. And in his fireside chat during his first month in office, Carter announced that he had instructed officials at the Department of Labor (DOL) and the Department of Health, Education, and Welfare (HEW) to "develop proposals for a new system which will minimize abuse, strengthen the family—and emphasize adequate support for those who cannot work and training for those who can."[25]

GEARING UP FOR REFORM

While DOL and HEW shared the responsibility of preparing the administration's proposals, President Carter charged HEW Secretary Joseph Califano with the task of coordinating the welfare reform efforts, aimed at a comprehensive plan that was "pro-work and pro-family" (Califano 1981: 325). Califano's previous service as a close adviser to President Johnson during the Great Society years gave him both substantive and political experience for a job everyone recognized as challenging and controversial. The reform effort was anticipated to be difficult because of the diversity of welfare critics and interest groups, and the lack of consensus over what to do about the system's complex problems. To help with the task, Califano established a twenty-eight-member group of representative of cabinet agencies, congressional committees, state officials, and interest groups. Califano instructed this welfare reform consulting group to overview the goals and practices of the nine existing income-security programs,[26] describe the characteristics of the low-income population, and discuss alternative approaches to income maintenance.

By February when the consulting group first met in Washington, it was already apparent to the HEW staffers assigned to support the group that its members were more interested in using the meetings to air their long-held opinions about social-service reforms than in listening to academic background papers on the welfare system. Califano subsequently allowed his staff to hold regular working meetings in private with analysts from other federal agencies in order to attempt to hammer out necessary analyses and develop a consensual administration proposal. The "insiders" group of analysts from HEW, DOL, the White House domestic policy staff, and the Office of Management and Budget (OMB) met every week on Monday, which gave them a chance to react to information generated at the public meetings of the consulting group on Fridays (Lynn and Whitman 1981: 53–58).

Throughout February, the Monday group began to boil down the number of reform approaches to four, each of which offered a different mix of benefits and job requirements for the working poor, for single-

and two-parent families, and for the elderly and disabled.[27] Quickly, a cabinet-level debate developed between DOL and HEW over the preferred policy for providing job incentives and opportunities as well as income assistance to needy individuals.

DOL Secretary Raymond Marshall and his top advisers were strong advocates of federal spending to create public service jobs and training programs as a way to reduce the welfare rolls. A "jobs approach" would require federal expenditures and tax incentives to bring about job creation in the public and private sectors. It would also necessitate a system for "tracking" the poor into different employment-relevant categories (e.g., a "triple-track system" would differentiate between the working poor, who needed an income tax credit to bring their income to the poverty line; unemployed households who were expected to work and would be offered a newly created job; and households not expected to work, who would receive a cash payment to bring their income to the minimum level). This approach reflected President Carter's own interest in finding work for the able-bodied poor and providing a decent standard of living for those unable to work (Lynn and Whitman 1981: 93.).

At HEW, Califano did not initially advocate one approach over another, but his top welfare reform advisers were encouraging him not to support an administratively complex and untested jobs approach. They argued that it treated the poor unequally and thus was inferior to an approach which awarded comparable cash benefits to households with similar demographic characteristics. The advisers at HEW also balked at building a large-scale, permanent jobs program as the core of the nation's income-security program. In part, this reflected a theoretical difference between HEW's income-maintenance economists and DOL's labor economists, but it also mirrored the jurisdictional interests of the departments they served. Some HEW advisers preferred an incremental reform strategy, involving a streamlined version of the complex eligibility rules for the existing welfare programs. This approach aimed to eliminate program overlap, fraud, and red tape and increase benefit payments for truly needy households. Other HEW advisers favored totally abandoning the existing structure of separate programs and replacing it with a guaranteed minimum income in the form of a simple cash payment. This concept of a negative income tax was in line with President Carter's support for a simplified administrative structure for the income-security system, as well as his hopes for bringing all poor households' income to the poverty line (Lynn and Whitman 1981).

Neither DOL staff nor HEW analysts had formulated a detailed plan or even strong, clear rationales for their department's preferred approach by early spring. Additionally, neither had hard data on the potential effectiveness or costs of a jobs or cash strategy. But each side did expect its approach to be better than the existing welfare programs in bringing households out of poverty.

Each group also expected to have to obtain an improved system at some cost. Here was the one area where both DOL and HEW agreed: that Carter's objective of reforming the welfare system at no increased cost was impossible. Carter and his advisers, however, refused to give in on that requirement, or the one that the agencies settle on a single compromise plan within a very short period of time. Carter wanted to announce the administration's reform principles in May, propose a bill in August, and have a new welfare reform law passed by Congress by September 1977. Consequently, analysts at both DOL and HEW set a frantic pace to attempt to produce such a plan and to analyze its impacts on the federal budget and the poverty populations.

THE ROLE OF ANALYSIS

Given the nature of this analytic assignment, the economists and policy analysts at both HEW and DOL were eager to use microsimulation models. From previous experience in other policy debates, many individuals at both agencies were familiar with the potential usefulness of models like MATH and TRIM. HEW, of course, had been using TRIM at its Office of the Assistant Secretary for Planning and Evaluation (ASPE) for several years. And while DOL analysts did not actually have MATH or TRIM within their agency at the start of the welfare reform effort, several of the top labor economists in the Office of the Assistant Secretary for Policy and Evaluation Research were familiar with how the models had been used in other program evaluations.

However, neither DOL nor HEW could simply use MATH or TRIM as such for this series of analyses. By design, these models were well suited for simulating current income-transfer programs but not for simulating ones which were as structurally different from them as a pure jobs approach or a pure cash approach would be. So the analysts had to be creative in adapting the existing microsimulation models for use in this round of welfare reform planning. "In developing the cost model, considerable emphasis was initially placed on developing the costing procedures in an open manner. In late February, HEW brought together a group of analysts from the Congressional Budget Office, DOL, OMB,the Treasury, the Council of Economic Advisers,the Urban Institute, and

Mathematica, Inc., to generate ideas about data bases and models that could be used to estimate the costs of welfare proposals" (Lynn and Whitman 1981: 93).

As it turned out, subsequent efforts by the primary agencies to cost out the proposals were considerably more combative than in the early days of the reform process. DOL eventually relied on a variation of the MATH model. HEW developed a new microsimulation model (the KGB model) based loosely on TRIM plus other new components. The decisions to use different although related techniques added an interesting twist to the larger process of collaborative but conflictual policy design by DOL and HEW. It meant that the interagency differences over programmatic goals and policy preferences were reinforced not only by the different world views of the agency employees (labor economists versus welfare economists) but also by the tools each group used to generate forecasts of the costs and effectiveness of alternative plans. "Countermodeling" by DOL and HEW analysts over the spring and summer of 1977 seemed to fuel agency rivalries and competitiveness rather than help to bring the "whiz kid" analysts at HEW and the "strike force" team at DOL closer together.

HEW'S "WHIZ KIDS" AND THE KGB MODEL

At HEW, the analytic work on welfare reform fell to the office of the new Assistant Secretary for Planning and Evaluation, economist Henry Aaron. Secretary Califano had recruited him from the Brookings Institution because of Aaron's strong reputation as an applied economist and his expertise in income-maintenance policy. Califano was eager to take advantage of the credibility and analytic rigor Aaron would bring to the job. To Califano, these qualities outweighed Aaron's political inexperience. Besides, other key advisers to Califano had extensive experience in government and politics (Califano 1981; Lynn and Whitman 1981).

At the ASPE office, Aaron found an already high-powered and sophisticated analytic staff. He added to its capabilities by appointing Michael Barth as his Deputy Assistant Secretary for Income Security Policy. Barth was a veteran in the welfare policy area: he had worked for the President's Commission on Income Maintenance Programs (1969), the Office of Economic Opportunity (1970), and the ASPE office under HEW Secretary Caspar Weinberger (1973). Barth had played an important role in designing and analyzing the plan for a negative income tax for Weinberger. Despite this past association with the negative income tax scheme, he tried to remain open-minded about how to attack the welfare reform problems.[28] Barth was highly regarded as a top-notch analyst and understood how to organize and manage the technical component of HEW's reform work. He brought in a number of other economists to help head the effort. He put his former ASPE colleague John Todd in charge of the Income Security Policy (ISP) staff.

Barth and Todd supported the continued use of microsimulation within ASPE. It was needed then more than ever because of the enormous challenge and pressure to devise a workable, mixed jobs-and-cash plan at no greater cost than the combined budgets of existing income-transfer programs. The ASPE staff, of course, had considerable experience working with both MATH and TRIM. Both had been implemented and used in-house for several years. But neither model could simulate a jobs program. ASPE analysts had to have some methodology for experimenting with changing income-transfer programs and for examining the employment responses of poor individuals to changes in program rules and benefit levels. Barth helped his staff obtain such a methodology when he recruited economist David Greenberg to work with ASPE economists Rick Kasten and Dave Betson to design a simple model capable of simulating an integrated cash and jobs program.[29]

Greenberg had already spent years researching and developing a theoretical model to predict demand for jobs. He worked with Kasten and Betson to write a computer program for the model (which was eventually named KGB after its designers). They worked day and night to build this program and to link it with a newly developed, simplified model of income-transfer programs, one which borrowed heavily from the logic and data-modification routines of MATH/TRIM. The specialized KGB model was operational within five weeks as a result of a marathon effort by Kasten and Betson, both of whom could design and program computer models.

When they wrote their model, Kasten and Betson intended it for their in-house use only and wasted no time in preparing documentation. It was ready in April—a remarkable achievement in such a short time, but one which came nearly too late, given President Carter's deadline for announcing the outlines of his welfare reform strategy by May 1. Assistant Secretary Aaron commented on how the timing of these events made the job of preparing the plan more difficult:

The May 1 deadline led [Secretary] Califano to insist on briefings and that meant we had to give them. But we were not able to give the kind of briefings that would have grasped Califano's attention because we lacked the necessary information. Until May we lacked the capacity to prepare estimates of costs or caseloads because the model we were going to use was still in preparation. We did not want to use older models that would produce estimates we would shortly have to disavow when the new model was finished. . . .

The key point is that we were hemmed in by two dates: the May 1 deadline which made briefings seem mandatory and precluded orderly development of a plan; and the earliest time at which the KGB model would be operational and, hence, at which cost and caseload estimates that we would be willing to live with would become available. In short, we became slaves of our analytic technology and a ridiculous deadline.[30]

The KGB model underwent continual changes as the ASPE analysts actually began to use it to simulate the choices individuals would make about taking a job as opposed to accepting cash payments under variable wage levels, lengths of employment, amounts of income assistance available during employment, and so forth. The model involved a choice algorithm which exposed each individual to a range of options and, assuming each person would attempt to maximize his/her household's income over time, calculated the level and composition of the demand for public-service and private jobs and the demand for cash assistance. Because of the rush to make the model operational early enough for it to be useful for designing and analyzing policy options before May 1, a number of technical problems remained. One, for example, resulted from the fact that Kasten and Betson didn't like the way MATH/TRIM aged the data bases. They chose not to use the data-aging procedures but didn't have time to redesign an alternative approach. Therefore, KGB produced program cost estimates using 1974 dollars, rather than dollars for 1981 when the reform plan would actually go into effect.[31]

With the help of the KGB technique, ASPE analysts explored a number of policy options that could satisfy Carter's demand for a no-additional-cost, mixed reform plan. The role KGB played has been described by analyst Richard Michel, a former TRIM manager at the Urban Institute who went to HEW to work on welfare reform:

The policy folks—people like Mike Barth, John Todd, myself, and others—would sit around and come up with ideas for what we wanted to see. Then we'd come up with a set of provisions we'd like to include as part of a plan. Then we'd run these provisions through the model. Inevitably, they'd cost too much. We'd have to decide what to change. We'd go through a process of examining the impact of changing discrete features to tone down costs, and then we'd run the simulations to see the marginal impacts of the changes. . . . Then we could provide a list of possible program adjustments to policymakers showing each one's cost impacts and their interactive effects. KGB was extremely useful for helping to show who'd be hurt and benefited by any change.[32]

All through the late spring, the staff worked feverishly to produce estimates of the regional distribution of jobs and cash support as well as the figures for the total costs of the various welfare reform packages. The staff kept Todd, Barth, and Aaron informed of the policy trade-offs and their effects. Barth and Aaron in turn briefed Califano on the major findings. Califano spent most of his energies testing the political waters surrounding alternative reforms and became involved with the technical aspects of designing the plan only in advance of presidential briefings. Califano has subsequently described this process:

My education faltered as other business interrupted our sessions, but also because abstract theories and intellectual disputes did not deal with the regional, local, partisan, legislative, and special interest politics. The contrast came home deeply on March 10, 1977, as I sat alone from 8:30 in the morning until 6:00 in the evening and heard witnesses in a public hearing on welfare reform. As I listened to a parade of contentious welfare mothers, labor leaders, Hispanics and blacks, handicapped citizens, program administrators, and congressmen, I wondered to myself about the computers that worked around the clock to help Aaron and his team analyze the consequences of various changes in the welfare laws. They were throwing out numbers just as Jackson Pollock splattered paint on a canvas: how many would remain poor or near-poor, who would be better off or worse off, what were the break-even points and marginal tax rates. Eventually they would provide a design. But would it be a design that attracted sufficient acclaim and consensus from the disparate, frustrated, sometimes angry critics? (Califano 1981: 329)

One reason why the ASPE analysts were cranking out numbers nonstop was that for a long period, Califano gave his staff little direction as to where he stood on alternative jobs-and-cash mixes. Apparently, he trusted and relied on the ASPE staff to work through the maze of options. However, many of the ASPE analysts felt that the Secretary made their job more difficult by declining to reveal his own policy preferences, if he had some. Barth and Todd had to struggle to present all alternatives as objectively as they could rather than advocate one particular approach. Barth described how his staffers conducted themselves even though many favored a negative income tax approach:"It was a new administration, a new Secretary, and they felt these people deserved good hard analysis, felt that they could provide it in an objective way, but also felt it important to appear objective. It was partially a matter of pride in their own abilities as good analysts and partially a sense that the appropriate policy levels ought to be making the policy calls and that they should be presented with the right information on which to base those decisions."[33]

A more cynical perspective on the difficulties in maintaining the image of neutrality was expressed by another staffer:

Aaron and Barth, I'm convinced, thought there would be a resolution of a lot of issues through the costing process, and Califano really believed that truth comes out of computers. References kept being made to "wait until the numbers come down." Califano felt that people who worked with computers were wizards; in fact, he gave a magic wand and T-shirts that said "Wizard" to Aaron, Barth, and Todd. This damn computer thing was the functional equivalent of the twelfth-century scholastics talking about the nature of the Trinity!

We couldn't find out what Califano wanted out of welfare reform. Did he want more income for poor people, and if so, for two-parent families? How much fiscal relief did he want? What was his conception of federal versus state roles in income maintenance? He just sort of superintended the decision-making process, which seemed to be one of somehow throwing all these issues in with costs [and having] an answer appear. If you put consultants together with a computer and get them to mate, welfare reform will be produced as a by-product.[34]

The norm of analytic objectivity was imposed upon the staff members by the Secretary's silence on policy and by Aaron's and Barth's consequent response as policy analysts par excellence. It increased the day-to-day work of the staff by necessitating that they systematically review every policy option, without a sense of which option was more important or viable than any other. It also made their task difficult because of the contrasting style and resources of their counterparts at the Department of Labor.

THE DOL "STRIKE FORCE" AND THE MATH MODEL

The analysts in DOL's Office of the Assistant Secretary for Policy Evaluation and Research (ASPER) were making their own forecasts of the impacts of the welfare reform options. Because of the bureaucratic rivalries associated with conflicting policy preferences, DOL officials wanted their own analytic capability, independent of the work going on across town at HEW's ASPE office. In previous welfare reform efforts, even ones with an employment component, HEW had always had control over the technical analytic work. This time, DOL officials wanted to play a more active role in policy analyses in order to make the department's interests heard during policy design.[35]

One reason for DOL's new aggressiveness in welfare reform was that DOL Secretary Raymond Marshall had appointed Arnold Packer as the new ASPER. Packer was an economist with strong opinions about how to use employment and training programs as the core of a federal income-maintenance policy. He decided "to stake out a claim—to a jobs policy and to policy analysis."[36] Packer already had experience in analyzing the costing out federal programs: he had formerly served as the Family Assistance Plan analyst at the OMB during the early 1970s, and more recently was chief economist for the Senate Budget Committee. Packer distinctly wanted "a piece of the action" and had Marshall's blessing to take an active role in the welfare reform effort.

To help him design and analyze a labor-oriented income-security plan, Packer hired a small but energetic and skilled staff: two labor economists, Alan Gustman and Gary Reed. Additionally, he contracted with Jodie Allen of Mathematica Policy Research to work with his staff as a full-time consultant. Allen had been involved with the Democratic presidential campaign and had expressed interest in a public service jobs approach to welfare reform. With Allen's assistance and her expertise in microeconomic techniques, Packer hoped to compete with HEW on comparable analytic terms.

Packer's "strike force," as the analysts were called, decided that DOL needed to use a computerized microsimulation model to prepare the agency's forecasts. This position meant a wholesale change from the way DOL had been performing policy analysis in the past. As Allen later explained:

There was huge resistance to the use of microsimulation before I came in. The bureaucrats didn't want it. . . . I knew of one guy who, when he first came into the program evaluation office, was told to fend off the modeling types. . . . The way was smoothed over by new people entering the system . . . [like] Packer and Marshall. . . .

We had a major war with Califano and the folks over at HEW. . . . Packer came in with a jobs approach, rather than a negative income tax approach, to welfare reforms. Packer had Marshall's support. Michael Barth and John Todd over at Income Security [at HEW] had their own version of TRIM. . . . And we knew that numbers beat no numbers every time. So we tried to get ahold of numbers just to be able to hold our own vis-à-vis the folks at HEW. We had to dig up a model.

By February, Allen was working on such a model with her colleague Ray at MPR. They designed a "JOBS" module for MATH which simulated a service employment program.[37] They developed it quickly with the help of programmers from the Hendrickson Corporation. The new JOBS module was constructed over several weeks and used MATH's data file processing components. Starting in April, this new version of MATH enabled DOL analysts to simulate households' choices between job and cash-payment options under study at HEW and DOL. DOL's model involved a complex individual choice routine which attempted to mimic how each household would decide which member (wife, husband, even children) was economically optimal for entering the labor force. It used MATH's aged data files to run the simulations. And, reported Allen, "we eventually produced a 'number'—a good one for our position. This enabled Arnie Packer to go and do war with HEW. . . . Because he believed in me, he trusted my numbers."[38]

MODELING WARS

Of course, the numbers generated by DOL's microsimulation model and HEW's microsimulation model were different. HEW's KGB model produced forecasts indicating that a strong jobs program would cost more than a simplified cash assistance program. DOL's version of MATH, with the JOBS module, projected that requirements for the able-bodied poor to participate in job training and public service employment would significantly reduce the size of the welfare population and would cost less than a guaranteed minimum-income approach. These disparities caused a new kind of war to break out between DOL and HEW—a war of numbers, with each side defending the soundness of its own calculations and challenging the integrity of the other agency's model. According to Allen:

[The DOL] labor supply model was well documented, clear. Everyone knew what we were doing with it. That was a characteristic their model never attained. We wanted our model to be visible; our system's code was readable, elegant. You couldn't do that with their model; you couldn't see its insides. There was no documentation. The system was filled with errors. For example, they had no women entering the labor programs. That made no sense since the most eligible in the program were women. . . .

At some point, science completely departed from this war. Their estimates would rise and fall by a million families; they were making totally random choices about participation, costs, population tapes. Their numbers were way off. . . . So we really needed our model to check their numbers.[39]

Each group of analysts, of course, viewed the other's model as biased, although no one at the time could point a finger at the source of bias. For one thing, the models were undocumented and constantly evolving during the process of utilization. Neither side could spend sufficient time to read the voluminous code of the other's model because of the pressure to use the models to turn out analyses.[40]

It is unclear whether the analysts would have even considered it a worthwhile activity to spend time evaluating the other agency's model in any technical detail, given the political context in which the countermodeling occurred. The production of conflicting estimates seemed, for a while at least, to be a tactical maneuver by partisans in the larger policy design battle. Even though DOL shared policymaking responsibility with HEW and the White House kept insisting that the agencies reach an agreement on an administration plan, the agencies acted more in defense of their programmatic turf than in a spirit of cooperation. Each agency, and each agency's welfare reform analysts, had a mission to protect. HEW's formal jurisdiction, of course, encompassed the traditional cash-based income-transfer programs. Additionally, HEW's ASPE office had a reputation of technical authority it wanted to preserve. DOL had to fight on multiple levels for a piece of the welfare reform action. It had to develop and justify a labor-oriented approach and then bring on its highly skilled analysts to wage the modeling war and discredit the other side's information and methodology.

On one side was DOL's strike force working for Packer, a man strongly committed to labor policies. Jodie Allen described how the DOL team functioned:

"We had a huge advantage over HEW. We never could have stayed in the game. We were only four people; we could see Ray [Marshall] anytime we wanted. We knew exactly what his parameters were so we were very efficient. We were the strike force, we came back and did cost estimates, wrote the memos, we didn't have any clearance process, and it was really very hard on Barth and Aaron because they didn't know what to do, whereas we could shoot from the hip."[41] Packer had the confidence in his staff and the trust of his boss to do battle with HEW over the jobs approach. Marshall explained: "Once we agreed on the general principles for the jobs program, Arnie represented me in negotiations. He produced several briefings for me and after sitting down and thinking the matter out, we found our views on welfare did not differ at all. . . . I felt comfortable delegating to Arnie."[42]

Packer had opinions, resources, and a strategy. He understood the political importance of numbers in the policy development process, and he set out to wage a battle of estimates. Packer began to send a constant flow of alternative plans over to HEW to be costed out. Over the next few weeks, the burden of analyzing these plans created considerable tension between HEW and DOL staff and some bitterness. An ISP staff member described what began to happen shortly after the April 11 meeting:

We met with Labor on the 13th, 16th, 21st, 23rd, and 25th, and I would literally be on the phone hour after hour getting a new plan. Barth's idea of fair play was to do a formal analytic piece on every proposal that they would come up with. So we would analyze the plan, and then they would come up with a new one—"Change the filing units, vary the parameters of the EITC [earned income tax credit]," and so on. . . . Conceptually, the changes were rather trivial but there was a lot of staff time spent treating them as if they were very important. Three analysts at the Labor Department were creating all this *Strum und Drang,* and Barth with his army was bogged down and tied up in knots. We couldn't be advocates because we were the analysts who were supposed to be fair and cost out all of these plans.

As we visualized it, they were on the other side of the wall and lobbing bombs over to us every day—"Here, have another one, you guys." It was a rational bureaucratic move for an advocate. In fact, it was a brilliant one, but it was very frustrating because there was nobody from top to bottom who was willing to say, "Enough, we anlayzed seventeen plans."

Packer, for his part, denied any intention of tying up the HEW staff. He saw the issue primarily on larger, conceptual grounds: "It wasn't anything as sophisticated as that. We would send them a proposal, which, incidentally, we would first have costed out in a rough model at Mathematica before sending it over to HEW. People at HEW would then find criticisms with the proposal." Packer's rapid adjustments inevitably fostered confusion in HEW. As Aaron observed: "Labor had a very different approach to the issue. . . . They would press on something and if you objected to that they would jump a long way off and try something completely different. So it was very difficult to have a sequential development of a proposal. It was inevitably disorderly, sometimes productive, and very hard to deal with." With regard to the directives they were receiving from Aaron and Barth, ISP staff commented: "Barth was giving us some direction. It wasn't particularly what we wanted and Packer was sort of running circles around him, but he was ordering us to be analytically responsive. . . . Aaron was playing the in-house Porodkey's analyst. A fine analyst, the best in the tribe, but largely functioning as a one-man analyst. He was not planning tactics or strategy, he was not saying, 'Look, here's how we handle this particular situation.' He was not functioning as a staff director" (Lynn and Whitman 1981: 108–110).

Across town, the whiz kids at HEW were playing the role of rational analyst. In the absence of clear policy direction or a delegation of authority from the Secretary's office, the ASPE analysts had to adopt the classic role of expert, whether or not they actually preferred to play a stronger advocacy role. On several occasions, Aaron and Barth had to keep their analysts "in line." One example occurred when, during the tense moments of late spring, Barth issued a memo reprimanding ISP staff members who were resisting cooperation with DOL staffers:

Let me make explicit that we have been directed by the President of the United States and the Secretary to examine a wide range of welfare reform options that could appeal to a wide range of persons and groups. Your job as a civil servant and an analyst is to provide analyses of these alternatives: costs and benefits, pros and cons. It is decidedly *not* to proselytize your colleagues against participating in such an endeavor.

The hallmark of the professional policy analyst is the ability to provide the elected and appointed officials to whom he or she reports with objective information. This could include analyses of plans that may not appeal to one's private, social, or political code. In performing such analyses, one has the dual responsibility to be responsive to one's superiors and honest with oneself.[43]

The hostilities between DOL and HEW staffs as well as the conflicting cost and caseload estimates became increasingly public, eventually making their way to the White House. As the May 1 deadline approached, Carter and his domestic policy advisers became annoyed with DOL's and HEW's internal bickering. Apparently, when Carter put Califano and his task force to work in January, he had intended for HEW and DOL to cooperate and reach some compromise on a reform package. But even toward the end of April, DOL and HEW were still submitting to the White House disparate program principles and grossly different figures on the cost of a mixed jobs-and-cash plan. In the course of one briefing in late spring, Carter charged Califano and Marshall to inform him as to which analyses were right. Each Secretary listed the components of the program being simulated and which existing programs would be dropped to offset the cost of the new program. There were descriptions of the methodologies each set of analysts had used, including their logic, their assumptions, and their results. Each Secretary tried to build the case for why his agency's analysts, model, and estimates were authoritative. According to one observer at the meeting:

People at the meeting began to realize that the models themselves were entirely malleable, that all the information could be fudged to come up with numbers to support the policy approach that agency wanted—whether or not the numbers were in fact fabricated. . . . But since there was no resolution between the agencies' positions, the models themselves lost favor. Their results were still presented, but neither agency had the luxury of saying its numbers were authoritative just because they'd come out of one of those models. After being a brief focal point of concern there at the White House, they lost credibility. Eventually . . . the focus of the discussion shifted to the principles behind each of the agencies' approaches to welfare reform. The numbers from the models were used occasionally to support or illustrate a point, but they were never used as some sort of definitive answer. Carter and his advisers concerned themselves with finding out who was going to be hurt or made worse off or mad by the plans.[44]

Soon afterward, Carter and his advisers settled on the principles of their welfare reform strategy, which Carter dubbed the "Program for Better Jobs and Income" in May of 1977. More precise planning and analysis continued for several months as the agencies hammered out the details of the administration's proposal for Congress. During this period, analysts at DOL and HEW cooperated with each other more than in the past, agreeing at least that they should utilize the same model to achieve some consistency in their forecasts. This reflected a growing awareness of and concession to the larger politics of welfare reform. The agencies began to recognize and accept that public battles between them might undermine the already weak chance for the administration's plan to survive congressional attacks. The domestic policy staff was pressuring DOL and HEW to agree on program content, and one way to foster an image of consensus was to at least use a single analytic methodology.

DOL's ASPER staff agreed to use HEW's KGB model. In part, Packer's staff accepted this approach because they agreed that KGB was relatively well suited for analyzing labor-force impacts of changes in cost benefit options. Additionally, DOL avoided a potentially touchy conflict-of-interest problem: in June, Jodie Allen left Mathematica Policy Research to work for Packer directly as his Deputy Assistant Secretary for Policy Evaluation and Research. Before long, she brought other MPR analysts, Ray Uhalde and Richard Hayes, to work with her at DOL. Allen believed ASPER should no longer contract with MPR, and she did not have sufficient time to bring MATH on-line on DOL's computers and make it work for that summer's analyses. She therefore agreed to DOL's using the KGB model. In so doing, Allen had to give up her agency's modeling independence because KGB could only be run on HEW's computer by HEW analysts. "This use of the KGB model had its disadvantages because we were dependent upon them to run our numbers. I hated that. We had trouble catching where there were problems in [decision] rules we didn't agree with. . . . If I had had any option at all, I wouldn't have let them do our numbers. You never let the enemy do your numbers for you. We couldn't get a check on their numbers. . . . Doing your own work keeps you independent and them honest."[45]

PROGRAM FOR BETTER JOBS AND INCOME

In the end, the KGB model provided the cost and caseload estimates which accompanied the public release of the administration's proposal. DOL and HEW officials and analysts had spent months of hard work arguing over the specific components of the Program for Better Jobs and Income (PBJI). Last-minute battles were waged over what assumptions to use in estimating the costs of the new program and in determining which existing programs to include in the tally of "offsets" (the budgetary "savings" associated with abolishing or revising existing programs as part of creating the new system).[46]

On August 6, 1977, President Carter announced the details of the PSJI. The new plan would center on a major jobs-creation program and a system for categorizing households according to their responsibility to participate in the work force. Households would be tracked into two tiers with different kinds of benefits: households whose members were expected to work and who would be offered a job or job training in the public sector; and households whose members were not expected to work (e.g., the aged, blind, disabled, and persons caring for young children) and who were eligible for cash benefits. The employment portion of the proposal would involve the establishment of new training programs and 1.4 million public service jobs a year. The total package was projected to cost $30.7 billion (1978 dollars), of which $27.9 billion would be offset by ending AFDC, food stamps, and a number of other existing programs.[47] This put the administration's final cost estimates for the PBJI at $2.8 billion over the cost of the current welfare system. (Carter had eventually conceded on the zero-cost constraint.)

Over the long run, the Program for Better Jobs and Income languished on Capital Hill. Despite initial optimism from various corners, critics began to rally around each plank of the program: the viability and effectiveness of the untested, massive job-creation program; the complexity and fairness of the dual-track system; the provisions for large, unrestricted cash payments to low-income households; the impacts on millions of households who would lose benefits; the uncertain equities of regional variation in benefits; and so forth. Each component stimulated a flood of criticisms from different interest groups. And key congressional leaders, including Congressman Al Ullman, chairman of the House Ways and Means Committee, and Senator Russell Long, chairman of the Senate Finance Committee, found serious faults in the program.

One of the few strong champions of the program was Congressman James Corman of the House Budget Committee. But even his support waned after the CBO released its evaluations of the plan. Corman had requested an independent analysis of HEW's cost estimates shortly after the administration released its proposal. Analysts John Korbell and Bill Hoagland of CBO's Human Resources and Community Development Division were by then familiar with microsimulation costing techniques. CBO was using MATH to analyze other income-transfer programs. But after facing the same kinds of difficulties DOL had experienced in using MATH's JOBS module to simulate PBJI, Korbell and Hoagland arranged to use the KGB model.

They released preliminary estimates in November. The CBO price tag for PBJI was $14 billion, five times the $2.8 billion figure HEW had issued in August. This gross discrepancy resulted from two factors: CBO used 1982 dollars in its estimates, instead of the 1978 dollars HEW had used (1982 would be the year the program would go into effect). This accounted for $4 billion of the difference. Also, CBO considered many of the programs on HEW's offset list as illegitimate savings from the new plan.[48]

Even though it was relatively easy to trace the sources of the discrepancies, the very fact of significantly different cost estimates clearly hurt PBJI's chances in Congress. Few people examined why the numbers varied. Instead, they saw that the administration was claiming its program would cost only two or three billion dollars over the existing system. Congressional analysts reported it would cost tremendously more. The situation worsened by January when HEW and CBO issued revised cost forecasts. After considerable pressure and criticism that it had deliberately underestimated the impacts of the program by using 1978 dollars, HEW published new estimates: PBJI would cost an additional

$8.8 billion, using 1982 dollars and the original list of offsets. CBO's final estimates, however, represented a $17.4 billion increase (after CBO had discovered it had originally overestimated the income tax receipts associated with PBJI). These high price tags effectively put an end to action on PBJI on Capitol Hill (Lynn and Whitman 1981). Even President Carter was silent on welfare reform in a listing of legislative priorities for 1978 in that year's State of the Union address. By spring of 1978, it was clear even to the most committed proponents in DOL and HEW that the Program for Better Jobs and Income was a lost cause.

CHAPTER SIX

MANAGERIAL AND POLITICAL IDEOLOGY IN MODEL USE

Macroeconomic modeling has become firmly institutionalized as a routine and important part of economic policymaking and fiscal analysis in the federal government. Analysts in the Council of Economic Advisers, the Department of the Treasury, the Office of Management and Budget, the Congressional Budget Office, and other federal agencies engaged in economic policymaking rely on computerized macroeconomic models.[1]

This chapter discusses the general nature of macroeconomic model use as a part of ongoing economic policymaking processes. The highly continuous nature of the federal budgetary process does not readily lend itself to case studies of specific episodes of model use for budgetary purposes. Rather, the use of macroeconomic modeling must be examined by focusing on the nature of cooperation and competition among macroeconomic modelers, policy analysts, and the policymakers they serve. This chapter explores these relationships and notes the major changes in routine uses brought about by recent ideological shifts that have influenced the federal government's policymaking. It focuses on use of the DRI model but also examines the roles played by other major macroeconomic models. However, before telling the story of federal macroeconomic model use, the chapter first reviews the two principal technical functions that macroeconomic models serve in the process of economic policy analysis.

PRINCIPAL POLICY APPLICATIONS OF MACROECONOMIC
MODELING

Macroeconomic models currently have two principal applications in federal policy making: they are used for forecasting and for
simulation. The most widely known use, at least in terms of general
public awareness, is for forecasting the likely conditions of the economy
at future points in time. Models typically produce forecasts of key economic variables such as Gross National Product, inflation, total employment, and changes in price levels and interest rates. These estimates
are critical to public planning and debates about fiscal and monetary
policy, because they provide information about what to expect in the
future, given certain assumptions about current policies and economic
performance.

However, forecasting even these basic values is not a simple
matter. The highly dynamic and interactive nature of the economic "system" ensures that every significant change in fiscal activity alters the
performance of the economy. Forecasts made at one point, even if they
are in fact "correctly" predicting economic conditions given existing
policies, can be invalidated by any subsequent changes made in those
policies. Moreover, the use of forecasts in the political context of fiscal
policymaking can have distorting effects on the outcomes of policies
through what some analysts characterize as an analog to Heisenberg's
uncertainty principle: the very act of measuring and "finalizing" a forecast about some aspect of the economy can change the behavior of
the thing being measured and forecast.[2] This is especially true in predicting changes in prices and interest rates. If forecasts say that prices
and interest rates will rise rapidly, and these forecasts are taken seriously by consumers and investors, their behavior may change in ways
unanticipated in the forecasts, and therefore there may be considerable
variation between the actual and predicted rates. Beyond this, the grave
difficulties of forecasting the future of an economic system that is not
fully understood, and therefore cannot be modeled with complete fidel-
ity, preclude consistent estimation of accurate future values of economic variables.

For all of these reasons, economists and policy analysts in federal agencies seldom attach too much importance to specific forecasts
from macroeconomic models. Model results serve as input to the forecasting process, but in nearly every case the actual forecasts that are
published are the results of "judgmental" forecasting done by economists looking at many different sources of information, including the
models (McNees and Ries 1983). Also, since the models used differ from

one another in their structures and assumptions and in the timeliness of their data, they usually give different forecasts for the same time periods; therefore, there is an almost universal tendency among users to analyze the forecasts of as many models as possible to see where their estimates agree and disagree.

This potential variance in forecasts, given models' different structures, data, and assumptions, is the basis of the second type of application among federal policy analysts: simulation of how the economy will behave and react if certain events take place. Simulation allows analysts to examine how forecast results vary when different models use the same assumptions, or when a single model is run using different assumptions.

Simulation, while less visible to the public and even to top policymakers, is the more important use of macroeconomic models as far as economists and policy analysts are concerned.[3] Through simulation, analysts can explore the likely impacts of many different policy options or different theories about the interrelationships among key variables. Simulation can help economists predict how the economy will behave in forthcoming quarters if certain policy choices are made or if certain "nonpolicy" (i.e., uncontrolled) events occur.

Economists may actually finalize their forecasts after judgmentally evaluating and modifying model-generated results, but the availability of information produced by econometric models has permanently altered such judgmental processes. Ever since the major econometric models became established in the analysis groups of economic policy-making agencies, the task of economic forecasting has become an amalgam of extensive simulation and judgmental interpretations of model results and other indicators. In the words of Samuelson: "However good is the qualitative judgment of myself or some person who follows events more closely than I, our judgment has been formed and is kept tuned up by looking at computer forecasts. I would no more dream of tackling the back of an envelope before I had looked at the Wharton, and Michigan, and St. Louis models than I would dream of doing so on the basis of tea-leaves or re-reading Alfred Marshall's *Principles*. In other words, we dwarfs of judgment see as far as we do because we stand on the shoulders of computer giants." (Samuelson 1975: 9). Macroeconomic models are influenced by judgmental analysts who recommend changes in the assumptions under which the models are run, while the judgmental analysts themselves are influenced in their judgments by the models' predictions.

Clearly then, while macroeconomic modeling requires highly

technical skills, forecasting that depends upon modeling is still very much a sophisticated art. This important fact is well known among economists and modelers, but it is often overlooked by those without economic training who read about economic forecasts in the news, and even by those in elected positions who are required to make policy affecting the economy. To economists and analysts, models are instruments that facilitate the difficult tasks of trying to understand how the economy functions and what is likely in the future. To policymakers, models are simply one of many sources of information they use to create expectations about the future. Economists and analysts who use models regularly tend to be at once more supportive of the general utility of models for analysis but less convinced by any single forecast that a model (or models) produces. Policymakers tend to be more concerned with the utility of specific forecasts, "believing" them when they fit with their own outlooks and discrediting them when they seem shaky or unsupportive of their own political ideologies or positions. The interplay of the perspectives held by analysts and policymakers has helped to institutionalize models as routine features of national economic policymaking.

The Institutionalization of Need for Macroeconomic Modeling in National Economic Policymaking

U.S. government agencies routinely use macroeconomic models such as the DRI model to provide analytical assistance in two policy areas: formation of fiscal policy (the creation of the federal budget and the means to finance it through taxes or borrowing), and the development of monetary policy (to help stabilize and strengthen the economy). These activities are highly interrelated in terms of their impacts on the national economy; but as a practical matter, responsibility for these different policy areas has come to be distributed over a number of separate agencies of the federal government.

THE CREATION OF FISCAL POLICY

The United States federal government exists to perform tasks that are needed, in the words of the Constitution, to "provide for the common defense" and "promote the general welfare" of the country. The taxes raised by the federal government and the expenditures it makes have important consequences for the national economy. The federal budget is large, representing between 7 and 8 percent of the country's gross national product, and it is highly diverse in its effects. The federal budget determines, for example, the fortunes of defense-related industries, the funding of massive public works projects, the foreign aid contributed to other countries, the national contribution to social security, health, and education, and the extent of transfer of income to the various segments of the population.

Similarly, the means used to finance the federal budget affect the economy in complex ways. Taxes take from taxpayers funds that might be used for other purposes, and changes in tax policy (e.g., marginal tax rates, deductions, credits) can encourage or retard capital investment, agricultural productivity, housing construction, and even family formation. When taxes and other directly collected revenue (e.g., tariffs and fees) fail to pay for the entire federal budget, the resulting deficit is covered either through borrowing (e.g., through Treasury securities) or by expanding the money supply. Deficit spending practices are commonly viewed as sources of economic difficulties, so Congress and the executive branch have historically attempted to take care that the demands of federal programs match the ability of the economy to meet them. Thus, creation of the federal budget has traditionally involved "the simultaneous consideration of the resource needs of individual programs, and the total outlays and receipts that are appropriate in relation to current and prospective economic conditions. (OMB 1981: 351).

Not only does federal fiscal policy affect the economy, but both budgetary and tax policies themselves are also strongly affected by the economy. Many long-standing federal programs contain statutory provisions that automatically adjust expenditures depending on economic conditions. For example, Social Security benefits have been indexed to changes in cost of living as indicated by the Consumer Price Index. This requires that budgeting for federal programs be based in part on expectations of what the condition of the economy will be during the fiscal year under consideration. Budgetary commitments that entail large sums over several years, such as major weapons procurement programs, must be made in light of expected inflation in order to provide sufficient funds to cover unavoidable cost increases. In the same manner, tax policy is affected by the economy. A strong economy with high employment and productivity will produce greater tax receipts than will a faltering economy. Thus there are built-in dynamic and powerful reciprocal relationships between the economy as a whole and the fiscal policies of the government. These interrelationships have been recognized by economists, policymakers, and members of the business community for many years, and as the science of economics has advanced since the late 1930s, it has been called upon to play a greater role in the development of federal fiscal policy. Over this same period the relatively rapid growth in the scope of the federal government, and hence the size of its budget, has also intensified the need to develop better means for making fiscal policy.

This combination of supply and demand for greater use of economics in fiscal policymaking can be clearly seen in the evolution of the process used to create the annual federal budget. What was once a comparatively simple task because of the smaller size of government and the relative dearth of systematic economic and policy analysis techniques has grown into a major enterprise employing hundreds and perhaps thousands of skilled economic analysts working throughout federal agencies.

THE BUDGET PROCESS

Federal fiscal policy is formalized by the congressional adoption and presidential signing of a budget bill and a tax bill, which are created through the budget process.[4] The federal budget and tax bills for any given fiscal year are prepared over an eighteen-month period prior to the start of the target fiscal year, and can be adjusted during the target fiscal year to meet unexpected conditions. This process determines the budget commitments and tax policies for the target fiscal year, and includes a planning horizon that stretches two years beyond to include longer-range commitments. Thus any given year's fiscal plan encompasses a planning scale of about four and half years (eighteen months prior to the target fiscal year, the fiscal year itself, and two years beyond).

Figure 6.1 provides a schematic of the budget process, which is explained briefly here. (Those boxes outlined in double lines indicate where economic analysis using macroeconomic models takes place.)

THE EXECUTIVE ROLE

The budget process begins in the executive branch. During the spring (eighteen months prior to the start of the target fiscal year), the Office of Management and Budget (OMB) coordinates the many different inputs to the President's budget proposal, including evaluations of programs and suggestions from the President, his advisers, government agencies, and others. Formal planning begins when an economic fore-casting group known informally as the Troika, made up of the depart-ment of Treasury, the OMB, and the Council of Economic Advisers (CEA),[5] prepares for the President projections of the state of the economy dur-ing the coming quarters. These projections are important for ascertain-ing the probable effects of the economy on the spending programs in the budget and the likely receipts of the Treasury, and they influence the directives the President gives to agencies for preparation of their budgets.

Within the Troika, use of econometric models takes place pri-marily at what is known as the T3 level. The Troika is subdivided inter-nally both by its three constituent agencies and by the vertical levels at which different analyses and policymaking activities take place. The top level, or T1, is composed of the Secretary of the Treasury, the director of the OMB, and the chairman of the CEA. The second level, or T2, is composed of the top division of office directors from the three agencies (e.g., the Treasury's director of the Office of Financial Analysis). The third, or T3 level, is composed of professional economists and policy analysts from the three agencies. It is at the T3 level where the actual running of models occurs.

Traditionally, the T3 Troika analysts have a number of models at their disposal. But primary responsibility for any given model has been divided among the agencies. The CEA has had primary responsibility for running analyses using the Federal Reserve's MPS model and the DRI model; OMB has run analyses using the Wharton model; Treasury has maintained the Chase Econometrics model. While other models are used periodically, these four have been the major ones used within the Troika.[6] This organization of responsibility was established mainly for conve-nience and economy, as well as to maintain proficiency with the indi-vidual models within their "home" agency. The fact that the models are complex and expensive, and that each model has its own unique char-acteristics, makes it necessary that the policy analysts who use them know the models and their operating characteristics very well.

The Troika makes its greatest use of macroeconomic models during the annual budget process when it prepares a forecast of eco-nomic conditions around which the budget and tax policies will be formed. As shown in figure 6.1, the analytical capabilities of the Troika are called into play in at least five places in the formal budget process. These incidents for formal review occur at the major steps in the executive branch's budget-planning process prior to initial planning in March, fol-

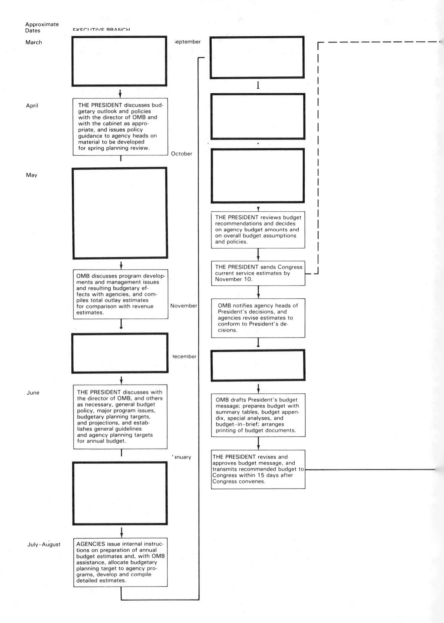

Figure 6.1. OVERVIEW OF THE FEDERAL BUDGET PROCESS

LEGISLATIVE BRANCH

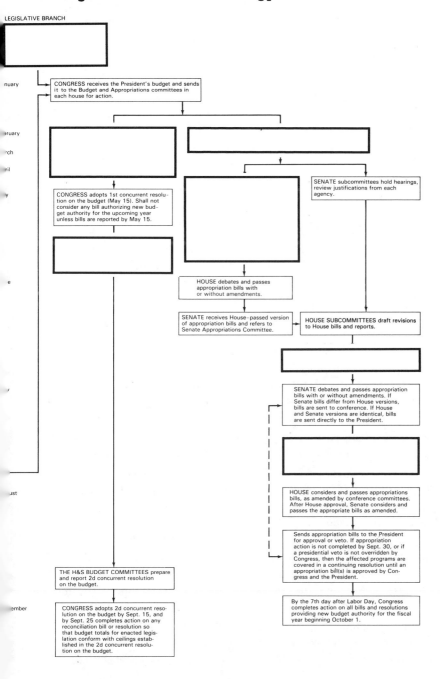

nuary

CONGRESS receives the President's budget and sends it to the Budget and Appropriations committees in each house for action.

ruary

rch

ril

y

CONGRESS adopts 1st concurrent resolu- tion on the budget (May 15). Shall not consider any bill authorizing new bud- get authority for the upcoming year unless bills are reported by May 15.

SENATE subcommittees hold hearings, review justifications from each agency.

e

HOUSE debates and passes appropriation bills with or without amendments.

SENATE receives House-passed version of appropriation bills and refers to Senate Appropriations Committee.

HOUSE SUBCOMMITTEES draft revisions to House bills and reports.

SENATE debates and passes appropriation bills with or without amendments. If Senate bills differ from House versions, bills are sent to conference. If House and Senate versions are identical, bills are sent directly to the President.

ust

HOUSE considers and passes appropriations bills, as amended by conference committees. After House approval, Senate considers and passes the appropriate bills as amended.

Sends appropriation bills to the President for approval or veto. If appropriation action is not completed by Sept. 30, or if a presidential veto is not overridden by Congress, then the affected programs are covered in a continuing resolution until an appropriation bill(s) is approved by Con- gress and the President.

THE H&S BUDGET COMMITTEES prepare and report 2d concurrent resolution on the budget.

ember

CONGRESS adopts 2d concurrent reso- lution on the budget by Sept. 15, and by Sept. 25 completes action on any reconciliation bill or resolution so that budget totals for enacted legis- lation conform with ceilings estab- lished in the 2d concurrent resolu- tion on the budget.

By the 7th day after Labor Day, Congress completes action on all bills and resolutions providing new budget authority for the fiscal year beginning October 1.

lowing initial program estimates drawn up by executive agencies and the OMB in early June, following the first comprehensive agency submissions of budget requests in October, after the President's directives to agencies for preparing their final budget submissions in December, and during the formal presentation the Troika makes to the House and Senate Appropriations committees in early February, after the President's budget has been forwarded to Congress. In addition to these regularly scheduled analytical tasks, Troika T3 staff conduct many special analyses in answer to questions that arise at the T1 level during ongoing economic planning in the executive branch.

THE CONGRESSIONAL ROLE

By law, the President must submit his proposed budget to the Congress within fifteen days after the start of the new congressional session in January. The Congress can approve, modify, or disapprove the President's budget proposals. It can change funding levels for different programs, eliminate proposals entirely, or add new programs it deems necessary.

Under the rules of the Congressional Budget Act of 1974, the Congress considers target budget and tax totals and settles them before considering individual appropriations. Standing committees of Congress are then required, by March 15, to submit to the House and Senate Budget committees budget estimates covering programs under their purview. By April 1, the Congressional Budget Office, established to assist Congress in the task of fiscal and budget analysis, must submit to both the Senate and House Budget committees a fiscal policy report containing analyses of both expected budgetary expenditures and expected government receipts given assumed economic conditions. Within CBO these analyses are conducted by the Fiscal Analysis Division (FAD) and the Budget Analysis Division (BAD).[7]

FAD's job is to produce two-year and five-year forecasts of the economy, which constitute the baseline from which the budgetary and expenditure forecasts are made by BAD. CBO's FAD is perhaps the most eclectic user of econometric models in the U.S. government. The large size of Congress (435 members of the House and 100 senators), and its organizational complexity (thirty-eight standing committees, nineteen special and select committees, and four joint committees in 1981), results in a great variety of demands for analysis using different assumptions and, in many cases, different models. As one senior staff member in FAD expressed it, "We [the CBO] have to subscribe to any model that has a member of Congress as a constituent." Thus CBO has subscribed to the DRI, Wharton, Chase, Evans, and Merrill-Lynch models, and negotiates for procurement of other models when they become popular with members of Congress having other economic ideologies (e.g., monetarist or supply-side economics). Despite this wide selection of available models, the CBO analysts tend to make greatest use of the large, well-established models (i.e., DRI, Wharton, and Chase) because of the availability of data, computing resources, and consulting assistance the larger modeling organizations provide and because they are also used by so many other federal agencies. In addition, these larger models have in the past served as the primary econometric modeling tools used by academic departments that train the government economists. The FAD will conduct analyses for individual members of Congress using any model or models a member specifies. The division's primary mission, however, is to create a set of forecasts that form a base for the budget policy analysis conducted by BAD. This is done by comparing and contrasting the various forecasts of the major models under different assumptions. To accomplish this, CBO has built a special analytical tool called the "consensus policy multiplier" which discounts some of the more questionable elements in each model while treating different kinds of fiscal actions uniformly across the models. The multiplier system, although often referred to as a model, is actually a data reduction algorithm that takes the results of four major models (DRI, Wharton, Chase, and the Fed's MPS) and creates a consolidated forecast from them. The result, not surprisingly, is that forecasts from the multipliers program tend to be about in the middle of the forecasts made by the four models, thus providing a "consensus" (actually an averaged) viewpoint of the various model builders' perspectives.

FAD then forwards this forecast to BAD where it provides the baseline for BAD's analysis of the expected costs of federal programs, given the economic assumptions of the coming quarters. Federal programs that are tied to the cost of living (e.g., Medicare, Social Security), that fluctuate depending on employment rates (unemployment benefits), or that involve large, multiyear construction programs (major weapons systems) are very sensitive to changes in the economy. Similarly, federal revenues, and therefore the amount of money available to fund federal programs, vary according to the state of the economy. Thus, minor fluctuations in the expected condition of the economy have major repercussions for the budget. The BAD's analyses were developed to provide an indicator of how, during the target fiscal year, federal budgetary policies fit the expected state of the economy, and hence federal revenues and expenses.

The analysis conducted by BAD is quite elaborate. For each budget year, BAD conducts an analysis of program cost for each of nearly 2,000 programs in the budget. The division estimates the impacts of economic conditions on program line items under four broad options: (a) the "current law option," which forecasts the effect of the economy on current programs that, by law, must keep pace with changes in the economy; (b) the "policy option," which forecasts economic effects on programs that are not formal entitlement programs and that can be altered by congressional budgetary policy; (c) the "President's option," which forecasts the economic implications on the budgetary programs contained in the President's budget; and (d) the "committee's option," which forecasts the economic effects on the budgetary proposals of the House and Senate Budget committees.

The analyses are conducted according to both the two- and five-year forecasts of the economy prepared by FAD, and each can be very detailed. Each program's budget is divided into a number of line item accounts (e.g., salaries, rents, travel), which are in turn run through "inflator" equations tailored to each kind of cost. The inflators used are built through analysis of historical inflation in each given cost category, tempered and adjusted by staff estimates of the effects of recent events on historical trends. Most of these cost data must be obtained from other sources, such as from DRI's time-series data bases, analyzed using DRI's Cost Forecasting Service model. Because DRI's cost forecasting model is designed to provide trends in six-year and ten-year increments, BAD analysts must change model assumptions to provide analyses for the one-, two-, and five-year projections it needs. Also, the DRI Cost Forecasting Service model is intricately tied to the DRI national macroeconomic model and uses inputs from it in many of its equations. Thus, BAD must take into account these inputs to ensure that they correlate with expectations of the FAD analyses.

FAD and BAD reports go into the preparation of CBO's analyses and forecasts, which go to the Congress for review. Congress must then adopt by May 15 an initial concurrent budget resolution to set the targets for total receipts and for programmatic budget outlays, both in total and by programs, and in some cases by line items within programs. The Congress then enacts program authorizations to establish the legal authority of agencies to carry out their missions for the target fiscal year. These authorizations do not typically establish the exact levels of funding, although they can put ceilings on the amount to be spent in different programs. Appropriations bills determine actual funding—the exact amount of money each program will receive. Appropriations must be made in approximate conformity to the initial budget resolution adopted on May 15, and in light of expected revenues being determined concurrently by other congressional committees. Differences between the appropriations and the budget "ceiling" and receipts "floor" set by the first concurrent resolution of May 15 must be reconciled through a second (or third, if necessary) budget resolution, which effectively finalizes the appropriations process. Once an appropriations bill is passed by both the House and Senate, it is forwarded to the President for approval or veto. Both the tax and budget bills become law in September when the President signs them. These laws then govern the taxation and expenditure behavior of the government for the target fiscal year.

CBO's role and its use of macroeconomic modeling in the budget process are analogous to those of the Troika. As shown in figure 6.1, the CBO is actively involved in several steps of the budget process. The most important contributions of CBO's modeling capability occur during the reviews of the Troika's forecasts by the Joint Economic Committee in December and January, the special hearings with Congress and the Troika in January and early February, the preparation of the first concurrent budget resolution by the House and Senate Budget committees in late February and March, the review of the effects of congressional action on budget targets in late May, and the redrafting and finalizing of House and Senate appropriations bills during June and July. Additionally, CBO is frequently called upon to perform special analyses with respect to specific programs under review by various congressional committees, both during the budget process and throughout the year.

The complex and demanding tasks of the preparation of budget and tax proposals require extensive economic analysis and forecasting. Macroeconomic modeling plays its most important role in three places: in the preliminary projections of economic outlook prepared by the Troika for the President; in the preparation of the CBO's reports to Congress regarding program cost and revenue projections; and in the deliberations within Congress during the preparation of the first and second budget resolutions and their attendant reconciliation. The competition among the major actors (i.e., the President, the House, the Senate, and the separate committees within these chambers) ensures the need for sophisticated, in-house economic analysis capability.

THE DEVELOPMENT OF MONETARY POLICY

Besides budget preparation and approval, the other major economic policymaking role of the U.S. government involves the establishment and maintenance of a stable monetary policy. As the only legal provider of U.S. currency, the federal government can influence the economy by controlling the amount of money in general circulation. While this control is often thought of as the government's ability to print money, control of the money supply actually has less to do with the amount of money printed than with the amount released into circulation.

Federal control over the money supply is based on the theory that monetary oversupply or undersupply can affect the economy in important ways. When there is an oversupply, the amount of money available to buy a given amount of goods and services increases, thereby lessening the amount of those goods and services that can be bought for a dollar. This results in a de facto devaluation of the dollar with respect to the things it can purchase and contributes to inflation. When there is an undersupply of money, dollars become scarce, resulting in capital shortages that drive up interest rates and make it hard for the economy to expand. While there has been a great deal of debate over how tightly the money supply should be controlled, most economists believe that the money supply should expand slightly ahead of economic growth to provide sufficient capital to continue economic growth. Under such a condition, the economy continues to grow into the space created by the slowly expanding money supply.

Control of monetary policy rests with the Federal Reserve System (the Fed), established by Congress in 1913 to give the country an elastic currency, to provide facilities for discounting commercial paper, and to improve supervision of banking.[8] Since that time the objectives of the Fed have been expanded to include promotion of economic stability and growth, maintenance of high employment levels, stabilization of purchasing power of the dollar, and maintenance of reasonable balance in financial transactions with foreign countries.

The Federal Reserve System consists of five major components: the Federal Reserve System Board of Governors; the Federal Open Market Committee; the Federal Reserve Banks; the Federal Advisory Council; and member banks.[9] Of these major components, monetary policy is primarily set by the Board of Governors and the Open Market Committee. The board's control comes through approval of discount rates set by the Reserve Banks (which heavily influence the interest rates member banks can charge their customers), setting of reserve requirements (which control the amount of a bank's assets it can release as loans), and setting of margin requirements on credit purchases in the stock market (to control the "leverage" in the buying of stock). The Open Market Committee's control comes through decisions regarding Fed purchase and sale of securities on the open market. Purchases of large dollar volumes of securities release capital into the open market, generally making capital more available and increasing the money supply, usually resulting in the lowering of interest rates. Sales of securities take capital out of the open market, making money less readily available and usually push interest rates upward.

Economic analysis is clearly important in the setting of board and committee policies. To determine whether the policy instruments of the Fed should be used to tighten up or loosen money supply, it is necessary to know the recent trends and current state of certain gross indicators of monetary conditions. The primary values used in these analyses are the amount of currency in circulation and the amount of money held in private demand deposits and other interest-bearing repositories of funds (e.g., money-market accounts). These values are thought to be determined by other, larger factors in the economy such as the trends in national income and product values, so these trends in basic economic indicators are also investigated to determine what changes in money supply are likely. Thus, the Fed uses traditional economic and econometric techniques (including modeling) to ascertain likely directions of the economy, and focuses especially on those aspects of economic activity that influence monetary conditions.

The Federal Reserve System employs a large number of economists to help determine the state of the economy, where it is going, and what actions the Fed should take to achieve continued and stable economic growth. Its main center of analytic activity is located at Fed headquarters in Washington. Headquarters staff also prepare analytical reports that go to the board and to the Open Market Committee.

The Fed's use of macroeconomic models parallels, to some degree, the Troika's modeling process. In the Troika, hands-on analysis is conducted at the level of the T3 staff economists and technicians with the results forwarded to the T2 senior economists, who forward their own summaries to the T1 policymakers. In the Fed system, a small number of modeling experts run model-based projections and simulations which are forwarded, along with the synthesized forecasts of about seventy-five "judgmental" staff economists, to the directors of the major Fed divisions concerned with forecasting and analysis. The package of forecast materials forwarded to these individuals typically consists of three elements:

1. A "pure" forecast from the Fed's own MPS model covering the coming quarters, with a short explanation of the model's predictions and the assumptions underlying them.
2. A survey of what the "outside" models (i.e., the DRI, Chase, and Wharton models) say, and a comparison of these forecasts with the forecasts of the judgmental analysts within the Fed.
3. A description of the differences between the results of the MPS model and the forecasts of the senior judgmental economists, with an analysis of the likely sources of these differences.[10]

Division directors then develop a set of information documents for the board or for the Open Market Committee. This set might contain all, some, or none of the staff's forecasting package, although board or committee members have access to any specific information they desire. Thus, as with model uses at the Troika and CBO, the end result of modeling at the Fed is the production of highly judgmental forecasts that are based upon extensive analysis using a number of the macroeconomic models.

However, the Fed's use of macroeconomic models differs in an important way from the uses made by the Troika and CBO. The Fed directly sets policies for monetary constraint or growth on an "as needed" basis—as often as once a month. It does not engage in an annual, procedurally regulated policymaking effort like the budget process. Therefore, the Fed's use of macroeconomic models tends to be more routine. Also, the Fed primarily concerns itself with analyzing the effects of changes in monetary policy, rather than fiscal policy. The Fed treats fiscal policies as independent variables, since the Fed exercises no real control over them. The Fed's focus on setting monetary policy on a fairly routine basis tends to isolate the Fed from the political debates surrounding the authorization and funding of federal programs. The net result of these conditions is a somewhat less hectic environment for macroeconomic modeling within the Fed than is found in the Troika or the CBO.

THE IMPORTANCE OF INSTITUTIONALIZED NEED
FOR MACROECONOMIC MODELING

There is little doubt that macroeconomic modeling has found a well-established and secure place in the making of national economic policy. The creation of dispersed, specialized analysis units in the various economic policymaking agencies of the federal government has helped to institutionalize both the need for macroeconomic modeling and the means whereby such analysis could be provided to policymakers. By 1980 these institutionalized centers of macroeconomic modeling capability, using the widely available commercial models (DRI, Chase, Wharton, and others) as well as specialty models (the CBO "multipliers" program and the Fed's MPS model), were employing hundreds of analysts and spending millions of dollars to provide analytical backup to federal policymakers. These centers had developed extensive and complex procedures for researching questions about the performance of the economy and providing forecasts of likely future economic performance given various policy assumptions.

Perhaps most important, the natural process of institutionalization has created a strong sense of established process and protocol in the conduct of economic policy analysis. Over many years, even the changing state of the national and world economies and the changing political philosophies that dominate the major economic policymaking agencies did not seriously disrupt the established roles and procedures of the centers of macroeconomic modeling within federal agencies. This sense of established process and protocol was disrupted substantially, however, by the 1980 national elections.

Macroeconomic Modeling
After The 1980 Election

Among the members of the macroeconomic modeling community in Washington, D.C., in 1981, there was a widespread sentiment that the election of Ronald Reagan brought numerous unanticipated changes to the established practices of economic policymaking in federal government agencies. Everyone knew the new President and his key advisers were socially and fiscally conservative, and it was expected that the President would attempt to make conservative reforms. Yet the 1980 election gave rise to three unexpected occurrences: the President's victory was very decisive, giving him at least a symbolic mandate for change; the Senate changed from a Democratic to a Republican majority, including the addition of several Republicans equally or more conservative than Reagan; and the Reagan administration, with backing from Senate Republicans, moved quickly and successfully in making major conservative budgetary and programmatic reforms.[11] These unanticipated occurrences created a climate of change in the top policy levels of the executive and legislative branches that went far beyond the changes of the recent past.

The election of Ronald Reagan placed the stamp of approval not only on Reagan as a political leader, but on his economic policies as well. Reagan's policies were based on the "supply-side economics" school of thought, a relatively recent arrival in the world of economics. "Supply siders" shook up the economic policy analysis and policymaking communities in Washington, which at the time were dominated by Keynesian economists of one hue or another.

J. M. KEYNES AND THE RISE OF THE COUNTER-KEYNESIANS

From the late 1940s until Reagan's election, the prevailing economic theories governing federal economic policymaking were those of John M. Keynes and his successors. These economists focused their attention on income and consumption as the major forces driving economic performance. Through the 1960s, Keynesian theories were fairly successful in predicting economic change and in guiding the development of sound economic policy. This led to the establishment of what has been described as "the mid-sixties economic orthodoxy," built heavily on the work of Keynes.[12] This economic orthodoxy came into question in the late 1960s and early 1970s in the aftermath of several radical destabilizing occurrences in the economy: increasing federal budget deficits resulting from the costly war in Vietnam, coupled with large domestic spending programs without sufficient tax increases; softening markets for U.S. products from intensifying industrial competition brought by the rapidly expanding industrial nations in Western Europe and Japan; and the inflationary effects of several major "energy crises" beginning with the first OPEC oil embargo in 1973 (Henry 1978). These events seriously upset the previously successful track record of the Keynesian-based prediction models, and opened new opportunities for critics.

At the time, the principal rivals for the throne of economic policy adviser were the monetarists, led by Professor Milton Friedman of the University of Chicago. The monetarists cannot really be called anti-

Keynesian; in fact, important aspects of monetarist theory build on Keynesian concepts. But monetarist philosophy differs from Keynesian philosophy in that it discounts the importance of income and consumption; monetarists concentrate instead on money supply as the key factor in economic performance. Monetarist theory contends that the money supply is a stronger economic force, because income and consumption are dependent variables that derive their values primarily from the nature of the money supply. Monetarism suggests that careful control of the money supply will prevent rapid economic expansion that leads to inflation, as well as rapid contraction that leads to recession or depression. With sound monetary policy the free market can be relied upon to balance investment and consumption in the most efficient manner. Thus, monetarists believe the fiscal policy of the government should not be considered as important as proper monetary policy.

Beginning in the mid-1950s, Friedman and his followers gained considerable influence in the shaping of federal economic policy, but even during the relatively conservative Nixon administration they never were sufficiently able to infiltrate the bastions of economic analysis and policymaking in federal agencies to compete with economists of the "mid-sixties orthodoxy." Monetarists were routinely represented in important economic policymaking boards such as the Federal Reserve Board of Governors and the Council of Economic Advisers, and they held important positions under Republican Presidents and on the Republican side of congressional budgetary and economics committees. But they never gained full control of economic policymaking.

Trouble for those of the "mid-sixties orthodoxy" school began when the U.S. economy started to act in unpleasant, unpredicted, and inconsistent ways during the early and mid-1970s. Most damaging was the emergence of combined inflation and stagnant economic growth. This phenomenon was difficult for orthodox Keynesian economists to explain, since it was contrary to their belief that inflation should go down when the economy went into recession. Thus, a major discrepancy between theoretical economic behavior and actual economic behavior opened the doors for "counter-Keynesians" to discredit major aspects of Keynesian theory.

During the 1970s, several major rivals of traditional Keynesian theory gained ground, and by 1979 two had emerged as strong competitors. One was standard monetarism, an updated version of the traditional monetarism of Friedman and his followers. The second was supply-side theory, a variant of monetarism, holding that short-run economic cycles are less important to economic growth than long-term trends, and that these long-term trends are most strongly influenced by the "incentive" effects on production and savings caused by marginal taxation rates and rates of return on investment. By 1981 it was generally recognized that there had emerged two competitive schools of thought, both with fundamentally monetarist tenets at their core, but differing in important respects (*Business Week* 1981).

THE "NEW ECONOMICS" OF THE REAGAN ADMINISTRATION
     Monetarist and supply-side economists traditionally have been welcomed into policy circles more ardently by Republican politicians than by Democrats, since monetarist and supply-side theories support fairly conservative "free enterprise" solutions to economic problems, and shy away from extensive direct federal intervention to deal with economic crises. The Republican party had moved demonstrably to the right of the political spectrum by the time of Reagan's nomination as the party's candidate for President in the 1979 campaign, and in adopting its platform for the 1980 election, the party wholeheartedly embraced the politically conservative aspects of monetarist and supply-side economics.

     The mood of the country seemed to be swinging right as well. The continuing economic problems evident during the Carter administration had cost the Democratic party considerable credibility. There was, it seemed, no easy way to beat the problems of high interest rates, high inflation, and high unemployment using the economic policies the Democratic party had advocated for years.

     The supply-side theorists provided Ronald Reagan with an economic philosophy and plan as unorthodox as the problems posed by the economy. The supply siders suggested that the best way to beat inflation and get the economy moving forward was to beef up productivity through massive infusions of private capital into investments in plant modernization and development of innovations. This capital would have to come from private investors, and the only way to generate sufficient capital would be to cut taxes. Individuals would put their extra income to work in the larger economy through savings which would boost the private lending pools and through investment in stocks and securities. The economic growth that would eventually result from tax cuts would lead to even greater tax revenues, thus enabling the federal government to met its budget commitments without major reductions in total federal spending. These dynamics would produce a balanced budget in the long run and help to drive down interest rates. As long as taxpayers behaved as expected—that is, as long as they invested their tax savings rather than use them to increase their consumption—the economy would improve over the long run. In important ways, the economic ideology of supply-side economics was a core component of the powerfully conservative political ideology of the new administration; and Regan's economic outlook and the programs it spawned soon became known as "Reaganomics."

Within the federal economic policymaking community the effects of the new approach were immediate and substantial. The most obvious change was the ascendancy of a large number of monetarist and supply-side economists into high-level positions previously held by economists of the "mid-sixties orthodoxy." Major changes in personnel took place in the Troika agencies, where important T1 and T2 positions were taken over by monetarist and supply-side economists, replacing nearly all of the post-Keynesian economists of the Carter administration era. These new economic advisers, with sympathetic support from the President, the Senate majority leadership, and a host of outsiders, brought with them a strong skepticism of the economic tools the Keynesians had used, including the DRI, Wharton, and Chase macroeconomic models.

The changes at the T1 and T2 levels of the Troika created considerable tension for the staff at the T3 level. Most T3 staff were permanent employees of their agencies, and as such were protected under civil service regulations from partisan firing by their new superiors.[13] Yet because they had been working for so long with the large computerized models now being criticized by new T1 and T2 officials, many felt that their professional standing and the usefulness of their work were jeopardized. During 1981, members of the T3 staffs of OMB and Treasury believed that their work was "up in the air," or it was as yet unclear what role the large macroeconomic models (and therefore their expertise with them) would play in the new administration.

The changes in leadership also created an environment ripe for the introduction of new models reflecting the economic philosophies of the new T1 and T2 Troika members. While none of the big three models (DRI, Chase, and Wharton) was being completely abandoned, their influence was greatly diminished and their future uncertain. Concurrently, a number of new models were being promoted by prominent supply-side economists.[14]

Further, the new interest in monetarist and supply-side economics sparked accelerated efforts by the traditional modeling organizations to come up with models to more fully incorporate these perspectives. For example, Michael Evans, who in 1980 had started his own modeling company, made a mark in the Reagan administration by developing versions of his model that catered to the monetarist and supply-side viewpoints. Similarly, DRI intensified its efforts to make its model more acceptable to the new economic policymakers, and received a substantial contract from the Senate Budget Committee to incorporate more of a supply-side perspective in its model. Finally, the change in political climate changed the role that models play and the way they are used in economic policymaking. These changes were particularly obvious in the making of the 1982 budget.

THE MAKING OF THE 1982 BUDGET

When President Reagan took office, his administration inherited planning for the 1982 budget that had been initially prepared by President Carter's staff. Reagan was determined to make good on his campaign pledge to cut federal spending, so the Carter budget was pushed aside and a forceful new budget preparation effort was begun by the new OMB director, David Stockman. The new budget was not merely a reworking of the Carter numbers. It constituted a drastic reorientation in both programmatic and total spending levels, meaning that many long-standing programs would have to be cut severely. Coupled with the President's pledge to increase defense spending, the new budget cuts meant that the hardest hit portions of the budget would be domestic programs, especially social welfare programs.

The presence of a supportive Republican Senate greatly aided the President in his budget-cutting efforts. The new Senate leadership made a conservative consensus with the President, and his budget became the Senate's budget. Initially, the Democratic leadership believed that the President could not succeed with his spending cuts. It felt that the House, still dominated by the Democrats, would not permit it. However, it soon became clear that many Democrats were interpreting the message of the voters in the 1980 election as a call for change, and they began to back the President's drive. During the first few months of 1981, Reagan's prospects looked brighter every day.

In the Troika, the use of the mainstream econometric models for fiscal analysis continued, but the pace of analysis slackened. There was even some speculation that the OMB and Treasury would stop using some of their major econometric forecasts, such as those produced by DRI. But there were few, if any, direct casualties of Reaganomics among the models or the modelers. Rather, agency analysts were asked to conduct studies related to the implementation of the President's political and economic goals. The basic ground rules were simple: the Carter 1982 budget proposals had to be cut by a large amount—about $30 billion. Defense spending was to increase substantially over the Carter budget. Certain programs that were very sensitive politically (e.g., Social Security) were to be left alone for the most part. The remaining programs were thereby open for cutting, and the cutting took place largely as across-the-board reductions in these programs. Specific programs that did not fit into the President's political philosophy were open for larger-than-average cuts, while other favored programs received below-average reductions. Since the objective of this approach to budget cutting was to cut predetermined levels of spending from specific programs and line items in the budget, it was not necessary to use econometric modeling (or even microsimulation) to forecast either the budgetary impacts of changes in program rules or the impact of cuts on program recipients.

After the President forwarded his budget to Congress in January 1981, the proposal worked its way through the congressional review process. The CBO's FAD and BAD began to conduct their forecasts of economic conditions, analyses of program requirements, and forecasts of anticipated effects of budget changes on programs. Both divisions, however, found themselves in a completely new operating environment. In previous years, BAD had to prepare six-month forecasts every January and July to assist Congress in creating the budget targets and the ceilings on spending and floors for revenues. To accomplish this, BAD used macroeconomic, model-based forecasts it obtained from the Troika and from the CBO's own AD, along with various DRI-supplied data. Normally, BAD sent the results of its analyses to the Senate and House Budget committees, which would use them to develop their own assessments of appropriate budget levels for specific program categories.

In early 1981, the Reagan administration and the new Senate leadership changed these ground rules. CBO analyses were forwarded as usual to both budget committees. But the Senate committee rejected CBO's assessments out of hand because they were based on forecasts using the DRI and other major models, run through the CBO's multipliers "model." These economic forecasts differed considerably from the assumptions and economic forecasts issued by the White House. The President's forecasts were optimistic, predicting that major spending and tax cuts would simultaneously reduce inflation and stimulate investment and new economic growth, thereby increasing federal tax revenues. The Senate Budget Committee accepted the President's forecast, with a minor adjustment of raising projected interest rates (the rates had, in fact, already gone up), and began to analyze the budget with its own staff using the President's forecast for their baseline assumptions.

The Democratic majority on the House Budget Committee, in an effort to counter the projections and budget plans of the President and the Senate committee, came up with its own forecasts, which fell between CBO's and the President's. The Democrats then began to barrage CBO with requests for analyses of program needs based on these new figures. CBO was required to go through revision after revision of its forecasts until the budgetary needs of programs coincided with the numbers contained in the House Budget Committee's forecast. Of course, it was also necessary for the CBO to run and rerun its analyses using the President's and the Senate Budget Committee's numbers, in order to see where the President's numbers might be strong (in answer to requests from Republicans) or weak (in answer to requests from Democrats).

This situation dramatically affected the CBO modelers. The most immediate effects were on their workloads. The processes CBO traditionally used to arrive at its forecasts were very extensive and refined, built up through six years of effort to create a solid, sophisticated, "non-partisan" forecasting capability.[15] They were also time consuming, since every effort had to be made to ensure accuracy. By law, CBO forecasts, and the procedures it uses to make them, have to be open to intense scrutiny by members of Congress and anyone else who cares to look at them. Even during "normal" years, the semi-annual forecast preparation periods had been frantic, with models being run ten hours or more each day. The sudden tidal wave of requests for analyses, many requiring alterations of the models in order to incorporate their assumptions, swamped the modeling capabilities of the analysts in FAD and BAD.

The second effect this battle of the budget had on CBO modelers was to place them on a battlefield with a constantly changing terrain that made modeling almost impossible. This was especially true for analysts in BAD. In order to prepare their forecasts of program impacts resulting from proposed budget changes, BAD had to get forecasts of basic economic conditions from FAD, which in turn derived its forecasts by running the DRI, Wharton, Chase, and other models. Since the actual costs of programs, especially entitlement programs, depend on the condition of the economy, it is essential to have a forecast of economic conditions downstream in the target fiscal year. Yet, in 1981, these very forecasts were the ones under assault by the new administration and the Senate. CBO analysts initially tried to follow their traditional analytic procedures. They accepted the forecasted values that came from the two budget committees and cranked them through their models. But the intensive workload and the changing terrain of battle made it necessary for them to bypass the delicate and carefully developed linkages between FAD and BAD which had been designed to refine and improve the internal consistency and technical quality of CBO forecasts. It quickly became clear that analysts in FAD, and especially those in BAD, were caught in the cross fire of a battle they could not win or even figure out how to fight.

The CBO analysts had discovered that modeling could slip back and forth between the roles of political weapon and analytical tool for policymaking. In prior years the role of forecasts had been comparatively routine and even predictable. The presidency might change party, but Congress had remained Democratic for several decades. Proposed budget changes were variants on a general theme. This created a relatively stable setting for macroeconomic analyses. The 1980 election changed everything. President Reagan and the new Senate leadership arrived with a mandate for major change. The changes they proposed were so sweeping and based on so many unorthodox assumptions that CBO's existing policy-modeling capabilities were simply inadequate for the task of providing careful policy analysis.

More important, as the budget process unfolded, it became even more clear that the new leadership in the White House and the Senate was more concerned with winning the battle than with what the models said. The opposition Democrats in the Senate and the House quickly followed suit. This became apparent in two interesting events.

First came a fight over whose economic forecast was correct. CBO published its forecast in January of 1981. As usual, this forecast resembled the forecasts of the major econometric models on which it was based. The President's forecast, said to have been based on a model created by John Rutledge of the Claremont Economics Institute in California, was very different from the CBO forecast. CBO and others around Washington (including the Fed) quickly tried to get a copy of the Claremont model in order to examine it and see how it worked. They could not, however, obtain the model, or even a diagram of its equations. One staff economist of the Joint Economic Committee claimed to have seen some of the equations and insisted that there was in fact a model (although he thought it might be a manual model instead of a computerized one). But other economists at CBO and elsewhere expressed doubts that the model existed at all. If it did exist, they claimed, it was probably too simplistic to be of great value.

Thus, in the middle of a major economic policy debate involving the President, the Senate, and the House, the question of where the estimates came from clouded the numbers themselves. A war of ideological prespectives emerged. On one side was the political philosophy of the new administration, with its adopted economic ideology of supply-side economics, and very meager modeling capabilities. On the other side was the political philosophy of the weakened Democratic Congress, with its established "mid-sixties orthodoxy" economics, and a mighty arsenal of macroeconomic modeling capabilities. The President's victory on his 1982 budget and tax bills demonstrated the power of his political and economic ideology, and the quickness with which those of the new ideology could seize and wield the political weapon of "model-based" forecasts irrespective of the opinions of those who traditionally did the modeling.

The other incident illustrating the overriding importance of winning was a brief battle over the projected deficit for the 1982 budget. The highly political battle over the President's budget and tax programs set off debates throughout Congress over the short-run and long-run economic consequences of these programs. Some Democrats felt convinced that the President's budget cuts would destablilize the economy, while the tax cuts would reduce revenues so much that the budget, even though cut, would still produce a large deficit. Democrats on the Joint Economic Committee (JEC) had several analyses run under various assumptions using the DRI model, and these projected large deficits for 1982 and 1983.

In the course of these forecasts, one analysis suggested that the President's program would result in a $100 billion deficit in 1982. This figure was picked up by a Democratic member of the JEC and held up to public view as evidence of the disastrous consequences the President's programs would have. There was considerable disagreement between the staff members for the Democratic and Republican sides of the committee over how big the deficit would be, but both sides were skeptical about the $100 billion figure. It simply seemed too high. Careful investigation revealed that a mistake in the running of that particular forecast had resulted in the high deficit prediction.[16] When the error was corrected, the projected budget fell to a level more in line with the hunches of the staff economists on the Democratic side, but still higher than the economists on the Republican side were forecasting. The Democratic member of the committee who had raised the issue noted the error and apologized in a letter to the Republican chair of the committee, and the issue blew over. But it had made a mark. Though the heat of battle had strained the established, model-based analytical processes to the point where major mistakes were likely, and even the results of error-free analyses were questionable, seasoned politicians could not resist the urge to use models and their results as political weapons. As one economist on the staff of the JEC remarked, "Members [of Congress] will use any number they can get their hands on to support their position, as long as they think it won't come back and bite them."[17]

In spite of the intense rivalries that have grown up in recent years between the different camps of modelers and their techniques, many long-term participants in the trenches of national economic policymaking believe in the staying power of the large-scale econometric models—even through the "assaults" of the Reagan administration. As a staff economist in the Council of Economic Advisers commented:

These large models [DRI, Chase, WEFA] are not threatened by the President's faith in supply-side theory because these are the only models we have that can make useful, detailed, short-run forecasts of the economy. Short-run forecasts are not important now [July of 1981] because a basic tenet of supply-side theory is that the long run is what is important, and there is no reason to concentrate on the short run at this time. But the President and his advisers will become very interested in short-run forecasts if their economic policies do not quickly produce the positive impact they hope for. As time goes on and the 1984 election draws near, the administration will start demanding short-run forecasts to explain and justify their position, and they will come back to these large models because they are the only place they can turn to get the analytical backup they need.[18]

CHAPTER SEVEN
ACCOUNTING FOR SUCCESSFUL MODEL USE

For well over a decade, federal agencies have demonstrated their eagerness to obtain computerized modeling capabilities in order to improve their ability to engage in sophisticated policy analysis and to wage effective political battles. The case studies of the use of the MATH/TRIM microsimulation models and DRI's macroeconomic modeling services provide ample evidence of agencies' keen interest in policy modeling for both technical and political purposes.

The two cases reveal different dimensions of agencies' use of modeling. The history of MATH/TRIM's use during food stamp debates in the mid-seventies and during the Carter administration's attempt to overhaul the nation's welfare system shows how microsimulation models came to play critical roles in intra-agency and interinstitutional partisan policy disputes at times of intense interest in welfare reform. In contrast, the DRI model and other major macroeconomic models gradually came to enjoy a more institutionalized status in federal economic policymaking, so that model-generated forecasts and policy simulations have become standard components of the highly complex and routinized processes of annual federal budget preparation and tax legislation efforts. Politics has certainly affected macroeconomic policy modeling, but in a less partisan and more ideological way than in the case of microsimulation models.

Partisan Use Of Models

LESSONS FROM THE FOOD STAMP DEBATES

Over the years 1975–76, the MATH model came of age as a fixture of the income-transfer policy analysis process. During this time, microsimulation gained acceptance by a corps of analysts and policy-makers who relied on it extensively for policy design and analysis. The MATH model displayed tremendous utility to analysts and managers who used it to achieve rationalist objectives. MATH was the most sophisticated method available to answer "What will happen if . . .?" questions at a time of great interest in welfare policy change but low consensus over means.

Because the model provided detailed information on who stood to win and lose from alternative policy changes—information of considerable interest to interest groups and politicians—MATH's forecasts had a natural and attentive audience in the political arena. The MATH model eventually became entangled in the larger political debate over food stamp reform when the Ford administration, which controlled the model and the public release of its results, used the estimates to justify complex policy choices. MATH and the information it generated became thorns in the side of Capitol Hill opponents who lacked comparable forecasting capabilities.

In the battle over food stamp policy changes, MATH constituted a tactical weapon which opponents had to reckon with on its own terms. Opponents had to fight forecasts with forecasts. The partisans waged a campaign of numbers, with each side's experts defending their own analyses and techniques and challenging the credibility of the other side's informants, methods, and information. In this skirmish, the political advantage the administration had temporarily enjoyed as a result of exclusive expertise and modeling capabilities became neutralized. Each side had its own retinue of trusted analysts as a technical component of a larger power base. Each side had its own forecasts reinforcing the reasonableness of its preferred policy stance. And each side challenged the objectivity of the other's methods, numbers, and analysts.

Outsiders looking in on the modeling war had a hard time understanding whose information and experts were in fact "right," because no one but the experts themselves could evaluate the merits of such complex "weapons" systems as MATH. But the very fact of contested information implied to many observers that the real objects of dispute fell beyond the realm of objective analysis anyway. On one hand, this led to a call for external evaluation of the "black box" methods themselves and, on the other hand, to a relegation of the model and its estimates to a more subordinate role in further policy discussions on food stamp reform.

The political attention span for such esoteric modeling disputes is relatively short. Over the year of GAO's evaluation of microsimulation models' use in welfare policy analysis, the partisans in the larger food stamp policy battle were moving on to other political turf. The evaluation findings came too late to capture the attention of many politicians, since they had already witnessed the resolution of the battle in which the models had played such a controversial role.

For the policy analysts, however, the eventual results of GAO's external review were ambiguous and unprovocative, reporting largely what many analysts already knew and believed: that MATH/TRIM contained some serious technical problems but that they were the best tools available to provide the kind of detailed budgetary and policy-impact information that politicians had by then come to expect.

The very act of having introduced microsimulation models, considering all of the flaws and barriers encountered in usage, into the policymaking arena meant a real change in the vocabulary of debate. This type of impact forecasting seemed to have a momentum of its own: once one group of participants had access to such detailed information, all other interested parties were at an "evidence" disadvantage until they too had such a capability. Also, models encouraged politicians to expect answers to complicated questions that might not be answerable with high levels of confidence, given the current state of the art. Many analysts have noticed this problem, which HEW's Michael Barth described:

Sometimes I wonder if these big complex models are worth all the trouble. They demand that you make strong statements about so many behaviors or relationships, many of which we don't really know enough about yet. . . . The simple models are good for gross estimates—which may also be strong statements in terms of their simplicity, but they do it without the pretense of seeming to know everything. The problem is that policymakers ask so many detailed questions that cannot be answered by simple models. They may not be able to be answered correctly by complex ones, but those models do produce an answer to the question asked. . . . So the real dilemma is how can we train the policymakers into not asking questions we can't answer when we lead them to believe we can?[1]

Not surprisingly, none of the analysts who expressed concern over this issue offered a suggestion for how to encourage politicians to use these models "correctly," since the very thing that attracts many politicians to microsimulation modeling capabilities is the models' and analysts' ability to provide detailed if inaccurate estimates of "what will happen if . . .?" Analysts seem to recognize that the individual who exposes the Emperor's new clothes risks losing his privileged position at the Emperor's ear.

The case study of model use during the food stamp debates illustrates several interesting dimensions of the politics of microsimulation modeling. Within this case of use and evaluation of a computerized planning technique, it is possible to identify numerous beneficiaries and multiple levels of impact.

On one level, the case represents the successful implementation of models into the income-transer policymaking process. For model vendors, this success had meant the transfer of modeling capability to agency users who have come to rely on the technique to conduct regular and salient policy analyses. The models and the technique gained attention—some favorable, some critical, but all ultimately attractive—at various points in the policy analysis process. This attention tended to reinforce the notion that the information provided by such models is useful, valid, and available for sale for policy and political use.

For the agency analysts, the MATH model was a new analytic technique, one which not only made their work more "interesting," "challenging," and "fun," but also enhanced the visibility and status of their role in the larger policymaking process. For some, their expertise in modeling gained them access to the offices of important agency officials and key committees of Congress. For agency administrators, MATH turned out to be a valuable resource in their campaign to rationalize the process of food stamp reform. It gave them information they could use to help convince administration officials of the possibility and reasonableness of selective surgery on the food stamp program rather than random stabs at the program's budget and beneficiaries.

For the administration, which eventually embraced and ultimately controlled the technique's use, the modeling capability provided a mystifyingly complex and temporarily exclusive weapon, one which could be deployed when its estimates served the interests of the administration and supressed or ignored or discredited when they didn't. The model itself appeared inconsistent in its biases toward overestimating or underestimating the impacts of various program changes. But control over its use and the access to its results gave users the flexibility to manage the data and parameters of the model to produce information in support of preferred policy choices. While the administration held monopoly control over MATH and its estimates, the modeling capability reinforced the existing informational advantage of the administration vis-à-vis its opposition on Capitol Hill. And its presence in the political battle over food stamp reform provoked others to get into the modeling business too, even if it meant using less sophisticated, ad hoc techniques to do so.

Thus, microsimulation modeling demonstrated a momentum of its own when used for political purposes: once introduced by one powerful and interested party, it became the currency of debate as other interested groups had to respond to the evidentiary challenge, adopt comparable techniques of their own, argue their positions by means of quantitative information (if only to discredit the authoritativeness of the other side's quantitative information), and then shift the focus of debate to other salient political issues. Here the presence of computerized planning models tended to focus political attention on what impacts were simulated by the models (strictly program costs and caseloads), to reinforce the political biases and interests of those who controlled the technique, and to exaggerate the importance and validity of computer-based information itself.

LESSONS FROM CARTER'S WELFARE REFORM INITIATIVES

When Carter's welfare reform proposals died in 1978, their failure resulted from a number of factors, not the least of which was the overwhelming difficulty of building consensus for a controversial redistributive program among politicians and interest groups with conflicting demands. Such political challenges arise for any administration attempting to change existing income-maintenance programs. But in the case of the Carter reform proposal, there were numerous other sources of problems; above all there was a lack of strong presidential activism or leadership toward a particular policy change. This in turn was mirrored by a lack of clear policy direction or political advocacy by the President's agent, HEW Secretary Califano, during the policy design process.

By extension, the welfare reform staff within HEW adopted a role of central analyst, examining every suggested combination of program elements and approaches. And the process of policy design became bogged down in the mire of technical analysis. The attention to detail and thoroughness was particularly problematic because of the rigid and unrealistic time and budgetary constraints imposed on the process by Carter. The staffers made a herculean effort to make the most of the limited time, and their control over such a complex data manipulation device as the KGB model assisted them in this end. Nonetheless, during all stages of the policy design process there was a sense of having to do a rush job.

HEW's workload was, of course, exacerbated by the turf battle between DOL and HEW. While Carter had put HEW Secretary Califano nominally in charge of the welfare reform effort, the President had expected—and insisted upon—joint problem-solving responsibility by the two agencies. DOL officials took full advantage of Carter's interests in a pro-work income maintenance strategy and interpreted "joint responsibility" as an endorsement for active involvement. Consequently, DOL bolstered its own analytic resources in order to be equal to those at HEW.

Both agencies had highly sophisticated staffs with access to complex analytic tools such as computerized microsimulation models. This situation was somewhat unusual among welfare reform efforts, where HEW had always enjoyed a monopoly over sophisticated and respected analytic resources. The act of decentralizing technical skills resulted in shifting power from HEW to DOL. Also, the different norms and styles of the two staffs had a similar impact. In contrast to the HEW staff members who were effectively forced by the agency leadership into playing the role of objective analyst, DOL staffers acted the part of committed advocates. DOL aides knew the clear policy orientation of their bosses and mobilized their skills and technical tools to advance their cause. DOL analysts used the MATH JOBS model as a political as well as technical resource, independently exploring ideas and preparing for interagency policy discussions, legitimizing their position as analytic equals with HEW's ASPE staff, and monitoring and countering the information produced by the KGB mode. Consequently, instead of cooperation and consensus building, competition and conflict—over programmatic approaches, over bureaucratic jurisdictional issues, and over the authoritativeness of analyses—became the hallmark of the 1977 welfare reform effort.

Microsimulation modeling was caught up in the larger clash between the departments. DOL used the MATH model as a weapon to combat HEW's KGB model for as long as DOL found it useful to play the role of agitator vis-à-vis HEW. In the early stages of policy design, DOL wanted to avoid the kind of reactive and therefore subservient relationship an analytically ill-equipped party would have to adopt with a technically superior party. Access to and control over its own model gave DOL independence and made DOL and HEW equal but competitive partners. Later in the process of policy design, after DOL had firmly established its position as an active participant and after it was becoming increasingly clear to everyone involved that the interdepartmental conflicts were threatening to undermine ultimate adoption of the Carter program, DOL officials and aides agreed to cooperate with HEW. This involved grudging acceptance of the use of the KGB model and its estimates in order to reestablish a single, consensual set of numbers representing the administration's point of view.

In the end, the process of analytic competition and counter modeling was a costly one. It was expensive in real dollar terms. According to agency analysts, HEW spent $1 million to develop and use the KGB mode for welfare reform analysis, while DOL's more abbreviated use of MATH cost $500,000.[2]

The process also was costly politically. Even though both sides' access to the models contributed to equalizing powerful resources between agencies, it helped to erode the political resources of the administration as a whole on this issue. Competition over models and estimates exacerbated the agencies' bickering and programmatic differences. Many outside observers of the internecine war got the impression that the Carter administration didn't know what it wanted in welfare reform, and external sources of support were difficult to muster in the end. Ultimately, the only way that countermodeling helped DOL and HEW achieve their objectives was in the ironic, even tragic sense that each agency prevented the other from getting its approach adopted. But neither one got what it wanted.

Ideology And Model Use

Utilization of macroeconomic models in federal economic policymaking has been less overtly partisan and politicized than that of microsimulation models. Macroeconomic model use is more heavily influenced by two particular ideologies. One we call managerial ideology; the other we call political/economic ideology.

MANAGERIAL IDEOLOGY AND MACROECONOMIC MODELING
We use the term "managerial ideology" to refer to a set of beliefs about appropriate uses for macroeconomic modeling in the federal government, and appropriate means by which modeling can be effec-

tively established and maintained to provide the analytical capabilities policymakers need. The managerial ideology evident in our case study of macroeconomic model use incorporates three beliefs:

1. Scientific techniques such as macroeconomic modeling can and should be used to help policymakers deal with difficult problems, such as the setting of national fiscal and monetary policy.
2. The most important requirement for providing macroeconomic modeling capability for policy analysis is the procurement of good technical people and adequate resources to build and run the models and interpret their results.
3. Modeling should be carried out in a consistent, reliable, and efficient manner that provides policymakers with need capability at reasonable cost.

The first tenet is illustrated by the establishment of formalized procedures for conducting economic analysis and the creation of offices specifically designed to carry them out. Every major agency engaged in making fiscal or monetary policy established its own, in-house, analytical unit to either use econometric models directly, or use the results of econometric modeling done by others. Agency economists believed that these models were useful, and they expected the institutionalized apparatuses for conducting econometric modeling to remain over time despite periodic changes in political ideology at the top.[3]

The second tenet is embodied in the fact that the Troika, CBO, and the Fed all established procedures for recruiting bright young economists and analysts from the "better schools," and for providing them with extensive and ready access to the modeling, data resources, and computing capability needed to conduct comprehensive analyses. Recruiting capable and well-respected economists and analysts was important to the agencies because of the complexities of macroeconomic modeling and forecasting, the controversies surrounding what models and assumptions are appropriate to answer certain questions, and the need for the agencies to maintain independent modeling capability of high quality to respond to questions from policymakers holding divergent views on economic policy. The Troika agencies also provided substantial and continuing support for procuring the best available modeling. They maintained contracts with most of the major model providers, and supported some in-house modeling using the Treasury's computing center. Additionally, CBO contracted with almost all available model providers, built its "multiplier" program to consolidate forecasts, and was spending 40 percent of its budget buying outside computing and data resources to support its analytical model activities.

The third tenet is illustrated by the fact that all of the agencies we studied carried out their modeling activities in a sound, businesslike manner. The Troika agencies divided responsibility among themselves for using various models. This provided comprehensive modeling capability within the Troika, and ensured that the individuals doing the modeling were deeply versed in the details of specific models, without each agency having to build a complete but redundant modeling capability. CBO built a smoothly running, in-house capability for macroeconomic analysis. This enabled CBO to keep up with the analytic demands of Congress arising from the statutory, procedural, and political requirements of the budget process. The Fed maintained a small but efficient in-house modeling staff to provide its judgmental analysts and top policymakers with model-based forecasts on a consistent and timely basis. Analysts in all of these agencies indicated a concern for controlling the costs of modeling while maintaining reliable and consistent modeling capability of high quality.[4] They said the analytic tasks they perform constitute an important part of the economic policymaking processes of government, and that they took care to preserve the carefully developed procedures designed to ensure efficient and effective macroeconomic analysis support for policymakers.

POLITICAL/ECONOMIC IDEOLOGY
AND MACROECONOMIC MODELING

Our term "political/economic ideology" refers to the basic political and economic philosophies that serve as ground rules for making judgments about what is happening with the economy and what ought to be done to improve economic conditions. Changes in political/economic ideology can have a strong influence on the conduct of macroeconomic modeling for policy analysis. In contrast to managerial ideology, which seems to take a common shape throughout the community of macroeconomic modelers and analysts, political and economic ideologies can take many different forms. A major change at the top levels of national policymaking from one prevailing political/economic ideology to another can bring major changes to the ways macroeconomic modeling is used.

We have four observations about this kind of influence from our analysis of the DRI case:

1. Economics is as yet a young and uncertain science. Any given economic theory, and the models that embody that theory, will be open to criticism whenever the results of that theory do not conform to the way the economy actually works.
2. Economic theories, no matter how academic, become a part of political ideologies as soon as they are applied to the making of national economic policy, which is ultimately a political and nonscientific process.
3. Political/economic ideologies heavily influence the ways in which macroeconomic analyses are called into play and used in policymaking because policymakers, who are partisans in policy debate, control the entry of model-based data into the debates.
4. Political/economic ideologies sometimes result in uses of macroeconomic model-based analyses that do not conform to the accepted scientific standards for modeling.

The first of these observations can be drawn from the history of macroeconomic modeling itself. Every macroeconomic model is an embodiment of a particular economic philosophy regarding the way the economy functions. Economists differ substantially in their beliefs about what makes economies behave the way they do; indeed, the history of economics has been filled with disagreement among economists over fundamental theories of economic behavior, fueled by discrepancies that arise between economists' explanations about how the economy operates and the way it actually does operate over time (Heilbroner 1953). This turbulence is a natural and healthy part of economics as an academic discipline, for it is only through such dialectics that the scientific paradigms needed to guide development of economic knowledge can be built.

This ecology of economic theories has been important for the development of macroeconomic modeling and its use in national economic policymaking. The first large model-building projects began in the early 1960s, during the heyday of the Keynesian and post-Keynesian economists. This was in part due to the fact that Keynesian economics was the prevailing theoretical viewpoint among most of the major econometric centers from which modelers came. Moreover, Keynesian concepts were the most extensively developed of economic theories, and were the most amenable to detailed reduction into mathematical models of economic behavior. Therefore, the Keynesian-based "mid-sixties orthodoxy" naturally dominated the creation of these large macroeconomic models. The only major competitor of this development of models with the Keynesian flavor was a monetarist model developed by the St. Louis Bank of the Federal Reserve System, and this was not developed until 1970—nearly a decade after the major burst of modeling based on Keynesian principles (Greenberger, Crenson, and Crissey 1976).

In addition to the basic theoretical differences in economic viewpoint between monetarists and "Keynesians," the models of these two camps have differed in important technical respects. By discounting the importance of the highly complex fiscal side of an economic system, and concentrating instead on the comparatively simple factors associated with money supply, the monetarist models tend to be much smaller than the Keynesian models. The St. Louis Fed model, for example, embodied only eight equations and three exogenous variables (Greenberger, Crenson, and Crissey 1976). Such small models have not fit into the quest for larger, more complex models many econometricians believe are required to accurately reflect the behavior of the real economy. This combination of important intellectual differences in economic philosophy between monetarists and Keynesians, and in their attitudes about the apparent strength or weaknesses of their models, greatly advantaged the Keynesian builders and users of large models throughout the 1960s and 1970s.[5]

The second observation—that economic theories become part of political ideologies once they are applied to the process of national economic policymaking—is illustrated by the fact that political leaders must accept and stand on only one basic policy position. Different economic theories support different policy positions in many cases, so a politician's decision to adopt a given policy reflects at least tacit acceptance of that policy's economic justification. Thus, economic theories become integral components in political debates whether economists want them to or not. The long-established tradition of Keynesian economics, and the analytical techniques it engendered, resulted in the creation of many centers of Keynesian-based macroeconomic analysis in federal economic policymaking agencies. The apparent stability of these centers served, in time, to obscure both the fact that there were competing theories about the behavior of the economy and the fact that the incorporation of Keynesian theories into policy analysis was itself a political act. As long as these theories remained predominant in policy analysis centers it was possible for those without detailed understanding of the economics discipline to assume that the theories embodied in the philosophies and models being used represented the "real" economics, and that competing theories were not seriously considered because they need not be taken seriously.[6]

By coincidence, the transition from the Carter administration to the Reagan administration provided interesting information about important aspects of modeling in political contexts. This change was not merely a change of political party in the White House and the Senate; it was a change within the Republican party toward an unusually conservative approach to the federal government's role in the economy. The manner in which Reagan's transition team adopted and applied the tenets of supply-side economics immediately made supply-side theory and its monetarist base a highly political issue. Suddenly questions about the validity and efficacy of supply-side theory went beyond the academic community and took on a new and powerful political character of great concern to people who had never heard of supply-side economics. Those who supported the Reagan campaign implicitly supported the ascendancy of one economic philosophy over another.

The third observation—that political/economic ideologies strongly influence the ways in which macroeconomic modeling for policy analysis is done—is shown by the experiences of CBO and Troika analysts following the 1980 election. Not only were traditional analytical practices disrupted, but fundamental questions arose about the very use of modeling for economic policy analysis. The question was asked whether it was sensible to use traditional macroeconomic models based on Keynesian economic constructs to perform analyses of policies based on the counter-Keynesian political/economic ideologies of the new President and the new Senate leadership. For example, most large macroeconomic models were designed to specify money supply as an endogenous variable, whose value is determined internally in the model as a result of exogenous factors such as policies of the Fed, the behavior of banks, and the size of the federal budget. Thus, changes in fiscal policy (e.g., tax rates, government spending) would result in major changes in the money supply. The monetarists claimed that money supply does not fluctuate as a result of these factors, so it should be input to the models exogenously, based on historical trends in the money supply itself. Entering money supply values exogenously would reduce the influence of fiscal policy on money supply within the models, bringing model structure more in line with what monetarists claim to be the case.

Thus, the major changes in political/economic ideology that swept into the top policymaking levels of the federal government following the 1980 election had serious ramifications both on the conduct of macroeconomic, model-based analysis and on the question of whether the prevailing, established models were in fact useful for developing policy under the new ideology.

The final observation—that changes in political/economic ideology can result in uses of macroeconomic modeling that do not fit accepted scientific standards for modeling—is illustrated by two experiences of model-using analysts following the 1980 election. One was the breakdowns that occurred in the long-established processes for doing analysis. These processes had grown up over time through efforts to improve the theoretical integrity of the modeling process and to ensure accuracy in the complicated tasks that advanced macroeconomic modeling requires. In the Troika the processes of modeling were almost suspended at one point during the creation of the 1982 budget, so the input of the major models were not felt at all. Those results of modeling that did not support the President's plan were simply ignored.

The other experience was the wholesale adoption of models as political weapons in the battle for the budget, irrespective of the technical details of modeling that are so critical to its technical utility as a tool for policy analysis. The forecasts of the condition of the economy provided by the executive branch were said to be based on one or more "supply-side models," but there is serious question as to whether those models even existed at the time the numbers were being promulgated. Subsequently, according to OMB director David Stockman, the forecasts provided by the President to Congress were not really based on detailed analysis at all, but instead were constructed to be convincing in support of the President's program.[7]

The behaviors of the Senate and House committees were equally at odds with accepted scientific standards for modeling and the use of model results. A fight erupted between the Democratic and Republican sides of the Joint Economic Committee of Congress over the probable size of the federal deficit in 1982 and 1983; the fight's major focus was on the results of a model-based projection, later found to be in error. The Senate Budget Committee rejected CBO's own forecasts because they were based on Keynesian macroeconomic models and accepted the President's forecasts after adjusting them to reflect what had already taken place in the economy. The House Budget Committee, in reaction, abandoned the CBO forecasts and settled on its own forecast that essentially split the difference between the CBO's and the President's forecasts.

These experiences were understandably frustrating to economists and analysts used to the traditional and established protocols for modeling and model use. Their reactions ranged from amusement at the blatant political behavior of the top elected and appointed policymakers in the executive and legislative branches, to apprehension over the implications of the political battle for the role of analysis in future policy efforts. The most significant concern voiced by the analysts was not that politics had supplanted analysis as a focus of their work; rather, it was that the carefully developed mechanisms of model-based policy analysis had been disrupted and perhaps even discredited during the political fray. As one CBO analyst expressed it, "I can't really see any reason for us to be doing these elaborate policy analyses when the questions people are concerned about have nothing to do with the programmatic impacts of budget cutting."[8]

INTERACTIONS OF THE IDEOLOGIES

Managerial and political/economic ideologies have major consequences for the ways modeling is conducted and the ways its results are used. We find that at different times, each of these ideologies prevails in the conduct of modeling.

The managerial ideology of modeling seems to be most influential when political/economic ideologies behind models and their use are stable. Such a condition prevailed for a fairly long period of time between 1960 and 1980 when the Congress was Democratic and the presidency was occupied by either moderate Republicans or moderate Democrats. This stability resulted in the creation of large, technically proficient modeling groups in many economic policymaking agencies. Once established, the major objective of these groups was to provide the best technical support possible for policymakers given the political perspectives of those policymakers and the economic ideologies they believed in. The managerial ideology was the primary influence on econometric modeling when economic ideologies and political ideologies surrounding economic policymaking were stable. Managerial ideology is, in a sense, the "default" dominating factor in the use of modeling; its influence will always emerge when political/economic ideologies stabilize.

Political/economic ideologies influence the use of modeling when theoretical disputes arise among economic advisers and policymakers who hold different ideologies about fundamental features of economic behavior. Since models rest on these economic theories, ideological disputes can disrupt modeling and model use. Modeling is a tool that can be used by economists of almost any ideology, but the basic focus of the Keynesian approach on the income and consumption side of the equation and the importance it attaches to the complicated fiscal behavior of the government have tended to make macroeconomic modeling a natural tool for federal policymakers who favor interventionist strategies. The monetarist and supply-side economists, who focus on more simple controls rather than complicated fiscal factors, regard modeling as somewhat less important. Therefore, economic philosphy has tended to divide modelers into two camps: the large camp of modelers using the Keynesian tradition, and the relatively smaller camps of monetarist and supply-side modelers.

Political/economic ideology appears to be the most powerful single factor influencing the role of modeling in policymaking, at least in the sense that changes in such ideology at the top positions can bring radical changes in the objectives and techniques of federal fiscal policymaking. Yet political changes such as the change from a Republican to a Democratic presidency do not necessarily result in major shifts of political or economic ideology as far as macroeconomic modeling is concerned. This is shown by the fact that macroeconomic modeling was well established and operational for almost twenty years, through five presidencies, and across two party changes. The major changes for macroeconomic modeling really began with the election of the Reagan administration and the Republican-dominated Senate. These newly ascendant Republican actors were more fiscally and socially conservative than had been the norm under previous, recent Republican Presidents. It was the degree of change in political ideology, in addition to the change in party affiliation, that so upset macroeconomic modeling activity in the Troika and the CBO. The economic ideology that had prevailed for twenty years was suddenly confronted with the emergence of both monetarist and supply-side economic philosophies backed up by a powerful political mandate and implemented by clever politicians and skilled new presidential appointees. The rationales behind the different ideologies were no longer at issue. Rather, the concern centered on which political/economic ideologies would prevail in the fight over the budget. The fight itself became so heated that the managerial and economic ideologies that governed the models and how they were used became of secondary concern, and modeling as science and art quickly took second place to the use of model results as weapons in the political fray.

The experiences of the model users in the Troika and the CBO contrasted sharply with those of model users in the Fed during this same period. The Fed is functionally separated from the executive and legislative branches of the government, and does not directly participate in the budget process. Thus, the Fed is buffered from the highly political battles over the budget in which the President, the Senate, and the House engage. Fed analysts watched the transition from the Carter administration to the Reagan administration from a safe distance, knowing that the nature of their work would not be directly affected by the change, at least in the short run. Fed analysts had both an intellectual and a professional interest in the changes, and they endeavored to acquire the Claremont Model, in order to analyze the model and the assumptions on which the President's forecasts were said to be based. But they did not experience any changes in their normal analytical operations. The impacts of changes in the political/economic ideologies within the White House and the Senate fell mainly on model users in the executive and legislative branches, where the changes themselves had taken place.

IMPLICATIONS OF CHANGE

Given the significance of the impacts on macroeconomic model use by federal policymaking agencies stemming from changes in political/economic ideology, a question arises as to the probable short-run and long-run changes in model use by these agencies. The answers are not clear, but we have two observations about how modeling will fit into future economic policy debates.

The first relates to the nature of debates among economists about which policies are appropriate for dealing with economic troubles. Despite the strong interest in the monetarist and supply-side theories inside the executive branch, most economists within and outside the government have refrained from supporting or even acknowledging the basic claims of these theories. This must be due, in part, to academic partisanship; traditional Keynesian-type economists cannot be expected to shift their allegiances to these theories simply because the President supports them. But more important, most of these more traditional economists feel that the monetarist and supply-side theories are not sufficiently developed and tested to provide reliable guidance for national policy interventions. Even if some of the basic tenets of the theories are reasonable, there is a dearth of empirical evidence to support the theories. Thus, many economists feel that the national economic policies based on these theories are at best experiments that will show whether or not the theories have merit. Some economists within the Fed, CBO, the Troika, and congressional committees have remained firmly convinced that the theories are not sound, and that the policies based on them will fail to solve current economic problems and will perhaps even exacerbate them.

The outcomes of these economic policy experiments will have importance for the future of macroeconomic modeling, and especially for the large established models, because the credibility of such modeling hinges on these outcomes. If the policies fail to work major structural improvements in the economy, and many economists believe in the likelihood of failure, the more traditional economic philosophies and the models that incorporate their theories will be "vindicated." As a result, the traditional use of macroeconomic models will be sustained and perhaps strengthened.

Of course, the corollary of this suggests that any unexpected successes of policies based on monetarist and supply-side theory will further jeopardize the use of the large, traditional macroeconomic models within federal agencies that now use them. But even the monetarist and supply-side economists within these agencies have always asserted that modeling as a tool is useful and needed. They might object to the forms and assumptions of many of the existing models, but they argue that macroeconomic modeling will remain useful and widely used as long as the models incorporate more monetarist and supply-side theory. In short, economists are supportive of modeling as long as the models used represent their philosophies. This attitude reflects a recognition of policymakers' demands for quantitative evidence to use as a basis of or a justification for economic policy decisions.

The second observation about the future of modeling has to do with the ecology of macroeconomic modeling as it has evolved over the past thirty years, and the managerial ideology of modeling as it has been applied to the tasks of economic policy analysis in the federal government. The large macroeconomic models are the products of a great deal of intellectual investigation and experience in building complex mathematical representations of the economy, and in creating the computerized means for producing forecasts and simulations based on them. The "modeling package" surrounding these large models is well developed, and this package has been adopted and incorporated into the routine analytical tasks of federal economic policymaking agencies. No such package exists for models based on supply-side or monetarist theories. The few models that do exist based on these theories simply have not received the same level of investment in their creation and refinement as have the larger, more established models. Even if it is theoretically possible to build powerful monetarist and supply-side models, many years of effort must be put into building them before they will reach the levels of sophistication and power found in the large models now available. This is critically important, given the fact that use of macroeconomic models takes place in the turbulent environment of national economic policymaking. The managerial ideology of modeling has grown up in a manner that naturally supported the larger, more refined models because they have reached a degree of development and utility that allows regular use for policy analysis. The routines of use are well established to meet nearly all the major demands made of the economic analysis centers in federal agencies, from long-run analyses of trends and impacts of policy options, to short-run assessments of economic conditions in the next one or two quarters. If modeling is used at all, the models used will almost certainly be those that are well developed both in theory and in the practical aspects of their use. The importance of the well established managerial ideology of modeling and the prevailing confidence among economists in the utility of the large macroeconomic models apparently is surviving the temporary disruption in their use.

CHAPTER EIGHT
CRITICAL FACTORS IN SUCCESSFUL MODELING

We began our study with the objective of clarifying our understanding of the factors that account for the wide-spread implementation and use of computerized planning models by federal agencies. As with many research projects, our work uncovered as many questions as we managed to answer.[1] We were, however, able to gain sufficient insight into the complex process of policy modeling to separate the critical variables from those that are less important. In this chapter, we summarize our conclusions about the relative importance of different variables in model implementation and model use uncovered by our research.

For discussion purposes we have organized our findings into the same four clusters of variables we identified in our conceptual frame-work (chapter 1) as being important to successful model implementation: the general environment of policy modeling; the organizations involved in policy modeling; the characteristics of modeling techniques; and the policies specifically adopted by modelers to facilitate model transfer.

Figure 8.1 shows the results of our attempt to distinguish between variables that are more or less important for successful model implementation. We have identified critical factors with the letter A. We have assigned the letter B to variables that, although important, are not as central to implementation. We have assigned a relative ranking of the same sort to the blocks of variables—to environmental preconditions, organizational attributes, and so forth. Since our case studies focused mainly on those we call "primary users" (i.e., those who are heavily involved in use of model-based analysis for policymaking support), our rankings of the variables reflect this focus. However, we believe that while some variables may not be critical for primary users, they may be important for secondary users (i.e., those who use modeling for general information or to "check up" on the analyses of primary users). We indicate in figure 8.1 which variables we think have special significance for secondary users.

Environmental Preconditions

Many features of the general environments in which models are developed, implemented, and used exert strong influence on the outcome of policy modeling. Our initial research indicated eight factors as potentially significant preconditions for the introduction and use of policy models in federal agencies. These preconditions are: (a) the state of development of substantive theory behind a model's structure; (b) the nature of funding support for development of policy models; (c) the status of computing resources needed to support policy modeling; (d) the availability of quality data resources required for policy modeling; (e) the predisposition to use analytic techniques in the policymaking process; (f) the competitiveness of organizations and institutions involved in policymaking and analysis; (g) the fluidity of movement of high-level professional policy analysts between the public and private sectors and among organizations that use policy models; and (h) the political saliency of the policy issues or questions being modeled.

Among this group, we found four to be especially important to implementation success: a well-developed substantive theory behind the model; adequate funding for model development and transfer; sufficiently developed computing technology; and availability of high-quality data. We believe that without any one of these factors serious and lasting modeling efforts cannot be mounted. The other variables—predisposition to technique, competitiveness among organizations, flexibility in personnel practices, and saliency of policy issues—are important from time to time, but do not carry the weight of the others.

Variable Group Weighting	Individual Variable Weighting		
A			Environmental Preconditions
	A		Substantive Theory
	A		Funding for Model Development and Transfer
	A		Status of Computing Technology
	A		Availability and Quality of Data
	B	S +	Predisposition to Technique
	B	S +	Competitiveness Among Organizations
	B		Flexibility in Personnel Practices
	B	S +	Saliency of Policy Issues
			Organizational Attributes
B			Features of the Modeler Organization
	A		Modeler's Reputation
	A		Modeler's Identification with a Model
	A		Modeler's Political Neutrality
	B	S +	Organizational Type
	B	S +	Division of Labor
A			Features of the User Organization
	A		Agency's Need for Analysis
	A		Fit of Model to Agency's Mission
	A		Internal Resources Available for Modeling
	A		User's Familiarity with the Technique
	A		Existence of Cooperative Arrangements for Model Implementation
A			Features of the Technology
	A		Nature of Model Error
	A		Characteristics of the Data
	A		Maintainability of the Model
	A		Accumulation of Knowledge
	B	S +	Cost of Model Acquisition and Use
	B	S +	Complexity of the Model
	B	S +	Intended Purpose of the Model: Product vs. Research
B			Transfer Policies
	A		Model Packaging
	B	S +	Marketing Styles and Strategies
	B	S +	Transfer Agent
	B	S +	Pricing
	B	S +	User Groups

A = High weighting; B = Lower weighting; S + = Possibly more important for secondary model users

Figure 8.1. RANKING OF VARIABLES IMPORTANT TO SUCCESSFUL MODEL IMPLEMENTATION

SUBSTANTIVE THEORY

All policy models rest on some body of substantive theory about the phenomenon being modeled. The state of development of this substantive theory is important for successful implementation of a model because it affects the willingness of analysts, advisers, and policymakers who adhere to that theoretical perspective to accept, acquire, or use a model built upon that theory.

Well-established economic theories, by definition, have been researched and refined by economists for long periods of time. Macroeconomic theories based on Keynesian concepts, for example, have been around for over six decades, and models based upon them are nearly as old. Adherents to this orthodoxy have dominated the U.S. economics community, and many have held high-level advisory positions to national policymakers. Many economic analysts in federal agencies have been trained in the Keynesian perspective, are familiar with the structural features of the major models based on Keynesian concepts, and accept these models as having an important role to play in the policy analysis process. These circumstances greatly facilitated the acceptance of macroeconomic models (such as the DRI model) in federal agencies over the past decade.

Models rooted in newer, still-evolving economic theories have faced greater resistance by federal users. This has been the case for monetarist macroeconomic models, which have been used by a limited number of agencies, and also for supply-side models, which entered the federal government on a limited basis only after 1980. It was also true for the TRIM and MATH microsimulation models, which have been incrementally implemented by a handful of federal agencies. What these models have in common is that they are all based upon theories in relatively early stages of development. Such models are not widely accepted among economists and analysts. These newer models entered into routine policy analysis processes only when supporters of the associated theoretical perspectives entered into key political, advisory, or managerial positions and were willing to commit their agencies' resources to bring those models in. For supply-side models, this abruptly occurred in 1981 when the Reagan administration brought in supply-side economists to high-level policymaking positions. For microsimulation models, it happened more gradually, as the original group of economists who helped to develop, adopt, and use the models moved into new organizational settings over the course of a decade.

FUNDING FOR MODEL DEVELOPMENT AND TRANSFER

All computerized planning models require substantial organizational support to move from the idea stage to the development stage, and on to implementation by user agencies. Three dimensions of support are especially important for successful implementation: level of funding, sources of funds, and flexible mechanisms of support.

The importance of adequate funding is well illustrated by both econometric and microsimulation models. For decades, the federal government has been a principal sponsor of the economic research upon which today's major econometric models are built. This research heritage provided a rich body of technical modeling experience later utilized by such entrepreneurial economists as Otto Eckstein, Lawrence Klein, and others who worked to build practical forecasting models. The early interest of agencies such as the Congressional Research Service, the Federal Reserve Board, the Bureau of the Budget, and the Department of the Treasury provided the background resources necessary to construct and refine these models, and a market for the information they produce.

Microsimulation modeling is newer and built on a smaller base of federal support. The seminal work of Guy Orcutt and his colleagues in the 1960s was supported by private funds. The federal government subsequently supported the first attempts to transform this research model into a practical technique, but inadequate funding levels inhibited model development and data collection. The Department of Health, Education, and Welfare (HEW) eventually recognized both the value and the problems of the model and underwrote a costly, long-term project to revise and maintain the TRIM model and make it a practical tool for in-house use. Other agencies funded incremental additions to TRIM and MATH, but they have resisted supporting model maintenance, have adopted a less patronlike attitude toward the model, and have actually used the models on a more sporadic basis.

The source of funding for model development and transfer also affects model implementation patterns. Private investment in designing models for actual planning applications has led in most cases to proprietary models, with model vendors controlling the conditions of users' access. Use of DRI's modeling services, built upon private venture capital, was regulated by DRI. Agencies could not actually purchase DRI's products and then take them in-house to use independently. DRI users had to subscribe to DRI's services, accessing them on a day-to-day basis only through DRI's time-sharing capabilities. This was not a problem, however, as many users of DRI's services appreciated their highly centralized nature. By using DRI's widely marketed services they kept abreast of what others had access to. As long as the modeling services were available at an affordable price and in a manner that facilitated easy use, the proprietary character of the model did not stand in the way of its implementation.

In contrast, access to the publicly funded microsimulation models like TRIM and MATH was open to anyone willing to pay the nominal costs of copying either model's code. Low cost facilitates physical transfer of the model, but MATH and TRIM were so large and complex that physical possession of a model's code was virtually useless without the help of consultants or agency staffers with hands-on experience in running the model.

Finally, the mechanisms used by federal agencies to acquire models also indirectly affect the model implementation process by helping to shape the structure of the modeling industry. During the late 1960s and early 1970s, when DRI first began to sell its modeling services and when the Urban Institute began to work on microsimulation models, federal agencies could issue sole-source, noncompetitive contracts to private firms. When an agency wanted a service and knew of a specific organization that could provide it, it could purchase the work without offering other organizations the opportunity to bid on the job. This gave the early, applied modeling efforts the implementation advantages of previous contracts and investment, practical experience, professional reputation, and contacts with federal agencies when, in the mid-1970s, the federal government changed its procurement policies to a predominantly competitive bidding system.

In summary, the size, complexity, and costly nature of development and deployment of large computerized planning models requires considerable, sustained financial support over a long period of time. This commitment can be costly, since it is not uncommon for the transfer and maintenance costs of a model to equal or exceed its development costs on an annual basis. Public support for the DRI, TRIM, and MATH models came primarily from a willingness of federal funding agencies to underwrite research on modeling techniques, and a willingness to freely procure modeling services for use in policy analysis once the models were ready for such uses. The proprietary versus public character of the models was less critical, given the manner in which these models were marketed and the support the federal government gave them as both patron and customer. It is difficult to estimate how implementation might have been different had research-funding levels been lower and marketing of modeling services been complicated by agencies' strict adherence to competitive bidding practices. However, we believe that any federal action that impairs the emergence and sustenance of highly qualified modeling groups would stifle development and refinement of sophisticated models for policy analysis and planning.

STATUS OF COMPUTER TECHNOLOGY

Large-scale models such as the TRIM, MATH, and DRI models are predicated on the availability of computing technology. There is nothing in the theoretical structures of these models that requires computing capability, but as a practical matter their use for policy analysis would be impossible without it. Five aspects of modern computing capability play key roles in the implementation of these models: computer processing power; high-speed secondary memory capability; sophisticated systems and applications software; input, output, and data communications capability; and effective policies for delivery and support of computing resources.

The advent of powerful second-generation computer processors in the mid-1960s was a major computing breakthrough affecting the development of large-scale models. These processors enabled for the first time the construction of very large modeling systems for practical use. Prior to this development, the sheer size of large models and the attendant time-consuming information-processing demands they created made model use cumbersome and slow. The more powerful processors made it possible to run very large programs in a much shorter time, thus facilitating the process of model construction and testing. The advent of third-generation interactive, time-shared computer processors further advanced model processing capability. The third-generation machines provided increased power at lower costs and allowed simultaneous use of processing resources by multiple users. By 1981, large third-generation computers formed the technical backbone of such models as TRIM, MATH, and DRI.

The development of high-speed, random-access secondary memory also was essential in enabling large-scale policy modeling. All such models require large amounts of data, which are much too large (and therefore too expensive) to store in the computer's main memory. It is essential to have the data stored in second memory in a manner that allows very rapid recall into main memory as needed. This capability is supplied by conventional high-speed disk technology. In 1981, DRI's modeling system had disk storage capacity exceeding seventy billion characters of data—the equivalent of more than fourteen million pages like this one.

Sophisticated systems software and applications software are also important in modeling. Systems software includes the operating system that allocates computing resources among all the users and manages machine operation (e.g., moving data back and forth between main and secondary memory) and provides users with such utilities (e.g., editors, compilers, and data management systems). Efficient operating systems are essential in providing computing power in a cost-effective manner, while the utilities enable users to accomplish their tasks. Applications software includes the programs that actually do the tasks users want done. The models themselves are applications programs containing all the equations for the model and the instructions to the computer regarding which data to use, what to do with the data, and how to organize useful output. Applications programs for modeling can be very large: DRI's Econometric Programming System contained more than 200,000 lines of instructions, while TRIM and MATH each had over 75,000 lines of instructions.

Input and output technologies, including terminals, printers, and tape devices, are essential in allowing users to give the computer instructions and data, and to return information in usable form. Data communications technology is necessary to allow users located away from the computer to communicate with the computer. While all three models we studied depended on these kinds of technology, the DRI system made especially heavy use of data communications technology because remote users had to access the central DRI system located in Lexington, Massachusetts.

Finally, successful use of computer-dependent models requires effective management of the computer resources that support the models. Effective management of computing is difficult, especially given large systems with many users, large data bases, and complex programs. Each component of the systems—the hardware, the software, and the data—must be maintained. Maintenance includes making repairs, upgrading the system to keep pace with technology or expanded needs, and extending system response to user demands for new capabilities. As a general rule, an amount equaling between 30 and 150 percent of a system's initial cost must be spent each year just to keep it running. For all the models we studied, maintenance of the modeling software has been critical to the success of the systems. In the DRI case, maintenance and upgrades were incorporated as a routine part of the operation; in the TRIM/MATH case, it took a financial commitment from HEW and a technical commitment from Mathematica Policy Research and the Hendrickson Corporation to provide this support.

AVAILABILITY AND QUALITY OF DATA

Useful computerized policy models require numerous large, detailed data files describing the system being simulated. The lack of appropriate data prevents a model from leaving the experimental stage.

Time-series data on major macroeconomic variables have been available to researchers for decades. The National Income and Product Accounts files have been collected and disseminated by the federal government since the 1930s, and they greatly facilitated the early development of applied econometric models. At present, public agencies collect thousands of regional, sectoral, and time-series data sets with usefulness for econometric modeling; a large percentage of these have been put on-line by DRI for use by its subscribers. This centralization of abundant data bases at a single, highly accessible location, and linked to an extensive modeling capability, increases the attractiveness of DRI's modeling services for users. (It also has resulted in the odd situation in which many data that originate in the public domain are available from a proprietary source.)[2]

In contrast, the historical lack of disaggregated census data inhibited the practical application of experimental microsimulation models for years. It was only after the Census Bureau agreed to release its raw data tapes to outside users in the late 1960s that analysts had the opportunity to run research models with real data sets. Even so, because the collection of detailed information about individuals' attributes, attitudes, and behavior is so costly and plagued with reporting problems, relatively few large-scale, nationwide household data files exist even at present, and each is at least partially out-of-date by the time of its release. This has generally dampened the implementation of microsimulation models.

Other data problems complicate the task of applying microsimulation to policy analysis. Microsimulation models can require as many as 30 million data elements for a given run. The Personal Income Tax Model of the Treasury Department uses 100 variables collected in a sample of about 100,000 tax filing units, for a total of about 10 million data items. The TRIM and MATH models use data on as many as 300 variables for sample populations of 100,000 or more, resulting in data bases of more than 30 million elements. Additionally, the data required for microsimulations often must be taken from different data bases that are not interconnected. Merging such data bases can be very difficult, and although there is considerable ongoing research to improve the means of linking data bases for microsimulation analysis, the task remains a major challenge.[3]

A final problem that, again, tends to plague microsimulation more than macroeconomic modeling stems from the fact that longitudinal, detailed data bases containing personal information on individuals can be sensitive from a privacy standpoint. Such data are automatically collected in the administration of many government programs, and, as long as they are used only on aggregate programmatic analyses, the privacy issue does not become so serious. However, when more elaborate analyses requiring the merging of sensitive data bases are attempted, the privacy issue emerges because the data may be used by agencies not directly involved in the purposes for which the data were originally collected. This problem, encountered by Treasury analysts using the Personal Income Tax Model when they needed Social Security data to study the effects of taxing Social Security income, can serve to inhibit policy applications of microsimulation.

Organizational Attributes

Our research also suggested that a number of features of organizations affect the successful transfer of computerized planning models by federal agencies (figure 8.1). Organizational variables are those structural and behavioral attributes of modeler and user organizations which influence whether any particular model will be implemented successfully by a user agency.

We identified ten organizational variables as potentially important to successful model implementation. The five variables associated with modeler organizations are the type of modeler organization, its internal division of labor, identification with the model, the reputation of the modelers, and the modeler's political neutrality. The five variables associated with the user agency are the agency's need for analysis, the fit of the model to the agency's mission, the internal resources available for modeling, the users' familiarity with the technique, and the users' cooperation with other agencies to obtain the model.

The organizational attributes of modeler organizations proved to be important to model implementation in some cases, but as a group they do not rise to the point of being critical to model implementation. Our case studies focused on primary users, where the attributes of the *user* organizations were more critical than the attributes of modeler organizations. Among the individual features of modeler organizations, a good reputation, identification with a particular model, and maintenance of political neutrality are more important than the others. The presence of a strong division of labor in the modeler organization is associated with modeling success, but we could not tell whether it contributes to modeling success (i.e., by allowing individuals to focus their attention on specific issues), or is a consequence of modeling success (i.e., growth resulting from success naturally leads to organizational differentiation). Organizational type seems to be important in some instances (e.g., the motivations for profit-oriented modelers affect their marketing strategies and are different from the motivations of the non-profit and government modeling groups), but the experiences of the new challengers to traditional macroeconomic modeling suggest that organizational type is less critical to long-run success than other variables such as modeler reputation.

The organizational attributes of user organizations proved to be very important to modeling success in the organizations we studied. Two items in particular stand out: the agency's need for analysis, and the fit of the model to the agency's needs. At one level, these observations seem trivial; after all, one would expect that the most successful instances of modeling would happen where models are needed and good models are available. But we believe that this simple observation carries critical weight because it is so often overlooked in the effort to analyze why models succeed or fail. Models often fail in implementation either because the user does not really need the model, or because the model does not fit the user's real needs. These two variables do interact with one another. Users that must have modeling capability are sometimes willing to "force fit" a model if it is the only one available. But the user generally will not change to fit the model. In all of our cases, the political, policy, and organizational contexts of the users dominated how they adopted and used their models.

The critical influence of need and fit tends to overshadow the other variables in this group, but other variables also proved important to modeling success. Successful modeling requires that user agencies have sufficient funds available for modeling, that they be sufficiently familiar with modeling techniques to make sensible use of models, and that they take advantage of cooperative arrangements for model implementation in the event that they cannot build extensive (and usually expensive) modeling expertise in-house.

AGENCY'S NEED FOR ANALYSIS

Federal agencies vary in their perception of the need for conducting policy analysis. Some have analysis as their central purpose (e.g., the Congressional Budget Office). Others engage in analysis in order to achieve other organizational objectives, such as providing advice (the Council of Economic Advisers), preparing programmatic budgets (the Food and Nutrition Service), forecasting economic conditions (the Federal Reserve Board), or analyzing impacts of program reforms (Department of Labor). Others do little policy analysis at all. In our study, the agencies that implemented and used computerized planning models most regularly and routinely were ones in which analysis was a central organizational purpose, or was essential to accomplishing organizational objectives.

Most of the agencies centrally involved in national economic planning maintain research and analysis units with teams of sophisticated analysts. These agencies include the Federal Reserve Board, CBO, and the Troika agencies (Office of Management and Budget, CEA, and Treasury Department). Models play a vital role in these agencies by providing information to policymakers either directly, in the form of model results, or indirectly, as input to the forecasts of judgmental economists within the agency. The economists in these agencies are knowledgeable, highly skilled, and reputed to be among the best in the federal government.

In the income-support policy area in the United States, two agencies play a central role in providing policy analysis. These two—HEW and CBO—have taken the lead in fostering support for acquiring models and in actually utilizing them for policy design and evaluation. Starting in the late 1960s, HEW's Office of the Assistant Secretary for Planning and Evaluation (ASPE) established itself as a center of high-quality policy analysis. HEW was an initial sponsor of development and maintenance of applied microsimulation models and has used them extensively since the early 1970s. HEW's analytic staff is first-rate, backed up by a "soup-to-nuts shop" of computer technicians and information and computing resources. The CBO has similarly established itself as a center of sophisticated and thorough policy analysis. CBO's Human Resources and Community Services Division began a lengthy process of implementing the MATH model soon after CBO was created in 1974, and in the intervening years has developed a small but skilled staff of model users.

Most other federal agencies lack the central organizational mandate to conduct policy analysis on these issues, but many prepare them routinely on specific programs, and sporadically when issues under their jurisdiction become critical problems. These agencies use computerized planning models with less regularity, less sophistication, and less resource support than agencies with central analytic missions. Among users of macroeconomic models, economists in GAO and the House and Senate Budget committees have access to the DRI model, but they use models infrequently and have experienced resistance to expanded reliance on them by other members of their organizations.

The situation is similar among the secondary set of users of the TRIM or MATH models. Many bureaus have been involved with these models over the past decade, but none has been completely successful in either transferring the models in-house or utilizing their results in policy analyses. The USDA's Food and Nutrition Service supported design of a food stamp module for MATH and then contracted with MPR to run the model extensively during debates about food stamp reforms over a two-year period. In another instance, the Department of Labor used MATH on an out-of-house basis for a short while during the late seventies, but only after internal staff resistance to microsimulation modeling was overcome by the introduction of new policymakers and analysts supportive of its use. In each of these cases, the analytic unit did not enjoy strong institutional support or a reputation for sophisticated policy analysis, and each one implemented the models with limited success.

FIT OF MODEL TO USER AGENCY MISSION

The technical appropriateness of a given model to the planning process of a federal agency depends upon the fit of the system being simulated in the model and the substantive mission of the agency. The first agencies to implement particular models are ones where there is a good fit. Subsequent adopters of the model tend to be ones where the fit is poorer but where there are interlocking programmatic ties or turf battles with the lead agencies in that policy area.

In our study, federal agencies tended to implement models in this sequence. Among the large number of agencies that currently use macroeconomic models of the U.S. economy, only a handful play a central role in analyzing fiscal or monetary policy. These agencies—CBO, the Fed, and the Troika—were among the earliest to adopt and use the major macroeconomic models. Many other agencies now also use these models, but they implemented the models later and they tend to primarily use them to keep abreast of the information available to the central fiscal and monetary policy agencies.

This implementation pattern roughly parallels that of the microsimulation models. The first federal user of a computerized microsimulation model was the ASPE office at HEW. HEW, of course, had primary, cabinet-level jurisdiction over income-maintenance programs, which both the TRIM and MATH models had been designed to simulate. Another early adopter of microsimulation models was the Treasury Department, whose Office of Tax Analysis is charged with analyzing the federal income tax system, also simulated in these models. After 1974, other agencies obtained TRIM or MATH. For the most part, these were organizations with authority over supplemental income-transfer or jobs assistance programs. These agencies contracted for revisions to TRIM or MATH to incorporate the interrelationships among the primary tax and welfare programs and other supplemental income-related programs. The only exception to this pattern of sequential adoption of microsimulation models is the relative lateness of CBO's implementation of MATH, beginning in 1975. CBO's mandate to analyze the budget proposals of all federal programs makes it the primary congressional unit engaged in analyzing federal income-transfer programs. This relatively late adoption is more a function of CBO's relatively late genesis (in 1974) than a noncentral role in analyzing income-transfer programs.

INTERNAL RESOURCES AVAILABLE FOR MODELING

Successful model implementation requires that agencies provide sufficient budgetary resources to procure a model, data, computing equipment, computer-operating time, and technically proficient personnel (either by training current employees or by hiring already skilled analysts, modelers, or operators). Commitment of extensive, internal modeling resources better enables an agency to implement the model efficiently and to conduct independent, competent, and timely analyses. Agencies unable to provide adequate organizational resources for modeling implement the models less successfully. Such agencies often have to rely on outside consultants to revise the models, to operate them, to perform analyses, and sometimes even to interpret model results. Modeling in these settings tends to be sporadic, inefficient, time consuming, and outside the direct control of the agency—all of which reduces the usefulness of modeling to these agencies.

Several of the agencies we studied provided relatively high levels of internal support for modeling. These agencies were the Federal Reserve Board and the Troika agencies (for macroeconomic models), HEW (for microsimulation models), and CBO (for both types of models). Each of these agencies actively uses models, maintains or contracts out for extensive computing resources, and employs highly skilled personnel who understand the technical features of the models they use.

Other agencies provide little or no internal resources for policy modeling. GAO, for example, subscribes to several macroeconomic models, although it runs them infrequently. GAO's economists are relatively inexperienced in using models, and the bulk of their contact with forecasting comes through reading periodic forecast results and reports issued by model vendors. When DOL ran MATH, it did so out-of-house because the agency needed model results quickly, it lacked appropriate computing facilities and personnel at the time, and it could obtain information most rapidly by contracting to outside consultants. This approach turned out to be an expensive way to conduct modeling, and DOL eventually hired its consultants to work as special aides within the agency. Similarly, the FNS contracted to MPR to revise and run MATH and to analyze its results, since FNS analysts were inexpert in modeling, and FNS could not commit a regular line position to hire someone who was an expert. In each of these cases, modeling failed to become institutionalized in the agencies.

USER FAMILIARITY WITH TECHNIQUE

Educated or experienced analysts know what models do, how they operate, what information they provide, and how they can fit into the policy analysis process. Among agencies without models, those with analysts or managers who are relatively knowledgeable and supportive of modeling tend to identify a place for modeling within their agency, to seek support for model acquisition, to undertake a search for a specific model to adopt, and to attempt to implement the model smoothly so that they can actually use it. Once the agency sets itself on a particular modeling path, the commitment to modeling and to any particular model tends to be reinforced by adopting employment policies aimed at building or maintaining the staff's experience with that model. Of course this only happens where the modeling efforts directly coincide with the analytical requirements of the agency.

We found that among users of macroeconomic models, the earliest major adopters were the Troika agencies, which have traditionally drawn their professional staffs from the nation's top graduate economics programs. These economists come to their jobs with a general understanding of macroeconomic models, and after a period of time on the job, they are able to identify ways in which forecasting and policy simulation can assist them in their work. These young managers and analysts tend to believe in the usefulness of quantitative methods for policy analysis, and these attitudes have stimulated a demand for bringing modeling capabilities in-house. Once modeling became a standard part of the analysis process, these agencies began to hire former employees of modeling firms to serve as staff economists, thereby strengthening agency experience with particular models and reinforcing agency commitment to them.

The implementation process worked somewhat differently for agencies that use microsimulation models, although we found that here too staffers' familiarity with modeling influenced successful model transfer. It is only relatively recently that the microsimulation technique has been applied to the welfare policy area. Few universities have offered graduate training in microsimulation modeling. Most economists and analysts skilled in microsimulation gained their knowledge from having participated in the actual development of the technique for practical policy work, or from having observed the involvement of these models in recent policy debates. The earliest users were analysts in HEW and Treasury who had worked with the RIM model at the President's Commission on Income Maintenance Programs. Over time, these analysts changed jobs and moved into new organizational settings, where they were receptive to initiatives by modelers to support adaptation of MATH to enable it to simulate new policy areas where the analysts now worked.

EXISTENCE OF COOPERATIVE MODELING
ARRANGEMENTS AMONG USERS

Many federal agencies acquire and utilize computerized planning models in cooperation with other agencies with similar institutional objectives or modeling needs. Cooperation can involve sharing the costs of developing and maintaining models and data bases, centralizing common computing facilities and personnel, and exchanging information about model results or modeling difficulties. Few agencies have such extensive modeling needs as to justify exclusive development of and support for a wide range of large, complicated data bases, sophisticated models, and computing capabilities. But many can benefit from having access to the full array of services, even if they use them on a sporadic or part-time basis. Many agencies have pooled their funds for modeling and coordinated their use of modeling services. Congressional users have been particularly successful in using common modeling contracts. All users on Capitol Hill have a blanket contract with DRI for access to DRI services. Congressional users of MATH also share a common contract. In another kind of cooperation, the three agencies of the Troika coordinate their use of the major econometric models in order to take advantage of the benefits of specialization and to keep costs down.

These cooperative arrangements have some disadvantages, however. At times they have imposed hidden political or managerial costs during the model-use phase, as agencies with common facilities but different interests have competed for control over model use or disposition of model results. Conflicts occurred, for example, between GAO and CBO when GAO was evaluating the MATH model, which CBO wanted to use.

Features of the Technology

Computerized planning models are complicated technologies that place heavy technical demands on organizations interested in acquiring and using them effectively. Models vary immensely, of course, and some of these differences affect how successfully they will be implemented by federal agencies. Our initial research pointed to five attributes of the modeling technology as possibly important for the implementation process: characteristics of the data, nature of model error, cost of model use, complexity of the modeling system, and intended purpose of the model (i.e., product versus research). We found that the underlying technical aspects of modeling are crucial to model success and added two more variables to this group: maintainability of the model and accumulation of knowledge.

We note above that the presence of strong substantive theory and adequate computational resources are key preconditions for success. In addition, modelers and users alike must thoroughly understand the technical potentials and limitations of modeling as a technology.

Computerized planning models are complicated technologies that place heavy technical demands on organizations interested in acquiring and using them effectively. Models vary immensely, of course, and some of these differences affect how successfully they will be implemented by federal agencies. Our initial research pointed to five attributes of the modeling technology as possibly important for the implementation process: intended purpose of the model (i.e., product versus research), characteristics of the data, cost of model use, the nature of model error, and complexity of the modeling system. We found that the underlying technical aspects of modeling are crucial to model success. We note above that the presence of strong substantive theory and adequate computational resources are key preconditions for success. In addition, modelers and users alike must thoroughly understand the technical potentials and limitations of modeling as a technology. In particular, users must understand the nature of the errors their models may generate and the characteristics of the data their models need to use, before models can make a legitimate and lasting contribution to the technical process of policymaking—the task of improving the quality of policy decisions through use of analysis. We were somewhat surprised to discover that the most solid and committed developers and users of models in our case studies were also those who were most aware of model limitations.

Another aspect of modeling that is important to success, at least in those agencies where model use is institutionalized, is the recognition that modeling is a highly dynamic business. Models are constantly evolving. In some ways it appears that the quality of a model's evolution is more important to long-lasting use than the quality of the model when it was first used. The two variables that come into play here are model maintenance costs and accumulation of knowledge. All the models we investigated required large investments in maintenance to keep them current and useful, and all the modeler and user organizations we studied had learned to institute policies that nurture the accumulation and retention of knowledge about modeling.

Model acquisition cost and model complexity turned out to be less critical than we had expected. Rather than devalue these variables, however, we believe their relatively low influence in the cases we studied was a result of the kinds of modeling situations we chose. All the user organizations we studied have well-developed needs for modeling, and are organizationally committed to bearing the cost of model use. These agencies deal with policies and programs involving millions or even billions of dollars, against which the costs of model acquisition and use pale. Moreover, the programs and policies being evaluated are themselves highly complex, so any effort to use analytical tools in improving policymaking is bound to be a complex undertaking. The complexity of models is an important factor that determines in part the level of investment required of a user agency, but if cost is little object, the investment is readily made. Issues of cost and complexity are likely to be much more serious impediments among secondary users who either do not need modeling as much or who cannot afford to spend as much on modeling as primary users.

Finally, the intended purpose of the model (product vs. research) proved to be an important factor in modeling success. Surprisingly, there are significant success stories in both categories. Successful models toward the "product" end of the spectrum include the DRI and MATH models; successful models toward the "research" end of the spectrum include the TRIM and PITM models. Once again, we believe the distinction between primary and secondary users is useful to explain the importance of the product/research distinction. Among primary users the selection among product and research models is primarily one of availability and convenience. If a product model is both available and convenient, the primary users will adopt it. But if there are no product models available, a primary user is likely to adopt or even build a research model to meet the need. We found that primary users were using a mix of product and research models, although there was a preference for the product models where they were available. Secondary users would probably be much more likely to adopt product models than research models. They would be more likely to be aware of the product models, they would probably find it easier to get information on the product models, and the packaging of the product would make adoption much easier.

Of the seven foregoing variables, three appear crucial to model success: characteristics of the data, nature of model error, and accumulation and maintenance of knowledge. Each is elaborated next.

CHARACTERISTICS OF THE DATA

All computerized planning models run on large data bases, which vary not only in their technical quality (e.g., representativeness of the sample or reliability of the responses) but also in terms of potential users' perceptions of the quality of the data (e.g., appropriateness of the measures used or the relative quality of the data compared with other data bases). Analysts adopt computerized planning models for forecasting or for policy simulations with the expectation that the models will provide valid information about the population or phenomenon they are analyzing. Given the significant potential problems associated with erroneous model assumptions or invalid parameter estimates, it is essential to start with data of sufficiently high quality to minimize data-related errors. Models that come with good data have an implementation advantage among users because analysts expect such models to yield fewer errors in analysis situations.

Among the agencies we studied, users' attitudes toward data quality varied by model type. Among macroeconomic modelers, DRI has historically provided an enormous inventory of data sets for its clients. This extraordinary set of eight to ten million time series, originally collected by numerous public and private groups, describes economic conditions in various countries, regions, and industries. DRI has consolidated and reformatted these data, cleaned and verified them, put them on-line, and organized them for easy, efficient use by its subscribers. Many federal users of DRI services report that the primary reason they subscribe to the DRI model is to obtain access to its abundant, centralized data resources.[4] DRI's unique data bases have given its subscription services an implementation edge over DRI's major competitors, Chase and Wharton, which provide their customers with data bases that are less comprehensive and less easy to utilize.

Both the actual and the perceived quality of microdata are generally high. Microdata are conceptually clearer and simpler than national income data, and more easily understood because they refer to individual characteristics that can be easily observed. Nevertheless, users admit that microdata sets impose considerable problems on users. First, microsimulation data sets are very large and unwieldy. Second, in many cases survey data are already out-of-date when they become available, and tricky and often difficult techniques for "aging" an old data base have to be applied to overcome this deficiency. Third, it is often necessary to merge two or more different microdata files to get a microdata file that is useful for the intended analysis, which is, again, a tricky and often difficult task that requires both ingenuity and considerable computing resources. A final problem is the limited and sometimes restricted availability of microdata. Privacy considerations often require that data files on households or individuals be stripped of individual identifiers, which again imposes severe problems for the creation of merged files.

NATURE OF MODEL ERROR

Since computerized simulation models are simplified, mathematical representations of complex systems, they all stand the chance of producing results that conflict with reality. Sources of possible error include leaving out important variables, improperly estimating the relationships among variables, and collecting an unrepresentative data sample. Models vary in the size and composition of their error terms. In the context of model use, they also differ in terms of users' perceptions about the significance of those errors. Models with a reputation for unknown but presumably low rates of predictive error realize greater implementation success than models perceived to have high error rates. Agencies still use models even though they are known or presumed to have prediction problems, but they tend to reduce their dependency on any given model by looking at other sources of information as well.

All of the models in our case studies have experienced prediction problems at one time or another. None of the major macroeconomic models anticipated the drastic 1973 oil price increases, and confidence in their predictive power suffered as a result of this important failing. Many agencies had implemented or begun to implement the DRI model which, previous to the oil embargo, had enjoyed a relatively good forecasting record. However, after 1973 the problems of all forecasts led many agencies to perceive the practical and political importance of diversifying the information provided to them. Generally, the agencies expanded their acquisitions of both model forecasts and of judgmental forecasts as well. The destabilizing influence of the oil price shocks resulted in most modelers, including DRI, running their model-generated forecasts through an internal team of senior economists before sending them out to the clients.

These activities underline the craftsmanship of econometrics, even though they have also been intended to build confidence among users that the error terms of these models have been reduced to a minimum by the combined talents of computer programmers and the best economic minds. Indeed, although the data on this matter are inconclusive, the actual predictive track records of the major Keynesian models seem to be slightly better on some measures than those of the major judgmental forecasters (McNees 1979a, b, 1982). Most prominent economists, and especially those with strong Keynesian roots, feel it is important to listen to what the major Keynesian models have to say (Samuelson 1975, 1980).

Microsimulation models are notorious for producing estimates that differ from reality, although it is difficult to determine the exact degree of error or why the error occurs. For one thing, unlike their macroeconomic brethren, they do not have a highly developed history of being regularly scrutinized over a long period of time. Microsimulation models are of more recent vintage and have been run less frequently. They have been used to estimate the costs, caseloads, and distributional effects of income-transfer programs, either as part of the routine budget preparation process or, more commonly, as part of the periodic program reform efforts. Yet because of this focus on routine policy analysis, microsimulation modeling has not built up a detailed, longitudinal forecasting record that could be carefully analyzed.

Neither macroeconometric nor microsimulation techniques allow analysts to predict the future with any certainty. Models occasionally produce forecasts or simulations that turn out to have been accurate, but more often the results are in error in important ways. This leads some to question the utility of such modeling, especially given the difficulties involved in its use. If the models do not provide accurate information, why are they used so extensively? The answer lies in the problematic nature of analysis and forecasting. There have never been any good methods for predicting the future, but expectations as well as intentions by definition are essential to planning. Forecasting has always been an essential part of policymaking; and even though judgmental forecasts often have been in error, there never has been an effort to do away with judgmental forecasting in planning. Modeling techniques offer refinements to the process of forecasting that most users and policymakers believe are worthwhile. They provide a reviewable framework of analytic discipline to the task of building profiles of future possibilities out of data from the past and present, and in some cases they appear to actually yield improved means of analyzing information to discern the very complex factors suspected to affect the course of the national economy or the incidence of large federal programs. Models do not as yet (and might never) provide the "solution" to problems of forecasting for policy planning, but most analysts that use them feel that they are the best techniques available and have firmly established them as important tools in the process of policy analysis.

MAINTAINABILITY OF THE MODEL

The high cost of system maintenance, a fact of life that has been accepted for large-scale software systems, does not yet seem to be fully recognized for large-scale computerized models. This seems odd, since these models are, in a sense, large and complex software systems. TRIM and MATH each have about 75,000 lines of service code. DRI's macroeconomic model has about 2,000 lines of code, but its operation depends on the EPS system, consisting of over 200,000 lines of code.

These models also undergo frequent change because of changes in underlying hardware and changes in the requirements of the users. Large models require considerably more user-related change than most software because of several peculiarities of modeling. The most prominent is the constant change in the models' underlying data bases. There is continual need to adapt the data base to the next available source of data. Also, many details in the models' structures need to be changed often because of changes in the environmental conditions on which policy judgments are based (e.g., new tax legislation). Finally, the questions addressed by model-based policy analysis exist in a highly political context that often shifts in its prevailing concerns and ideologies. These changes must be accommodated through steady adjustments to the models to keep them relevant to the tasks to which they are applied. All developers and users must find some way to maintain their models, or even a relatively good model will become nearly useless within a short time. All the models studied here met the challenge of maintenance through one means or another.

The TRIM modelers at the Urban Institute received extensive maintenance support from HEW over a six-year period; maintenance efforts cost approximately the same amount per year as was spent on TRIM's initial development. Despite this substantial support, the institute found it hard to maintain the model and had to use funds from other institute contracts to maintain TRIM. The MATH developers faced similar problems but found different solutions. MATH developers thoroughly redeveloped the model around improved technical standards that decreased the model's technical maintenance demands. Second, they offered the MATH model on a subscription basis in an attempt to obtain adequate revenues for maintenance tasks that included a quarterly release of the latest MATH version, complete with updated documentation.

The maintenance activity surrounding the DRI model is extremely high. The model is updated every month, with an update consisting of as many as 150 minor and sometimes major adjustments to the model's structures and equations. This updating is done by a small group of econometricians and software people in consultation with up to fifteen senior DRI economists. DRI has always been able to afford these high maintenance costs because of two mechanisms. One is its package of service offerings which has made it possible to occasionally subsidize maintenance costs by profits from the other services, such as the time-sharing systems. Second, DRI marketed subscriptions to its model. The clientele for these subscriptions is large, which has made it possible for DRI to charge relatively low subscription rates even though the costs of maintaining the model are very high.

ACCUMULATION AND MAINTENANCE OF KNOWLEDGE

Modeling is a sophisticated technology, demanding for both modelers and users. It took new users of TRIM and MATH two full years to learn and understand either of these models. In the field of econometrics, Brian Crissey has reported that it took him about half a year to gain a detailed understanding of the structure of a big econometric model, exclusive of its behavior in operation (Crissey 1977). Accumulation and maintenance of modeling knowledge is critical to modeling success, and this knowledge primarily resides in knowledgeable people.

However, accumulated knowledge is not just in the brains of experienced people. It is also embedded in the models themselves. During the continual process of model evolution and refinement, faulty specifications and other problems are replaced by improvements, and often these improvements are themselves replaced with improvements at a later date. New features are added to meet user requirements, and periodic evaluations of former performance often cause changes to be made in models. In econometrics, such refinement procedures have become something of a professional standard, and all the micromodels we studied have experienced similar pressures. The models themselves thereby become embodiments of knowledge, and the whole package of models, people, and service infrastructure represents a very substantial accumulation of knowledge.

Both users and developers of successful models have to keep their knowledge edge over their competitors. The most obvious way of doing this is to maintain policies that promote continuity in personnel, since most of the knowledge is in the heads of the people involved with models. But this policy is risky if it is pursued at the expense of other approaches. An organization can become too dependent on a few knowledgeable people. In the case of the Urban Institute, Jodie Allen and Harold Beebout left to start a new enterprise based on the institute's publicly available TRIM model. Their extensive experience plus their knowledge of the model enabled them to start a new microsimulation policy analysis venture that successfully competed with the institution.

Transfer Policies

Not all computerized planning models succeed in being used outside the organizations where they were created. Some miss because their designers never intended them for outside use or never publicized them in such a way as to inform outsiders of their model's utility. Others fail despite the modelers' hope to make them useful for policy analysis because the models do not incorporate design features that make them truly transferable. Still others fail because conditions in the implementation environment change, and a model that once seemed a worthwhile investment never actually get incorporated because of withdrawal of the resources needed to use it effectively.

Many models succeed, however, and federal agencies have implemented a wide variety of econometric and microsimulation models over the past decade. We discovered in our case studies that successful model implementation can be facilitated by a set of decisions and practices, made by modelers and users alike, that are intended to aid the transfer and use of the models. We call these decisions and practices "transfer policies."

From our case study research, we were able to identify six variables that seemed important to the success or failure of model implementation: marketing styles and strategies, model packaging, transfer agent, pricing strategies, user groups, and ongoing management of the transfer process.

Overall, however, these variables proved to be less critical than we expected when we began this work. Only one variable, model packaging, proved to be of critical importance in all the cases we studied. Users do not want models; they want modeling capability, which comes only in a package containing the models themselves and everything else required for model use. Also, a sophisticated modeling package allows users to choose their relative level of model use. The less comprehensive the modeling package supplied by the modeler, the greater the user investment required to make the minimum modeling package viable. DRI is clearly a leader in the packaging of its services, but MPR's success also is due in major part to its efforts to package its products.

Other transfer policy variables are important to modeling success, although not as important as packaging. The marketing styles and strategies used by DRI and MPR were important in spreading their models around, but their competitors are still in business and their models are still being used. The presence of a transfer agent is important, but we found that the role of assisting in the adoption and implementation of a model varies from time to time and place to place. Pricing tended to be of little consequence in the agencies we studied, although it occasionally was a factor in retaining one or another model against competitors. The existence of user groups was of some importance, but mainly for the convenience and enhancement of modeling activities. The participants in the user groups had been using models before the groups were created, and could probably continue to use models if the groups disappeared.

Here too we believe the distinction between primary and secondary users affects the interpretation of our observations. Model packaging is important to both primary and secondary users, but it is especially important to secondary users. Without a package of services available from the modeler organization, any secondary users would find it impossible to adopt and use models. The same is true for the other variables here. While primary users are not greatly affected by marketing styles and strategies, such styles and strategies could make an important difference in a secondary user's awareness of a model's existence and its utility. Similarly, the presence of an agent to assist in the transfer could be important to a less knowledgeable secondary user. Secondary users, because they are not as dependent on modeling, are likely to be more price sensitive. And such users are also more likely to need the support of user groups in acquiring the necessary skills to deal with modeling on more than a modest scale.

MODEL PACKAGING

Modelers make a decision about whether to conduct research, to produce a product, to perform a service, or to do some combination of all three. One outcome of such a decision—to produce a model that is an experimental technique, a practical tool, or a mixed breed—is related to implementation success. Product models are implemented more successfully by federal agencies than research models.

DRI and MPR have both adopted model-packaging policies. DRI's early decision to combine a diverse array of modeling and data capabilities into an organized package was truly innovative. Historically, this is what distinguished DRI from other modeling endeavors. From DRI's inception, its founders foresaw a potential market for a ready-to-use, commercial forecasting product accompanied by a comprehensive set of supporting services. This package would be both standardized and personalized at the same time, offering a combination of DRI-generated economic forecasts, user-controlled forecasting and simulation capabilities, extensive centralized data resources, and personalized economic consultation. The package would be designed for ease and efficiency of use. Users might need only a portion of the package's components, but if the price of the entire package were low relative to the price consultants charged for performing separate customized services for individual clients, users might be willing to purchase the whole package. Apparently, DRI analyzed the market well. Federal users were indeed willing to purchase a comprehensive package of goods and services from DRI. Most federal agency users reported that acquiring the full set of products and services was worthwhile, even if they used them irregularly.

Although not as extensive nor as widely implemented as DRI's package, MPR's subscription service for MATH is somewhat analogous. It is a standardized package of products and services available to clients for a fixed rate. All MATH subscribers receive the newest version of the full model, data bases, technical descriptions, user manual, regular model updates, and a fixed number of hours of consultation. Users may also contract with MPR for special model design work at an additional charge. But subscribers generally benefit from the products of these model development contracts when the new routines become part of the standard, updated version of MATH. MPR undertook the subscription service with two objectives in mind. It would assist in model implementation by supporting agencies' adoption or retention of the MATH model. It would also assist in achieving MPR's commercial goals of surviving organizationally and economically between model development contracts, and charging users for part of the costs of maintaining the models. So far, its model-packaging policy has helped to achieve those objectives.

Summary

Our analyses reveal three groups of variables to be of dominant importance in modeling success: environmental preconditions, organizational attributes of user organizations, and features of the technology. Together they tell us that modeling success is most likely when the necessary conditions (theoretical and technical) for usable modeling have been met, where the necessary ongoing resources (data and user knowledge) for model use are available, where there is a strong need among users for the model, and where there is a model that fits those needs. This comes as no great surprise; after all, even without our study, we could have predicted that modeling only happens when it is possible and when someone wants it badly enough to pay the cost of doing it. The value of the findings comes from the insight they provide into the dynamics of the variables and how they interact. Among the model users we studied, we found that need for modeling outweighed most other factors. In these agencies, if modeling was possible, it was used. Modeling in these agencies is very much demand driven, and the characteristics of modeler organizations and policies for transfer are of less consequence than the actions the agencies took within the context of the opportunities and constraints of their policymaking arenas.

On the other hand, our analyses provided us with an opportunity to indirectly evaluate the importance of the variables to model success in secondary user organizations. When applied to secondary user organizations, the rankings of our variables might change significantly. Of course, modeling is still only possible when the theoretical and technical bases are established, and models will be adopted only as long as they serve some purpose for the user. But in secondary model-using organizations, the supply-side factor of modeler attributes and transfer policies are probably quite important. Among primary users, strong demand for modeling overwhelms most other factors, and makes the user agencies willing to heavily invest in acquiring technology, people, and data in support of modeling activities. Secondary users are less willing to invest large sums in modeling, and generally will adopt only well-packaged, product-oriented models that are backed up by modeler organizations which can provide the expertise they need.

We believe these findings are significant, because they illustrate that the most important factors in model success are features of the user organizations. Given that modeling is technically feasible in a given situation, the question of whether it will be used depends on circumstances of the user. If the user must have modeling capability, other considerations become opportunities or obstacles in the development of that capability. If, however, the user does not have a great need for modeling capability, the other factors become much more important in the determination of whether modeling will be used. Our use of the term "need" here is quite broad. It includes technical need, in the sense that a model is required to improve the substantive quality of a decision (e.g., determining more accurately how much money to budget for a program). But it also includes political and ideological need, in the sense that a model is needed to gain a political advantage over an opponent or to counter the opponent's use of models.

CHAPTER NINE
COMPUTER MODELS AND POLICYMAKING

Computerized planning models and the information they produce have become increasingly important in federal policy discussions in recent years. Agencies now spend millions of dollars on modeling. Many now have specialized staff and complex procedures for maintaining and running models, for using them to simulate policy options or forecast future conditions, and for interpreting their results for policymakers. By all appearances, then, it would seem that modeling has taken hold in the institutions of policymaking in Washington.

In this chapter we discuss the "successful" outcomes of model implementation among federal agencies. By "successful," we mean that the models are actually being used and, in some cases, have become institutionalized in federal policymaking processes. We conclude that modeling is here to stay, for it serves the various political, organizational, and professional interests of those who directly participate in the policy analysis community.

Model Use

Actual use of a computerized planning model by an agency of the federal government seems to us an appropriate if minimal measure of implementation success. For models to reach the point of actual use, agencies have to have made decisions and taken actions indicating that modeling might be useful to them politically or technically, that they understand how they might use models, and that they are willing to make a commitment of resources so they can use them. The use of models results from such steps. Our research also shows that model use is an intermediate step in a continuous, dynamic process of implementation, with agencies' experience in transferring or using a model often leading to changes in the model itself or in how the agency uses it.

Under a simple definition, models that have been adopted and used for policy analysis at least once fall into the category of successfully implemented models. By design, all of the models we studied in our cases fall into this category, although the extent of use of the model varies. The DRI macroeconomic model, for example, has achieved a phenomenal record of use, constituting an estimated third of all instances of macroeconomic modeling in federal agencies in 1978 (GAO 1979). Many agencies that use DRI's package also subscribe to other econometric models (particularly the Chase and Wharton models), as well as other types of computerized planning models. The microsimulation models MATH and TRIM have been used by a smaller number of agencies, but by all agencies directly engaged in federal income-maintenance policymaking. The PITM has been used by only one agency, but it has been used heavily and continuously because there are no other models that meet the needs it was designed to meet.

Computerized planning models are widely used, but how they are used differs considerably across models and across agencies. As we have seen, agencies vary in their motivations and capabilities for modeling. Their motivations and capabilities affect their choice of models, their behavior in implementing them, and the manner in which they actually utilize them.

TYPES OF MODEL USE

Federal agencies utilize computerized economic planning models for various purposes, some conforming to a managerial ideology of model use, some fitting into a political ideology of modeling, and others serving both approaches.

A managerial ideology of modeling presumes that the quality of decisions that emerge from the policymaking process depends at least in part upon the quality of the information entering the system, and that improvements in the information available to decision makers may lead to improved policy choices. According to this ideology, computerized planning models deserve a place in the policymaking process because they enhance the diversity of information available to analysts, managers, and policymakers; they provide a systematic means to reduce uncertainty about the future, given certain identifiable assumptions about the present; and they provide detailed if not altogether scientific answers to "What will happen if . . . ?" questions.

Many of the agency analysts who actively use (or have used) the models in our study cited such reasons for doing so. And many of their actual uses of macroeconomic and microsimulation techniques fit into a managerial ideology. For example, CBO, the Troika agencies, and the Federal Reserve Board all utilize the DRI and other macroeconomic models to make forecasts of future states of the U.S. economy. This is perhaps the most standard application of these models—to answer "What will happen" questions, given current policy and certain assumptions about the behavior of key economic forces. Similarly, CBO, HEW, and USDA use MATH or TRIM to make budget projections of future costs for major entitlement programs in the welfare system. In most agencies these forecasts are part of larger information collection processes where analysts attempt to increase the number of reputable sources of information available to them and to managers, and thereby reduce the risk of too-heavy reliance on any single information source. Analysts tend to temper the results of their models' forecasts with other information, including their own judgment or intuition.

Simulation techniques are important for predicting the impacts of alternative policy changes in estimates of interest to policymakers, and for exploring how sensitive different variables are to changes in assumptions. This is perhaps the most common use of PITM, MATH, and TRIM. Treasury, HEW, USDA, DOL, and CBO have all used microsimulation models to forecast program costs and caseloads of income-transfer programs, using alternative eligibility rules and benefit levels. Federal users of DRI and econometric models also use their models for simulation. The Troika and CBO use them to forecast the impacts of federal budget proposals on key economic conditions (such as unemployment or productivity), while the Fed simulates the performance of the national economy using alternative interest rates. These modeling applications contribute to a larger process of policy design by enabling analysts to explore the marginal impacts of alternative policy configurations. Analysts often use these simulation techniques to fine-tune policy proposals, or to determine the mix of program elements (e.g., eligibility rules) that would produce a desired program objective (e.g., total case-load size or total program cost).

All of these more or less technical applications of models—for forecasting, for policy simulation and design, for maximizing available information—support a managerial ideology of modeling. They provide extensive, detailed, and quantitative information about the costs and benefits of alternative public policies, and once they have been imple-mented, they do so relatively efficiently, although with an uncertain amount of error.

These applications serve other purposes as well, ones that sup-port a political ideology of modeling. This ideology acknowledges that the policymaking process is a system that produces decisions about who wins and who loses as a consequence of governmental actions. Therefore, it is a political system whose members compete for power, at least as a proximate goal, using whatever weapons they have at their disposal, including information. Information is useful for decisions to the extent that it provides answers to politically relevant questions: Who will be adversely or positively affected by a decision, and in what ways? Where do these people live? What policy options do different groups favor or oppose? How intensely do they care about them? Information can also be politically useful to the extent that it is consistent with policymakers' biases and therefore can be used as arguments or justi-fications for their positions. Moreover, a political ideology of modeling presumes that mechanisms that provide such information, such as com-puterized planning models, will find support among members of the pol-icymaking community, who will utilize these tools strategically to achieve political objectives.

The cases of model use by federal agencies reveal numerous instances where modeling interacted with elements of the political and institutional environment to support a political ideology of model use. In the early 1970s, for example, welfare analysts noted a distinct increase in the attention politicians paid to the results of their microsimulation analyses after they presented the data in charts showing the break-down of income-maintenance program beneficiaries by region. This led to a tendency for analysts to routinely report, along with more aggre-gated impact forecasts (e.g., total program costs), the location of the "winners and losers" of proposed income-security program changes in as much geographical detail as possible. Over the long run, this treat-ment of data generally made the information more salient to politicians and helped to build the constituency of individuals in favor of a methodology that could produce such relevant details.

Other examples of political uses of computerized planning models abound. During the mid-seventies debates over food stamp reforms, the Food and Nutrition Service (FNS) deliberately bolstered its information and analytic capabilities so that it could present a case for selective program cuts to others in the administration who favored across-the-board reductions in the food stamp caseloads. FNS's use of the MATH model give it an efficient and exclusive numbers-generating capability. FNS controlled the operating assumptions of the model, the actual analyses performed, and the dissemination of quantitative information to outsiders within the administration and on Capitol Hill. As sole dispenser of "hard evidence," the FNS had the enviable attribute of authoritativeness, and its numbers remained unchallenged by any other set of estimates of similar detail or "scientific" origin.

In partial recognition of (and reaction to) the informational power the numbers game gave to FNS, the Department of Labor decided to engage in countermodeling when it agreed to work with the Department of Health, Education, and Welfare on welfare reforms in 1977. Because DOL and HEW supported different reform strategies, and because DOL policymakers wanted "a piece of the action," DOL administrators reasoned they could not afford to let HEW be the sole provider of detailed, quantitative analyses. HEW, of course, had TRIM, and it was developing the KGB model especially for this reform initiative. DOL used (at least for a while) a revised version of MATH to perform its own analyses in-house, to build a quantitative case for its position, and to try to discredit the information coming out of HEW. Using MATH helped DOL enhance its position vis-à-vis HEW, but this dissension within the executive branch also seemed to have the effect of undermining the overall stature of the administration's position vis-à-vis opponents in Congress.

Our case studies revealed other examples of countermodeling as a phenomenon of an agency's acquiring and using a model different from the one their "opponents" use. Instead of using MATH for its analyses of 1976 food stamp proposals, the House Agriculture Committee decided to build and use its own simple, ad hoc forecasting model, and thereby avoid internal committee fights over whether MATH had the "liberal" biases the conservatives on the committee said it had. In 1977 conservative Republican Jack Kemp attacked the large "Keynesian" macroeconomic models used by CBO as inaccurate sources of information on which to base budgetary decisions. And in 1981, when the

Reagan administration brought in "supply-side" economics as the theoretical justification for its new tax and budget program, administration
analysts touted a new "supply-side model" (the Claremont model) as a
counter to the traditional Keynesian econometric models that then dominated the economic modeling scene in Washington.

Other instances of a political ideology of modeling occur, as with
"accountability modeling," where an agency implements the same model
another agency is using in order to keep that other agency "honest"—
to monitor the information available to the rival agency and the credibility of the numbers in the reports the rival agency issues. CBO has
cited this as one of the rationales for why it adopted MATH and TRIM
for its income-security analyses: CBO wanted to use the same models
on-line at HEW. Similarly, CBO used the KGB model in 1977 to analyze
the administration's welfare reform proposals because it wanted to monitor
HEW's estimates using HEW's own technique and thereby reduce forecasting differences introduced by using different methodologies. Numerous users of econometric models state that a key reason they subscribe to the DRI modeling package is because DRI is used in all of the
major economic policy agencies of the federal government, and they
want access to the same information. Moreover, CBO made an early
decision to reduce potential controversies inside Congress over the
credibility of its economic forecasts and to help build its image as a
nonpartisan analytic unit by subscribing to any macroeconomic model
that had a member of Congress as its constituent. This helps CBO avoid
unexpected and unanswerable challenges to its projections and aids in
preparation of conservative "consensual forecasts" based on the projections of several major econometric models of the U.S. economy, although it substantially increases CBO's modeling costs.

FREQUENCY OF MODEL USE

Not all models are used all of the time even by agencies that
have fully implemented them. Some agencies routinely use the DRI model
to produce periodic forecasts of future states of the economy. Others
only use models during periods of high interest in an issue, as with
HEW's use of the KGB model during the 1977–78 welfare reform debates. All of the macroeconomic and microanalytic models we studied
can be considered successfully implemented, since each has actually
been used for managerial or political objectives by at least one agency
besides the organization that developed it.

In another sense, however, models that are frequently used give the impression of greater implementation success if frequency of use is a criterion for success. The PITM model of Treasury may be the most heavily used of all major microsimulation models, with 1,000 to 1,500 runs per year for over a decade. Among the models used for broader analytical applications, the macroeconomic models as a class seem more successfully implemented than the TRIM and MATH models, since the former are run more often and are used by a wider number of federal agencies. But frequency of use alone can be a misleading indicator of success because in large part it results from the differences in the systems that various types of models simulate, and the changes in the importance of the issues the models deal with over time in the national policymaking agenda. How often and how intensely agencies actually use individual models depends upon a number of independent variables, such as the level and kinds of resources they generally have available for certain tasks, the importance to them (or to outside resource providers) of a particular issue, and the ability of the model to produce information relevant to analyzing or solving a particular problem. Thus, it takes a mixed set of measures to evaluate the nature of model implementation success.

To this end we have developed a matrix to characterize contextual factors that affect patterns of agencies' use of computerized planning models (figure 9.1). The axes represent relationships between characteristics of models and the modeling environment. The horizontal axis denotes the frequency with which the system being simulated in the model is an intensely salient issue in the national policy agenda. At one end are issues of high, continuous saliency, such as the condition of the U.S. economy, or the composition and size of the annual federal budget. Many models have relevance for these types of issues, among them macroeconomic models that simulate the interaction of key variables (e.g., federal spending) with other important economic variables (e.g., monetary conditions, international trade, and GNP). At the other end of the continuum are issues that are more episodic in nature, being highly salient only at certain times—such as effort to enact or revise welfare policies—and less important in the national policy agenda at other times. For HEW and for certain interest groups, welfare policy has been and will remain an issue of continuing high importance, but in terms of the overall U.S. policy agenda, interest in welfare reform waxes and wanes over time. Support for modeling of welfare programs correspondingly varies with political interest in the area.

The vertical axis of figure 9.1 represents another major charac-

		Frequency of High Political Interest in Policy Area Simulated in Model		
		Continuous		*Episodic*
Breadth of Acceptance for the Model by Community of Analysts in Policy Area	Broad acceptance	DRI ⎤ by Troika; Chase ⎟ by CBO; Wharton ⎦ by Treasury MATH ⎤ by HEW TRIM ⎦ or CBO		MATH ⎤ by DOL TRIM ⎦ or USDA DRI ⎤ Chase ⎟ by GAO Wharton ⎦
		PITM		
		Fed MPS		
	Narrow acceptance		Claremont Model	KGB

Figure 9.1. PATTERNS OF MODEL USE

teristic of model techniques: the breadth of acceptance for particular models within the community of model users. Some models are relatively old and well established and have a strong clientele of users. Examples include the DRI, Chase, and Wharton macroeconomic models, and the PITM, MATH, and TRIM microsimulation models. These are the models most often used within their respective policy analysis arenas. In contrast, at the other end of the continuum are models that are relatively new, undergoing significant change, poorly documented, and used by few agencies. The clientele for these models is small, as is the case for the Claremont model of the U.S. economy or the KGB microsimulation model.

When the models we investigated are plotted on the matrix, the pattern indicates frequency of use of individual models over time relative to use of other competing models. A cluster of macroeconomic models (i.e., DRI, Chase, Wharton) enjoys routine, continuous use by a large community of agency analysts. The PITM model is heavily used, but only within one agency. Others (e.g., MATH) have a strong, broad support among many agencies' analysts, but they are used routinely or intensively only during erratic episodes of high interest in the policy issue they simulate. Models like the Claremont model have a narrow base of support and enjoy routine use only under extraordinary environmental conditions (i.e., the rise to power of supply-side economists in the Reagan administration's federal budget proposal of 1981). Still others with narrow support are used for specific episodes of specialized policy reforms (as with the use of KGB during 1977). We believe that models which are frequently used and broadly supported are more likely than others to become institutionalized as regular features of the policy analysis process.

The Institutionalization of Modeling

While the actual use of a model at least once by an agency is a minimum measure of implementation success, a more comprehensive measure is what we call the institutionalization of models and of modeling per se. Successful model implementation in this broader sense is the result of a complicated coexistence and interaction of "demand pull" by agencies for modeling resources and a strong "supply push" by modelers for transfer of specific models. Over the past two decades, these forces have resulted in the institutionalization of certain models and certain kinds of modeling in U.S. federal agencies. At the same time, significant barriers to model transfer and use continue to exist for many agencies. Modelers who are able to reduce these obstacles seem to experience greater implementation success.

It is worth noting that the increasingly widespread use of computerized planning models has led to several interesting impacts on the policymaking process.

"DEMAND PULL" FOR MODELING
Federal agencies' demand for computerized planning models and the quantitative information they generate is high and has been strong for some time. Over the past two decades, in response to a number of pressures to increase the amount or quality of "objective" information available to policymakers, most agencies have enhanced their analytic capability. They have bolstered their in-house analytic staffs, increased their use of outside consultants, and expanded their use of sophisticated analytic techniques. Strong demand for information, experts, and models as technical tools and as political weapons has led to great investment in the development of policy-relevant models and trained personnel, and in the adoption, transfer, and use of models in the policy-analysis process.

Some federal agencies have had more experience and greater success than others in building their analytic capabilities and in using them effectively. We have found that agencies' opportunities for and interest in implementing policy models result to a large extent from two external political factors: the saliency of the policy area that constitutes an agency's mission (e.g., continuously strong interest in the U.S. federal budget among congressional and Troika agencies, or episodic instances of high public interest, such as welfare policy under HEW's jurisdiction), and the nature of competition among actual and potential model users (e.g., whether partisan or bureaucratic opponents have a modeling or numbers-generating capability).

The saliency factor affects model implementation in several ways. At any given time, sudden, intense national political interest in an issue, such as the growing cost of the food stamp program, the need for energy information following an oil embargo, or the size of the federal deficit during a time of economic stress, tends to increase the resources available to the relevant federal agencies trying to solve these problems. Such interest focuses external attention on how particular policies or programs are doing and on how alternative approaches might improve the situation. For example, sharp increases in the number of food stamp participants in 1974 and 1975 led to demands for reform. The Food and Nutrition Service (FNS) came under pressure to determine what had happened in the food stamp program, to estimate what future caseloads and costs were likely to be, and to generate proposals for reform. FNS needed quantitative information for both managerial and political purposes. Moreover, it needed this information fast, since focused, intense political interest tends to reduce the time an agency has to investigate a problem and come up with solutions. Political crises demand some kind of response, even if it is only the appearance of action in the form of studying the problem. At such times, agencies tend to react by devoting increased resources for rapid information collection and analysis and for acquiring expertise (either on the staff or off) to help provide that information and credibility. In the case of FNS, this meant conducting new, ad hoc surveys of the food stamp clientele, contracting for the development of a food stamp module for the MATH model, and supporting the staff and management time necessary to rapidly develop a computing capability to use MATH for policy analysis and political evidence.

A similar phenomenon occurred in the early 1970s when the high costs of the Vietnam War and the mounting burden of Great Society social welfare programs created concern over the growth of the federal budget. Agencies with major portions of the budget (e.g., HEW and Defense) were pressured to come up with better means of forecasting and controlling costs, while the congressional and executive agencies responsible for budget analysis were forced to come up with better indicators of the costs of programs. In all major agencies, the primary response was to improve analytical capability by expanding analytical staff and investing in analytical tools such as computerized models.

Federal agency responses to hot political issues are also shaped by the nature of political competition that exists among the participants engaged in analysis and policymaking. FNS needed quantitative evidence because program critics (i.e., in the media, in OMB, and on Capitol Hill) had numbers they were using to attack the program. At first, FNS didn't have detailed numbers and was at a political disadvantage as a result. It had to acquire a number-generating capacity just to maintain an equal footing. To get into a position of strength, FNS was eager to find a way to get "better" numbers (e.g., Where did program recipients live? Which ones would lose benefits if the program rules changed? How much money would individual congressional districts lose as a result of changes?). Generating such numbers was a costly and technically problematic proposition, but the political heat enabled FNS to justify the effort.

FNS, of course, was not the first federal agency to acquire a microsimulation capability, although it was the first to introduce that technique into the food stamp policy area. The FNS modeling efforts are an example of a larger model implementation sequence we observed among competing types of organizations within discrete policy areas. In any given issue area, the first agency to implement a model is usually the one with the primary programmatic responsibility in that area. This organization is drawn by strong managerial and political objectives to acquire data analysis and policy simulation capabilities. Often, the agency even provides support for model development or for revising existing research models to meet more applied policy analysis needs. These lead agencies then create the organizational infrastructure needed to contract with a dedicated outside modeling agency to provide the service they need (as the FNS did with MATH), or to bring the model in-house and use it independently (as HEW did with TRIM).

This pattern has also emerged in the use of macroeconomic models. The first adopters of the DRI macroeconomic model in the federal government were the staff agencies to the two competing institutions in the budgetary process—the Congressional Research Service in the Congress, and the Treasury Department in the executive branch. And it was the largest mission agency—Defense—that supported DRI's building of the cost-forecasting service to analyze the downstream costs of major procurements when Congress became concerned with cost overruns.

Agencies that later adopt and use these models do so in part because the lead agency in that policy area has already adopted the modeling capability. These second-stage model implementers often are agencies that want models predominantly for political objectives. In a national-level policy war (between administrative agencies or between branches or political parties), information—particularly detailed, quantitative evidence generated by sophisticated techniques—is a powerful weapon, especially if one participant has it and the other does not. So when one party has a model, the other has a strong political incentive to seek parity by acquiring a modeling capability for itself. Second-stage model implementers pursue one or more political objectives: to keep track of the information available to the lead agency, as with CBO's acquisition of the same econometric models used by the Troika agencies; to gain in-house, analytical independence from the other agency, as with CBO's implementation of TRIM and MATH, both of which were then used by HEW; to discredit or at least to challenge the numbers generated by the lead agency's model, as did DOL by use of MATH in response to HEW's use of KGB; and to build evidence for and advocate an alternative policy, as the Reagan administration and the Senate Budget Committee did in their use of the Claremont model.

Once the lead agency in a given policy area has introduced a model into the analysis and policymaking process, the other participants in the process feel strong pressure to engage in modeling. Thereafter, model-generated information becomes one of the standard pillars of evidence in policy debates in that area. The political competition at the heart of the policymaking process works together with a strong, generalized demand for "objective" or quantitative evidence to encourage the spread and institutionalization of modeling among agencies of the federal government.

"SUPPLY PUSH" FOR MODELING

Of course, model developers and vendors are not neutral bystanders in this process. Historically, agencies' strong "demand pull" for information and for techniques of analysis has been matched by a powerful "supply push" by modelers for model implementation. The behavior and practices of individual modelers who are oriented toward policy applications—not to mention commercial success—of their models have greatly influenced the spread of modeling generally and especially the implementation success of those individual models.

Our study revealed that modelers who are more strongly motivated by economic incentives (as opposed to scholarly interests) develop a more aggressive strategy in seeking consumers for their models. They seek out agencies that will not only support model development and acquisition, but also actually implement and use a model over time. These modelers orient their activities to enhance their goal of selling their goods and services to agency users. They adopt policies that encourage transfer, such as structuring their organization toward servicing clients' needs, designing a comprehensive package of wares, and promoting and pricing the package in such a way as to obtain customers.

In our study, DRI stands out as an archetype of a successful user-oriented modeler. DRI is a private commercial firm, established to sell a product (i.e., access to its models, forecasts, and data bases) to paying customers. DRI's principals designed its services with the user in mind, combining a wide array of models, data bases, and consulting services into a simple-to-use package, priced to attract a large set of public users. DRI organized its personnel into specialized teams whose primary responsibility has been to market the package and provide assistance to specific clients. DRI has continuously revised and upgraded its product line and the quality of its services to meet the demands of its important customers. It has allowed for lateral movement of personnel to and from user organizations and academic institutions, and has maintained good relations and contacts across a wide range of organizations, as well as improving its understanding of the changing needs of users. This has enabled DRI to adapt its services to the changing political, economic, and technological environment in which its customers operate.

Key factors in DRI's success in transferring its model to a wide clientele in Washington and in realizing the goal of actual agency use are the commercialization of its modeling enterprise (for which DRI is largely responsible) and DRI's adoption of the specific transfer strategies noted above. Its competitors, such as Chase Econometrics and the Wharton Economic Forecasting Associates, have followed DRI's lead in these practices, but these firms have lacked DRI's unique data resources, its user-centered software and systems, and its enviable position of having been the first commercial firm to develop a large clientele of users.

Among microsimulation modelers, MPR and its MATH model have historically achieved the greatest implementation success among a diverse set of agencies. Like DRI, MPR is a private consulting firm offering a user-oriented product package, as well as customized modeling services. MPR's original top personnel had extensive agency experience and understood users' need for analysis for both managerial and political purposes. Like DRI, they used this knowledge in the design of their services.

MPR's most effective transfer policies have related to a need to adjust the process of implementation to a key defining feature of the technique itself: its complexity. Because MATH is so complicated and time consuming to learn to use, MPR has developed important strategies to overcome this barrier. It has developed an organizational structure which focuses on users' needs, and it has developed and marketed a subscription service containing a standard, low-priced model, accompanied by user-oriented documentation, training, and consultation. More important, perhaps, MPR has adopted a policy of "personal transfer" which encourages trained personnel to move between modeler and user organizations and which facilitates the movement of such personnel between user agencies.

MPR's gradual development of this subscription package and marketing style distinguishes it from its major competitor, the Urban Institute, a nonprofit research firm. The institute's main transfer policy has been to allow for personal transfer. It has historically been less aggressive than MPR in marketing its TRIM-related services, although recent cutbacks in funds for social science research have been prompting the institute to take a more active role in finding markets for its services.

The strong "personalized transfer" policies of the organizations involved in microsimulation modeling have helped decentralize expertise in such modeling, thereby spreading understanding of and interest in it across a wide range of organizations. However, personalized transfer provides a fragile base of support for modeling in the income-transfer policy areas as compared with the highly institutionalized base that exists among organizations engaged in macroeconomic modeling; this difference corresponds to the fact that particular microsimulation models are usually focused on narrow policy issues (e.g. income-transfer policy) which are the domain of just a few agencies and which tend to be episodic in their political saliency.

INTERACTION OF "DEMAND PULL"
AND "SUPPLY PUSH" FOR MODELING

Thus, a number of factors had converged in Washington, D.C., to foster the implementation of computerized planning models among federal agencies. By the mid-seventies, models had become institutionalized, routine fixtures of the policy analysis process. The period from the late sixties through the mid-seventies was the golden age of policy analysis, with administrators eager to adopt more systematic management techniques and quantitative tools for program analysis. Politicians wanted to know hard facts about how federal programs were doing and what the impacts of their decisions might be.

Within the welfare policy area, this situation translated into demands for estimates of the costs and number of people served by social support programs, as well as evidence on the status of the "war against poverty." The seventies were a period of intense concern over the effectiveness of the nation's large, complex, and costly welfare system. Nearly all interested groups agree that something had to be done to reform the system, but few people could agree on the best way to provide assistance to the poor while also controlling the size of the welfare budget. This interest in welfare reform and the controversy over how to do it eventually combined with a generalized thirst for systematic policy analysis, to make microsimulation modeling an attractive tool for social welfare policy analysis in Washington.

The strong "demand pull," of course, helped foster the development and implementation of the TRIM and MATH models. These two models were the only microsimulation models being utilized for federal income-maintenance policy analysis in the mid-seventies. Their virtual monopoly in this arena had largely resulted from several factors. Microsimulation was a relatively new technique for economic analysis, and a limited number of economists had technical training in microanalytic modeling. The key developers of the earliest applied policy models were still directly involved in modeling work. They had strong modeling experience and expertise, and records of service which gave them a competitive edge over newcomers to the field. While other analysts had access to MATH and TRIM (both publicly funded projects), the very complexity of these models meant significant start-up costs for outsiders who wanted to get into the microsimulation modeling business.

In competition for agency contract work, other firms couldn't underbid more experienced outfits like the Urban Institute or Mathematica Policy Research (MPR), nor could they claim greater analytic expertise. User agencies had been working with individuals at the institute and MPR for years and had developed strong ties. In many cases, the "revolving door" employment tradition in the income-security analysis community meant that many agency analysts were in fact former employees of these two firms, or vice versa. The institute had a solid reputation for high-quality applied research, and MPR had become known as an aggressive and capable provider of packaged, user-oriented services.

These "supply push" factors associated with modelers' work interacted well with the agencies' "demand pull' for quantitative analyses, facilitating the process of implementing these microsimulation models for use in actual policy analysis. Therefore, by 1976 TRIM and MATH enjoyed strong support and use.

In the macroeconomic policy arena, the demand for and supply of analytic techniques also interacted to spread macroeconometric models across the terrain. A number of circumstances enabled a supply of modeling capability to become available for policy use. Several decades of theory building and research in econometric methods led to the development of numerous macroeconomic models. The creation of major economic data bases served as input to the models. Large-scale advanced computing capability allowed for the construction of more complex models and the ability to process huge time-series data files. Successive cohorts of economists and planners gained exposure to econometric techniques in graduate schools and led to the emergence of a professional community of skilled econometricians and data analysts.

As tools for economic analysis became more refined and those with knowledge of them moved into positions of advice and authority in economic policy agencies in Washington, demand for improved access to high-quality information began to rise. But most who wanted to use large data bases for forecasting or policy simulation purposes faced serious obstacles, such as difficulty obtaining information from decentralized sources of economic data, insufficient resources or skills to create reliable models of complex economic systems, and lack of access to appropriate data processing facilities.

Eventually, by the late sixties, a handful of senior economists with an entrepreneurial bent and considerable experience in giving advice to federal policymakers began to recognize the existence of this growing public market for economic information and analytic services. They established private for-profit firms dedicated to providing services to federal economic analysts. These analysts were eager to possess the ability to make credible economic forecasts and simulations of fiscal and monetary policy options so as to better answer the questions of economic policymakers concerned with reducing the uncertainty and risks in their decisions.

DRI designed a package of services to meet the analysts' needs and aggressively marketed its services to key users long before there was any competition from other "full-service" economic consulting firms. DRI's early market entry and its success in getting the key economic policymaking agencies to subscribe to its services made it attractive to other agencies as well. They wanted to become clients so that they could have access to the same information as the Office of Management and Budget, the Department of the Treasury, and the Council of Economic Advisers. Thus, it was not only the marketing strategies and the data, modeling, and consulting services DRI provided that fostered the firm's success throughout federal agencies; it was also the fact that key actors in the economic policy community believed that DRI forecasts and data bases met important analytical and political needs, and then actually relied on DRI's services to perform critical and sometimes visible analytical tasks.

BARRIERS TO SUCCESSFUL MODEL IMPLEMENTATION

In spite of the evidence for a gradual move toward increased reliance on modeling, we see several political and technological obstacles in the way of broader implementation of models, both in terms of the number and diversity of agencies that adopt models and also the frequency of agencies' use of models. We have identified four types of barriers: complexity of the modeling system and its use; problems with the data; perceived inaccuracies of the model; and little relevance of results for policymaking.

The more complex the computerized modeling system is from the user's perspective, the greater the difficulties associated with model transfer and use. Complex systems are harder to learn to use and pose numerous operational problems. Many users of models cite model complexity as the largest obstacle in the implementation process. This is especially true if the complexity of the model itself makes use of the model for analytic purposes intricate, time consuming, and cumbersome.

Curiously, there appears to be a paradox in agencies' attraction to and difficulties with complex models. Many users want models that are technically sophisticated in order to achieve certain managerial objectives (e.g., to simulate the behavior of complex systems, such as the effects of changes in food stamp policy on the tax and welfare programs) and political purposes (e.g., building credibility of economic forecasts through the use of state-of-the-art analytic techniques). Many agencies seem attracted to particularly complex systems with the aim of capturing the benefits of controlling a "black box"; yet they discover that this very attribute actually prevents them from controlling the technology promptly or efficiently after model acquisition. The MATH model, for example, requires a two-year investment in training time for personnel to become competent enough to operate the system independently. This high learning cost has often meant that agencies either "use" MATH long before transferring it in-house (through the assistance of MPR's staff who run it at (MPR) or attempt to hire MATH analysts away from MPR or other user agencies. In either case, the new user agency has to postpone its sense of control over this complex methodology until either the new employee is socialized into the life of the organization or existing personnel become sufficiently competent to take over operation of the modeling enterprise.

The complexity of computerized microsimulation models such as MATH and TRIM seems to limit the spread of the technology to new users and to inhibit use by adopters because so few people have thorough knowledge of the methodologies and the techniques for using them. In contrast, many economists are taught the techniques of econometric modeling in universities and can identify the differences between models fairly rapidly. Moreover, the major econometric models, although complex, often have sophisticated software routines that make their use relatively straightforward. DRI is particularly sophisticated in this regard, and many subscribers to DRI services report that one of its greatest selling points lies in its ease of use. Indeed, one of the keys to DRI's success is the fact that its designers aimed at ease of use when designing the software systems that manage user interactions with the complex array of DRI models, data bases, and report generators.

Problems with the quality and usability of data processed and generated by computerized planning models may be retarding expanded implementation of models. Critics of the MATH/TRIM microsimulation models, for example, have cited data problems such as unrepresentativeness of samples, invalid responses, old and missing data, and imputed information as significant drawbacks to policymakers' reliance on the results of model runs (GAO 1976a). Microsimulation modelers agree that these problems exist. They argue, however, that most microsimulation problems result not from the microsimulation methodology, but from the high costs and reporting difficulties unavoidably associated with the collection of large, detailed samples of U.S. households—problems that are common to all disaggregated analyses of the behavior of the population affected by complex phenomena such as income-transfer programs. Given the market that exists for analyses of this population, they contend, microsimulation models do the best job they can of processing the huge data sets which are required to obtain representative samples of the population at risk.

The accuracy and utility of model results have to do with the quality of the data processed, the design of the model itself (i.e., the structural relationships among variables), and the end users' belief in the model's accuracy. Herein lies a further obstacle to model implementation: models face resistance when potential users of the information they generate believe the results are biased.

Our research leads us to conclude that anytime model results are used in policy disputes or political battles, some partisans are going to be suspicious of the objectivity of the model. But even in the context of nonpoliticized policy modeling, model objectivity can be a problem for users.

The issue of perceived model bias is critical for two reasons. First, models' actual predictive accuracy is difficult if not impossible to determine because the systems they simulate tend to be dynamic. Forecasts of complex economic and social phenomena can actually change the behavior of the participants in the system modeled during the forecasted period, thereby reducing the "accuracy" of the original forecast. In such cases, it is difficult to know whether the error in prediction resulted from the system's response to the information provided by the forecast, or from faults in the design of the forecasting model itself, or both. Moreover, although there is generalized interest among members of the policymaking community to know the accuracy of various computerized planning models, there are few instances where specific organizations care enough to fund thorough assessments of the accuracy of model forecasts. For example, criticisms of the major commercial econometric models abounded after their well-publicized failure to predict the radical changes in energy prices in the early 1970s. Yet this resulted in neither a widespread rejection of these models nor a concerted effort to investigate the predictive accuracy of individual models. The work of McNees (1981, 1982; McNees and Ries 1983) of the Federal Reserve Bank of Boston indicates that the computerized macroeconomic models perform slightly better than do judgmental forecasts, while the GAO's longitudinal study to systematically monitor and evaluate the prediction records of the major models and the judgmental forecasters concluded that both techniques do about equally well. There have been no such efforts to evaluate the long-term accuracy of microsimulation forecasts, although the GAO has investigated these models' results carefully. The funds that agencies have been willing to invest in microsimulation models have been primarily for development, manufacture, and use, and seldom for evaluation.

Perceived bias in model forecasts detracts from model implementation in a second way, one that fits more into a political ideology of modeling. Analysts and policymakers who strongly believe that a model reflects a particular economic theory (e.g., Keynesian) or political perspective (e.g., liberal) will reject or discredit it if they do not share the same assumptions. Beyond this, they may not be able to use such models even when the model's results fit their own view of the world. Our study indicated that potential users who wanted to utilize a model that was reputedly biased in line with their own views decided against using it because they expected their political opponents would attempt to discredit any results produced by the model. This happened during congressional food stamp debates in the mid-seventies when the Democrats on the House Agriculture Committee opted not to use MATH because of vocal claims by Republicans that MATH had a liberal bias.

A final obstacle to model use has to do with analysts' and policymakers' acceptance of model-generated information as relevant to their own analytic or decision processes. Unless a modeler can convince a policy analyst that the products and services he provides are useful and worth the asking price, the analyst will not implement the model. And unless an analyst can use the modeling services to provide answers to questions of interest to policymakers, his analyses will be irrelevant and ignored. Under such conditions, support for modeling in the policymaking organization will break down.

From our case studies, it appears that microsimulation models which are focused on one specific program, such as the PITM model, are the most likely models to capture and hold the interest of agency policymakers. These models are highly focused on particular aspects of the programs they are built around; they relate directly to issues which agency leaders are interested in; they use data bases developed and maintained by the agency itself (and in which the agency has confidence); and they often are buffered from political warfare because of their narrow, embedded role in the analyses of their home agency. The more generalized policy models, including income-transfer simulation models like MATH and TRIM, are less likely to be met with such immediate trust. MATH and TRIM modelers recognized this issue not long after the models were introduced to federal agencies. To overcome the lack of interest in their work among politicians, these modelers began to reorganize the results of policy simulations into a format which elected officials could more easily grasp. They produced "winners and losers" tables, indicating the location and socioeconomic status of groups likely to be affected by different policy changes. Ever since, politicians have expected to learn how their own constituents might be harmed or benefited by policy changes, in addition to hearing about overall programmatic or budget impacts. Yet such politicized use of these models has placed modelers in the uncomfortable position of having to attach qualifiers to their model-generated results and explain their models' inherent limitations to policymakers who want to know the "true" answer to some question of political importance. Policymakers rebel when they hear information "contaminated" by qualifiers about the size of the possible estimating errors. They want precise answers—"point estimates"—even if the questions they ask are vague and the model methodologies are incapable of producing error-free estimates.

IMPACTS OF MODELING ON THE POLICYMAKING PROCESS

Our study reveals that computerized planning models have a solid footing in Washington, D.C., at least until future technological innovations surpass their ability to produce quantitative information about policy choices in a politically useful form. Model-generated "evidence" is now part of the standard vocabulary of policy debates. Models have been institutionalized in agencies throughout the federal government, and analysts strongly believe that at present there are no better tools to help them provide the information policymakers want.

One reason for our conclusion that computerized planning models are here to stay is that most of the actors involved in the modeling-for-policy analysis enterprise have a stake in keeping models on board. Obviously, modelers have commercial, intellectual, and professional interests in designing usable models and in offering them in forms attractive to analysts and policymakers. Analysts as a group also show a strong commitment to modeling, because it tends to make their jobs more stimulating and to enhance their organizational status. Policymakers appreciate the information that models provide, whether it be for decision-making purposes (according to a managerial ideology of modeling) or for ammunition for political battles (according to a political ideology of modeling). Although policymakers and analysts are cynical about the accuracy of models' estimates, they nonetheless support model use because they believe that even if they don't use models and argue in numerical terms, their opponents can and will use them. And in politics, "some numbers beat no numbers every time." In such a system, all of the participants have a stake in keeping modeling going, and no one can afford to take an isolated stand as an objector to the numbers game.

This issue is important because computerized planning models are clearly powerful techniques in terms of technology, economics, and politics. These are sophisticated methodologies capable of processing and analyzing enormous, complex data bases. They enable those who control them to produce information that seems to reduce uncertainty about the future, which, in turn, gives the modelers and analysts personal and organizational power in the form of specialized knowledge. And it gives the organizations that control the models a resource with high political utility and one that they often use to promote narrow organizational goals.

Computerized planning models also represent a significant amount of political and economic power for those who directly benefit from their sale and use. These are costly tools. Not all groups in a policy war can afford to acquire or implement them. They also represent an enormous social investment, although it is difficult to say just how great an investment, given the diverse number of models available, the large number of agency users, and the lack of centralized data about model expenditures. But individual agencies' estimates of the cost of using one model over a one-year period can point to the magnitude of the social investment: CBO reportedly spent over $1 million on DRI services in 1980. HEW apparently spent $1 million of computer time alone using the KGB model during 1977. These are but the tip of the iceberg of the costs of computerized planning modeling, an enterprise strongly supported by agencies of the federal government and showing signs of becoming more institutionalized over time.

Some Lessons from Our Study

The implications of this study are many, but we focus here on three: the implications for the modeling field in general, including both decision support systems (DSS) and planning models;[1] the implications for model builders; and the implications for policymakers and analysts.

IMPLICATIONS FOR THE MODELING FIELD

Our study has several implications for the policy modeling field, especially with regard to large-scale models implemented in complex organizational and political environments.

The first is that the prevailing perspectives for understanding policy models in vivo need to be broadened. The conventional view is quite rationalistic in character, with even the most sensitive accounts assuming that some order can be made from the chaos of conflicting views and opinions of policymakers. Planning models, in this view, are intended to provide better information and "what if" kinds of analytical support to the difficult task of strategic planning. This viewpoint is not naive; it acknowledges the problems inherent in doing strategic planning, and takes into account various behavioral issues in the implementation of modeling systems designed for decision support. But studies of the behavioral aspects of modeling tend to be concerned with the success or failure of system implementation strategies, or the "fit" between characteristics of the systems and the needs of their users. They seldom address the implications of behavioral factors on the overall utility of planning models.

The use of macroeconomic and microanalytic models in national social and economic policymaking suggests that the context of application sometimes supersedes all considerations of the appropriate or sound methods of implementation. As the complexity, magnitude, and political import of problems to be addressed increases, the role of planning models becomes less predictable, and the strategies for implementing them become less certain to produce improved decisions. The managerial ideology of model use as described in the case studies conforms to the common view of where and how such systems fit within the policymaking process. In the case of the macroeconomic models, this ideology was eclipsed following the 1980 election by a number of powerful contextual factors related to the political and economic ideologies of new national leaders. These political/economic ideologies were not new; they had been latent in the policymaking apparatus of the federal government for many years. But because these ideologies had never been resident in the dominant political coalitions of government during the period of economic model development, they were not represented in the institutionalized economic modeling activities of government agencies. The only major modeling effort that embodied some of these views was the St. Louis Fed model, and it was never incorporated into routine analyses in the Troika or the CBO. Even the Fed relied more heavily on the traditional models than on the monetarist St. Louis Fed model. Only after the 1980 election did the relative dearth of economic models embodying monetarist and supply-side views become apparent.

Second, *planning models, like other computerized systems designed to support organizational activities, are inherently political instruments* (Danziger, Dutton, Kling, and Kraemer 1982; Dutton and Kraemer 1985). Moreover, these planning-oriented models are more closely bound to political issues than operations-oriented models because they are aimed at the highest level of decision making in organizations. This fact is not readily apparent during periods of stable political ideology because the models developed during these periods tend to reflect the biases of prevailing coalitions. Major changes in ideology at top policy levels reveal the extent to which embedded models are bound up in particular ideological viewpoints.

This fact reveals a prevailing paradox in the effort to create planning models in support of policymaking in complex environments. On the one hand, the purpose of these models is to provide informational and analytical support to help decision makers better understand the facts surrounding decision problems. Understanding such facts, in turn, should help decision makers arrive at decisions that yield preferred outcomes. On the other hand, facts in the context of planning models are artifacts of information processed through the models, which embody some view of how the world works. The information input to these models might indeed be factually correct, but the models used to derive meaning from information take their cues from theories that are subject to debate. The paradox lies in this: the act of making decisions is the process of eliminating alternatives, but the use of modeling is intended to elucidate and even expand the base of alternatives available for consideration. In fields like economics, different models for interpreting data often embody contradictory assumptions, and no single model can be expected to represent all relevant viewpoints. In the end, the models used in policymaking must conform to one of two states. Either the models used are consistent in their assumptions and underlying theories, thereby excluding rival views; or a variety of models must be used to represent rival theories, thereby specifically embedding the models in the political environment of the moment. It is a delusion to assume that a single model can simultaneously represent all conflicting theoretical and policy viewpoints. It is also a delusion to assume that any model or array of models can maintain ideological neutrality.

A question arises, then, as to what difference policy modeling makes in national policymaking. The cynical view would be that it makes no fundamental difference in the prevailing debates, because in the end modeling must embody the theoretical differences of opinion underlying those debates. They become, in a sense, extensions of those debates with technological trappings. But this view is neither charitable nor fair. Social and economic models can and often do provide meaningful support to policy debates in four important ways.

First, they provide a means of clarifying the positions of various parties in the debate; an important first step in any conscientious effort to determine which course of action to take in a complex decision situation. Planning models, for all their faults, at least force the assumptions underlying various ideologies onto paper or into computer code in a consistent and coherent format. This assists those on various sides of debates by focusing attention on the underlying assumptions involved. Models thereby serve as formal position statements of the views of their builders and users. Such clarification can serve an important role in policy debates, particularly by making clear what is and is not understood about the issues at hand.

Second, they enforce the discipline of data analysis in the course of issue determination and resolution. Even conflicting theories must take account of the facts represented by data on existing and past conditions. The selection of a variable as relevant to an analysis establishes that variable as a consideration that cannot easily be ignored in subsequent analyses. Emphasizing or discounting the importance of a variable must be justified by theoretical or factual reasons, which makes it more difficult for important factual data to be overlooked, suppressed, or improperly emphasized. Moreover, the use of models forces attention on the systematic relationships between variables. These relationships must be specified in the model, which means that must be taken seriously in the process of analysis.

Third, planning models provide the ability to dynamically test the sensibility of different theoretical views about the behavior of the system being modeled. The availability of large data bases and computer processing power makes it possible to repeatedly test, under different scenarios, the underlying models of behavior to determine whether the results they yield are reasonable. This has two advantages. One is the contribution such simulations make to improve the understanding of social and economic phenomena. Simulations help in the refinement of models, and more refined and accurate models are useful in social and economic research. The other is the contribution of simulation to the testing of proposed social or economic policies. Even though such simulations cannot be relied upon to produce a precise forecast of the outcome of policy adoption, they can play a critical role in establishing the boundaries around likely outcomes. This helps in avoiding the adoption of policies that would be likely to have catastrophic outcomes, and also helps policymakers understand the sensitivities inherent in their proposals.

Finally, social and economic models provide policymakers with new tools for stimulating the dialectics inherent in policy debates. Of course, the protocols for appropriate exploitation of these models can be destroyed when political debates get heated. But over time, the use of planning models can strengthen the pluralistic policymaking process by bringing to policymakers refined tools for evaluating their own proposals and critiquing their opponents' proposals. To the extent that these models make such contributions, they assist in the policymaking processes of the user organization.

IMPLICATIONS FOR MODELERS

Our study has implications for the construction and deployment of large-scale, complex models, whether under the rubric of DSS, operations research, statistical, or planning models.[2] These implications should be of particular importance to model builders and operators.

The first is that *the models in this study illustrate the critical importance of having all the major components of the "package" developed and available for the use of the user analysts who depend on the system.* Ideally, the package would include the computerized model and its documentation, the data bases required to operate the model, computing and telecommunications support to operate the model at the user's site, and staff support to assist the users in adapting the model and the data bases to their policy problem.

The fact that such complete packages are seldom constructed is probably due as much to the vagaries of timing and providence as to planning by model builders. In the case of DRI, the development of a successful package occurred at the intersection of several major streams of effort: the widespread belief in the utility and need for macroeconomic models, the general availability of trained econometricians, the presence of skilled and farsighted technicians, advances in computer and time-sharing technology, the privatization of economic data bases, and the availability of venture capital to begin a modeling and data service company. Convergence of such key forces at one time is uncommon but important.

Second, *the technical support function of modeling need not be organizationally tied to the user environment.* Although much of the management science, operations research, and DSS literature contains a bias toward in-house modeling, the success of a planning model sometimes stems in part from the fact that it came from an organization outside of its primary user environment. This was again illustrated by the DRI case. DRI was a private firm providing businesslike services to the federal government, which gave the company an image of independence amid the highly political environment in which its modeling services were applied. This suggests that successful planning models need not be developed in an environment where the systems personnel and users are organizationally bound together. Rather, the successful transfer of DRI's services to federal agencies occurred because of close disciplinary ties between the economists in DRI and those in the federal agencies. This close interaction was dramatically enhanced by the extensive movement of personnel among the various organizations involved, from universities to federal agencies to DRI.

Third, *policy modeling requires a culture of independence between modelers and users, especially when the modeler is a private company and when multiple, possibly competing, organizations use the same modeling service.* One way of maintaining such independence, which successfully worked for both DRI and MPR and their government clients, is to form, for each user agency, service groups that are independent from one another but that can each consult with the model builder who developed the model in the first place.

Fourth, *utility is of critical importance in successful model implementation; and utility is a function of the model package being useful, usable, and used.* For example, at the time the DRI services were fully operational, model-based analysis was becoming a routine part of federal economic policymaking. The models were *useful* aids to judgment because they provided a means by which large amounts of economic time-series data could be quickly reduced and analyzed in light of prevailing theories about the behavior of economic systems. The models also were *usable* because DRI provided a full range of modeling, data, computer, and technical analysis support to user agencies. Therefore, user agencies could choose the level of support based upon their needs and ability to pay. Finally, the models were *used* because they had demonstrated they could provide support to the various actors in the policymaking environment, and this support was specifically aimed at giving analysts the tools to construct their own analyses to fit their own biases. Use by one agency stimulated use by others and, eventually, stimulated use of both the DRI and other models by the key federal agencies concerned with economic policymaking.

IMPLICATIONS FOR POLICYMAKERS AND ANALYSTS

Finally, our analysis has implications for policymakers and analysts who seek to determine whether to undertake policy modeling and to improve the quality of advice they receive from modeling enterprises.

Whether or not to undertake policy modeling is an interesting question. This is especially the case because systematic studies of the forecasting performance of planning models show that they generally perform no better than expert judgment (Ascher and Overholt 1983). Yet the use of large-scale, complex models has steadily increased within the federal government over the last twenty years and shows no signs of abating. What then is the motivation to use modeling?

Our analysis shows that it is fundamentally, and appropriately, political. For both substantive and purely partisan reasons, policymakers and their analysts seek modeling assistance as the political saliency of policy issues increases. Sometimes it is to seek assistance in choosing a policy; other times to bolster and justify a policy choice already made; still other times to be able to respond to potential arguments against the policy from the opposition, or to attack the opposition's policy, or both. What makes policy modeling fundamentally political, however, is not simply the political context of policy modeling. It is that there is often no single correct way to make forecasts; that modeling is rife with core assumptions that determine forecast accuracy more than any other considerations; and that these core assumptions are matters of *both* expert and political judgment.

Once they have decided to engage in modeling, policymakers and analysts can take several steps to bolster the quality of policy advice that can be obtained from modeling. First, they should *encourage greater pluralism of models concerned with a policy problem.* As pointed out by Ascher and Overholt (1983), the two functions of modeling—to produce consistently reasonable forecasts and to anticipate counterintuitive outcomes—can rarely be pursued by the same model at the same time, but can be pursued as separate enterprises.

Second, they should *encourage greater pluralism of modeling groups concerned with a policy problem.* Policymakers, analysts, and modelers all benefit when modeling is characterized by a pluralistic approach with lots of modeling going on by lots of people. In both the microanalytic case and macroeconomic case, the modeling enterprises benefited from the fact that there were multiple groups working with similar models. In the case of MATH/TRIM, the modelers and analysts were in different agencies and used the models to promote competing policies. The competition among agencies sharpened the modelers', analysts', and policymakers' understanding and helped to reveal critical assumptions in the models. In the case of the macroeconomic models, different agencies generated independent forecasts using different models and then met regularly to discern how and why their forecasts disagreed. Thus, modeling benefits from the involvement of multiple user agencies.

Third, they should *encourage greater competition and cooperation among modelers, analysts, and policymakers involved in policy arenas.* Modeling benefits from both competition and cooperation among user agencies. Competition among user agencies helps to raise questions about the core assumptions, parameters, and alternatives considered in the models. Cooperation among analysts provides a forum for resolving technical issues so that models can be somewhat divorced from politics at a technical level. One approach to cooperation is illustrated by the Energy Modeling Forum, where different modeler and user agencies voluntarily cooperated in exchanging information about energy models, running tests of the models using common scenarios, and assessing model performance (Hogan 1979; Sweeney and Weyant 1979). Moreover, competition and cooperation also are beneficial at the policy and political levels because sometimes there are answers to competing policy choices in the numbers; by focusing attention on particular choices, policymakers and analysts can sometimes get answers that inform policymaking, or at least learn that there are no definitive answers.

Fourth, they should *recognize that modeling is a "package" which requires substantial and continuing investments in several components,* including computing, telecommunications, software, data bases, and staff expertise. The more large-scale and complex the models, the more expensive, cumbersome, time consuming, and difficult they are to use and to manage. Consequently, user agencies should realize that policy modeling is no small affair. Generally, it will require several years and millions of dollars to acquire competent modeling capability. Thus, large-scale planning models require substantial and continuing financial investments. However, when the programs being evaluated by the models involve hundreds of millions of dollars, as they often do, investment of millions in modeling to evaluate policy options appears relatively insignificant.

Fifth, they should *encourage systematic model validation and assessment by independent agencies* not formally associated with the model builders or users. Validation and assessment are different though related. Validation of a model attempts to establish how closely the behavior of the model mirrors the real-world system being modeled. Assessment of a model attempts to establish a process by which interested parties who were not involved in a model's development and implementation can determine, with some level of confidence, whether or not the model's results can be used in decision making (Gass 1983).

Despite the frequent intonation by modelers that model validation and assessment are required, they seldom get done. Various arrangements for validation and assessment have been suggested and rejected over the years. For example, in a 1979 survey (Roth, Gass, and Lemoine 1979:216), three propositions involving bureaucratic intervention in the modeling field were put to expert model practitioners in university, nonprofit, for-profit, and government organizations. These propositions involved the establishment within the government of a model testing, verification, and validation center, a modeling research center, and a model postreview panel. All three were soundly rejected by the respondents. Yet some progress has been made as illustrated by the assessments of economic models by the American Statistical Association and the National Bureau of Economic Research (Su and Su 1975) and by the assessments of energy models by the National Research Council (1978), the Energy Modeling Forum (Hogan 1979; Sweeney and Weyant 1979), and the MIT Energy Laboratory (Kresge 1979; Wood 1980). Both validation and assessment should be performed by independent agencies within the government, universities, or private organizations. Because they require special expertise and independent financial support, validation and assessment are best performed in a few centers that can garner the required resources rather than be left to the marketplace.

Given all the above considerations, user agencies are well advised to consider the following specific strategies for dealing with the implementation of policy models:

1. *Use personal transfer*—hiring someone already expert in the model you want—as a means of getting in-house expertise quickly. Such a person usually will exist in the modeler organization, another government agency, or a university.

2. *Use an outside model repeatedly before bringing it in-house.* This will allow the user agency to become familiar with the model and assess its utility for the policy problem at hand. Also, bringing a model in-house can involve financial commitments considerably greater than using outside modeling services.

3. Where possible, *use simpler, more aggregate models* rather than complex and highly disaggregated models.

4. *Where policy problems do not lend themselves to simple, aggregate models, use a family of models;* that is, use a series of small, aggregate models each of which addresses a part of the policy problem, and use verbal argument to link and interrelate the various parts (Dalkey 1965).

5. *Use experienced, expert analysts,* whether in-house, elsewhere in the government, or in a modeler organization. The policy modeling arena requires considerable technical sophistication on the part of user agencies because of the diversity in operating modes, model forms, and model functions. For example, the operating modes vary from manual to automated, to automated plus judgment, to automated plus judgment plus adjustments for parameter drift. Similarly, model forms vary from simple, aggregate models to families of models, to large-scale, complex models. And model functions may be able either to produce consistently reasonable forecasts or to anticipate counterintuitive outcomes. The analyst has to be able to choose the proper mode and model form for a policy problem. Moreover, the analyst must be able to "recognize which models' outputs are to be regarded as most consistently and plausibly likely, and which are designed to be ultrasensitive to possible surprises even at the risk of a worse overall record of accuracy" (Ascher and Overholt 1983:113).

Conclusion

Perhaps the real lesson from our study is that the evolution of model use depends on many factors, but the most important factors are the presence of the means to do modeling and the desire of bureaucrats and politicians to use model-generated information. This is no surprise, on the one hand, since supply and demand account for nearly everything here. But our study indicates that the most critical supply factors are primarily enabling factors. Without them, modeling cannot occur, but even when they are present, modeling still might not occur. The important demand factors seem to be dominant in the question of whether modeling will take place. If the means to develop models are not present, modeling cannot take place, regardless of a desire to use models. But powerful government interests backed up by large amounts of money can encourage and sometimes even command the development of modeling capability to serve the interests of bureaucrats and politicians. As demand for modeling grows, either to meet serious information needs for policy analysis or to take the offensive or defensive in political fights, the supply will usually grow to fill the need.

Demand for modeling has been a key to model success in the U.S. experience. Years before agencies actually had computerized planning models to generate forecasts and develop policy simulations, there was a prevailing demand among U.S. government and private organizations for improving quantitative analysis skills. When DRI assembled its service company to meet the needs of private organizations, it was well placed for the sudden and explosive growth in demand for modeling by federal agencies. The infrastructure for microsimulation modeling was nonexistent in U.S. federal agencies when a presidential commission needed a technique to help forecast demand for social services and to simulate the effects on demand of changes in welfare program rules. But an applied modeling effort was mounted to attempt to equip the organization with needed analytical techniques.

Where the means to do modeling were weak but the desire to use models strong, government agencies have heavily invested in the creation of new modeling efforts. It is likely that if government interest in using models were to wane, either because models failed to show sufficient practical utility or because they failed to retain their political potency as weapons, it is doubtful that the concerted efforts of modeling suppliers could sustain the modeling market.

We think modeling is here to stay and the use of models will continue to grow. The demand for models continues to be fed by the fact that modeling as a science and art is becoming more refined, thus resulting in models that are more likely to provide genuine analytical assistance to those locked into difficult planning situations. As long as models continue to prove their value as useful tools for planning, in the rationalistic sense of the term, their political potency as weapons in debate will remain. However, in cases where models eventually prove to be no better than guesswork, the demand for models will eventually wane and disappear because their practical and political value cannot be sustained. This brings us back to the fundamental fact that modeling technology must provide genuine practical value to its users if it is to survive and persist in use. In the end, the fate of models is not decided by the nature of model providers, or the political needs of model users. Models survive or die based on their ability to help policy analysts and policymakers choose appropriate courses of action from among many complicated alternatives. High-pressure sales tactics from modelers as well as flagrant political uses of models by politicians can catapult a model to stardom, but unless the model continues to prove its value on the hard ground of forecasting and simulation, its stardom will be short-lived indeed.

INVENTORYING PROPOSITIONS ON SUCCESSFUL MODELING

Our investigation of recent studies, surveys, and cases of implementation and utilization of computerized planning models by federal agencies makes it clear to us that these are complex, dynamic processes. Model implementation and use are subject to influence by a wide variety of factors, each of which might be important in some circumstances but not in others. Our research has revealed a modest list of propositions about the variables that seem to lead to successful model implementation and use in federal agencies.

This appendix draws together the full array of propositions we found important in our review of the literature, our in-depth case studies of the DRI and the TRIM/MATH models, and our brief encounters with other policy models. It therefore complements chapter 8, "Critical Factors in Successful Modeling." Whereas chapter 8 focused on a few factors found to be "critical" to successful modeling, this appendix presents a comprehensive array. As in chapters 1 and 8, we have grouped our discussion of the propositions into the same four clusters of factors we identified in chapters 1 and 8 as being important to successful model implementation: the general environment of policy modeling; the organizations involved in policy modeling; the characteristics of modeling technologies; and the policies adopted by modelers to facilitate model transfer.

Environmental Preconditions

Many features of the environments in which modeling takes place are important influences on the outcome of policy modeling. Our research reveals eight propositions about the preconditions for the introduction and use of policy models in federal agencies (see figure A.1).

Proposition #1: *Models based on theories that are relatively well established, stable, empirically grounded, and widely accepted by members of the discipline are implemented more broadly and more easily than new or evolving models.*

All policy models rest on some body of substantive theory about the phenomenon being modeled. The state of development of this substantive theory is important for successful implementation of a model because it affects the willingness of analysts, advisers, and policymakers who adhere to that theoretical perspective to accept, acquire, or use a model built upon that theory.

Well-established economic theories, by definition, have been researched and refined by economists for long periods of time. Macroeconomic theories based on Keynesian concepts, for example, have been around for nearly six decades. Adherents to this orthodoxy have dominated the U.S. economics community, and many have held high-level advisory positions to national policymakers. Economists in federal agencies have been trained in the Keynesian perspective, are familiar with the structural features of the major models based on Keynesian concepts, and accept these models as having a role to play in the policy analysis process. These circumstances facilitated the acceptance of macroeconomic models (such as the DRI model) in federal agencies.

Models rooted in newer economic theories have faced greater resistance by federal users. This has been the case for monetarist macroeconomic models, supply-side models, and the TRIM and MATH microsimulation models. What these models have in common is that they are all based upon theories in relatively early stages of development and are not widely accepted among economists and analysts. These

Factor	Variable
Environmental Preconditions	1. Substantive Theory
	2. Funding for Model Development and Transfer
	3. Status of Computing Technology
	4. Availability of Quality Data
	5. Predisposition to Technique
	6. Competitiveness of Organizations
	7. Flexibility of Personnel Practices
	8. Saliency of Policy Issues
Organizational Attributes	9. Organizational Type
	10. Division of Labor
	11. Identification with the Model
Modeler Organization	12. Reputation
	13. Political Neutrality
	14. Need for Analysis
	15. Fit of Model to Agency Mission
User Organization	16. Internal Resources Available for Modeling
	17. Familiarity with the Technique
	18. Existence of Cooperative Arrangements for Modeling
Features of the Technology	19. Intended Purpose of the Model: Product vs. Research
	20. Characteristics of the Data
	21. Cost of Model Acquisition and Use
	22. Nature of Model Error
	23. Maintainability of the Model
	24. Complexity of the Model
	25. Accumulation of Knowledge
Transfer Policies	26. Marketing Styles and Strategies
	27. Model Packaging
	28. Existence of Transfer Agent
	29. Pricing of Modeling Services
	30. User Groups

Figure A.1. LIST OF PROPOSITIONS ON SUCCESSFUL MODEL IMPLEMENTATION

newer models entered into routine policy analysis processes only when supporters of the associated theoretical perspectives entered into key political, advisory, or managerial positions and were willing to commit their agencies' resources to bring those models in.

Proposition #2: *Generous public funding levels, combined with noncompetitive contracting mechanisms, increase the chance that individual models will be implemented by many federal agencies.*

All computerized planning models require substantial organizational support to move from the idea stage through to implementation by users. Three dimensions of support are especially important for successful implementation: level of funding, sources of funds, and flexible mechanisms of support.

The importance of adequate funding is well illustrated by both econometric and microsimulation models. For decades, the federal government has been a principal sponsor of the economic research upon which today's major econometric models are built. This research heritage was later utilized by entrepreneurial economists who worked to build practical forecasting models. The early interest of key fiscal agencies provided the resources necessary to refine these models, and a market for the information they produce. Microsimulation modeling is newer and built on a smaller base of federal support. Although the original work was supported by private funds, the federal government supported the first attempts to transform this research model into a practical technique. HEW underwrote a costly project to revise and maintain the TRIM model and make it a practical tool for in-house use. While other agencies funded incremental additions to TRIM and MATH, they have adopted a less patronlike attitude toward the model.

The source of funding for model development and transfer also affects model implementation patterns. Private investment in designing models has led in most cases to proprietary models. Use of DRI's modeling services, built upon private venture capital, is regulated by DRI; users subscribe to DRI's services, accessing them on a day-to-day basis only through DRI's time-sharing capabilities. Apparently, as long as the modeling services are available at an affordable price and in a manner that facilitates easy use, the proprietary character of the model does not stand in the way of its implementation. In contrast, access to the publicly funded microsimulation models like TRIM and MATH is open to anyone willing to pay the nominal costs of copying either model's code.

Finally, the mechanisms used by federal agencies to acquire models also affect model implementation indirectly by helping to shape the structure of the modeling industry. Before the early 1970s, federal agencies could issue sole-source, noncompetitive contracts to private firms. When an agency wanted a service and knew of a specific organization that could provide it, it could purchase the work without offering other organizations the opportunity to bid on the job. This gave the early, applied modeling efforts the implementation advantages of previous contracts and investment, practical experience, professional reputation, and contacts with federal agencies when, in the mid-1970s, the federal government changed its procurement policies to a predominantly competitive bidding system.

Proposition #3: *Successful implementation of these models is highly dependent on stable availability and affordability of user-oriented computing systems.*

As a practical matter, large-scale models such as the TRIM, MATH, and DRI models are predicated on the availability of computing technology. Five aspects of modern computing capability play key roles in the implementation of these models: computer processing power; high-speed secondary memory capability; sophisticated systems and applications software; data communications capability; and effective policies for support of computing resources.

The advent of powerful second-generation computer processors in the mid-1960s was a major computing breakthrough affecting the development of large-scale models. These processors made it possible to run very large programs in much shorter time, thus facilitating the process of model construction and testing. The advent of third-generation interactive, time-shared computer processors further advanced model processing capability because they provided increased power at lower costs and allowed simultaneous use of processing resources by multiple users. Large third-generation computers form the technical backbone of such models as TRIM, MATH, and DRI.

The development of high-speed, random-access external memory was also essential in enabling large-scale policy modeling. All such models require large amounts of data, which are much too large to store in the computer's main memory. It is essential to have the data stored in second memory in a manner that allows very rapid recall into main memory as needed.

Sophisticated systems software and applications software are also important in modeling. Systems software includes the operating system that allocates computing resources among all the users, manages machine operations, and provides users with system utilities. Efficient operating systems are essential in providing computing power in a cost-effective manner, while the utilities enable users to accomplish their tasks. Applications software includes the programs that actually do the tasks users want done. Applications programs for modeling can be very large: DRI's Econometric Programming System contains more than 200,000 lines of instructions, while TRIM and MATH each have over 75,000 lines of instructions.

Data communications technology is necessary to allow users located away from the computer to communicate with the computer. The DRI system requires heavy use of data communications technology because remote users must rely on it to access the central DRI system located in Lexington, Massachusetts.

Finally, successful model use requires effective management of the computer resources that support the models. This is difficult, especially given large systems with many users, large data bases, and complex programs. Each component of the systems—the hardware, the software, and the data—must be maintained. Maintenance includes making repairs, upgrading the system to keep pace with technology, and extending system response to user demands for new capabilities. For all the models we studied, maintenance of the modeling software has been critical to the success of the systems.

Proposition #4: *The availability of high-quality data bases enables the successful implementation of computerized planning models by federal agencies by creating the opportunity to transform research models into more practical tools that provide information useful for policy analysis.*

Useful computerized policy models require numerous large, detailed data files describing the system being simulated. The lack of appropriate data prevents a model from leaving the experimental stage.

Time-series data on major macroeconomic variables, which have been available to researchers for decades, greatly facilitated the early development of applied econometric models. Public agencies collect thousands of regional, sectoral, and time-series data sets with usefulness for econometric modeling; a large percentage of these have been put on-line by DRI for use by its subscribers. This centralization of abundant data bases at a single location, and linked to an extensive modeling capability, increases the attractiveness of DRI's modeling services for users.

In contrast, the historical lack of disaggregated census data inhibited the practical application of experimental microsimulation models for years. Only after the Census Bureau released its raw data tapes to outside users in the late 1960s could analysts run research models with real data sets. Even so, because the collection of detailed information about individuals' attributes, attitudes, and behavior is so costly and plagued with reporting problems, relatively few large-scale household data files exist. This has dampened the implementation of microsimulation models.

Proposition #5: *A positive attitude toward technique is important for successful model implementation because it creates an environment generally supportive of the introduction and use of quantitative analytic techniques.*

Over the past several decades, numerous techniques have been developed for analyzing the characteristics of public policies. There are techniques that measure the efficacy of current programs, project the budgetary costs of program options, and estimate the economic costs and benefits of policy alternatives. This kind of information can help policymakers with evaluating policy options according to criteria they care about personally, or legitimating decisions they have made on non-technical grounds. Policymakers who find model-based information relevant or useful have been willing to invest their individual and collective resources in developing and improving these techniques, in making them accessible to policy analysts, and in institutionalizing them as part of the policymaking process.

The major policymaking institutions of the federal government exhibit a generally positive attitude toward analytic techniques. Starting in the 1960s, federal agencies began to introduce and experiment with quantitative techniques of information generation, program evaluation, and policy analysis. Policy analysis grew as an academic and professional movement. Congress bolstered its analytic capabilities in the 1970s by increasing its in-house professional staff, establishing research and analysis units, and creating a formal budget review process. As part of these trends, several agencies built and/or acquired capabilities in computerized forecasting models.

This predisposition toward technique reflects a more generalized faith among Americans in the ability to solve social problems through the application of technical knowledge. Public attitudes strongly favored science and technology during the 1960s, and although there was some erosion of confidence in technical experts and professionals during the 1970s, faith in technique has remained strong. These conditions have helped create a policymaking environment generally receptive to expertise, analysis, and quantitative date, and to techniques and processes that endow policymaking institutions with these resources.

Proposition #6: *Competition among the organizations engaged in policymaking and the modeling process aids in successful model im-*

plementation because competitive relationships provide strong incentives for the participants to engage in politically useful activities, such as analysis and modeling.

Competition among policymaking institutions and groups enhances successful model implementation by making it politically attractive for organizations to engage in modeling and to seek to control the dissemination of a model's results. Models can generate politically relevant information about policy issues over which organizations disagree. Results produced by models are not only used by organizations for internal analysis and informational purposes, but also in partisan policy battles with opponents in the other party, or in rival agencies or branches of the government.

By design, the institutions of the U.S. federal government compete for political power. Political competition takes many forms: institutional competition between the legislative and executive branches; interdepartmental competition among executive agencies; and partisan competition among parties and among interest groups. All of these forms of competition can affect the processes through which federal agencies implement models.

With respect to institutional competition, our research showed economic modeling began at different times in the executive and legislative branches. Executive agencies, which historically have been the primary locus of collection and analysis of detailed information on national economy and on federal programs, were early adopters of commercial macroeconomic models and microsimulation models in the early 1970s. Several years later, Congress took steps to enhance its informational and analytic capabilities, partly in an attempt to correct a perceived imbalance of information-based power vis-à-vis the executive branch. The establishment of the CBO in 1974 institutionalized the congressional role in analysis, and facilitated the acquisition of DRI's modeling services and the MATH and TRIM models.

Interdepartmental relations also affect agencies' efforts to implement these models. Among agencies engaged in income-security policy, HEW has traditionally been the lead administrative unit; it was also the first to acquire microsimulation modeling capabilities. Other federal agencies with jurisdiction over income-transfer programs (e.g., USDA's FNS over the food stamp program, DOL over employment-related programs) have also used microsimulation models to give themselves analytic independence from HEW.

Partisan competition also affects model implementation. Republicans in the House and Senate insisted that CBO carefully scrutinize the cost figures attached to the Carter administration's welfare reform proposals. With 1981's change to a Republican majority in the Senate and to a Republican administration, traditional Keynesian macroeconomic models began to lose favor after the influx of "supply-side" economists and their models.

Highly competitive political situations increase examples of what we call counter-modeling, advocacy modeling, and accountability modeling. When only one political group has a sophisticated number-generation capability, this group's numbers have the advantage of being exclusive and therefore "authoritative." The other side has an interest in obtaining some modeling capacity: either the same model in order to monitor the information available to the other party or to check the accuracy of the estimates, or a different model in order to challenge the authoritativeness of the other side's numbers. This desire to ensure that rival agencies do not hold a monopoly on sophisticated analytical capability has helped to institutionalize modeling in federal agencies.

While political competition affects the demand for models, economic competition among modelers stimulates implementation by increasing the supply of available models. The DRI, TRIM, and MATH models have historically dominated their respective industries, enjoying substantial market success. DRI was the first commercial econometrics venture and remained the sole supplier of commercial services for several years, establishing a lead over prospective competitors in the field. DRI's early position as supplier to the key policy agencies gave it a decided market advantage. Similarly, Mathematica Policy Research (MPR) and the Urban Institute have operated in a rather noncompetitive microsimulation industry. Although publicly funded and thus available for use by potential competitors, both MATH and TRIM are large, complex models requiring enormous investments in personnel training to use them efficiently. Later on the initial set of model designers, operators, and analysts had the advantage of knowledge, experience, and contacts with users. This meant market success first for the Urban Institute, and later for MPR, when the modelers switched organizations in the mid-seventies. As the pool of model specialists has slowly expanded, the possibility for market competition has also grown, and by 1981, several well-connected TRIM/MATH analysts had opened new, competing firms.

Proposition #7: *The successful implementation of complex models is enhanced where user and modeler agencies allow lateral movement* *of model specialists between modeler and user agencies and across user organizations.*

Flexible personnel practices facilitate successful model implementation because they help potential user agencies to rapidly overcome the significant technical obstacles to model use. MATH and TRIM model users who had not been personally involved in designing those models needed two years to understand them well enough to use them independently. This long learning time stands as an impediment to new user agencies. In some cases, agencies initially had to use MATH out-of-house because they lacked the necessary time to fully implement the model before they needed results. Other agencies overcame the time obstacle by hiring knowledgeable personnel laterally, either from a modeling firm or from another agency that already used the model. In DRI's case, even the built-in advantages of widespread econometric training of economists and user-oriented DRI software did not mitigate the need to have "experts" in model-using agencies. Familiarity with the model is essential to being able to use it rapidly and effectively in complicated policy analyses.

In addition to shortening the model-learning time, lateral hiring practices often lead to a movement of experienced personnel who are committed to using a particular model into an agency which has not yet made a decision to implement that model. This familiarity with and support for a given model can lead to a new location of model use. Flexible personnel practices create an organizational environment hospitable to the mechanism of model implementation we call "personal transfer."

Proposition #8: *The political saliency of policy areas influences successful model implementation by shaping the demands and resources of federal policymaking agencies for information and analysis about specific issues.*

High political interest in an issue to which model-based analysis can be applied enhances successful implementation by increasing policymakers' willingness to invest in modeling, in the hope that model results will help resolve the issue or at least quiet the controversy attached to it. The more salient an issue, the greater the demands of policymakers for information about what is happening in the problem area, who is being affected, and who is likely to be affected by policy changes.

Political saliency varies in intensity for distinct policy issues over time and across policy issues at any given time. Fiscal policy, for example, has high saliency in the federal government year after year. Preparation and approval of the annual federal budget takes place through an almost continuous budget process in which groups likely to be affected by the budget's size and composition move into and out of the political fray. There has long been a strong interest in upgrading the informational and analytic capabilities of the federal budgetary process, and macroeconomic modeling has been an important feature in those upgrades.

Political interest in other policy areas, such as social programs or environmental policy, waxes and wanes. Here, the level of political interest and policymaking activity depends upon changes in social, economic, or physical conditions, with crises often leading to high political interest and active attention. The provision of resources for welfare policy models, such as the RIM model or its redesign as TRIM, came episodically during periods of high political interest in reforming income-transfer programs. Revision of TRIM to incorporate new policy areas, such as development of the food stamp module or labor component for MATH, occurred incrementally at times of high political interest in those issues and programs.

Organizational Attributes

Our research suggests that a number of features of organizations affect the successful transfer and use of computerized planning models by federal agencies. Organizational variables are those structural and behavioral attributes of modeler and user organizations which influence whether any particular model will be implemented successfully by the user agency.

We have identified ten organizational variables that relate to successful model implementation (see figure A.1). Five variables are associated with modeler organizations and five are associated with the user agency.

FEATURES OF MODELER ORGANIZATIONS

Model developers and vendors differ according to their organizational structures, products, reputation, clientele, and market success.

Several of these characteristics influence the ways in which modelers interact with potential model users and the ways in which users implement their models.

Proposition #9: *Commercial modelers experience greater success than nonprofit modelers in implementing their models in user agencies.*

Modeler organizations are either private, for-profit firms or nonprofit (public or private) groups. Their status affects their incentives and the strategies they adopt to transfer their model to outside users. For-profit, private firms have a clear financial interest in finding consumers for their product or services. Commercial status necessitates the creation of strategies for determining the market demand for models and modeling services, designing products to fit the needs of potential model users, and marketing modeling wares to specific clients—all of which enhance model transfer.

The two private vendors we studied (DRI and MPR) both exhibited such strategic behavior. Each adapted its services and products over the years to respond to changing environmental conditions (e.g., political interest in different policy areas or growth of competition from other modelers). Both attempted to build into their products and services features that make them unique among their competitors: DRI carefully packaged its time-sharing and modeling capabilities with extensive data resources and consulting services; MPR established a subscription service for its model. Both firms have pursued internal policies to give employees a stake in their company's success. Early on, the principals at DRI could acquire company stock, and at MPR, many employees participate in a profit-sharing program.

We also found that several not-for-profit organizations have also succeeded in developing models for use by federal agencies. These organizations include: private, nonprofit research groups, such as the Urban Institute (TRIM model) and the Brookings Institution (SSRC/Brookings model); a public advisory task force, the President's Commission on Income Maintenance Programs (RIM model); and research units in public agencies, such as the Fed's Division of Research and Statistics (MPS model), HEW's Office of the Assistant Secretary for Planning and Evaluation (KGB model), and Treasury's Office of Tax Analysis (PITM model).

Although these organizations are not a homogeneous lot, their nonprofit status distinguishes them from commercial firms in terms of their goals, incentives, and orientation toward promoting their models. The primary goals of applied research institutes are to foster their members' contributions to the production of knowledge and to enhance the professional reputations of the organization and its researchers. These goals orient the organizations toward developing and refining techniques useful for problem solving. They promote their products through publishing books and articles and preparing reports for agencies that sponsor their research. They tend to develop models for general usefulness, rather than specific applications. This sometimes creates a mismatch between the services provided and actual needs.

Modelers in research units of mission-oriented public agencies, like those in private firms, work to develop models for actual use in policy simulation and forecasting. But unlike private firms, agency research units target their model development to narrow, highly specific applications. They design their model exclusively for in-house use, change it continually during its operational period to fit evolving organizational demands, and rarely publicize, document, or release it for outside use.

Proposition #10: *Modeler organizations that have personnel and practices specialized in transfer function are more successful than non-specialized organizations in transferring their models to user agencies.*

Because of the complexity of the model-designing, -building, -operating, -marketing, and -training tasks, no single individual can do all that is required. All modeler groups interested in effectively transferring their products or services must divide their labor to deal with these varied tasks. Modeler organizations that are structured for model transfer can offer users full-time attention to user-oriented activities, including marketing, training, continuity of service, and assisting in model operations and applications. In comparison, modeling organizations without this specialization have less experienced, less knowledgeable, and less efficient transfer operations, and are less successful in implementing their models among users.

Two modeling organizations in our study have deliberately created user-oriented organizational structures. DRI's Washington, D.C., office was established specifically to solicit and service federal government users. DRI employs a team approach for handling clusters of federal clients. Teams of consultants, knowledgeable in economic analysis and the technical aspects of the DRI service package, work with users in the executive branch. Another team services clients on Capitol Hill. DRI bases this approach on the assumptions that clusters of users share certain attributes (procurement practices, informational resources, and political or institutional perspective) that are relevant for their acquisition and utilization of models, and that DRI can better handle user needs through a specialization of function. MPR also has a user-oriented organizational structure, although on a smaller scale. One individual at MPR is responsible for maintaining communications between modelers and users, servicing users' technical needs, handling training, and monitoring users' application of and changes in the model.

None of the other modeler organizations we studied have specialized in the transfer function.

Proposition #11: *Strong organizational identification with a model increases the organization's efforts to promote and successfully implement the model.*

All modeling organizations produce a set of goods and services, of which perhaps only a portion relate to policy modeling. Firms whose activities are concentrated around a single product (i.e., a model and its related services) tend to identify strongly with that product, for it provides a significant share of the firm's work. In such cases, the organization's reputation depends upon the quality of the modeling enterprise and the performance of key staff who have a strong personal attachment to the model. Firms with strong identification with their models depend upon the successful transfer of their models for their commercial or professional survival and invest in activities geared toward model transfer.

In our study, the organizations with widely implemented models identify strongly with their models and related services. DRI was built around a modeling enterprise that has remained a focal point of the organization's activities. The Washington office of MPR was founded by former TRIM developers who wanted to rebuild the model in a new organizational setting more aggressively geared toward selling the model to users. By contrast, the Urban Institute has weaker organizational attachment to the TRIM model, which has been transferred to only a handful of federal agencies. For the institute as a whole, TRIM has accounted for a relatively small share of the organization's work, revenues, and reputation.

Proposition #12: *For modelers offering computerized policy models, success in implementing their models among federal users depends upon having built a reputation based on both the technical and* *professional reputation of individual modelers in the organization, and the ability of the organization to service user needs in a businesslike manner.*

A modeler's reputation strongly influences users' willingness to adopt and use a particular model. Computerized economic planning models such as MATH and the DRI model are politically useful, but they are also expensive and technically complex. Few policy analysts can evaluate the technical quality of the models or the modelers who built them without having worked with the models extensively. Potential users need a way to choose among models and modelers, and price alone frequently is considered an inappropriate or insufficient criterion for selection. The professional reputation of a modeler organization or its modelers is sometimes a useful indicator of the quality of the expertise available for hire. Also, because users have to depend upon modelers to explain the model, operate it, and interpret its results during intitial phases of the implementation process, users will choose modeler organizations with a strong user-oriented reputation in hopes of facilitating the learning and communications processes. Finally, users who want models to produce numbers with potential political usefulness also want their models to be associated with authoritative modelers who have high status in the segment of the political community of interest to those users.

All of the modeling organizations involved in our study have enjoyed good reputations, although the sources of their status have varied considerably. DRI has established a strong reputation as a technically competent, businesslike firm whose model package is widely used. DRI's reputation was originally founded on the names of its two principal economists, both of whom were respected in the economics community and well connected to the policy community. DRI's early success at selling its services also made it possible for DRI to develop a track record impressive to subsequent users. The fact that "everybody who was anybody" used DRI services enhanced its reputation greatly.

Both MPR and the Urban Institute also enjoy solid professional reputations, but based on different strengths. The Urban Institute's reputation as an innovative developer of policy models was established in the early 1970s when the principal economists concerned with practical applications of this technique converged there to work on the TRIM project. The institute's reputation in this particular area proved to be fragile, however, depending as it did on whoever was working at the institute at the moment. When several key microsimulation personnel left to go to MPR, they took their status with them. MPR's reputation as a progressive microsimulation organization was further enhanced by its orientation toward serving client needs.

    Proposition #13: *Model developers that maintain political neutrality with regard to the policy issues their models are used to analyze are likely to experience wider acceptance and use of their models in sensitive policy analyses.*

    All of the models we studied were developed and/or used in highly political environments. The cases illustrate that the taking of strong political stands by a model developer can destroy clients' trust in the models, and in some cases weakens client support for sophisticated analytical instruments in general.

    In the TRIM/MATH cases, both the Urban Institute and MPR generally restricted themselves to pure analytic positions with respect to sensitive issues and tried to avoid controversy. The institute even declined to do work for the legislative branch, since its primary clients were in the executive branch. MPR was more aggressive: it marketed to both branches and did not attempt to restrict the use of its model, but it usually abstained from advocating policy positions.

    One exception to this code of conduct occurred when, during the food stamp debate, Jodie Allen from MPR wrote a strong editorial on the food stamp program in the *Washington Post.* The ensuing controversy was damaging for both MPR and for its model. MATH users began to fear that MPR's analyses might be influenced by the opinions of MPR staffers, and the MATH model itself came under suspicion as a model with a liberal bias. GAO was asked to investigate the models. MPR had to make a concerted effort to "prove" to its clients that the model itself was neutral. Allen herself never changed her position on food stamps, but she did acknowledge that her deviation from political neutrality was a real problem for the model, and that, as a rule, modelers ought not to take political stands on issues for which they conduct analyses.

    In the DRI case, the model and its outputs have become something of a political issue in themselves. DRI's economic outlooks, like those of other major macroeconomic forecasters, are regularly cited in the news media, and forecasters have become institutionalized in the public discussion of economic policy. Thus, in one sense, the macroeconomic modelers are indirectly involved in the politically sensitive process of making economic opinion and policy. However, the behavior of macroeconomic modelers tends toward political neutrality. The nonpartisanship of the major Keynesian macroeconomists came into question only briefly when, after the 1980 national elections, a new group of supply-side economists, modelers, and models (e.g., the Claremont model) came into favor by the Reagan administration. The other major modelers subsequently attempted to depoliticize their models by promising to incorporate aspects of the newly powerful political/economic ideology into their modeling packages.

FEATURES OF USER ORGANIZATIONS

Like modeler organizations, user organizations differ along a number of dimensions which affect decisions to acquire models and the success of model implementation efforts. Our research suggests there is a strong relationship between the broad characteristic of user demand for modeling and how a model was acquired and used in policymaking. This concept of "demand pull" reflects the extent to which a user agency wants to use modeling and is willing to acquire the means necessary to do so. The five factors described below (propositions #14–18) relate to this user demand.

Proposition #14: *Agencies with a strong need for policy analysis show a relatively high interest in implementing innovative analytic techniques such as models. They adopt them sooner, experience less resistance to implementing them, and use them more extensively, as compared with other agencies.*

Federal agencies vary in their perception of the need for conducting policy analysis. Some have analysis as their central purpose. Others engage in analysis in order to achieve other organizational objectives, such as providing advice, preparing programmatic budgets, forecasting economic conditions, or analyzing impacts of program reforms. Others do little policy analysis at all. In our study, the agencies that implemented and used computerized planning models most regularly and routinely were ones in which analysis was a central organizational purpose, or was essential to accomplishing organizational objectives.

Most of the agencies centrally involved in national economic planning maintain sophisticated research and analysis units. These agencies include the Fed, CBO, and the Troika agencies (OMB, CEA, and Treasury). Models play a vital role in these agencies by providing information to policymakers either directly, in the form of model results, or indirectly, as input to the forecasts of judgmental economists within the agency. In the income-support policy area, two agencies play a central role in providing policy analysis. These two—HEW and CBO— took the lead in acquiring models and utilizing them for policy design and evaluation.

Most other federal agencies lack the central organizational mandate to conduct policy analysis on these issues, but many routinely prepare them on specific programs, and sporadically when issues under their jurisdiction become critical problems. These agencies use computerized planning models with less regularity, less sophistication, and less resource support than agencies with central analytic missions.

Proposition #15: *Key agencies in a substantive policy area have a relatively strong technical rationale for acquiring information about that particular area and for implementing methodologies to provide such information. Lead agencies provide strong support for development and implementation of appropriate models compared with secondary agencies, which may implement the same model at a later time.*

The technical appropriateness of a given model to a federal agency depends upon the fit of the system being simulated in the model and the substantive mission of the agency. The first agencies to implement a particular model are ones where there is a good fit. Subsequent adopters tend to be agencies where the fit is poorer but where there are interlocking programmatic ties or turf battles with the lead agencies in that policy area.

In our study, federal agencies tended to implement models in this sequence. Among the large number of agencies that currently use macroeconomic models of the U.S. economy, only a handful play a central role in analyzing fiscal or monetary policy. These agencies were among the earliest to adopt and use the major macroeconomic models. Many other agencies now also use these models, but they implemented the models later and they tend to use them primarily to keep abreast of the information available to the central fiscal and monetary policy agencies. This implementation pattern roughly parallels that of the microsimulation models.

Proposition #16: *Relatively generous internal organizational support for analytic, modeling, and computing activities is related to successful implementation of computerized planning models in federal agencies.*

Successful model implementation requires that agencies provide sufficient budgetary resources to procure and support a model. Commitment of extensive internal resources better enables an agency to implement the model efficiently and to conduct independent, competent, and timely analyses. Agencies unable to provide adequate resources for modeling implement the models less successfully; they often have to rely on outside consultants to revise and operate the models, to perform analyses, and sometimes even to interpret model results. Modeling in these settings tends to be sporadic and time consuming, which reduces the usefulness of modeling to these agencies.

Several agencies in our study provided relatively high levels of internal support for modeling. These agencies were the Fed and the Troika agencies (for macroeconomic models), HEW (for microsimulation models), and CBO (for both types of models). Each of these agencies actively uses models, maintains extensive computing resources, and employs highly skilled personnel who understand the technical features of the models they use. The other agencies we studied provide little or no internal resources for policy modeling, and modeling failed to become institutionalized in the agencies.

Proposition #17: *Agencies with employees who are relatively familiar with models experience greater demand for model acquisition and use than agencies whose staffs are less educated or experienced in modeling.*

Educated or experienced analysts know what models do, how they operate, and how they can fit into the policy analysis process. Among agencies without models, those with analysts or managers who are relatively knowledgeable and supportive of modeling tend to identify a place for modeling within their agency, to seek support for model acquisition, to undertake a search for a specific model to adopt, and to attempt to smoothly implement the model so that they can actually use it.

We found that among users of macroeconomic models, the earliest major adopters were the Troika agencies, which have traditionally drawn their professional staffs from the nation's top graduate programs in economics. These economists come to their jobs with a general understanding of macroeconomic models, and after a period of time on the job, they are able to identify ways in which forecasting and policy simulation can assist them in their work. These young managers and analysts tend to believe in the usefulness of quantitative methods for policy analysis, and these attitudes have stimulated a demand for bringing modeling capabilities in-house.

For microsimulation models also, staffers' familiarity with modeling influenced successful model transfer. Because few universities have offered graduate training in microsimulation modeling, the economists and analysts skilled in microsimulation have had to gain their knowledge through participating in the actual development of the technique for practical policy work, or through observing the involvement of these models in recent policy debates.

Proposition #18: *The existence of cooperative arrangements for modeling among user agencies helps to promote successful model implementation.*

Many federal agencies acquire and utilize computerized planning models in cooperation with other agencies with similar institutional objectives or modeling needs. Cooperation can involve sharing the costs of developing and maintaining models and data bases, centralizing computing facilities, and exchanging information about model results or modeling difficulties. Congressional users have been particularly successful in using common modeling contracts. All users on Capitol Hill have a blanket contract with DRI. Congressional users of MATH share a common contract.

Features of the Technology

Computerized models are complicated technologies that place heavy technical demands on organizations interested in acquiring and using them effectively. Models vary immensely, and some of these differences affect how successfully they will be implemented. Five attributes of the modeling technology seem to affect the implementation process (see figure A.1).

Proposition #19: *Models designed explicitly for transfer and use, and offered as a packaged product, are transferred more successfully by federal agencies than models designed for research purposes or for one-shot analyses.*

Models are designed for a variety of purposes. The ones we call "research models" are built for the direct, personal use of the modelers rather than for use by outside policy analysts. The primary purpose of research models is to advance the development of theory and the state of the modeling art. In contrast, "product models" are produced expressly for policy applications and for ongoing use by various organizations.

The presence or absence of certain attributes is what classifies any individual model as a pure product or pure research model. (Models actually fall along a continuum, and may combine features of both types. For these mixed breeds, implementation is facilitated to the extent that they resemble product models.) Product models are deliberately designed for practical applications; are based on well-established theory; are well documented; employ "user-friendly" software; are available as a package of products and services (e.g., the basic model, data bases, documentation, training); and are well publicized and promoted through scholarly journals, advertisements, conferences, and personal marketing calls. Research models lack these attributes and are noted for being associated with methodological research and theory development; having a continuously evolving structure; having poor (if any) documentation; lacking an organized package of services to accompany the model if and when it is acquired by outsiders; and being publicized principally via scholarly journals and academic conferences. Product models experience greater success in being implemented by federal agencies because, in short, their designers have paid serious attention to the practical requirements of model use.

The product versus research-model distinction, when used to classify the models in our study, also tends to distinguish the successfully implemented models from the poorly implemented ones. The DRI model is a nearly perfect example of a pure product model. MPR's MATH model comes close to it, especially after the subscription service was started in 1976. Its predecessor, TRIM, and the two other commercial econometric models (the Chase and Wharton models) are hybrids, with a mixture of features from the product- and research-model categories. Three other models—the St. Louis Fed model, the RIM model, and HEW's KGB model—most closely resemble the research type, although none fits it perfectly.

These differences in features and intended purposes of the models somewhat parallel the variations in their implementation successes. DRI clearly dominates federal usage of macroeconomic models. The Chase and Wharton models are also widely implemented among federal agencies, but not to the extent of DRI. Few agencies have adopted the St. Louis Feds model. MATH is the most widely implemented among the microsimulation models, with every agency that conducts microsimulation analysis having used it at one time or another. By contrast, TRIM has been implemented only at HEW and CBO. The KGB model was developed within and used by HEW's ASPE office, although it was used for a short time by DOL but never formally transferred to it.

Proposition #20: *Models that are accompanied by relatively high-quality data, measured specially in terms of users' belief in the quality of the data, experience greater implementation success than models with poor-quality data bases.*

All computerized planning models run on large data bases, which vary not only in their technical quality but also in terms of potential users' perceptions of the quality of the data. Analysts adopt such models for forecasting or policy simulations with the expectation that the models will provide valid information about the population or phenomenon they are analyzing. Models that come with good data have an implementation advantage because analysts expect such models to yield fewer errors in analysis situations.

Among the agencies we studied, users' attitudes toward data quality varied by model type. Among macroeconomic modelers, DRI has historically provided an enormous inventory of data sets to its clients and organized them for easy, efficient use by its subscribers. Many federal users report that the primary reason they subscribe to the DRI model is to obtain access to its abundant, centralized data resources.

Microdata are conceptually clearer and simpler than national income data and more easily understood because they refer to individual characteristics that can easily be observed. Still, users admit that microdata sets impose considerable problems on users. First, these data sets are very large and unwieldy. Second, in many cases survey data are already out of date when they become available. Third, it is often necessary to merge two or more different microdata sets to get a file that is useful for the intended analysis.

Proposition #21: *High costs of model acquisition impede model transfer, and high costs of model maintenance and use can undermine successful model implementation.*

From the perspective of initial model transfer, the relevant model implementation costs are the agency's direct costs of acquiring and transferring the model for its own use. But ongoing model use depends heavily on the costs of maintaining, operating, and revising the model over time. All other things being equal, high costs of model acquisition impede successful model transfer because they stand as a large capital-expenditure barrier which must be justified and appropriated before an organization obtains the model. Similarly, high costs of fully implementing the model undermine successful routinization and use over time. When ongoing costs are high, use of the model tends to be limited to analyzing only truly critical problems. This in turn decreases users' familiarity with model operation, increases the average cost of model runs, and reduces the economic benefit-to-cost ratio of modeling—making it difficult for management to justify model support.

The models we studied tend to be expensive to implement. All of the major macroeconomic models, including DRI, Chase, and Wharton, are commercial, proprietary models with restricted access to outside users. The rates charged by DRI are substantial, although federal users consider them to be fair compared with what DRI's major competitors charge and what it would cost users to provide equivalent capabilities on their own. DRI has also managed to keep its price down by offering blanket contracts to clusters of federal agency customers. This gives such customers access to the basic services for a relatively low fee, with each agency paying the marginal costs of its own use of the modeling, data, and consulting services.

The cost to users of gaining basic access to the major microsimulation models is remarkably low. MATH and TRIM were developed with public funds and can be obtained for a nominal fee. However, the total cost of implementing these models is quite high because of the expense associated with learning to use the models effectively. Inexperienced users of MATH or TRIM reported that it took them two to three years to become sufficiently competent in understanding the model to fully allow in-house operation and interpretation of model results. To avoid this long lead time, many agencies have hired employees already familiar with the models, thus taking advantage of "personal transfer."

Agencies wanting to use microsimulation routinely face another cost hurdle: these models are usually expensive to operate. Each one depends on an enormous data file which must be read, reduced, reformatted, aged, and then reread during a single policy simulation. MATH users report that machine costs range from $600 to $1,500 for a partial run (1980 dollars) and more than $3,000 for a full model run using a large data file. TRIM is cheaper to run ($300 to $500 for a partial run, up to $2,400 for the most costly simulation), because HEW financed a six-year project costing over $600,000 to rewrite the more inefficient portions of the model's programs. These high operating costs limit agencies' use of these models generally, making it worthwhile to run the models extensively only during times of high interest in welfare policy reform.

Cost appears to be a relative factor in model implementation and use, dependent on the perceived criticality of the issue being analyzed. The greater the saliency of an issue, the less important cost becomes in the decision to use a model in policy analysis. Policy analysis related to economic policy and to big-ticket budget items, such as income-transfer programs, confronts analysts with policy cost consequences that dwarf the costs of modeling. A policy decision to alter food stamp eligibility requirements can result in increases or decreases of hundreds of millions of dollars in the federal coffers. It is understandable that most analysts in policymaking agencies consider the task of improving policy analysis more important than keeping down costs in the use of analytic tools.

Proposition #22: *Models with low or unknown errors in prediction experience greater implementation success than models perceived to have high levels of errors.*

Since computerized simulation models are simplified, mathematical representations of complex systems, they all are likely to produce results that conflict with reality. Models vary in the size and composition of their error terms and, in the context of model use, in terms of users' perceptions about the significance of those errors. Models with a reputation for low rates of predictive error realize greater implementation success than models perceived to have high error rates.

All of the models in our case studies have experienced prediction problems at one time or another. None of the major macroeconomic models anticipated the drastic 1973 oil price increases, and confidence in their predictive power suffered as a result. Such problems led many agencies to perceive the practical and political importance of diversifying the information provided to them. Generally, they expanded their acquisitions of both model forecasts and of judgmental forecasts.

Microsimulation models are notorious for producing estimates that differ from reality, although it is difficult to determine the exact degree of error or why the error occurs. Microsimulation models are of more recent vintage and have been run less frequently than their macroeconomic brethren. They have been used to estimate the effects of changes in income-transfer programs, either as part of the routine budget preparation process or, more commonly, as part of the periodic program reform efforts. Because of this focus on routine policy analysis, microsimulation modeling has not built up a detailed, longitudinal forecasting record that could be carefully analyzed.

Proposition #23: *Models that have well-developed maintenance procedures and an organizational commitment to maintenance will be implemented more easily and will stand a greater chance of survival in use.*

The high cost of system maintenance seems yet to be fully recognized for large-scale computerized models. These models are enormous: TRIM and MATH each have about 75,000 lines of service code; and DRI's macroeconomic model depends for its operation on the EPS system consisting of over 200,000 lines of code. These models also undergo frequent change as a result of alterations in underlying hardware and user requirements. There is a continual need to adapt the data base to the next available source of data. Further, many details in the models' structures often need to be changed because of changes in the conditions being forecast or simulated. All developers and users must find some way to maintain their models, or even a relatively good model will become nearly useless within a short time. All the models studied here met the challenge of maintenance through one means or another.

The TRIM modelers at the Urban Institute received extensive maintenance support from HEW over a six-year period. Despite this substantial support, the institute had to use funds from other institute contracts to maintain TRIM. The MATH developers faced similar problems but found different solutions. They thoroughly redeveloped the model to decrease its maintenance demands and offered the model on a subscription basis in an attempt to obtain adequate revenues for maintenance tasks.

Maintenance of the DRI model is extremely costly. The model is updated in minor and major ways every month by a group of econometricians, software people, and senior DRI economists. DRI has always been able to afford these high maintenance costs because of two mechanisms. First is its package of service offerings, which has made it possible to occasionally subsidize maintenance costs by profits from the other services. Second, DRI marketed subscriptions to its model.

The clientele for these subscriptions is large, which has made it possible for DRI to charge relatively low subscription rates.

Proposition #24: *Highly complex modeling systems present barriers to users that impede their successful implementation by outside organizations.*

Models that simulate social or economic phenomena tend to be complex systems, capable of analyzing large disaggregated data bases containing numerous interrelated variables. One reason many analysts seek the aid of computerized analytic tools is that computers can quickly analyze many variables and process enormous data sets more efficiently than individuals making the calculations by hand, and in many cases they offer capabilities for analysis that would otherwise be impossible. Complex computerized systems also carry an aura of authority that mortal analysts sometimes lack, which is an attractive feature to some users. Yet the very power of such systems can impede their implementation success when they are so complicated that they require large start-up costs before analysts can ever actually use them.

This latter sense of the term "complexity" primarily refers to the practical difficulties which confront a user when actually conducting analysis, and not necessarily the intellectual or technical complexity of the modeling technique. The DRI and TRIM/MATH models are both intellectually and technically complex, but they differ considerably in terms of the complexity users face when using them. This is the type of complexity that impedes model implementation.

The DRI macroeconomic model is a large, highly integrated modeling system backed by software systems that have been designed to reduce the complexity of model use by providing extensive "front end" assistance to the user in the form of a fairly straightforward, "user-friendly" set of computing routines that call into action the larger components of the system. Thus, the highly complex DRI system has been engineered to appear relatively simple to the user. In fact, users repeatedly reported to us that a major selling feature of DRI is its ease of use.

TRIM and MATH lack the elegant "front-end" software systems available to DRI users; users must personally see to many kinds of details that are taken care of for DRI users by the software. And the size and complexity of TRIM and MATH (100,000 to 150,000 lines of source code) make it impossible for novices to understand their structure, assumptions, and operations. Therefore, agencies must hire experienced TRIM or MATH operators, designers, or users away from other agencies or wait two to three years for novices to learn to use the systems.

This difference between the DRI model and the TRIM and MATH models illustrates an important aspect of implementing complex model systems. Potential users need to see results soon after acquiring a model or they will be unable to sustain investment in it. Recognizing this problem early on, DRI designed its systems to be simple for users. The investment in these systems was considerable, but it paid off by facilitating widespread adoption of the DRI system. Resource constraints at the Urban Institute and Mathematica Policy Research precluded investments of the kind made by DRI, so alternative means of expediting user acquisition of modeling capability had to be used. One means was the refinement of the TRIM and MATH software so that it was more easily employed by an experienced user. The other means exploited by MPR but not the institute was the institution of a variety of services (e.g., documentation, user guides, and training) to help users gain a more rapid understanding of the system. This strategy seems to have given MATH an implementation advantage over TRIM.

Proposition #25: *Modeling efforts that have the ability to accumulate and maintain knowledge relevant to modeling are relatively likely to achieve success.*

Modeling is a sophisticated technology, demanding for both modelers and users. It requires the accumulation of knowledge not just in the brains of experienced modelers but also embedded in the models themselves. During the continual process of model evolution and refinement, faulty specifications and other problems are replaced by improvements, and new features may be added to meet user requirements. In econometrics, such refinement procedures have become something of a professional standard, and all the micromodels we studied have experienced similar pressures. Thereby, the models themselves become embodiments of knowledge, and the whole package of models, people, and service infrastructure represents a very substantial accumulation of knowledge.

Transfer Policies

Not all computerized planning models succeed in being used outside the organizations where they were created. Some were never intended for outside use or never publicized in such a way as to inform outsiders of their utility. Others intended for policy analysis have failed because they do not incorporate design features that make them truly transferable. Still others fail because conditions in the implementation environment change, and a model that once seemed a worthwhile investment never actually gets incorporated because of the withdrawal of the resources needed to use it effectively.

Many models succeed, however, and federal agencies have implemented a wide variety of econometric and microsimulation models over the past decade. We discovered in our case studies that successful model implementation can be facilitated by a set of decisions and practices, made by modelers and users alike, that are intended to aid the transfer and use of the models. We call these decisions and practices "transfer policies." We have defined six transfer-policy variables that seem important to the success or failure of model implementation. (see figure A.1.)

Proposition #26: *Modelers experience greater success in implementing their models when they deliberately market their products and services.*

Decisions about marketing strategies influence model implementation. Modelers who actively publicize their models through standard advertising techniques experience greater implementation success than those who promote their models in more passive ways, such as through articles in scholarly journals or in responses to agency requests for proposals. Successful model promoters carefully target their publicity and marketing efforts by identifying, courting, and gaining support from individuals in potential user organizations whose jobs could be enhanced through access to a modeling capability. Finally, modelers are more successful in marketing their models when they encourage "personal transfer" in the form of lateral movement of their employees into and out of potential or actual user organizations. All three techniques improve the network of personal contacts between the modelers and agencies, enhance modelers' knowledge of users' needs, and make it more likely that the modeler can design useful and usable products.

In our study, the most successfully transferred macroeconomic and microsimulation models were those offered by private, commercial modeling firms that engaged in aggressive marketing programs. DRI, the exemplar in this respect, has used a combination of marketing techniques to build a clientele for its services and products. DRI has a marketing division whose activities include sales brochures, publications, press releases, media events, conferences, contract proposals, and direct marketing calls. DRI's name regularly appears in the media. Many of DRI's employees have previous federal agency experience, and many former DRI economists now work in user agencies. DRI's major econometric competitors use less aggressive marketing strategies, and are generally less well known than DRI.

Like DRI, MPR stands out as the most active and most successful promoter of its type of model. While MPR has a less centralized marketing effort, MPR publicizes its work through brochures, conferences, workshops, contract proposals, scholarly articles and books, and direct marketing calls. Many of MPR's principals have previous agency experience and therefore have many contacts and an orientation toward designing services and products useful to agency clients. The movement of analysts between modeler and user agencies also has created a wide network of individuals who are aware of the MATH model and a core group of knowledgeables who are supportive of using MATH. This personal transfer also helps lessen the high start-up costs agencies face in beginning to use MATH, thereby increasing the chances that an agency will actually implement the model.

MPR's major competitor, the Urban Institute, is not a commercial firm. Its main methods of promoting TRIM are papers, scholarly publications, and research proposals. The institute also allows personal transfer but has not encouraged it actively, and personnel shifts have only occured between the Urban Institute and HEW. The institute has been less successful than MPR in implementing its model in other agencies.

Proposition #27: *The policy of a modeler to produce and package a set of goods and services for sale to outside customers aids in successful transfer and implementation.*

Modelers decide whether to conduct research, to produce a product, to perform a service, or to do some combination of all three. One outcome of such a decision—the production of a model that is an experimental technique or a practical tool—is related to implementation success: product models are implemented more successfully than research models.

DRI and MPR have both adopted model-packaging policies. DRI's early decision to combine a diverse array of modeling and data capabilities into an organized package was truly innovative. From DRI's inception, its founders foresaw a potential market for a ready-to-use, commercial forecasting product accompanied by a comprehensive set of supporting services. This package would be both standardized and personalized at the same time: a combination of DRI-generated economic forecasts, user-controlled forecasting and simulation capabilities, extensive centralized data resources, and personalized economic consultation. The package would be designed for ease and efficiency of use. Apparently, DRI analyzed the market well. Federal users were indeed willing to purchase a comprehensive package of goods and services from DRI.

Although not as extensive nor as widely implemented as DRI's package, MPR's subscription service for MATH is somewhat analogous to DRI. It is a standardized package of products and services available to clients for a fixed rate. Users may also contract with MPR for special model design work at an additional charge, the products of which generally become part of the standard, updated version of MATH.

Proposition #28: *The existence of a special transfer-agent position in the modeler organization greatly enhances the successful implementation of a firm's model.*

DRI and MPR also differ from other modelers in our study for having created a formal "transfer agent" function within their organizations. This involved establishing a position (or cluster of positions) specifically responsible for performing the tasks associated with the model implementation process. The agent focuses on taking care of users' needs, and thereby gains experience with the problems users encounter in implementing the model and the ways in which they resolve these problems. This knowledge can be applied to new implementation settings and can aid in the redesign of the firm's services.

DRI has a highly organized team approach for servicing its clients. Each team has a service representative who acts as the day-to-day manager of DRI's relations with individual users. DRI has organized its team system around clusters of users with similar institutional ties or needs. For example, one team services users on Capitol Hill while others service the federal administrative branch. MPR also has a specialized transfer agent, although on a more modest scale. One individual serves as an external mediator between user organizations and MPR, and acts as an internal coordinator between model designers and model technicians. The creation of this formal coordinating function became necessary when MPR undertook its subscription service.

Proposition #29: *Modelers improve the likelihood of implementation of their models by pricing their products and services in such a* *way as to minimize the initial costs of acquiring and transferring the model.*

High model costs act as a deterrent to implementation because they force potential users to identify great benefits from model use in order to justify these costs. The most obvious costs to potential users are the price of acquiring access to the model, the expense of obtaining appropriate computing capabilities, and the costs of either training current staff or hiring experienced personnel. When the up-front costs are relatively low, agencies are more willing to invest in the model.

Both MPR and DRI have priced their services strategically with adoption and implementation in mind. Each offers its model as part of a standard package of basic services, and each has set fixed prices for what it provides to similar groups of clients.

DRI's basic fees are relatively low, even enabling potential but marginally committed model users to justify the expense of subscribing to DRI's basic package. DRI's blanket contracts for clusters of federal agency users are relatively inexpensive compared with what DRI charges private customers for comparable services—a pricing strategy based partly on the assumption that having extensive government usage of DRI's forecasts makes DRI's services attractive to private users, and partly on the expectation of economies of scale in serving all the users on the Hill under a blanket contract. Now that DRI has several commercial competitors, some of whom offer services at a lower price, DRI has been careful to position its public-user price below a point where current subscribers would find it worthwhile to pay the high cost of switching over to use a cheaper modeling service.

MPR has also made strategic pricing decisions for the services it provides, although they differ from DRI's policies. For one thing, MPR does not have proprietary rights to MATH. Whatever revenues MPR collects from its MATH work must be generated from its contracts with individual agencies for custom modeling work (e.g., for model development or revision) and from the fees for its subscription service. For the model development contracts, MPR bases its bids on a cost-plus formula, adjusted for MPR's evaluation of the bids, reputations, and capabilities of its competitors. MPR set its subscription price by spreading the costs of model maintenance across the plausible set of subscribers, for whom the cost would be relatively low. Whatever number of actual subscriptions MPR sold would bring in revenues it had previously subsidized. In fact, the subscription service has not had enough members to fully cover MPR's costs in maintaining MATH, but it does provide a substantial base for MPR's microsimulation work, enabling it to keep its bids on custom modeling proposals relatively low. This has helped MPR market and successfully sell its modeling services to agency users.

Proposition #30: *Establishment of and participation in model-user groups enhance successful model implementation by helping to institutionalize the base of support for modeling across agencies.*

Policy modeling sometimes takes place in an organizational and political environment at least partially hostile to quantitative methods of analysis. Many participants in the policymaking process want clear answers to often ambiguous questions, and they seek numbers to help them justify their choices; but they also have a disdain for analytic approaches that oversimplify or misrepresent their view of reality, and they are quick to criticize techniques that produce numbers that conflict with their positions on issues. This makes the environment of policy modeling fragile and unstable. One way some modelers have coped with this instability is to attempt to institutionalize a base of support for modeling in agencies by organizing user groups.

Microsimulation modelers have been particularly active in promoting a sense of community among model users and developers. Various individuals at the Urban Institute and MPR have helped to organize a TRIM/MATH users forum, with participants from the federal agencies that have used one of the models. The forum affords modelers and users the chance to share technical information and intellectual interests. MPR also recently organized a microsimulation conference, with formal papers presented by users, modelers, and scholars. Such efforts seem to reinforce a strong sense of commitment among microsimulation analysts. They know each other professionally and socially, participate in an active "personal transfer" system, and consider themselves part of a group. These efforts seem especially important for creating a stable base of support for modeling, given the youth of the microsimulation modeling field and its application environment.

Curiously, the user group concept now evident in microsimulation modeling parallels a similar movement among macroeconomic modelers in the 1960s. At that time the major macroeconomic modelers were involved with scattered modeling efforts that came together, at least symbolically, in the SSRC/Brookings model. A number of regular meetings were held around the model experience, and two resulted in published books. Since then, the field of macroeconomic modeling has solidified and stabilized around a number of major academic and commercial modeling efforts. Now that econometrics has become institutionalized as a standard part of the economic forecasting process in Washington, D.C., it no longer demands the community building required by microsimulation modeling at present.

SUMMARY

The foregoing thirty propositions represent our assessment of the factors that contribute to successful implementation of policy models. While this inventory of propositions is comprehensive, we do not presume that it includes all of the factors relevant to successful model implementation. Rather, it includes those factors that are identified in our research and supported by existing literature. In this appendix, we made no attempt to rank the various factors for their relative importance. We presented them as all of potentially equal importance. As we discussed in chapter 8, however, our research suggests that these factors are all not of equal importance. Some factors are clearly more critical than others in successful modeling. We have attempt throughout *Datawars* to focus on these more critical factors in order to improve our understanding of model implementation.

NOTES

1. Implementation and Use of Planning Models

1. The General Accounting Office (GAO) survey, completed in 1979, revealed that nineteen federal agencies were using national economic modeling, spending about $1 million per year in contract costs for models ($340,000 fixed costs and $650,000 variable), and employing eighty-three full-time employees on such modeling efforts (GAO 1979). Estimating conservatively at a cost of $36,000 per employee (mainly in the GS 13–16 levels), the labor cost at that time was $3 million. Hence the estimate of $4 million per year for national economic model use alone. We consider this estimate highly conservative, since it probably underestimates contract and personnel costs and further omits many related cost categories (e.g., computing, data collection, and storage costs, contributed staff time of analysts and policymakers). Moreover, our research interviews with one of the major providers of national economic models, Data Resources, Inc., revealed that the Department of Defense *alone* was contracting with DRI for over $2 million per year for econometric modeling services in 1980.

2. Some authors have used attitudinal measures such as perceived success or intended use as their outcome measure, but even these are not consistently defined. Bean et al. (1975) define "perceived success" by a multi-attribute attitude measure, whereas Manley (1975) operationally defined the measure as the perceived probability of successful implementation. Schultz and Slevin (1975) define "intended use" as the perceived probability of one's own use versus the perceived probability of others' use. In contrast, Sounder et al. (1975) describe intended use as willingness to adopt.

Radnor, Rubenstein, and Tansik (1970) focused on the "degree of implementation" as the model moved through five phases in time. White (1975) measured the degree of implementation by the extent to which the model moved through several phases of legitimacy. "Policy use" was studied by Fromm, Hamilton, and Hamilton (1974), Greenberger, Crenson, and Crissey (1976), and Pack and Pack (1977a, b). "Policy accomplishment" was studied by Fromm, Hamilton, and Hamilton (1974); and "political use" was studied by Pack and Pack (1977a, b) and Greenberger, Crenson, and Crissey (1976).

3. Other outcomes which are frequently attributed to the modeling process include education, research, and technique development. These outcomes are deliberately excluded from our definition of successful implementation, since the focus of our research is on implementation of planning models *for policymaking*.

4. Indeed, the DRI econometric model, which is the subject of one of our cases, is used extensively by the private sector as are the other major econometric models.

5. Judith de Neufville makes this point in the context of federal, state, and local statistics for policymaking (de Neufville 1975, 1981, 1984). She also argues that the design of any policy

indicator is at least in part a political process. This is because so much often hinges on what the statistics show and because there is often no single correct way to make many estimates and projections (e.g., federal, state, and local population estimates).

2. Political and Technical "Demands" for Models

1. For an excellent description of Orcutt's early work, see Greenberger, Crenson, and Crissey (1976:108–112).

2. Interview with Nelson McClung, Division of Tax Analysis, Department of the Treasury, Washington, D.C., July 10, 1980.

3. Interview with Jodie Allen, Deputy Assistant Secretary for Policy Evaluation and Research, Department of Labor, Washington, D.C., July 17, 1980. See also Harris (1978:5–7).

4. The President's Commission on Income Maintenance Programs was also known as the Heineman Commission, after its chairman, Benjamin Heineman, Sr.

5. "Aging" a data base refers to use of statistical techniques to take an actual data base recorded at one point in time and, based upon evidence from past trends, project it forward to another time period by changing the values of the major variables. Thus, through the technique of aging, a data base collected on the population today can be "aged" according to expectations based on historical or conjectured trends, and, with luck, it will closely resemble the population at the later time of interest. This "sample of future population" can then be analyzed to determine the effects of possible policy changes during that time period. Aging is a crucial component of microanalytic simulation modeling, and one of the most problematic. The slightest misestimation in the process of aging an important variable in the data base can drastically distort the characteristics of the "aged" sample of the population.

6. Interview with Jodie Allen, July 11, 1980.

7. *Ibid.*

8. Frank Gorham, the first Assistant Secretary for Planning and Evaluation, Department of Health, Education, and Welfare, under the Johnson administration, was instrumental in establishing the Urban Institute. Worth Bateman also came to the Urban Institute from ASPE.

9. Interviews with Jodie Allen, July 17, 1980; and Nelson McClung, July 10, 1980.

10. Interview with Richard Michel, the Urban Institute, Washington, D.C., July 20, 1981.

11. Interview with Harold Beebout, Mathematica Policy Research, Washington, D.C., July 8, 1980.

12. The data modification modules were needed to combine different data files into a single unified data base and to modify the records so that they were representative of the population in the year of interest in the model simulation. The data sources used are the March Current Population Survey, covering 47,000 representative households (approximately 130,000 individuals) for every year since 1968, and including questions on a wide variety of demographic, social, and economic variables; the Survey of Economic Opportunity, which includes 30,000 households and was conducted in 1967 by the Census Bureau for the Office of Economic Opportunity; and the Census Bureau's Decennial Census of the Population (Public Use Sample), collected only once in ten years and providing detailed data on households' income, living conditions, and health.

13. Interviews with Richard Michel, July 20, 1981; and Heather Pritchard, Sistemis, Washington, D.C., July 22, 1981.

14. Interview with Richard Wertheimer, the Urban Institute, Washington, D.C., July 16, 1980.

15. Interview with Joan Turek-Brezina, Division of Computation and Modeling, Office of the Assistant Secretary for Planning and Evaluation, Department of Health and Human Services, Washington, D.C., July 8, 1980.

16. At the time, only the Urban Institute, HEW, and MPR had working versions of TRIM. The Treasury Department had its own Personal Income Tax Model.

17. Interview with Jodie Allen, July 17, 1980.

18. "Institute president Frank Gorham was afraid of congressional users. It had never been

done before. Previously, the administration was the only buyer and producer of numbers. Gorham didn't want to alienate his clientele." Interview with Jodie Allen, July 17, 1980.

19. MPR obtained a joint contract with SRI, Inc., from ASPE to conduct and analyze the Seattle and Denver income-maintenance experiments. MPR's portion of the contract amounted to nearly $300,000 over several years and constituted "the lifeblood of the Washington office" during its initial period. These experiments were intended to explore the labor supply responses of individuals receiving a negative income tax and eventually provided data that MPR analysts used much later to build a labor supply module for MATH.

20. According to Harold Beebout, MPR's main competition for the SRS bid came from the Research Triangle Institute, a firm which had obtained a copy of the TRIM model.

21. Interview with Jodie Allen, July 11, 1980.

22. Interview with William Hoagland, Human Resources and Community Development Division, Congressional Budget Office, Washington, D.C., July 9, 1980.

23. *Ibid.*

24. Interview with Carolyn Merck, Mathematica Policy Research, Washington, D.C., 1981.

25. Interviews with Harold Beebout, July 8, 1980; Myles Mayfield, Mathematica Policy Research, Washington, D.C., July 20, 1981; and Richard Hayes, the Policy Research Group, Washington, D.C., July 23, 1981.

26. Interview with William Hoagland, July 9, 1980.

27. Interview with Patricia Doyle, Mathematica Policy Research, Washington, D.C., July 16, 1980.

28. According to several users, Beebout had accurately analyzed the political importance of users' controlling the model's use. Bill Hoagland of CBO said: "One reason [CBO wanted to subscribe to the model] is that I'm a cheapskate. Those contracting organizations are very costly to the government. More important, CBO has technically knowledgeable people, very capable of figuring substantive issues. However, we have lacked computing expertise and we needed training. I didn't want to be captive of another organization. . . . There's another reason too: when a proposal comes up on the Hill, they want CBO's analysis the next morning. We can't do that if we contract out. We need to have our own capability. . . . But I didn't want to be completely independent because we also want to reap the benefits of what resources DOE and DOL and other contractors and consultants are putting into MATH. So the subscription contract works well for that balance of independence and contact" (interview with William Hoagland, July 19, 1980).

29. Users on the annual MATH subscription service received the latest version of the model code and subsequent updates; the MATH Codebook; the MATH Technical Description; MATH User's Guide; MATH Technical Bulletin; and thirty hours of technical and analytical consultation. All other services, including model development, model installation, and additional training or consultation, cost extra.

30. Interview with Nelson McClung, July 10, 1980.

3. The "Push" for Model Implementation

1. The basis of modern economics rests on systems concepts, and the genesis of these concepts can be traced back several centuries. However, it was not until the late nineteenth and early twentieth centuries that it became possible to represent economic systems concepts with mathematical statements. Since this time, mathematics has become a critical tool (and often a focus) of economic research (Heilbroner 1953).

2. An important assumption in this view of the predictability of economic behavior is that the behavior of major aspects of an economy under study remains stable for significant periods of time. This stability is critical because it is only through observing actual economic behavior under stable conditions that the complex interactions of economic systems components can be identified. When an economy begins to behave in unstable ways, it becomes much more difficult to model accurately using prevailing systems concepts.

3. More detailed discussions of the history and field of econometrics and econometric

modeling are found in Greenberger, Crenson, and Crissey (1976); Klein and Burmeister (1976); Kmenta and Ramsey (1981); Omerod (1979).

4. The late Otto Eckstein noted that the Harvard ABC indicators project (a study during the mid-1920s of leading and lagging economic indicators) did in fact predict a major economic downturn prior to the crash of 1929, but that the economists running the project did not believe the results and did not publish them. Interview with Otto Eckstein, December 1981.

5. This history of DRI was assembled using one major documentary source (Greenberger, Crenson, and Crissey 1976), augmented by interviews with present and past employees and affiliates of DRI. In some cases the documentary source and the individuals interviewed did not agree with one another. Thus this history must be seen as a well—intentioned approximation of how DRI came to be, not as a final reference source on the history of the company.

6. Considerable disagreement exists between the account of Otto Eckstein and Gary Fromm over what happened in the early days of DRI. This disagreement is particularly acute in the case of Fromm's role in the creation of the company and his responsibility for its success. The account here reflects our synthesis of opinions from Eckstein, Fromm, and seven others familiar with the early days of the company. Other points of disagreement are noted below.

7. Marron's early concept for this service included Bill Moyers to handle domestic political affairs and Henry Kissinger to handle international political affairs. Eckstein was to handle economic affairs. Partly as a result of the movement of Kissinger to the Nixon administration, these political components of the plan did not materialize. The economic part of the plan prospered, however. Interviews with Charles Warden, Stephen Browne, and G. Dennis O'Brien, December 1982.

8. This is a point of major disagreement between Fromm and Eckstein. Both claim to have been first to come up with the basic idea.

9. The $1.1 million in initial capital came primarily from two venture capital sources (one company and one individual investor, for $500,000 each) and from Mitchell Hutchins ($100,00). The early principals (e.g., Fromm and Eckstein) also contributed comparatively small amounts of capital and in-kind services as investments.

10. The connection between DRI and the Wharton group is interesting. One story about the connection suggests that the Wharton modeling group was willing to go along with DRI and put the Wharton model on DRI's system, but the Wharton trustees eventually turned the deal down (the reasons are unclear), thus necessitating the development of an in-house DRI model. Another story is that DRI "tied up" plans among some at the Wharton group to go commercial with the Wharton model by arranging to put it on the DRI system, thereby fending off competition until the DRI model was ready. In any case, Wharton did sign a three-year contract with DRI to place its model on the DRI system for a once-per-year payment and a share of time-sharing revenues. The deal fell apart in the third year, and Wharton sued DRI for the final payment.

11. DRI's competition was not strong or well organized. For example, Daniel Suits and his group at Michigan had been continuing the refinement of their model and issuing forecasts periodically, but these forecasts were available on almost a "public information" basis. Similarly, the Klein group at Wharton was issuing forecasts and holding workshops for "sponsors" who paid $5,000 per year to support the Wharton modeling effort. The early workshops were held at the Wharton School at the University of Pennsylvania, but when the Wharton operation split off to become a separate entity called Wharton Economic Forecasting Associates, the workshops moved to WEFA. In both cases, as with the other modeling efforts, these organizations were not pursuing commercialization of their efforts at the time DRI got started.

12. Ahlstrom selected the Burroughs machine because it featured a technical innovation called virtual memory. Virtual memory is a means of dividing up large computer jobs into "pages" that can be stored outside of the computer's main memory on high-speed secondary storage devices; these pages are called as needed into the main memory for processing. Thus programs that would normally be too large to run on a given computer's main memory could be run through use of this virtual memory. Virtual memory made the Burroughs machine practical for DRI's needs

and was less expensive than nonvirtual memory machines of equivalent processing power. In this case a technical innovation resulted in the improvement of price/performance ratios of computing, putting sufficient computing resources within reach of the young company.

13. Craig's innovations in the collection, processing, and management of data were instrumental in DRI's establishment. An example of these innovations can be observed in the data input format Craig developed for entering the latest values for a given set of time-series variables. The computer would provide the data entry clerk with a screen showing the individual variables in a column down the left side of the screen. Next to each variable were the second to last entry, the last entry, and a space for the current entry, each in its own column. This provided the clerk with a check on the previous two values for each variable, allowing quick assessment of the new value to see if it was within reasonable bounds. Also, the computer kept a "blind" total (i.e., it wasn't printed on the screen) for each column, and would compare the total for the new column with the totals for the previous two columns to see if the total was within reasonable bounds. If it was not, the computer would alert the data entry clerk to check for problems with the new entries. Such techniques made it possible to enter new data into data banks rapidly and accurately.

14. The ability of MODEL to keep track of the values of variables for multiple runs under different assumptions was a key feature of the system. Without this feature each specific run would have to be done separately to keep the individual variable values straight. With MODEL it was possible to do essentially the same run with a number of different values for key exogenous variables and get the result in a single output. This streamlined the analyst's tasks considerably.

15. The development of "user-friendly" software was an important goal adopted by the founders of DRI. As stated by Fromm, "We wanted it to be able to be used by idiots." Interview with Gary Fromm, September 1981. The DRI software systems were indeed the most advanced of their kind, and have remained so to this day. The programs (excluding the actual equations and including only executable lines of source code) were enormous: MODEL, 4,000 lines; MODSIM, 20,000 lines; AID, 5,000 lines; EPS (initial version), 240,000 lines. The impetus to build such sophisticated systems appears to have come largely from Ahlstrom and Lacey. Both had recognized how critical it was to allow users to do their own programming and to make their own analytical runs. As Lacey commented, "I knew the only leverage you could get from the modeling system was to give clients software tools that would enable them to write one command and have it execute $3,000 worth of computing use." Lacey's hunch paid off, as illustrated by the phenomenal success in implementation of EPS in 1977. There had been concern that users would be reluctant to move to EPS because of the need to learn new features of the system. Instead, the users rushed to get on and use the new system. EPS was brought up in January of 1977, and by June of that year it accounted for more than half of the system usage. By mid-1978 EPS was accounting for more than 90 percent of system usage. Another indicator of EPS success was the fact that users avidly began to write and retain their own programs for later use. DRI estimates that over one million lines of user-created code reside in EPS, and in fact, most of the routines that were originally part of EPS were written by DRI employees who were not programmers. Interviews with Robert Lacey and James Craig, April 1982.

16. Charles Warden related two examples illustrating the way these early marketing efforts took place. The first demonstration of the DRI system at the Congressional Research Service took place in the old Library of Congress building where the CRS offices were located. Warden and his group brought in their terminal and equipment and set things up to connect the terminal to the DRI computer over the telephone. They then discovered that the Library of Congress building, which was built before the turn of the century, was wired entirely with direct current instead of alternating current. Their equipment would not work. The CRS staff, deciding that anyone who went to the trouble to bring all that equipment down for a demonstration probably had a working system, bought the service. When Warden and Fromm took the equipment to the Treasury, they met with Murray Weidenbaum, then an Assistant Secretary of Treasury. Fromm was busy explaining the mathematical details of the DRI model, and Weidenbaum appeared to be uninterested in these details. Warden then turned on the system and showed Weidenbaum how the system could fore-

cast GNP and plot out the results. Weidenbaum was amazed that the system could plot the results in such a nice, readable form, and bought the service on the spot. Interview with Charles Warden, December 1981.

17. Interview with Eric Williams of DRI, December 1981. Williams had spent considerable time marketing DRI services in Europe.

18. The difficulties that the major modelers have in coming up with precise and accurate forecasts abound. A survey by the *Los Angeles Times* of ten model-based forecasts (including DRI's) of the 1981 GNP ranged from a predicted decline of 1.0% to a predicted gain of 2.0%. The actual GNP change (estimated as of December 1981) was a gain of 1.9%. The forecasts of the same models for the 1982 GNP ranged from a decline of 1.0% to a gain of 1.0% (DRI's 1981 forecasts were +0.8 for 1981, and −0.6 for 1982.) Magnuson (1982: part V, p. 1).

19. G. Dennis O'Brien, who did marketing work in the Washington office in the mid-1970s, claims that DRI had all the major federal agencies as users by the end of 1974.

20. Gary Fromm left DRI in 1974 because of a dispute over the work he had performed and the compensation he felt he deserved. A lawsuit against DRI by Fromm followed, which was decided in favor of Fromm. Despite his departure from the company, Fromm retained DRI stock.

21. Eckstein felt Fromm received an unfairly large among of money considering Eckstein's assessment of Fromm's contribution to the company. Fromm saw things differently. The dispute was aggravated by the fact that the amounts of money involved were so large. Fromm reportedly received in excess of $7 million for his share of DRI, while Eckstein is said to have received more than $20 million for his.

22. William Raduchel, vice president for information technology products at DRI, said that as of 1981, DRI had close to ten million time series available on-line.

23. DRI's computing and information systems capabilities were considerable. At the time of our study, the company's Lexington computing center operated four Burroughs B7800 Model III central processors with six megabytes of main storage each. Connected to these were over 200 disk drives, possessing a total of forty billion characters of storage capability. The central processors were connected through data communications processors to DRI's remote network (called DRINET), through which users throughout the U.S., Canada, and parts of Europe and the Far East could use the system. All DRI computer-based products and data bases were on-line. Beyond these capabilities, the company was undergoing a major reorganization and expansion of its computing operations. Plans included a move toward use of large IBM equipment, and away from Burroughs. (The B7800s were to be replaced with IBM 4341/IIs and subsequently with IBM 3081s.) The main machines would be linked together with a new internal communications network to increase flexibility and reliability in processing assignments, and the data storage operations would be coordinated through a special "file machine" DRI was building based on SEL 32/7780 computers. Disk storage capability would be increased to about seventy-seven billion characters. This expansion was planned to take over two years. In an effort to capitalize on the increasing popularity of microcomputer-based systems, DRI also was developing a user workstation containing an Onyx microprocessor and input/output devices that would enable local processing as well as communications with the Lexington facility. Interview with Jan Prokop, December 1981.

24. Robert Harris at the Congressional Budget Office noted that, at one point, between 70 and 80 percent of the time-sharing service billings from DRI to CBO were for disk storage on DRI's system. Many analysts had built their own little models or had copied into their disk space various components of DRI's models in order to use them for their analyses. Harris sought DRI's help in getting CBO analysts to be more conscientious about their use of disk storage, and issued internal CBO directives to that effect. These efforts reduced disk storage costs somewhat, but they remained a major component in CBO's payments to DRI. Interview with Robert Harris, July 1981.

25. This observation was made by an economist with the Council of Economic Advisers, and was echoed by economists at the Office of Management and Budget and the Congressional Budget Office, during interviews in July of 1981.

4. Accounting for Implementation Success

1. Nearly every person interviewed for the TRIM/MATH case study used the phrase "incestuous group" to describe the community of modelers and users of MATH and TRIM.

2. Interview with Myles Maxfield, Mathematica Policy Research, July 20, 1981.

3. Interview with Harold Beebout, Mathematica Policy Research, July 20, 1980.

4. Interview with Richard Hayes, the Policy Research Group, Washington, D.C., July 23, 1981.

5. Estimate provided by Joan Turek-Brezina, director of the Division of Computation and Modeling, Office of the Assistant Secretary for Planning and Evaluation, Department of Health and Human Services, July 8, 1981.

6. This notion of a "package" to describe the implementation of an innovation has become a primary theme in the characterization of technological innovations in work conducted over the past eight years by researchers at the Public Policy Research Organization at the University of California at Irvine. The package concept developed from an observation made by Ivan Illich about the problems encountered in transferring educational innovations in primary and secondary education from developed to developing countries (Illich 1971), and was refined in a study by Stewart of the transfer of physical technologies to developing countries (Stewart 1977). It has since been articulated in a number of articles (cf. King and Kraemer 1978, 1981, 1985; Kling and Scacchi 1979, 1981; Scacchi 1981).

7. The Federal Reserve System's MPS model is now available to anyone who wishes to see it, and the Fed will even make a copy of the model for those who want it. The only things the Fed now keeps confidential are the values the Fed supplies to the model for their analyses, since these might indicate where the Fed is moving in its decisions about control of the money supply. Interview with Flint Brayton, Federal Reserve System, July 1981.

8. This observation was made by Mark Therber, an economist with the Congressional Budget Office, and was corroborated by other federal agency users. Interviews with Mark Therber, August 1980 and July 1981.

9. Several informants pointed out the importance of DRI's ability to do rapid analyses of the possible impacts of various policy changes. Otto Eckstein told one story about how he received notice from a friend in Washington a few hours in advance of President Nixon's announcement of the imposition of wage and price controls in August of 1971. DRI analysts produced extensive analyses of the probable impacts of these controls within a few hours of the announcement, gaining national visibility for being the first economic forecasting group to predict the consequences of this surprising action by the President. Interview with Otto Eckstein, December 1981.

10. Most of the macroeconomic forecasting groups have their senior economists review, and if necessary alter, their forecasts before they are published. The extent to which this is considered reasonable or unreasonable depends on the observer's bias about what the role of a "good" model should be. Some argue that the model results should be published exactly as they come from the machine; others argue that postrun adjustments are needed to fine-tune the model's results to account for factors that the models cannot incorporate. The fine-tuning of model results has been a controversial aspect of macroeconomic modeling, but most of those in the modeling community believe it is sensible and even necessary (see, for example, Greenberger, Crenson, and Crissey 1976; McNees 1982).

11. David McLain, Steve Brooks, and other former members of DRI agree that the needs of business clients are different from those of federal agency users. Federal agency users are generally well versed in what the models are trying to do and are more concerned with manipulating the models to see what results they produce under simulation of various conditions. Business users, in part because they do not feel they have much control over national economic policy, and in part because they are usually concerned more with what forecasts imply for their companies, desire greater interpretation of the forecasts issued directly by DRI. Interviews with David McLain, December 1981, and with Steve Brooks, July 1981 and December 1981.

12. The term "providence" in this context is intended to convey the fact that the coming

together of the various components that resulted in the success of DRI happened in such a timely and coherent manner. It by no means slights the vision and efforts of the founders and builders of DRI in creating the company and making it successful.

13. The people who contributed to the creation of this short list of people generally did not include Gary Fromm in the list. This seems in part due to the fact that some of those who commented on this list as it was being developed did not work with Fromm and lost contact with him when he left the company in 1974, and in part because of the differences of opinion between Eckstein and Fromm regarding Fromm's role in the company's formation. He is included here because, based on interviews with him and comments from others familiar with DRI's early days, it seems he was instrumental in the development of the initial concept for the company and in helping to create the modeling base for its products.

14. The number of top econometricians is certainly larger than indicated here. The small "clique" referred to contains only those econometricians who were experienced model builders and operators, and who understood not only how to construct models but how to build the necessary supporting infrastructure to make them useful.

15. Wharton, when it changed to WEFA, began more actively to pursue a market-oriented approach. However, it began to do so much later than did DRI, and it has never been so active in this regard as has DRI. Interviews with Gary Fromm, September 1981, and Steve Brooks, December 1981.

16. It should be noted that the DRI model, along with other large models, has come under criticism from the monetarist and supply-side economists as being "too Keynesian" in its formation. This criticism is not new. According to Doug Beck of DRI's Washington office, the criticism from monetarists began in the early 1970s, when the emergence of inflation problems and concern about capital supply began to influence economists' thinking about the importance of the monetary component of the economy. The election of Ronald Reagan to the presidency in 1980, and the subsequent rise to power of monetarists and supply-side economists in his administration, heightened this debate. Chapter 6 discusses the consequences of Reagan's election for economic modeling.

17. This opinion is expressed in Greenberger, Crenson, and Crissey (1976), and was reiterated by several former DRI employees in interviews in August 1980 and July and December 1981.

18. It is useful to note that another user at CBO felt that much of the money being spent for DRI and other modeling services was being wasted. Not everyone needs a "DRI Cadillac," he said. This opinion was also stated by an economist in the Department of Commerce.

19. There are exceptions to this, of course. Most of the disputes between team members and clients have less to do with the substance of economics or modeling than with the financial arrangements for providing services. Interviews with economists in the CBO, OMB, and DRI Washington office, August 1980.

20. This DRI policy of not deliberately hiring away staff of its federal clients is acknowledged by federal agency users, and is appreciated by them. Nevertheless, many such movements from clients to DRI have taken place at the initiative of the individuals who made the move. DRI does not turn down applicants for positions if the applicants will make worthwhile additions to the DRI team. Those we talked to both in the user agencies and in DRI felt that the movement of key people is both advantageous and troubling. It is troubling in that good staff people sometimes leave for a "better opportunity," leaving gaps in the staff that can be hard to fill. But it is advantageous in that the movement of these key people spreads talent around and facilitates close working relationships among all the members of the "invisible college" of economists and analysts.

21. Interviews with Jered Enzler of the Fed and Gail Mackinnen of the General Accounting Office, August 1980.

22. A useful review of the strengths and weaknesses of model-based forecasting can be found in McNees (1982) and McNees and Ries (1983).

23. This observation was made both by an economist in DRI's Washington office and by an economist with the Congressional Budget Office.

24. This comment was made by an economist in the Department of Commerce.

5. Partisan Politics and Model Use

1. Interview with Carolyn Merck, Mathematica Policy Research, Washington, D.C., July 20, 1981.

2. *Ibid.*

3. *Ibid.*

4. *Congressional Quarterly,* August 9, 1975, p. 1790.

5. Interview with Carolyn Merck, July 20, 1981.

6. Interview with James Springfield, U.S. Department of Agriculture, Washington, D.C., July 17, 1980.

7. Interview with Carolyn Merck, July 20, 1981.

8. Interview with James Springfield, July 17, 1980.

9. Interview with Wendall Primus, Senate Budget Committee, July 18, 1980.

10. Interview with James Springfield, July 17, 1980.

11. The bill the House Agriculture Committee reported out included these provisions: eligibility limited to those with net income at the poverty line ($5,496 for a household of four in 1976); sliding deductions based on household size; extra deduction for the elderly, for child care expenses, for working families; elimination of purchase requirement for the elderly, while other households pay 27.5 percent of their net income to purchase food coupons. The bill would save the program $100 million a year: 1.5 million people would be dropped from the program; 0.7 million would come in; 8.5 million would receive increased benefits; and 3.3 million would receive the same benefits. *Congressional Quarterly,* August 14, 1976, p. 2236.

12. The Senate compromise bill involved limiting eligibility to households with net income below the poverty line ($5.496), allowing a standard deduction of $100 per month for all households plus a $25 per month deduction for workers, and requiring all recipients to purchase coupons with 27.5 percent of their net income. The bill would cut out 1.4 million people but expand benefits to the recipients. CBO estimated the savings at $630 million per year; FNS estimates were for $360 million per year. *Congressional Quarterly,* March 20, 1976, p. 618.

13. Interview with Carolyn Merck, July 20, 1981.

14. Interview with Jodie Allen, Deputy Assistant Secretary for Policy Evaluation and Research, Department of Labor, Washington, D.C., July 17, 1980.

15. Interview with Carolyn Merck, July 20, 1981.

16. Interview with Jodie Allen, July 17, 1980.

17. Interview with Bruce Thompson, Frank Capece, and Nick Lanier, General Accounting Office, Washington, D.C., July 9, 1980.

18. The GAO report explained these criteria in detail:

    a. Model documentation: scope and content of documentation; its availability and accessibility to users of varying skill and expertise; its costs.

    b. Computer program verification: extent to which verification took place during actual development and implementation of the model; extent to which errors were discovered and corrected.

    c. Technical validity: identification of model assumptions; ways in which and extent to which assumptions diverge from reality; and extent to which data is appropriate, complete, and accurate.

    d. Operational validity: impacts of alternative assumptions on model results.

    e. Dynamic validity: adequacy of provisions for maintaining, reviewing, and modifying the model.

    f. Usability: extent of practical usefulness of the model, including ease of use, ease of understanding, availability and cost of data, transferability to different computer systems. (GAO 1977: 55–60)

19. Interview with Bruce Thompson, Frank Capece, and Nick Lanier, July 9, 1980.

20. Interview with Michael Barth, ICF, Inc., Washington, D.C., July 23, 1981.

21. Interview with Nelson McClung, Office of Tax Analysis, Department of the Treasury, Washington, D.C., July 10, 1980.

22. Interview with Bill Hoagland, Human Resources and Community Development Division, Congressional Budget Office, Washington, D.C., July 9, 1980.

23. Letter from Harold Beebout, Mathematica Policy Research, to Harry Havens, Program Analysis Division, GAO, August 22, 1977 (GAO 1977:104–105).

24. Letter from Richard Michel, the Urban Institute, to Frank Capece, General Accounting Office, September 19, 1977 (GAO 1977:103).

25. *Congressional Quarterly,* February 5, 1977, p. 211.

26. These nine programs included Aid to Families with Dependent Children (AFDC), Medicaid, food stamps and other nutrition programs, Supplemental Security Income (SSI), General Assistance, veterans' pensions, housing assistance, basic educational opportunity grants, and earned income tax credits (*Congressional Quarterly,* February 19, 1977, pp. 337–338).

27. *Congressional Quarterly,* April 30, 1977, pp. 795–796.

28. Interview with Michael Barth, July 23, 1981; see Lynn (1980); Lynn and Whitman (1981).

29. Information on the development of the KGB model was obtained from interviews with Richard Kasten, ASPE office, Department of Health and Human Services, Washington, D.C., July 23, 1981; Michael Barth, ICF International, Washington, D.C., July 24, 1981; and Heather Pritchard, ASPE office, Department of Health and Human Services, Washington, D.C., July 22, 1981. An additional source was Betson, Greenberg, and Kasten (1980:153–188).

30. Henry Aaron, letter to David Whitman, May 10, 1979, quoted in Lynn and Whitman (1981:73–74).

31. Interviews with Richard Kasten, July 23, 1981, and Lynn and Whitman (1981:92).

32. Interview with Richard Michel, the Urban Institute, Washington, D.C., July 20, 1981.

33. Barth, quoted in Lynn and Whitman (1981:76).

34. Anonymous Income Security Policy staff member quoted in Lynn and Whitman (1981:92).

35. Interview with Jodie Allen, July 17, 1980, and Lynn and Whitman (1981).

36. Interview with Richard Hayes (former ASPER staff member), the Policy Research Group, Washington, D.C., July 23, 1981.

37. Information on the "JOBS" module came from the following interviews: Jodie Allen, ASPER office, DOL, Washington, D.C., July 11, 1980; Ray Uhalde, ASPER office, DOL, Washington, D.C., July 21, 1981; Richard Hayes, July 23, 1981; Myles Maxfield, Jr., Mathematica Policy Research, Washington, D.C., July 20, 1981.

38. Interview with Jodie Allen, July 17, 1980.

39. *Ibid.*

40. A post hoc sensitivity test of the two models by Myles Maxfield, Jr., of Mathematica Policy Research, indicated that one significant source of variation was in how the two models estimated the costs of current income-transfer programs. This was politically important because abolishing programs with a total cost of "x" would allow "x" dollars to "offset" the costs of the new proposed welfare plan. If the new program cost less than or equal to "x," it met Carter's criteria for a "no additional cost" reform.

41. Jodie Allen, quoted in Lynn and Whitman (1981:71).

42. DOL Secretary Raymond Marshall, quoted in Lynn and Whitman (1981:72).

43. Letter from Michael Barth, quoted in Lynn and Whitman (1981:145).

44. Interview with James Fallows, former chief speech writer to President Carter, Washington, D.C., July 13, 1980.

45. Interview with Jodie Allen, July 17, 1980.

46. Interviews with Michael Barth, July 24, 1981; Jodie Allen, July 17, 1980; and Richard Hayes, July 23, 1981.

47. The itemized cost of the Program for Better Jobs and Income was:

Employment and training programs	$ 8.8 billion
Cash assistance	19.2 billion
Earned Income Tax Credit	1.5 billion
Emergency assistance block grant	.6 billion
Child care deduction	.6 billion
	$30.7 billion

The existing programs included in the "offsets" tally were:

Aid to Families with Dependent Children (AFDC)	$ 6.4 billion
Supplemental Security Income (SSI)	5.7 billion
Food stamps	5.0 billion
Earned Income Tax Credit (EITC)	1.3 billion
Portions of comprehensive employment Training Act (CETA) jobs	5.9 billion
Extended unemployment insurance	.7 billion
Reduced regular unemployment insurance	.4 billion
Increases in Social Security contributions—new workers	.3 billion
Fraud, abuse eradication efforts	.4 billion
Reduced demand for housing subsidies	.5 billion
Rebates to poor for wellhead taxes	1.3 billion
(proposed at time)	$27.9 billion

SOURCE: White House estimates accompanying PBJI announcement, reported in *Congressional Quarterly,* August 13, 1977, p. 1702.

48. CBO refused to accept savings from CETA, the proposed wellhead tax, reduced welfare fraud, and extended unemployment insurance as directly related to PBJI. These programs added up to nearly $7 billion. Lynn and Whitman (1981).

6. Managerial and Political Ideology in Model Use

1. These are not the only federal users of econometric models. A 1979 report of model users listed, in addition to the Council of Economic Advisers, Treasury, the Office of Management and Budget, and the Congressional Budget Office, the following agencies as model users: Agriculture, Commerce, Defense, Energy, General Services Administration, Education, Health and Human Services, Housing and Urban Development, Interior, Labor, the Council on Wage and Price Stability, the Environmental Protection Agency, and the Interstate Commerce Commission.

2. The uncertainty principle of Heisenberg states, in general, that it is impossible to empirically determine the simultaneous position and speed of an electron because the act of measuring its position or speed alters its position and speed. This is a succinct natural sciences example of a broader principle of uncertainty that obtains in all empirically validated fields of inquiry: the act of measurement, the very means one uses to empirically measure something, and the reporting of results can distort the behavior of the phenomenon being measured or the measurement being taken.

3. This opinion was voiced by virtually every economist we interviewed. All the economists acknowledged that the exciting and well-known uses of the models center on forecasting, but the real contributions of the models for policymaking come from their simulation applications. An excellent account of this can be found in Gass (1983).

4. A more complete review of the budget process followed in any given fiscal year can be found in the annual *Budget of the United States Government* for that fiscal year. This account was based in part on the *Budget of the United States Government: Fiscal Year 1981* (OMB 1981:349–366), and in part on *A Glossary of Terms Used in the Federal Budget Process* (GAO 1981).

5. The Troika traditionally has been composed of the Council of Economic Advisers, the Treasury Department, and the Office of Management and Budget. President Carter added to the

Troika the Departments of Labor and Commerce for a total of five agencies. President Reagan removed Labor and Commerce from the Troika, returning it to its traditional form.

6. The Reagan administration brought into power economists of the so-called monetarist and supply-side schools. These economic perspectives have never been as heavily represented in the Troika as they are now. Because monetarists and supply-side economists have fundamental disagreements with models based primarily on Keynesian orthodoxy, they have begun to insist on Troika use of other models that reflect their economic persuasions. This change is discussed later in the chapter.

7. These descriptions of congressional use of modeling were provided by Steve Zeller and Mark Therber of the CBO.

8. These descriptions of Fed activities come from Board of Governors (1974).

9. The role of each part of the Federal Reserve System is as follows: The *Federal Reserve System Board of Governors*—seven members appointed by the President and confirmed by the Senate for fourteen-year terms. The board formulates monetary policy and has broad regulatory powers over activities of commercial banks and the operations of Federal Reserve Banks. The board establishes reserve requirements for members banks, reviews and approves discount rates of the Federal Reserve Banks, sets policies governing the administration of the "discount window" at those banks, and sets margin requirements on credit purchases in the stock market.

The Federal Open Market Committee (FOMC)—twelve members, including seven members of the board plus five members from Federal Reserve Banks. The FOMC determines what transactions the Federal Reserve will conduct in the "open market" (i.e., buying and selling of government securities and other selected financial paper), which is the primary vehicle by which the Fed controls money supply.

The Federal Reserve Banks—twelve banks located around the country, with twenty-four additional branch banks. The banks execute changes in the discount rate (the rate at which they loan money to member banks) and set interest rates on loans made to depository institutions. The banks perform other services such as distributing currency into the payments system, processing checks and conducting electronic transfers of money for depository institutions, acting as the U.S. government's banker, helping to regulate the banking system in states, and conducting research.

The Federal Advisory Council—twelve members, one from each Federal Reserve Bank district. The FAC provides advice to the Board of Governors on economic and banking matters, and suggests improvements in operations of the Federal Reserve System. Member banks—consisting of about 6,000 out of the nation's 14,000 banks—can use Fed facilities and services, including borrowing; using check processing, clearinghouse, and funds-transfer facilities; and obtaining new currency and coin; and they can participate in the election of some members of the board of directors for the Federal Reserve Bank in their district.

10. Interview with Flint Brayton, July 1981.

11. The rapid success of President Reagan in enacting major changes appears to have resulted from his decisive margin of victory; the fact that the Senate became more Republican and more conservative, and thus supportive of his changes; and the creation of an administratively competent transition team that had many of the changes planned in detail before Reagan was inaugurated. The new administration surprised many longtime observers of the Washington scene by quickly exploiting its politican strengths in pursuit of policies that would alter the status quo substantially. This fact and unexpected change occurred in the informal processes of policymaking as much as in the policies of the executive branch, which led to changes in the roles computerized modeling would play in those processes.

12. The term "mid-sixties orthodoxy" comes from Frank Deleeuw of the U.S. Commerce Department, who provided valuable background on many economic issues in macroeconomic modeling.

13. An exception was the Council of Economic Advisers, which has greater flexibility in personnel matters than other departments of the executive branch because its employees are not civil servants. At the same time, however, CEA staff employees are not strictly political appointees,

either. Usually a staff member comes to the CEA and stays for a few years, then departs to industry or academia. When there is a change of party in the White House there is likely to be a complete turnover, but there are exceptions to this. Some staff members remain for ten years or more and become valuable because of their deep knowledge of CEA operations and analytical tools.

14. Among the new models considered by the new administration were the Claremont model of John Rutledge; a model by M. Ture, a former consultant who had become an Assistant Secretary at Treasury; and a revised model by Michael Evans, based on his former models.

15. Strictly speaking, the CBO operations are supposed to be unbiased and nonpartisan. However, since the CBO was created and staffed during the period when both houses of Congress were dominated by Democrats and hence by the economic persuasions of the "mid-sixties orthodoxy," these subtle biases appear to have affected CBO analyses.

16. The mistake occurred when analysts at DRI's Washington office failed to convert current dollars to constant dollars for government expenditures in moving from a short-term forecast to a long-term forecast, according to economists at DRI and at the Senate Budget Committee. An extensive discussion of events where ideology played a larger role than mistakes is found in Stockman (1986).

17. This remark seemed to carry two meanings. One was an obvious facetious implication that the members do not care as much about the truth as they do about what looks good for them. But a more basic message, revealed in further discussion, was that members do not have the time or training to understand what the models do or what the numbers they produce mean. Members depend heavily on their staff people to come up with the "right" numbers and to be sure that these numbers are not going to prove embarrassing to them later on.

18. This was an observation made by longtime CEA staffer Mike Munroe, who had the unique opportunity to observe CEA operations through four administrations. Interview with Mike Munroe, July 1981.

7. Accounting for Successful Model Use

1. Interview with Michael Barth, ICF, Inc., Washington, D.C., July 24, 1981.

2. HEW's cost estimate provided by Richard Kasten, Office of the Assistant Secretary for Planning and Evaluation, Department of Health and Human Services; DOL's cost estimate provided by Ray Uhalde, Office of the Assistant Secretary for Policy and Evaluation Research, Department of Labor, July 21, 1981.

3. Most members of the econometrics and modeling communities feel that models will remain because they are needed, and that no individual is strong enough to remove modeling from the policymaking process. It is interesting to note, however, that there is a precedent for the politically motivated destruction of modeling efforts. Otto Eckstein recalled that a former executive from General Motors, serving as an Assistant Secretary of Defense in the Eisenhower administration, single-handedly destroyed almost all federal government use of input/output modeling (a technique developed by the Russian-born Leontief) because he believed such planning-oriented modeling was socialistic. Interview with Otto Eckstein, December 1981.

4. The question of how high modeling costs should be has entered into the considerations of managers and model users in executive agencies, the CBO, and the Fed, and there has been concern that model use be kept within reason because it is expensive. However, the prevailing objective was to do whatever analysis necessary to provide a solid assessment of conditions and options in support of policy formation, and this usually limited cost-control efforts to eliminating obvious extravagances such as unnecessary disk storage charges. Some agency analysts felt that the government-wide efforts to cut costs brought by the Reagan administration would result in greater attention to controlling modeling costs, but by 1982 no regulations dealing with modeling had emerged. Any reductions in modeling costs that had materialized were due to reductions in the use of certain models for ideological reasons, not economic reasons. At the same time, the new supply-side and monetarist models were being introduced and used, and we saw no evidence that net reductions in modeling costs had been achieved.

5. The relative advantage of the Keynesian models in this regard derives primarily from the fact that these models have a long and highly developed history. Thus these models naturally have a more refined intellectual base that is somewhat independent of whether the forecasts of the models are in fact more "accurate" than the rival models.

6. There had been controversy for some time over the extent to which the large models adequately deal with economic reality. Conservative Republican Congressman Jack Kemp (New York) criticized the use of these models on the floor of the House in 1977, even quoting Keynes' observation (from *The General Theory of Employment, Interest, and Money*) that "a large proportion of recent 'mathematical' economics are mere concoctions, as imprecise as the initial assumptions they rest on." Kemp went on to claim that CBO's analyses were based on such faulty economic models, and suggested that Congress either "abandon the use of econometrics entirely . . . or develop a model which can more closely approximate the real world" (Kemp 1977: 6835).

7. Interesting accounts of David Stockman's experiences in the creation of the Reagan administration's fiscal policies can be found in Greider (1981), and Stockman (1986).

8. This remark was made by BAD analyst Mark Therber shortly before he left CBO. Interview with Mark Therber, July 1981.

8. Critical Factors in Successful Modeling

1. See chapter 8 for an inventory of the full array of variables in our research and the propositions we explored in our analyses.

2. A former employee of the Urban Institute remarked that DRI had strongly lobbied against a federal government plan to create an integrated, on-line data service of federal data, on grounds that the government should not do tasks that the private sector was already handling well. The federal data service was never adopted. Interview with B. Teitel, July 22, 1980.

3. The Treasury Department, the Brookings Institution, and HEW have all worked on the problem of linking diverse data sets. Useful overviews of these efforts can be found in Wertheimer (1978), Pankoke-Babatz (1980), and Paass (1982a,b).

4. It should be noted that the positive attitude of users toward DRI data quality stems more from the data's technical accuracy and reliability than from their substantive quality. There are a number of severe problems associated with national account data, and there is a large base of literature on these problems. Major problems include conceptual ones (e.g., "What does this variable mean?"), measurement problems ("unobservable results"), methodological problems (making seasonal adjustments), and never-ending revisions in the definitions of variables, making the task of historical comparisons a genuine adventure. Oskar Morgenstern's classic *On the Accuracy of Economic Observations* (1950) is a good reference on the general problems of data accuracy in economic observations. Other useful references related to data accuracy in macroeconomic models are: Cochran (1962), Durbin (1954), Denton and Kuiper (1965), and Zarkovitch (1966). There is a comparable but smaller body of work on problems in microdata. A good reference is Hansen, Hurvitz, and Bershad (1961).

There is a subtle issue of data quality at stake in both macroeconomic models and microsimulation models that should be mentioned here. This has to do with the question of required data accuracy given the model's intended application. Macroeconomic models are fundamentally driven by the economic theories and empirical developments over time that are embodied in the model's equations. Theoretical issues and comparability over time tend to be somewhat more important to model outcomes than the microlevel precision of the data that are used in these models.

The national accounts data, for example, contain many conceptual, measurement, and estimation errors. Morgenstern once remarked that "economics [based on national accounts data] is a one-digit science," by which he meant that only the first digit in an economic statistic was to be trusted. But data errors seem to threaten microanalytic simulation models in a manner different from the threats posed to macroeconomic modeling. Microsimulation models are more dependent on the quality of data used because the data, in a sense, "drive" the models. The initial data base forms the foundation on which all "future populations," derived by aging an old data set, are based. Problems arise because of data reporting and recording problems in the data collection portions of these systems. Microsimulation files contain primary data on individual participants in a given program or system such as food stamps. There are many subtle sources of systematic error that can creep into such data bases. For example, the Treasury's PITM relies for its data on income tax filings. While such data might be a useful representation of income tax system behavior, and may in fact be the only useful source of such data, the data remain approximations of what they are used to represent. As one economist at the Treasury Department observed concerning the PITM model's data base, "It isn't a data base on taxes; it is a record of how people fill out tax returns."

9. Computer Models and Policymaking

1. We feel that our study has implications for DSS models as well as for planning models. In chapter 1, we argued that the large-scale planning models used by government agencies were similar to the large-scale DSS recently developed for industry. Our study indicates that significant examples of successful implementation of large-scale, complex DSS can be found, provided one broadens the use of the term "DSS" to include the major computerized policy-modeling systems in the federal government. Given the size of the econometric and microanalytic simulation models we studied, their considerable extent of use, and their diffusion within government, it is fair to say these models are probably among the most successful large-scale DSS to date. In size and complexity, they are similar to the energy-forecasting models developed during the 1970s and now also used extensively in government and industry (Greenberger 1983; Ascher and Overholt 1983).

2. See the discussion in chapter 1 regarding "Focus on Planning Models" and "Research Methods and Case Studies." Also, see Gass (1983) and Kraemer and King (1986).

REFERENCES

Aaron, H. 1978. *Politics and the Professors: The Great Society in Perspective.* Washington, D.C.: Brookings Institution.

Abernathy, W. and J. M. Ulterback. 1978. Patterns of industrial innovation. *Technology Review,* June-July, pp. 41–47.

Abt, C. C. 1965. *Survey of the State-of-the-Art: Social, Political, and Economic Models and Simulations.* Cambridge, Mass. Abt Associates.

Allen, J. T. 1974. Factors determining welfare costs and caseloads. MPR Working Paper No. E-8 (November), Mathematica Policy Research, Washington, D.C.

—— 1975. Reforming the food stamp program. *Washington Post,* February 1, p. A-14.

Allen, J. T. and H. Beebout. 1974. Problems in estimating costs and caseloads for current and proposed welfare programs: Three case studies. MPR Working Paper No. E-24 (November), Mathematica Policy Research, Washington, D.C.

Archibald, R. W. and R. B. Hoffman. 1964. Introducing technological change in a bureaucratic structure. Paper delivered at the annual meeting of the Academy of Management, Chicago, December 28–30.

Ascher, W. 1978. *Forecasting: An Appraisal for Policy-Makers and Planners.* Baltimore: Johns Hopkins University Press.

Ascher, W. and W. H. Overholt. 1983. *Strategic Planning and Forecasting.* New York: Wiley.

Balogh, T. 1980. Economists in the long run: Is Keynes dead? *The New Republic* (June), 7:15–18.

Barker, W. G. 1973. The use of models in urban transportation. Washington, D.C.: Department of Transportation (NTIS No. PB-222 893).

Bean, A. S., R. D. Neal, M. Radnor, and D. A. Tansik. 1975. Structural and behavioral correlates of implementation in U.S. business organizations. In R. L. Schultz and D. P. Slevin, eds., *Implementing Operations Research/Management Science.*

Beebout, H. 1975. Analyses of the cost and caseload impacts of eliminating the food stamp purchase requirement. Study proposal submitted to the U.S. House Committee on Agriculture, July 24.

—— 1977a. The MATH welfare model: Executive summary. MPR Working Paper No. E-46 (February), Mathematica Policy Research, Washington, D.C.

—— 1977b. The MATH welfare model. MPR Working Paper No. E-45 (February), Mathematica Policy Research, Washington, D.C.

—— 1977c. Microsimulation as a policy tool: The MATH model. Policy Analysis Series No. 13 (February), Mathematica Policy Research, Washington, D.C.

—— 1980. Food stamp policy modeling: An application of MATH. In R. Haveman and D. Hollenbeck, eds., *Microeconomic Simulation Models for Public Policy Analysis,* pp. 45–72.

Betson, D., D. Greenberg, and R. Kasten. 1978. An analysis of the economic efficiency and distributional effects of alternative program structures: The negative income tax versus the credit income tax. HEW Staff Working Paper (December 14).

—— 1979. A simulation of the Program for Better Jobs and Income. Technical Analysis Paper No. 17 (January), Office of Income Security Policy/ASPE/HEW, Washington, D.C.

—— 1980. A micro-simulation model for analyzing alternative welfare reform proposals: An application to the Program for Better Jobs and Income. In R. Haveman and D. Hollenbeck, eds., *Microeconomic Simulation Models for Public Policy Analysis,* pp. 153–188.

Blau, P. and R. Scott. 1962. *Formal Organizations.* San Francisco: Chandler.

Board of Governors. 1974. *The Federal Reserve System: Purposes and Functions* (September), Washington, D.C.: Federal Reserve System.

Boyce, D. E., N. D. Day, and C. McDonald. 1970. *Metropolitan Plan Making: An Analysis of Experience with the Preparation and Evaluation of Alternative Land Use and Transportation Plans.* Philadelphia: Regional Science Research Institute.

Brewer, G. D. 1973. *Politicians, Bureaucrats, and the Consultant: A Critique of Urban Problem Solving.* New York: Basic Books.

—— 1974. *An Analyst's View of the Uses and Abuses of Modeling for Decision-Making.* Santa Monica, Calif.: Rand Corporation.

—— 1977. Review of the DOD modeling effort and modeling as a profession. Paper presented at a workshop held at the National Bureau of Standards, Gaithersburg, Md., April 28–29.

—— 1978. Operational social systems modeling: Pitfalls and perspectives. *Policy Sciences* 10:157–169.

Brewer, G. D. and M. Shubik. 1979. *The War Game: A Critique of Military Problem Solving.* Cambridge: Harvard University Press.

Bruckel, S. and W. Schwartz. 1975. *Personalfluktuation in Grobforschungseinrichtungen eine personalstatische Analyse.* St. Augustin: Gesellschaft für Mathematik und Datenverarbeitung.

Bungers, D. 1979. *Microanalytic Simulation Models as Tools for Legislative Planning. BAFPLAN: A Planning System for the German Federal Student Aid Program.* Bonn: Institute for Planning and Decision Systems, Gesellschaft für Mathematik und Datenverarbeitung.

Bungers, D. and P. Hoschka. 1977. Mikromodelle: Ein DV-Instrument zur Planung von Gesetzen. *GMD-Jahresbericht,* pp. 43–47. Bonn: Gesellschaft für Mathematik und Datenverarbeitieng.

Burke, V. and V. Burke. 1974. *Nixon's Good Deed: Welfare Reform.* New York: Columbia University Press.

Business Week. 1981. Where the big econometric models go wrong. March 30, pp. 70–77.

Califano, J. 1981. *Governing America: An Insider's Report from the White House and Cabinet.* New York: Simon and Schuster.

CBO (Congressional Budget Office). 1979a. Creation of a 1980 data base for purposes of determining the relative impact of the Social Welfare Reform Amendments of 1979 (final draft, August) Mathematica Policy Research, Washington, D.C.

—— 1979b. The utilization of microsimulation techniques for welfare reform analyses. Paper presented by G. W. Hoagland, Symposium on Government Planning, November.

—— 1982. Creation of fiscal year 1980 and 1984 current services micro data bases. Mathematica Policy Research, Washington, D.C.

Center for Water Resources, University of Texas. 1976. Effectiveness of technology transfer programs. National Technical Information Service, Springfield, Va.

Chaiken, J. 1977a. *Implementation of Emergency Service Deployment Models in Operating Agencies.* Santa Monica, Calif.: Rand Corporation.

—— 1977b. *Transfer of Emergency Service Deployment Models to Operating Agencies.* Santa Monica, Calif.: Rand Corporation.

Chaiken, J., T. Craybill, L. Holliday, D. Jaquette, M. Lawless, and E. Quade. 1975. Criminal justice models: An overview. Santa Monica, Calif.: Rand Corporation.

Chakrabarti, A. K. 1973. Some concepts of technology transfer: Adoption of innovations in organizational context. *R and D Management* 3(3):11–120.

Chow, G. 1977. A programmer's's primer to TRIM. Institute Paper, pp. 996–1005. Washington, D.C.: Urban Institute.

Churchman, C. W. and A. H. Schainblatt. 1965. The researcher and the manager: A dialectic of implementation. *Management Science* 11:B69–87.

Cochran, W. G. 1962. Errors of Measurement and Statistics. *Technometrics* 10:637–666.

Committee on Merchant Marine and Fisheries, 94th Congress. 1975. *Computer Simulation Methods To Aid National Growth Policy.* Washington, D.C.: PO.

Comptroller General of the U.S. 1977. *An Evaluation of the Use of the Transfer Income Model—TRIM—To Analyze Welfare Programs.* Report to the Congress, PAD–78–14 (November 25). Washington, D.C.: General Accounting Office.

—— 1979. *Uses of National Economic Models by Federal Agencies.* Report to the Congress, PAD–79–24 (May 16). Washington, D.C.: General Accounting Office.

Congressional Quarterly (August 9, 1975), 33(32):1790.

—— (March 20, 1976), 34(12):618.

—— (August 14, 1976), 34(33):2236.

—— (February 5, 1977), 35(6):211.

—— (February 19, 1977), 35(8):337–338.

—— (April 30, 1977), 35(8):795–796.

—— (August 13, 1977), 35(34):1702.

—— (November 19, 1977), 35(47):2449.

—— (December 25, 1977), 35(52):2602.

Control Analysis Corporation. 1978. A study for assessing ways to improve the utility of large scale models—task 3 report: Reviewer opinion and discussion report of alternate improvement possibilities. Palo Alto, Calif.: Control Analysis Corporation.

Costello, T. W. 1971. Change in municipal government: A view from the inside. *The Journal of Applied Behavioral Sciences* (March-April), 7:131–145.

Crissey, B. 1977. Models in the policy process: A framework. Paper presented at a workshop held at the National Bureau of Standards, Gaithersburg, Md., April 28–29.

Czepiel, J. A. 1974. Word of mouth processes in the diffusion of a major technological innovation. *Journal of Marketing Research* 11:172–180.

Dalkey, N. 1965. *Families of Models.* Santa Monica, Calif.: Rand Corporation.

Danziger, J. N., W. H. Dutton, R. Kling, and K. K. Kraemer. 1982. *Computers and Politics.* New York: Columbia University Press.

de Neufville, J. I. 1975. *Social Indicators and Public Policy: Interactive Processes of Design and Application.* New York: Elsevier.

—— 1981. Federal requirements and local planning capacity: The case of CDBG. Working Paper No. 365. Berkeley: Institute of Urban and Regional Development, University of California, Berkeley.

—— 1984. Federal statistics in local governments. Working Paper No. 439. Berkeley: Institute of Urban and Regional Development, University of California, Berkeley.

Denton, F. T. and J. Kuiper. 1965. The effect of measurement error on parameter estimates and forecasts. *Review of Economics and Statistics* 47:198–206.

Department of the Army. 1971. Review of selected army models. Washington, D.C.: Department of the Army.

Department of Commerce Memorandum. 1979. To: Members of Subcommittee on Micro-Simulation, Federal Committee on Statistical Methodology. From: Milo Sunderhauf. RE: Meeting to Consider Agenda for Subcommittee, March 20.

—— 1977. Software requirements for an improvement in transfer and adaptability of models. Paper presented at the NBS workshop on the utility and use of large-scale mathematical models, Gaithersburg, Md.

—— 1978. Implementation strategies for socio-economic models. Paper presented at the Institute de Recherche en Informatique et Automatique (IRIA) Symposium of Systems Optimization and Analysis, Paris.

—— 1979a. Strategies for standardization in socio-economic modeling. In B. P. Zeigler, M. S. Elzas, G. J. Klir, and T. I. Oren, eds., *Methodology in Systems Modeling and Simulation,* pp. 161–168. Amsterdam: North-Holland.

—— 1979b. Toward standardization in socio-economic modeling. *Technological Forecasting and Social Change* 13(4):321–331.

—— 1986. Implementation by legal demand: The BAFLAN case. Irvine: Public Policy Research Organization, University of California.

Dickhoven, S., ed. 1976. Modellierungssoftware: Proceeding of a GMD state-of-the-art workshop on modelling software. GMD Report IPES 76.206. Bonn: Gesellschaft für Mathematik und Datenverarbeitung.

Downs, G. W. and L. B. Mohr. 1975. Conceptual issues in the study of innovation. Discussion paper prepared for delivery at the annual meeting of the American Political Science Association, San Francisco, September 2–5.

Doyle, P. 1979. Creation of a 1980 data base for purposes of determining the relative impact of the Social Welfare Reform Amendments of 1979. Washington, D.C.: Mathematica Policy Research.

Doyle, P., D. Edson, N. Pappas, and B. Boulding. 1980. Creation of 1980 and 1984 data bases from the March 1978 Current Population Survey. Ch. 1. Mathematica Policy Research, prepared for Congressional Budget Office, U.S. Congress, February 16.

Doyle, P. and K. Neyland, eds. 1979. MATH technical description. Washington, D.C.: Mathematica Policy Research.

Drake, J. W. 1973. *The Administration of Transportation Model Projects.* Lexington Books Studies in Transportation and Regional Science, pp. 243–246. Lexington, Mass.: Heath.

DRI (Data Resources, Inc.). 1981. Product Description. Lexington, Mass.: Data Resources, Inc.

Duesenberry, J. S., G. Fromm, L. R. Klein, and E. Kuh, eds. 1965. *The Brookings Quarterly Econometric Model of the United States.* Chicago: Rand McNally.

Durbin, J. 1954. Errors in variables. *Review of the International Statistics Institute* 1::23–32.

Dutton, W. H., J. N. Danziger, and K. L. Kraemer. 1980. Did the policy fail? The selective use of automated information in the policy-making process. In H. M. Ingram and D. E. Mann, eds., *Why Policies Succeed or Fail.* Vol. 8 of Sage Yearbooks in Politics and Public Policy. Beverly Hills, Calif.: Sage Publications.

Dutton, W. H. and K. L. Kraemer. 1977. Technology and urban management. *Administration and Society* 9(3):305–340.

—— 1979. The automation of bias: Computers and local government budgeting. *Information Privacy Journal* 1(7):303–311.

—— 1985. *Modeling as Negotiating.* Norwood, N.J.: Ablex.

Emshoff, J. R. and R. L. Sisson. 1970. Design and use of computer simulation models. New York: Macmillan.

Eveland, J. D., E. M. Rogers, and C. A. Klepper. 1977. The innovation process in public organizations: Some elements of a preliminary model. Final Report (March), University of Michigan. Grant No. RDA-7517952, National Science Foundation.

Fainstein, N. I. and S. S. Fainstein. 1972. Innovation in urban bureaucracies: Clients and change. *American Behavioral Scientist* 15(4):511–531.

Feely, M. M. 1978. The New Haven direction center. In R. R. Nelson and D. Yates, eds., *Innovation and Implementation in Public Organizations,* pp. 39–68.

Fliegel, F. C. and J. E. Kivlin. 1966. Attributes of innovations as factors in diffusion. *American Journal of Sociology* 72(3):235–248.

Frendewey, J. O., Jr., R. W. Duea, Jr., D. E. Monarchi and R. H. Taylor. 1977. General guidelines regarding the transferability of computer based socio-economic, land use, and environmental models. Springfield, Va.: National Technical Information Service.

Fromm, G., W. L. Hamilton, and D. E. Hamilton. 1974. *Federally Supported Mathematical Models: Survey and Analysis.* Washington, D.C.: GPO.

Fromm, G. and L. R. Klein, eds. 1975. *The Brookings Model: Perspective and Recent Developments.* New York: American Elsevier.

GAO (General Accounting Office). 1973a. *Advantages and Limitations of Computer Simulation in Decision Making.* Washington, D.C.: General Accounting Office.

—— 1973b. *Auditing a Computer Model: A Case Study.* Washington, D.C.: General Accounting Office.

—— 1976a. *Improvement Needed in Managing Automated Decision Making by Computers Throughout the Federal Government.* Washington, D.C.: General Accounting Office.

—— 1976b. *Review of the 1974 Project Independent Evaluation Systems.* Washington, D.C.: General Accounting Office.

—— 1976c. *Ways to Improve Management of Federally Funded Control Analysis Computerized Models.* Washington, D.C.: General Accounting Office.

—— 1976d. General Accounting Office Memorandum. To: OCR; From: Frank Capece, supervisory mathematician, OPA) RE: Meeting to Discuss the Committee's Interests in the Transfer Income Model, June 1.

—— 1976e. General Accounting Office Memorandum. To: Director, OCR. From: Harry Havens, director, Program Analysis Division. RE: PAD Review of TRIM, November 8.

—— 1977. *An Evaluation of the Use of the Transfer Income Model—TRIM—To Analyze Welfare Programs* (November 25). Appendix I, pp. 103–105. Washington, D.C.: General Accounting Office.

—— 1979. *Uses of National Economic Models by Federal Agencies.* Washington, D.C.: General Accounting Office.

—— 1981. *A Glossary of Terms Used in the Federal Budget Process.* 3d ed. (March). Washington, D.C.: General Accounting Office.

Gass, S. I. 1977. Evaluation of complex models. *Computers and Operations Research* 4(1):27–35.

—— 1983. Decision-aiding models: Validation, assessment, and related issues for policy analysis. *Operations Research* 31(4):603–631.

Gass, S. I. and R. L. Sisson. 1975. *A Guide to Models in Governmental Planning and Operations.* Potomac, Md.: Sauger Books.

Gass, S. I., ed. 1979. *Utility and Use of Large-Scale Mathematical Models: Proceedings of a Workshop.* NBS Special Bulletin 534. Washington, D.C.: U.S. National Bureau of Standards.

GMD (Gesellschaft für Mathematik und Datenverarbeitung). 1979a. Implementation plan for the IMPMOD (model implementation and impact research) project. Bonn: GMD.

—— 1979b. Structural plan for the planning models program. Bonn: GMD.

—— 1980a. Modellbanksystem Version 1.3, Benutzerhandbuch (Users Guide). Bonn: GMD (Report IPES 80. 203).

—— 1980b. Arbeiten und Ergebnisse des Instituts für Planungs- und Entscheidungssysteme. Bonn: GMD (Internal Report IPES 90. 209).

Greenberg, D. 1978. Participation in guaranteed employment programs: An exploratory simulation. In J. Palmer, ed., *Public Service Employment, Supported Work, and Job Guarantees.* Washington, D.C.: Brookings Institution.

Greenberger, M. 1983. *Caught Unawares: The Energy Decade in Retrospect.* Cambridge, Mass.: Ballinger.

Greenberger, M. and M. A. Crenson. 1973. *The Study of Simulation Modeling in Socio-Economic Policy Research.* Baltimore: Johns Hopkins University.

Greenberger, M., M. A. Crenson, and B. L. Crissey. 1976. *Models in the Policy Process: Public Decision Making in the Computer Era.* New York: Russell Sage Foundation.

Greider, W. 1981. The education of David Stockman. *Atlantic Monthly* 248(6):27–54.

Gupta, J. and N. D. Gupta. 1977. Management science implementation: Experiences of a practicing OR manager. *Interfaces,* May, pp. 84–90.

Hall, G. and S. Loucks. 1977. A developmental model for determining whether the treatment is actually implemented. *American Educational Research Journal* 14(3):263–276.

—— 1978. Innovation configurations: Analyzing the adaptations of innovations (November). Austin: University of Texas, Research and Development Center for Teacher Education.

Hall, O. P., Jr. 1975. A policy model appraisal paradigm. *Policy Sciences* 6(2):185–195.

Hansen, M. H., W. N. Hurvitz, and M. A. Bershad. 1961. Measurement errors in censuses and surveys. *Bulletin de 1 Institute International de Statistique* 38(2):359–374.

Harris, R. 1978. Microanalytic simulation models for analyses of public welfare policies. Urban Institute Paper on Income Security, No. 819–1. Washington, D.C.: Urban Institute.

Harvey, A. 1970. Factors making for implementation success and failure. *Management Science* (February), 16:B312–321.

Hauff, V. 1980. Staatliche Forschungspolitik und Grossforschungseinlichtungen in den 80er Jahren. Unpublished manuscript of a speech of the Federal Minister of Research and Technology, May 7, Heidelberg, West Germany.

Havelock, R. G. 1969. *Planning for Innovation Through Dissemination and Utilization of Knowledge.* Center for Research on Utilization and Scientific Knowledge (CRUSK), Institute for Social Research. Ann Arbor: University of Michigan.

Haveman, R., and D. Hollenbeck, eds. 1980. *Microeconomic Simulation Models for Public Policy Analysis.* New York: Academic Press.

Hayes, F. and J. E. Rasmussen. 1972. *Centers for Innovation in Cities and States.* San Francisco: San Francisco Press.

Hayward, G., O. H. Allen, and J. Masterson. 1976. Characteristics and diffusion of technological innovations. *R and D Management* 4(1):15–24.

Hegelheimer, A. 1981. Einsatz und Erfahrung mit Modellen in der Bildungsplanung. Paper in GMD lecture series Possibilities and Limitations of Planning Models (October). Bonn: Gesellschaft für Mathematik und Datenverarbeitung.

Heilbroner, R. L. 1953. *The Worldly Philosophers.* New York: Simon and Schuster.

Heilemann, U. 1980. Econometric model practice in the U.S. *Jahrbücher für Nationalokonomie und Statistik* 195(1):61–76.

Hendricks, G. and R. Holden. 1976. The role of microanalytic simulation models in projecting OASDI costs. *Proceedings of the Business and Economic Statistics Section, American Statistical Association.* Washington, D.C.: American Statistical Association.

Henize, J. 1980. Modeling large-scale socio-economic systems: Can we begin to do better? *Large Scale Systems* 1:89–105.

Heinze, J. 1982. Balancing the conflicting goals of economic efficiency, social justice, and individual liberty: A comparison of contrasting values of U.S. and German society. In H. Stachowiak et al., eds., *Bedürfnisse, Werte und Normen im Wandel,* Munich: W. Fink/F. Schonigh Verlag.

Henry, J. 1978. The future hustle. *The New Republic* (February), 4:16–20.

Herzfeld, E. 1981. Das Wohngeldbemessungssystem des BMBau. Paper in GMD lecture series Possibilities and Limitations of Planning Models (September). Bonn: Gesells-chaft für Mathematik und Datenverarbeitung.

HEW (Health, Education, and Welfare Administration). 1977. Comments of the Depart-ment of HEW on the GAO draft report *An Evaluation of the Transfer Income Model,* Comptroller General of the U.S., Report to the Congress, PAD–78–14 (November 25). Washington, D.C.: General Accounting Office.

Hickmann, B. G., ed. 1972. *Econometric Models of Cyclical Behavior: Proceedings of a Conference.* New York: National Bureau of Economic Research.

Hogan, W. W. 1979. The energy modeling forum. In S. I. Gass, ed., *Utility and Use of Large-Scale Mathematical Models,* pp. 137–161.

—— 1980. Alternatives to transfer of large-scale models. Paper presented at the annual meeting of American Association for Advancement of Science (symposium on "Outlook for Large-Scale Energy Models"), San Francisco, January.

Hollis, M. S., W. H. Dutton, and K. L. Kraemer. 1978. Fiscal impact budgeting systems: A technical assessment. Irvine: Public Policy Research Organization, University of California.

Hoschka, P. 1977. DV-Unterstützung politischer Planung (Planning Paper). Bonn: Gesellschaft für Mathemalik und Datenverarbeitung.

Hoschka, P. and U. Kalbhen, eds. 1975. *Datenverarbeitung in der politischen Planung.* Frankfurt: Campus.

House, P. W. 1974. Diogenes revisited—the search for a valid model. *Simulation* 23(4):117–125.

House, P. W. and J. McLeod. 1977. *Large-Scale Models for Policy Evaluation.* New York: Wiley.

Illich, I. 1971. *Deschooling Society.* New York: Harper and Row.

Jahnke, E. 1981. Okonometrisches Modell der deutschen Bundesbank. Deutsche Bun-desbank, Internal Report (February), Frankfurt.

Jick, T. D. 1979. Mixing qualitative and quantitative methods: Triangulation in action. *Administrative Science Quarterly* (December), 24:602–611.

Katz, D. and R. Katz. 1967. Organizational change. In D. Katz and R. Kahn, eds., *The Social Psychology of Organizations,* pp. 390–451. New York: Wiley.

Katz, E., M. L. Levin, and H. Hamilton. 1963. Traditions of research on the diffusion of innovation. *American Journal of Sociology* 28(2):237–253.

Kemp, J. 1977. Speech by Jack Kemp to the House, March 9. *Congressional Record,* House, 123(6):6835.

Keen, P. G. W. 1981. Value analysis: Justifying decision support systems. *MIS Quarterly* 5(1):1–16.

Keen, P. G. W. and M. Scott-Morton. 1978. *Decision Support Systems.* Reading, Mass.: Addison-Wesley.

King, J. L. 1977. Centralization vs. decentralization of computing: An empirical assess-ment in city governments. Ph.D. diss., Graduate School of Management, University of California, Irvine.

—— 1983. Successful implementation of large-scale decision support systems: Comput-erized models in U.S. economic policy making. *Systems, Objectives, Solutions* 3(4):183–205.

—— 1984. Ideology and use of large-scale decision support systems in national policy-making. *Systems, Objectives, Solutions* 4:81–104.

King, J. L. and K. L. Kraemer. 1978. Electronic funds transfer as a subject of study in technology, society, and public policy. *Telecommunications Policy* 2(1): 13–21.

—— 1979. Operations research technology transfer: The urban sector experience. Irvine: Public Policy Research Organization, University of California.

—— 1981. Cost as a social impact of information technology. In M. L. Moss, ed., *Telecommunications and Productivity*, pp. 93–130. Reading, Mass.: Addison-Wesley.

—— 1985. *The Dynamics of Computing.* New York: Columbia University Press.

Klein, L. R. and R. M. Young. 1980. *An Introduction to Econometric Forecasting and Forecasting Models.* Lexington, Mass.: Lexington Books, D. C. Heath.

Klein, L. R. and E. Burmeister. 1976. *Economic Model Performance.* Pittsburgh: University of Pennsylvania Press.

Kling, R. and W. Scacchi. 1979. Recurrent dilemmas of computer use in complex organizations. *Proceedings of the 1979 National Computer Conference* 48:107–116. New York: AFIPS Press.

—— 1981. The web of computing. Irvine: Public Policy Research Organization, University of California.

Kmenta, J. and J. Ramsey, eds. 1981. *Methodology of Macroeconometric Models.* Amsterdam: North-Holland.

Kraemer, K. L. 1977. Local government, information systems, and technology transfer: Evaluating some common assertions about computer applications transfer. *Public Administration Review* (July-August), 37(4):368–383.

—— 1981. The politics of model implementation. *Systems, Objectives, Solutions* 1(4):161–178.

Kraemer, K. L., J. N. Danziger, and W. H. Dutton. 1979. Automated information systems and urban decision making. *Urban Systems* 3(4):177–190.

Kraemer, K. L., J. N. Danziger, W. H. Dutton, A. Mood, and R. Kling. 1976. A future cities survey research design for policy analysis. *Socio-Economic Planning Sciences* 10(5):199–211.

Kraemer, K. L. and W. H. Dutton. 1979a. The interests served by technological reform: The case of computing. *Administration and Society* 2(1):180–186.

—— 1979b. Urban technology, executive support, and computing. *The Urban Interest* 1(2):35–42.

Kraemer, K. L., W. H. Dutton, and J. Matthews. 1975. Municipal computers: Growth, use, and management. *Urban Data Service Report,* vol. 79, no. 11. Washington, D.C.: International City Management Association.

Kraemer, K. L., W. H. Dutton, and A. Northrop. 1980. *The Management of Information Systems.* New York: Columbia University Press.

Kraemer, K. L. and J. L. King. A critical assessment of urban technology transfer: The case of computing applications in U.S. local governments. Irvine: Public Policy Research Organization, University of California. (Published in *Transfer 4,* the West German Journal of Applied Social Science, as Transfer von Informationstechnologie: Amerikanische Erfahrungen. Bonn: Westdeutscher.)

—— 1980. An international comparative study of computing policies and impacts in cities. Irvine: Public Policy Research Organization, University of California.

—— 1986. Computer-based models for policy making: Uses and impacts in the U.S. federal government. *Operations Research* (forthcoming).

Kraemer, K. L. and J. Perry. 1979. The federal push to bring technology to the cities: The case of computers. *Public Administration Review* 39(3):260–276.

Krelle, W. 1980. Möglichkeiten und Grenzen okonometrischer Modelle. Paper in GMD lecture series Possibilities and Limitations of Planning Models (June). Bonn: Gesellschaft für Mathematik und Datenverarbeitung.

Kresge, D. 1979. The EPRI/NBER energy model assessment project. In S. I. Gass, ed., *Utility and Use of Large-Scale Mathematical Models,* pp. 123–135.

Krupp, H. J. 1980a. The role of public employment in an integrated mid-term-programme for recovery of full-employment in the Federal Republic of Germany. Paper presented at the congress "Public Employment and Public Finance" of the International Federation of Information Processors (IFIP), Jerusalem, Israel, August.

—— 1980b. Möglichkeiten und Grenzen mikroanalytischer Modelle. Paper in GMD lecture series Possibilities and Limitations of Planning Models (December). Bonn: Gesellschaft für Mathematik und Datenverarbeitung.

Krupp, H. J., H. P. Galler, H. Grohmann, R. Hauser, and G. Wagner, eds. 1981. *Alternativen der Rentenreform '84.* Frankfurt: Campus.

Kübler, K. 1981. Einsatzmöglichkeiten von Energiemodellen für die Energiepolitik. Paper in GMD lecture series Possibilities and Limitations of Planning Models (May). Bonn: Gesellschaft für Mathematik und Datenverarbeitung.

Lambright, W . H. 1977. *Adoption and Utilization of Urban Technology: A Decision-Making Study.* Syracuse, N.Y.: Syracuse Research.

Larsen, J. K. and R. Agarwala-Rogers. 1977. Reinvention of innovative ideas: Modified? Adopted? None of the above? *Evaluation* 4:136–140.

Larson, L. 1977. Model implementation. Paper presented at the National Bureau of Standards workshop on the utility and use of large-scale mathematical models, Gaithersburg, Md.

Lee, D., Jr. 1973. Requiem for large scale models. *Journal of the American Institute of Planners* 39(2):136–174.

Lepper, F. 1981. Ein Simulationsmodell für sozialpolitische Entscheidungen. *Datenverarbeitung und Recht* 10(3):221–229.

Lipinski, H., R. Amara, and K. Spengler. 1978. Communication needs in computer modeling. *World Simulation Conference 78: Proceedings,* Tampa, Fla.

Little, J. D. C. 1970. Models and managers: The concept of a decision calculus. *Management Science* 16(8):466–485.

Livingston, R. G. 1982. Wie berechenbar ist Ronald Reagan? *Die Zeit* 24:3.

Lucas, H. C. 1975. Behavioral factors in system implementation. In R. L. Schultz and D. P. Slevin, eds., *Implementing Operations Research/Management Science,* pp. 203–215.

Lynn, L. 1980. *Designing Public Policy: A Casebook on the Role of Policy Analysis.* Santa Monica, Calif.: Goodyear.

Lynn, L. and D. Whitman. 1981. *The President as Policy Maker: Jimmy Carter and Welfare Reform.* Philadelphia: Temple University Press.

McKay, C. 1978. Micro analytic simulation system technical documentation. Bethesda, Md.: Hendrickson Corporation.

McKinsey and Co. 1973. Ausrichtung der Ausbildungsforderung auf die Zukunft. International Study for Federal Ministry of Education and Science (BMBW), Düsseldorf, West Germany.

McNees, S. 1976. An evaluation of economic forecasts: Extension and update. *New England Economic Review,* September-October, pp. 30–44.

—— 1977. An assessment of the Council of Economic Advisers' forecast of 1977. *New England Economic Review,* March-April, pp. 3–7.

—— 1979a. The forecasting record for the 1970s. *New England Economic Review,* September-October, pp. 1–21.

—— 1979b. The accuracy of macroeconomic models and forecasts of the U.S. economy. In P. Omerod, ed., *Economic Modelling,* pp. 245–264.

—— 1981. The recent record of thirteen forecasters. *New England Economic Review,* September-October, pp. 5–21.

—— 1982. The role of macroeconomic models in forecasting and policy analysis in the United States. *Journal of Forecasting* 1:37–48.

McNees, S. K. and J. Ries. 1983. The track record of macroeconomic models. *New England Economic Review,* November-December, pp. 5–18.

Magnuson, E., D. Beckworth, and D. Brew. 1981. A visit to the woodshed. *Time,* November 23, pp. 10–13.

Magnuson, R. 1982. Battered in 1981, economic forecasters resolve to do better in 1982. *Los Angeles Times,* January 3, part V, p. 1.

Maher, T. J. 1972. Power to the states: Mobilizing public technology. *State Government* 45(2):124–134.

Malcom, D. G. 1965. On the need for improvement in implementation of OR. *Management Science* (February), 11:B48–58.

Manley, J. H. 1975. Implementation attitudes: A model and measurement methodology. In R. L. Schultz and D. P. Slevin, eds., *Implementing Operations Research/ Management Science.*

Maxfield, M. 1979. Microsimulation modeling. Chapter 7 in *A Research Design for the Employment Opportunity Pilot Projects.* Princeton, N.J.: Mathematica Policy Research.

Mayntz, R., ed. 1968. *Bürokratische Organisation.* Cologne: Kiepenheur-Witsch.

Mayntz, R. and F. Scharpf, eds. 1973. *Planungsorganisation.* Munich: Piper.

Menzel, D. 1975. Scientific and technological dimensions of innovation in the American states. Paper presented at 1975 Annual Meeting of the American Political Science Association, May 1–3, Chicago.

Menzel, H. and E. Katz. 1955. Social relations and innovation in the medical profession: The epidemiology of a new drug. *Public Opinion Quarterly* 19:337–352.

Methlie, L. B. 1983. Organizational variables affecting DSS implementation. In G. Huber, ed., *Proceedings of DSS '83,* Boston, pp. 75–85.

Mihram, G. A. 1972. Some practical aspects of the verification and validation of simulation models. *Operational Research Quarterly* 23(1):17–29.

Mintzberg, H. 1979. Beyond implementation: An analysis of resistance to policy. In K. B. Haley, ed., *O R '78,* pp. 106–162. Amsterdam: North-Holland.

Moeller, J. F. 1973. TRIM technical description. Urban Institute Working Paper (February). Washington, D.C.: Urban Institute.

Mohr, L. B. 1969. Determinants of innovation in organizations. *American Political Science Review* 63(1):111–126.

Monarchi, D. E. and R. H. Taylor. 1977. Final Report: Models Transfer Project. Springfield, Va.: National Technical Information Service.

Morgenstern, O. 1950. *On the Accuracy of Economic Observations.* Princeton, N.J.: Princeton University Press.

Moynihan, D. 1973. *The Politics of a Guaranteed Income: The Nixon Administration and the Family Assistance Program.* New York: Vintage Books.

MPR and THC (Mathematica Policy Research and the Hendrickson Corporation). 1978. *MATH Technical Bulletin,* vol. 1, March 22.

MPR and SSS (Mathematica Policy Research and Social Scientific Systems). 1979. MATH Users Workshop, handouts. November-December.

—— 1980. *Math Technical Bulletin* (Spring), vol. 3, no. 1.

Munson, F. and D. Pelz. 1980. *Innovating in Organizations: A Conceptual Framework.* Ann Arbor: University of Michigan.

National Research Council, Committee on Nuclear and Alternative Energy Systems, Modeling Resource Group. 1978. Energy modeling for an uncertain future. Supporting Paper 2. Washington, D.C.: National Academy of Sciences.

Naylor, T. H. 1983. Strategic planning and forecasting. *Journal of Forecasting* 2(2): 109–118.

Nelson, R. R. and D. Yates, eds. 1980. *Innovation and Implementation in Public Organizations.* Lexington, Mass.: Lexington Books.

NSF (National Science Foundation). 1978. Program announcement for extramural research. Washington, D.C.: Division of Policy Research and Analysis.

—— 1980. "Dear Colleague" letter from Alden S. Bean. Washington, D.C.: Division of Policy Research and Analysis.

OMB (Office of Management and Budget). 1980. *Budget of the United States Government: Fiscal Year 1980.* Washington, D.C.: PO.

—— 1981. *Budget of the United States Government: Fiscal Year 1981.* Washington, D.C.: PO.

Omerod, P., ed. 1979. *Economic Modelling.* London: Heinemann Educational Books.

Orcutt, G., S. Caldwell, and R. Wertheimer. 1976a. *Policy Exploration Through Microanalytic Simulation.* Washington, D.C.: Urban Institute.

—— 1976b. Microanalytic simulation. Urban Institute Working Paper No. 1217–4 (September). Washington, D.C.: Urban Institute.

—— 1977. A microanalytic simulation system. New Haven, Conn.: Institute for Social and Policy Studies, Yale University.

Orcutt, G., A. Glazer, R. Harris, and R. Wertheimer. 1980. Microsimulation modeling and the analysis of public transfer policies. In R. Haveman and D. Hollenbeck, eds., *Microeconomic Simulation Models for Public Policy Analysis,* pp. 81–106.

Orcutt, G., M. Greenberger, J. Korbel, and A. Rivlin. 1961. *Microanalysis of Socioeconomic Systems: A Simulation Study.* New York: Harper and Row.

Paass, G. 1982a. Comparison and evaluation of statistical matching methods. GMD Report IPES 82.0202. Bonn: Gesellschaft für Mathematik und Datenverarbeitung.

—— 1982b. Statistical match with additional information. GMD Report IPES 82.0204. Bonn: Gesellschaft für Mathematik und Datenverarbeitung.

Pack, H. and J. R. Pack. 1977a. The resurrection of the urban development model. *Policy Analysis* 3(3):407–427.

—— 1977b. Urban land-use models: The determinants of adoption and use. *Policy Sciences* 8:79–101.

Pack, J. R. 1975. The use of urban models: Report on a survey of planning organizations. *AIP Journal* (41)3:191–199.

—— 1978. Urban models: Diffusion and policy application. Philadelphia: Regional Science Research Institute.

Pankoke-Babatz, U. 1980. Einsatz mikroanalytischer Simulationsmodelle in den USA. GMD Report IPES 80.212. Bonn: Gesellschaft für Mathematik und Datenverarbeitung.

Pappas, N. G. 1978. A microsimulation model of the Medicaid program. Washington, D.C.: Mathematica Policy Research.

Pechman, J. 1965. A new tax model for revenue estimating. In A. Peacock and G. Hauser, eds., *Government Finance and Economic Development,* pp. 231–244. Paris: Organization for Economic Cooperation and Development (OECD).

Pelz, D. and F. Munson. 1980a. A framework for organizational innovating. Paper presented at annual meeting of Academy of Management, Detroit, August.

—— 1980b. Level of originality and the innovating process in organizations. Ann Arbor: University of Michigan.

Perry, J. 1978. Cooperation in intergovernmental networks and the diffusion and transfer of computer applications. *Urban Analysis* 5:111–129.

Perry, J. and J. N. Danziger. 1980. Adoptability of innovations: An empirical assessment of computer applications in local governments. *Administration and Society* 2(4):461–492.

Perry, J. and K. L. Kraemer. 1978. Innovation attributes, policy intervention, and the diffusion of computer applications among local governments. *Policy Sciences* 9(2):179–205.

President's Commission on Income Maintenance. 1979. Technical Studies (November). Washington, D.C.: PO.

Public Affairs Counseling. 1976. Factors involved in the transfer of innovations: A summary and organization of the literature. Washington, D.C.: Office of Policy Development and Research, Department of Housing and Urban Development.

Pugh, R. E. 1977. *Evaluation of Policy Simulation Models.* Washington, D.C.: Information Resources Press.

Quade, E. S. 1982. *Analysis for Public Decisions.* 2d ed. New York: Elsevier.

Radnor, M., I. Feller, and E. Rogers, eds. 1978. The diffusion of innovations: An assessment. Final Report. Evanston, Ill.: Northwestern University.

Radnor, M., A. H. Rubenstein, and D. Tansik. 1970. Implementation in operative research and R and D in government and business organizations. *Operations Research* 18(6):967–981.

Raduchel, W. and O. Eckstein. 1981. *Economic Modeling Languages: The DRI Experience.* Lexington, Mass.: Data Resources, Inc.

Robinson, J. 1978. Global modeling-modeler client relationship. *IASA-Information.* International Institute for Applied Systems Analysis.

Roessner, J. D. 1975. Federal technology transfer: An analysis of current program characteristics and practices (July). Washington, D.C.: Committee on Domestic Technology Transfer, Federal Council for Science Engineering and Technology.

—— 1979. Federal technology policy: Innovation and problem-solving in state and local governments. *Policy Analysis* 5(2):181–200.

Rogers, E. M. 1962. *Diffusion of Innovations.* New York: Free Press of Glencoe.

Rogers, E. M. and G. M. Beal. 1957. The importance of personal influence in the adoption of technical changes. *Social Forces* (May), 36:329–334.

Rogers, E. M. and F. Shoemaker. 1971. *Communication of Innovations: A Cross-Cultural Approach.* 2d ed. New York: Free Press of Glencoe.

Roth, R. F., S. I. Gass, and A. J. Lemoine. 1979. Some considerations for improving federal modeling. In B. P. Zeigler et al., eds., *Methodology in Systems Modeling and Simulation,* pp. 166–175. Amsterdam: North-Holland.

Rothe F., ed. 1971. *Bundesausbildungsforderungsgesetz,* Cologne: Kohlhammer.

Rothman, J. 1974. *Planning and Organizing for Social Change: Action Principles from Social Science Research.* New York: Columbia University Press.

Rowe, L. and W. Boise, eds. 1973. *Organizational and Managerial Innovations.* Pacific Palisades, Calif.: Goodyear.

Sadowsky, G. 1977. *MASH: A Computer System for Microanalytic Simulation for Policy Exploration.* Washington, D.C.: Urban Institute.

Samuelson, P. A. 1975. The art and science of macromodels over 50 years. In G. Fromm and L. R. Klein, eds., *The Brookings Model.*

—— 1980. A Nobel for forecasting. *Newsweek* (November), 18:72.

Sartore, A. B. 1976. Implementing a management information system: The relationship of participation, knowledge, performance, and satisfaction in an academic environment. Ph.D. dissertation. Graduate School of Administration, University of California, Irvine.

Scacchi, W. 1981. The process of innovation in computing. Ph.D. dissertation. Department of Information and Computer Science, University of California, Irvine.

Schatz, H. 1978. Das politische Planungssystem des Bundes—Idee, Entwicklung, Stand. In H. C. Pfohl and B. Rurup, eds., *Wirtschaftliche Messprobleme.* Cologne: Hanstein.

Schmidt, H. 1978. *Das Sozialinformationssystem der Bundasrepublik Deutschland.* Eutin: Adl Verlag.

Schmidt, W. 1975. DV-gestützte Bildungsplanung in BMBW. In P. Hoschka and U. Kalbhen, eds., *Datenverarbeitung in der politischen Planung.*

Schrage, M. 1985. How you can profit from the coming Federal InfoWar. *Washington Post,* October 29, pp. B1–B4.

Schultz, R. L. and D. P. Slevin. 1975. A program of research on implementation. In Schultz and Slevin, eds., *Implementing Operations Research/Management Science.*

Schultz, R. I. and D. P. Slevin, eds. 1975. *Implementing Operations Research/Management Science.* New York: American Elsevier.

Shepard, H. A. 1967. Innovation-resisting and innovation-producing organizations. *Journal of Business* 40(4):470–477.

Shipp, P. R. 1980. Discussion. In R. Haveman and D. Hollenbeck, eds., *Microeconomic Simulation Models for Public Policy Analysis.*

Shubik, M. and G. Brewer. 1972. *Models, Simulations, and Games: A Survey.* Santa Monica, Calif.: Rand Corporation.

Smith, R. 1977. Middle management use of computer services: The influence of organizational distance and workflow dependence. Ph.D. diss., Graduate School of Administration, University of California, Irvine.

Sommer, M. 1981. *System Dynamics und Makroökonometrie.* Bern, Switz.: P. Haupt.

Souder, W. E., P. M. Maher, N. R. Baker, C. R. Schumway, and A. H. Rubenstein. 1975.

An organization intervention approach to the design and implementation of R and D: Project selection models. In R. L. Schultz and D. P. Slevin, eds., *Implementing Operations Research/Management Science.*

Stewart, F. 1977. *Technology and Underdevelopment.* New York: Macmillan.

Stockman, D. A. 1986. *The Triumph of Politics: Why the Reagan Revolution Failed.* New York: Harper and Row.

Strotz, R. 1978. Econometrics. In W. H. Kruskal and J. M. Tanur, eds., *International Encyclopedia of Statistics,* pp. 188–197. New York: Free Press.

Su, V. 1978. An error analysis of econometric and noneconometric forecasts. *Proceedings of the American Economic Statistical Association* 68(2):306–312.

Su, V. and J. Su. 1975. An evaluation of ASA/NBER Business Outlook Survey forecasts. *Explorations in Economic Research* 2(4):588–618.

Subvetta, M. 1976. An analyst's guide to TRIM. Institute Paper. Washington, D.C.: Urban Institute.

Sweeney, J. L. and J. P. Weyant. 1979. The Energy Modeling Forum: Past, present and future. EMF PP 6.1. Stanford, Calif.: Energy Modeling Forum, Stanford University.

Szyperski, N. 1979. State of the art of implementation research on computer based information systems. In N. Szyperski and E. Grochla, eds., *Design and Implementation of Computer Based Information Systems,* pp. 5–28. Alphen aan den Rijn, Netherlands: Sijthoff and Noordhoff.

Tinbergen, J. 1939. A method and its application to investment activity. In vol. 1 of *Statistical Testing of Business Cycle Theories.* Geneva: League of Nations.

Tornatzky, L., D. Roitman, M. Boylan, J. Carpenter, J. D. Eveland, W. Hatzner, B. Lucas, and J. Schneider. 1979. Innovation processes and their management: A conceptual, empirical, and policy review of innovation process research. Washington, D.C.: National Science Foundation, Division of Policy Research and Analysis.

Turek, J. 1979. Agenda for microsimulation users' forum meeting (December 5). Washington, D.C.: Office of the Assistant Secretary for Planning and Evaluation, Department of Health, Education, and Welfare.

Uebe, G. 1976. Survey of macro-econometric models in chronological order. In S. Dickhoven ed., Modellierungssoftware.

Umweltbundesamt. 1978. *UMPLIS-Verzeichnis rechnergestützter Umweltmodelle.* Berlin: Erich Schmidt.

Urban Institute. 1971. *The Struggle To Bring Technology to the Cities.* Washington, D.C.: Urban Institute.

U.S. House Memorandum. 1975. To: Members of the Food Stamp Study Group. From: Jim Springfield, staff of House Committee of Agriculture. RE: Proposed Food Stamp Study Contract, November 3.

Van Maanen, J., ed. 1979. Reclaiming qualitative models for organizational research: A preface. *Administrative Science Quarterly* (December), 24:520–526.

Venture. 1979. Econometricians who forecast profits. November, pp. 48–50.

Voorhees, A. M., and Associates. 1973. A simulation city approach for preparation of urban area data bases (November). Washington, D.C.: U.S. Environmental Protection Agency.

Walker, J. L. 1969. The diffusion of innovations among the American states. *The American Political Science Review* 63(3):880–899.

Webb, R. and G. Chow. 1978. TRIM user's guide. Working Paper (September). Washington, D.C.: Urban Institute.

Wegener, M. 1979. The use of computers for urban and regional planning in West Germany: A review. Paper presented at PAR 79, Berlin, May 7–10.

Wertheimer, R. F. 1978. Methodological issues in building microsimulation models. Paper presented for Gesellschaft für Mathematik und Datenverarbeitung, Bonn, October.

—— 1979. Microsimulation research at the Urban Institute. Paper presented at the Users' Forum on Microsimulation Models, December.

White, M. T. 1975. *Management Science in Federal Agencies: The Adoption and Diffusion of a Socio-Technical Innovation.* Lexington, Mass.: Lexington Books, D. C. Heath.

Wilensky, G. 1969. An income transfer computational model. In President's Commission on Income Maintenance Programs, Technical Studies.

Wood, D. O. 1980. Model assessment and the policy research process. In S. I. Gass, ed., *Utility and Use of Large-Scale Mathematical Models,* pp. 23–63.

—— 1981. Energy model evaluation and analysis: Current practice. In S. I. Gass, ed., *Utility and Use of Large-Scale Mathematical Models,* pp. 123–135.

Yin, R. K., K. Heald, M. Vogel, P. Fleischauer, and B. Vladeck. 1976. *A Review of Case Studies of Technological Innovations in State and Local Services.* Santa Monica, Calif.: Rand Corporation.

Zaltman, G., R. Duncan, and J. Holbek. 1973. *Innovations and Organizations.* New York: Wiley.

Zarkovitch, S. S. 1966. *Quality of Statistical Data.* Rome: Food and Agriculture Organization of the United States.

Zarnowitz, V. 1978. On the accuracy and properties of recent macroeconomic forecasts. *Proceedings of the American Economic Association* 68(2):313–319.

INDEX